Performing
Microsoft® Excel

Comprehensive Course

Iris Blanc
New York City Board of Education

Cathy Vento
Computer Education Consultant

Thompson Steele
Harvard Massachusetts

COURSE TECHNOLOGY
TM
THOMSON LEARNING

COURSE TECHNOLOGY
25 THOMSON PLACE
BOSTON MA 02210

Australia • Canada • Denmark • Japan • Mexico • New Zealand • Philippines • Puerto Rico • Singapore
South Africa • Spain • United Kingdom • United States

**COURSE
TECHNOLOGY**
™

THOMSON LEARNING

Performing with Microsoft Excel 2002, Comprehensive Course

by Iris Blanc, Cathy Vento, and Thompson Steele

Senior Vice President
Chris Elkhill

Sr. Product Manager
Dave Lafferty

Development Editor
Thompson Steele, Inc.

Marketing Manager
Kim Wood

Directors of Production
Becky Herrington
Patty Stephan

Production Manager
Doug Cowley

Editorial Assistant
Jodi Dreissig

Production Editor
Kristen Guevara
Ellana Russo

Print Buyer
Denise Sandler

Cover and Internal Design
Ann Small
A Small Design Studio

Illustrations
Ferruccio Sardella

Compositors:
Kellee LaVars
Myrna Zambrano
Andrew Bartel
Michelle French Linder

Printer
Banta

Announcing the Performing Series!

Give Your Best Performance with Iris Blanc and Cathy Vento!

This new series on Microsoft® Office XP provides an innovative instructional tool designed for introductory and advanced courses. Using a unique approach to learning, these texts offer Microsoft Office User Specialist (MOUS) certification for both the core and expert level in all applications.

NEW! Performing with Microsoft Office XP by Iris Blanc and Cathy Vento
75+ hours of instruction for beginning through intermediate features on Word, Excel, Access, PowerPoint, FrontPage, Outlook, Windows, and Internet Explorer.
0-619-05853-6   Textbook, Hard Spiral Cover, Core MOUS Certification
0-619-05854-4   Instructor's Resource Kit (IRK) CD-ROM Package
0-619-05867-6   Review Pack (Data CD-ROM)
0-619-05931-1   Annotated Instructor's Edition

NEW! Performing with Microsoft Office XP, Advanced Course by Blanc, Vento, and Thompson Steele
75+ hours of instruction for intermediate through advanced features on Word, Excel, Access, PowerPoint, FrontPage, Outlook, Windows, and Internet Explorer.
0-619-05855-2   Textbook, Hard Spiral Cover, Expert MOUS Certification
0-619-05856-0   Instructor's Resource Kit (IRK) CD-ROM Package
0-619-05868-4   Review Pack (Data CD-ROM)
0-619-05932-X   Annotated Instructor's Edition

NEW! Performing with Microsoft Word 2002, Comprehensive Course
0-619-05857-9   Textbook, Hard Spiral Cover, Expert MOUS, 35+ Hours
0-619-05856-0   Instructor's Resource Kit (IRK) CD-ROM Package

NEW! Performing with Microsoft Excel 2002, Comprehensive Course
0-619-05859-5   Textbook, Hard Spiral Cover, Expert MOUS, 35+ Hours
0-619-05856-0   Instructor's Resource Kit (IRK) CD-ROM Package

NEW! Performing with Microsoft PowerPoint 2002, Comprehensive Course
0-619-05861-7   Textbook, Soft Spiral Cover, Expert MOUS, 35+ Hours
0-619-05856-0   Instructor's Resource Kit (IRK) CD-ROM Package

NEW! Performing with Microsoft Access 2002, Comprehensive Course
0-619-05863-3   Textbook, Soft Spiral Cover, Expert MOUS, 35+ Hours
0-619-05856-0   Instructor's Resource Kit (IRK) CD-ROM Package

NEW! Performing with Microsoft FrontPage 2002, Comprehensive Course
0-619-05880-3   Textbook, Soft Spiral Cover, Expert MOUS, 35+ Hours
0-619-05856-0   Instructor's Resource Kit (IRK) CD-ROM Package

NEW! Performing with Microsoft Office XP, Projects for the Entrepreneur by Iris Blanc and Cathy Vento
0-619-05865-X   Textbook, Perfect Soft Cover, 35+ Hours of Instruction
0-619-05866-8   Instructor's Resource Kit (IRK) CD-ROM Package
0-619-05869-2   Review Pack (Data CD-ROM)

Join us on the Internet at
www.course.com

PREFACE

The *Performing with Microsoft® Office XP* series teaches Office tools through a unique set of task-oriented exercises and project-based applications built around a business theme. Students focus on the skills they need to know to complete practical, realistic applications and create materials suitable for portfolio evaluation. In this Comprehensive Course text, the software skills developed meet both the "Core" and "Expert" MOUS (Microsoft Office User Specialist) certification requirements for Excel 2002.

Performing with Microsoft® Office XP is a new and different approach based on the premise that students successfully assimilate and retain computer skills when they understand why the skills are useful. *Performing with Microsoft® Office XP* presents skill sets within the framework of engaging projects and tasks that teach the software and business competencies needed to succeed in the workplace, thus providing a real-life context for learning. Through this task- and project-based approach, students develop critical thinking, analysis, problem solving, and information and resource management skills. With the Internet activities that appear throughout the text, they learn research and communication skills—essential tools for today's workplace. College or college-bound students will find that these software, business, and and thinking skills will serve them in their coursework, internships, and professional careers.

Rather than focus solely on software features, this series emphasizes the project or task and develops those software skill sets needed to accomplish it.

OBJECTIVES

Performing with Microsoft Excel, Comprehensive Course is intended for a half year Computer Applications course. No experience with this software is assumed. The objectives of this book are:

- To use a three-phase approach to develop MOUS competencies:
  - ✦ Tryouts: Learners practice software skills using a step-by-step tutorial approach.
  - ✦ Rehearsals: Learners apply software skills to an illustrated business task.
  - ✦ Performances: Learners use technology to complete a business project.

- To use tasks and projects to develop SCANS (Secretary's Commission on Achieving Necessary Skills) competencies:
  - ✦ Acquire and evaluate data
  - ✦ Organize and maintain files
  - ✦ Interpret and communicate information
  - ✦ Apply technology to specific tasks
  - ✦ Apply critical thinking and problem solving
  - ✦ Work with members of a team

- To provide a text that may be used for independent study.

When students complete a Computer Applications course using this text, they will have Expert MOUS and workplace competencies.

ORGANIZATION OF THE TEXT

Performing with Microsoft® Excel 2002 Comprehensive Course begins with an Introduction to Computers unit that gives the foundation for an understanding of computers. Thereafter, the Introductory Excel Lessons 1–7 are followed by the Advanced Excel Lessons 8–14. If your class needs practice with basic Office skills, such as opening, saving, and printing files, as well as Internet basics, have the students complete the three lessons in the Performing Basics unit found in the Appendix.

The lessons in Introductory and Advanced Excel are organized by a series of categories that cover the following types of outcome-based projects:

- Business Forms
- Accounting Records
- Data Analysis
- Financial Reports
- Charts
- Integration
- Budgets and Templates
- Data Tables
- Data Lists
- Marketing and Sales Reports
- Data Analysis
- Accounting Department: Shared Files

Lessons use a three-phase pedagogy. The first phase, **Tryout,** introduces the software features necessary to complete document production in the lesson category (i.e., correspondence). It also includes software concepts, illustrations, step-by-step directions, and short, easy exercises, **Try it Out!,** that provide practice with software features. Students should read all software concepts on a topic before completing the related **Try it Out!** exercise.

In the second phase, **Rehearsal,** students apply the software skills practiced in the Tryout phase to a series of tasks in which they produce model professional documents. What You Need to Know information and Cues for Reference guide learners in completing the activities on their own, thus helping them build skills and confidence in accomplishing the Rehearsal activity. The Rehearsal phase produces tangible results that represent actual professional documents within the lesson category.

In the third phase, **Performance,** students complete challenging work-related projects (either independently or as a team) for one of nine companies. In this phase, students must apply critical thinking and problem-solving skills and integrate the software skills and business concepts learned to produce the documents required by the company-related scenarios. This phase can be used as evidence of lesson mastery.

This text is an innovative approach to teaching software skills through a project-based, applied learning process. This approach is unique because it teaches the Core MOUS skills by applying software features in various work-based contexts. The opportunity to use the skills independently and creatively will enable students to survive and thrive in a high-performance workplace.

SPECIAL FEATURES

- **Keyboarding Reinforcement Unit** (found on the Data CD) contains 18 exercises of drill and practice material covering the entire alphabet for those who wish to learn the keyboard or improve their keyboarding skills quickly.
- **Speech Recognition Unit** (found on the Data CD) provides basic concepts and activities to develop skills in the use of Dragon Naturally Speaking voice recognition software.
- **End-of-Lesson Performance activities** use a project-based approach to reinforce the concepts and applications learned in the lesson and require critical thinking and Internet skills.
- **Data files** (found on the Data CD) allow learners to complete many of the activities without keyboarding lengthy text.
- **Directories** list file names alphabetically with corresponding lesson numbers, as well as document sample pages.
- **Vocabulary words**—both MOUS and project-related—for each lesson.
- **Portfolio-building projects** found in the Performance sections of each lesson.
- **Multiple-Choice, True/False, Matching and Completion Objective test questions** as part of the Encore review.
- **Appendices** that include the following:
  - ✴ MOUS Correlation Chart
  - ✴ File Management
  - ✴ Using the Mouse
  - ✴ Toolbars, Menus, and Dialog Boxes
  - ✴ Selection Techniques
  - ✴ Portfolio Basics
  - ✴ Proofreader's Marks
  - ✴ Task Reference
  - ✴ Glossary

A first course text is available: *Performing with Microsoft® Office XP, Introductory Course.* This allows a full year's course on introductory Microsoft Office instruction. A second book, Performing with Microsoft Office XP, Advanced Course, is also available. Also, as part of this series, there are stand-alone, comprehensive texts on Microsoft Word, Excel, PowerPoint, Access, FrontPage, and Publisher. To help with additional projects, there is Performing with *Microsoft® Office XP: Projects for the Entrepreneur.*

ACKNOWLEDGMENTS

For the many people who have played a role in the production of this quality book, we owe our gratitude and appreciation. First and foremost among them are Dave Lafferty, Sr. Product Manager; Kim Wood, Marketing Manager; and Kristen Guevara, Production Editor for their professionalism, guidance, and support throughout this project.

Our heartfelt thanks go to those who have made significant contributions and assisted us with the production of this book:

- To the contributing writer: Diane Bukatko.
- To the production team at Thompson Steele: Sally Steele, Nicole Barone, Deb Thompson, Karla Maki, and Penny Jollimore, who kept everyone on track and on time, and did so with support and guidance all along the way.
- To the production team at Course Technology: Becky Herrington, Doug Cowley, Kellee LaVars, Ellana Russo, Andrew Bartel, Michelle French Linder, Myrna Zambrano and Alisha Ferraro.
- To our reviewers: Maurice Henderson, Susan Long, Kim Newport, and Joyce Smith.
- To Marie Michele for her wonderful illustrations.
- To the Donnelly family for permission to adapt the Keyboarding Reinforcement unit from the work of the late Frank Donnelly.
- To our families for their love, encouragement, inspiration, and above all, for their patience.

Iris Blanc
Cathy Vento

ABOUT THE AUTHORS

Iris Blanc is currently the Director of Virtual Enterprises, International, a New York City Board of Education program. Formerly, Ms. Blanc was assistant principal/department chair of business education at Tottenville High School, a New York City public high school.

Ms. Blanc has taught business education and computer applications at the high school and college levels for over 25 years. Ms. Blanc conducts seminars, workshops, and short courses in applied learning strategies and methods of teaching and integrating technology at conferences nationwide.

Catherine Vento is currently working as a consultant for the New York City Board of Education and as a staff developer for the district. She is also an adjunct instructor for the Human Resources Development Institute for the State of New Jersey. She was formerly the assistant principal/department chair of Business Education at Susan Wagner High School, a New York City public high school.

Ms. Vento has taught business education, accounting, and computer applications at the high school level. She has presented seminars, workshops, and mini-courses at conferences, colleges, and business schools nationwide.

Ms. Blanc and Ms. Vento have co-authored numerous computer application texts and reference guides for over 15 years. The Performing series represents their combined pedagogical talents in an innovative, new approach to develop workplace skills and competencies. Over their many years as educators and authors, they have discovered that students learn best what they need to know!

LESSON 2

Lesson outcome

Indicates the workplace-related goal for learning MOUS software skills.

Correspondence

In this lesson, you will learn to use features found in Word to format correspondence, create an envelope and labels, and send e-mail. Correspondence includes written communications such as letters, memos, and e-mails.

▶ **Upon completion of this lesson, you should have mastered the following MOUS skill sets:**

✶ Set margins Ⓜ
✶ Insert the date and time Ⓜ
✶ Use smart tags
✶ Use horizontal text alignments
✶ Create envelopes and labels Ⓜ
✶ Use templates Ⓜ
  ✶ Open existing templates
  ✶ Create your own template
✶ Use wizards
✶ Send e-mail
  ✶ Create a new message
  ✶ Send a Word document as e-mail

Lesson skills sets

Lists MOUS and Office XP skills sets that the learner needs to know to complete the work-related activities. An "M" notation indicates MOUS skills.

Terms
Document-related
Full-block business letter
Enclosure notation
Justified text
Delivery address
Letterhead
Logo
Memorandum
E-mail
MOUS-related
Portrait orientation
Landscape orientation
Template
Placeholder
Wizard

Terms

Lists MOUS/ software-related and document/file-related terms. Terminolgy is introduced on a need-to-know basis.

Lesson summary

Summarizes the lesson's objectives and workplace-related applications

Phase One

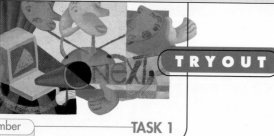

TRYOUT

Goals

Lists the skill sets practiced in the task.

▶ **GOAL**
To practice using the following skill sets:
⚹ Set margins
⚹ Date and time
⚹ Smart Tags

TASK 1

Task number

Identifies the task number within the lesson. Each lesson consists of up to four tasks that will develop skills needed to complete the lesson goal.

WHAT YOU NEED TO KNOW

Set Margins

> The blank area at the edge of a page is the margin. Standard paper measures 8.5" wide by 11" long. Standard paper that is positioned to be taller than it is wide is considered to be *portrait orientation*. Paper positioned to be wider than it is tall is said to be *landscape orientation*.

> The default margins for portrait orientation are 1" top, 1" bottom, 1.25" left, and 1.25" right.

> To change margins, select File, Page Setup. In the Page Setup dialog box that displays, as shown in Figure 2.1, click the Margins tab and enter the desired top, bottom, left, and right margins in the appropriate text box after you choose the page orientation (portrait is the default). You can apply margin changes to the Whole document (the default) or From this point forward.

TRY*it* OUT

1. Open **2.1pf letter** from the Data CD.

2. Click **File, Page Setup.**

3. Click the **Margins tab.**

4. Enter **1.5"** in the left and right text boxes.

5. Click **OK.**

6. Do not close the file.

Try it Out

A short, step-by-step exercise that allows learners to practice immediately the software feature described in the What You Need to Know section.

What You Need to Know

Explains the software feature and related concepts needed to complete the task.

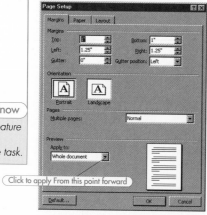

Click to apply From this point forward

Figure 2.1 Page Setup dialog box

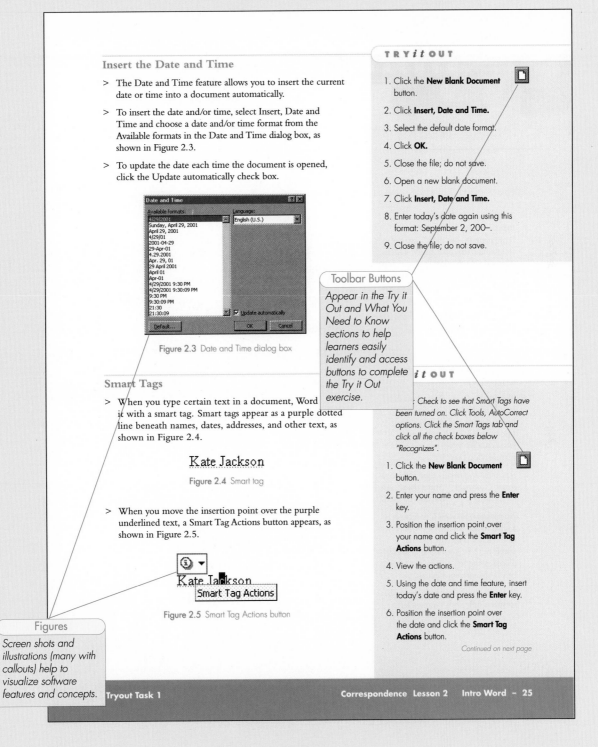

Insert the Date and Time

> The Date and Time feature allows you to insert the current date or time into a document automatically.

> To insert the date and/or time, select Insert, Date and Time and choose a date and/or time format from the Available formats in the Date and Time dialog box, as shown in Figure 2.3.

> To update the date each time the document is opened, click the Update automatically check box.

Figure 2.3 Date and Time dialog box

Smart Tags

> When you type certain text in a document, Word it with a smart tag. Smart tags appear as a purple dotted line beneath names, dates, addresses, and other text, as shown in Figure 2.4.

Kate Jackson

Figure 2.4 Smart tag

> When you move the insertion point over the purple underlined text, a Smart Tag Actions button appears, as shown in Figure 2.5.

Kate Jackson
Smart Tag Actions

Figure 2.5 Smart Tag Actions button

Figures

Screen shots and illustrations (many with callouts) help to visualize software features and concepts.

T R Y *it* **O U T**

1. Click the **New Blank Document** button.

2. Click **Insert, Date and Time.**

3. Select the default date format.

4. Click **OK.**

5. Close the file; do not save.

6. Open a new blank document.

7. Click **Insert, Date and Time.**

8. Enter today's date again using this format: September 2, 200–.

9. Close the file; do not save.

Toolbar Buttons

Appear in the Try it Out and What You Need to Know sections to help learners easily identify and access buttons to complete the Try it Out exercise.

it O U T

Check to see that Smart Tags have been turned on. Click Tools, AutoCorrect options. Click the Smart Tags tab and click all the check boxes below "Recognizes".

1. Click the **New Blank Document** button.

2. Enter your name and press the **Enter** key.

3. Position the insertion point over your name and click the **Smart Tag Actions** button.

4. View the actions.

5. Using the date and time feature, insert today's date and press the **Enter** key.

6. Position the insertion point over the date and click the **Smart Tag Actions** button.

Continued on next page

Tryout Task 1

Correspondence **Lesson 2**   **Intro Word** – 25

Phase Two

REHEARSAL

TASK 1

Rehearsal goal
Identifies the outcome of the applications.

GOAL
To create a full-block business letter

SETTING THE STAGE/WRAPUP

Margins: 1.5" left and right
Start line: At 2.5"
File name: 2.1employment

Setting the Stage/Wrapup
Identifies file names and/or settings needed to begin the Rehearsal application.

Task number
Each task includes a Rehearsal that applies all the software features practiced in the Try it Out phase.

WHAT YOU NEED TO KNOW

> The layout of a letter is called a format. There are a variety of letter formats, but most have the following parts: date, inside address, salutation, body, closing, name and title of the writer, and reference initials of the writer and the person who prepares the document.

> In a *full-block business letter,* all parts begin at the left margin.

> The date generally begins 2.5" down from the top of the page. (The At indicator on the status bar displays 2.5").

> The margins used depend on the length of the letter. Short letters use wider left and right margins; (more than 1"), whereas longer letters use narrower left and right margins (less than 1").

> Sincerely is generally used to close a letter. "Cordially," "Yours truly," and "Very truly yours" can also be used.

> An *enclosure notation* is indicated on a letter when something in addition to the letter is included in the envelope. The notation is generally placed at the left margin, two lines below the reference initials.

> In this Rehearsal activity, you will format a full-block business letter.

DIRECTIONS

1. Open a new blank document.

2. Set the margins.

3. Press the **Enter** key to advance the insertion point to 2.5".

4. Use the Date feature to insert the current date. Use this format: September 3, 200–.

5. Enter the letter as shown on the facing page. Press the **Enter** key between letter parts as shown.

6. Correct spelling errors.

7. Preview the document.

8. Save the file; name it **2.1employment**.

9. Close the file.

Directions
Clear instructions that guide learners to complete the application. These instructions are less detailed than those in the Try It Out phase, requiring students to build skills and confidence.

What You Need to Know
Explains business-related concepts and provides information needed to complete the application.

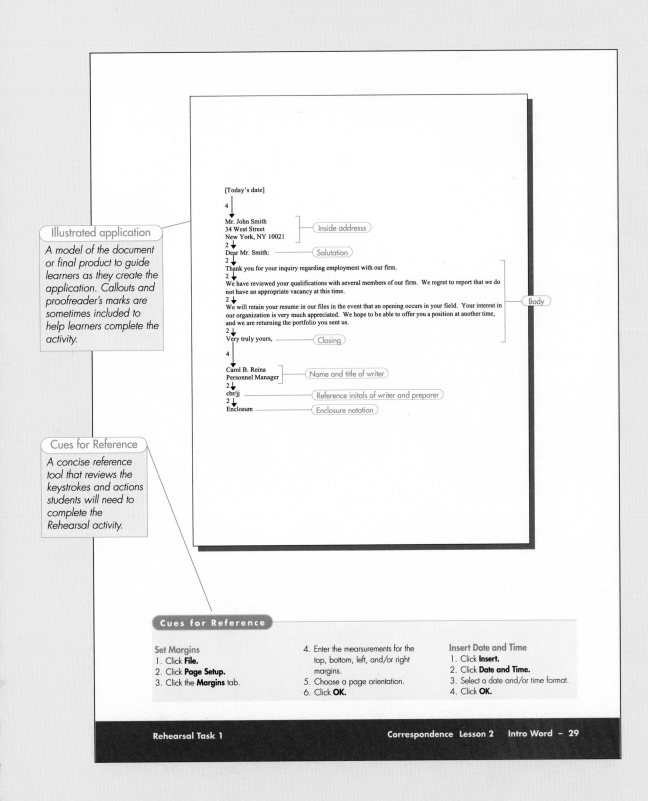

Illustrated application

A model of the document or final product to guide learners as they create the application. Callouts and proofreader's marks are sometimes included to help learners complete the activity.

Cues for Reference

A concise reference tool that reviews the keystrokes and actions students will need to complete the Rehearsal activity.

[Today's date]

4

Mr. John Smith
34 West Street
New York, NY 10021 ————— (Inside address)

2

Dear Mr. Smith: ————— (Salutation)

2

Thank you for your inquiry regarding employment with our firm.

2

We have reviewed your qualifications with several members of our firm. We regret to report that we do not have an appropriate vacancy at this time.

2

We will retain your resume in our files in the event that an opening occurs in your field. Your interest in our organization is very much appreciated. We hope to be able to offer you a position at another time, and we are returning the portfolio you sent us. ————— (Body)

2

Very truly yours, ————— (Closing)

4

Carol B. Reina
Personnel Manager ————— (Name and title of writer)

2

cbr/jj ————— (Reference initals of writer and preparer)

2

Enclosure ————— (Enclosure notation)

Cues for Reference

Set Margins
1. Click **File.**
2. Click **Page Setup.**
3. Click the **Margins** tab.

4. Enter the mearsurements for the top, bottom, left, and/or right margins.
5. Choose a page orientation.
6. Click **OK.**

Insert Date and Time
1. Click **Insert.**
2. Click **Date and Time.**
3. Select a date and/or time format.
4. Click **OK.**

How to Use This Book

Phase Three

PERFORMANCE

▶ **SETTING THE STAGE/WRAPUP**
Act I File name: 2.p1dallas
Act II File names: 2.p2alslet
2.p2sanfran
Act III File name: 2.p3osha

Setting the Stage/Wrapup

Identifies file names and/or settings needed to begin the activities, which are listed as "Acts." There may be one to four Acts in this phase.

WHAT YOU NEED TO KNOW

In the Performance phase of each lesson, you will assume that you work or correspond with one of the companies listed in the front of this textbook. A description of the company, its logo, and the company's communication information is indicated there. In subsequent exercises, only the logo will be presented, so if you need to review company information, you will have to refer in the front of this textbook. Your performance in preparing documents and projects that are typically used in business will apply the skills you have developed in the previous phases of this lesson.

Scenario

Introduces the business problem.

Act I

You are interested in traveling to Dallas, Texas, in May. Write a personal letter to Ms. Robin Byron of the Air Land Sea Travel Group in New York. Request that they send you the famous *Travel Guide 2003*. Tell them you are particularly interested in visiting the Arts District, Civic Center, and the Farmer's Market and would like any additional information they might have about those areas.

air land sea
travel group

Company logo

Identifies the company that the students are "working for" in the scenario. The company information is outlined on the "To the Student" pages and may be used for reference.

Follow these guidelines:

✻ Use your own name, address, and phone information for the letterhead.

✻ Use any desired margins, an appropriate letter style, and an appropriate closing.

✻ Save the file; name it **2.p1dallas.**

✻ Prepare an envelope.

✻ Print one copy of the letter and envelope.

Guidelines

Lists the requirements, specifications, and/or tips needed to complete the project.

ENCORE

Review questions

Provides review of software concepts learned within the lesson. Review questions may include multiple-choice, true/false, or completion type questions.

MULTIPLE CHOICE

Identify the letter of the choice that best completes the statement or answers the question.

1. **The inside address of a letter is:**
   A. The name and address of the person to whom you are sending the letter.
   B. The name and address of the person writing the letter.
   C. The name and title of the person who signs the letter.
   D. None of the above

2. **A placeholder is:**
   A. A template.
   B. An empty box that identifies the placement and location of text and contains preset text formats.
   C. An easy way to create a letterhead.
   D. A place to enter an e-mail message.

3. **You can create labels for:**
   A. File folders.
   B. Business cards.
   C. Name badges.
   D. Floppy disks.
   E. All of the above

4. **If you need to create a customized document, you first create a:**
   A. Wizard.
   B. Full-block letter.
   C. Template.
   D. Placeholder.
   E. Smart tag.

5. **To guide you through the steps for creating a template document, you would use:**
   A. A template.
   B. A placeholder.
   C. A wizard.
   D. The Office Assistant.
   E. None of the above

6. **When something in addition to the letter is included in an envelope, you must include the following notation on the letter:**
   A. Courtesy copy.
   B. "Re" line.
   C. Subject line.
   D. Attention line.
   E. Enclosure.

7. **A written communication sent within a company is a:**
   A. Template.
   B. E-mail.
   C. Memorandum.
   D. Courtesy copy.
   E. Wizard.

8. **When text is aligned evenly at the left and right margins, it is said to be:**
   A. Right-aligned.
   B. Left-aligned.
   C. Justified.
   D. Centered.

Appendices

These include information, illustrations, and reference material on:
- *MOUS Certification Correlation Chart*
- *File Management*
- *Using the Mouse*
- *Toolbars, Menus, and Dialog Boxes*
- *Selection Techniques*
- *Portfolio Basics*
- *Proofreaders' Marks*
- *Task Reference*
- *Glossary*

Encore   Correspondence Lesson 2   Intro Wor

WHAT'S NEW AND IMPROVED IN MICROSOFT® OFFICE XP

Microsoft Office XP has many powerful new features as well as significantly improved interfaces to the features with which you are already familiar. Complex operations such as mail merge are now much easier. Improved Web access from all applications means you can integrate Web resources with your Office files. Sharing the information or data in your Office applications via the Web is now practically seamless. Office XP includes improved tools to enhance collaboration when you work on projects with other people.

The many new and improved Office XP features include:
- Improved data recovery in case of system or application failure.
- Smart tags that automatically pop up to display your options.
- Task panes with easy-to-follow instructions and access to special features.
- Office Clipboard task pane for viewing the contents of the clipboard while you work.
- Smart Tag Paste options display your options whenever you copy information from one application to another.
- New File task pane displays all your options for creating or opening files.
- Enhanced template library with hundreds of formats to choose from, as well as a link to more Microsoft Office templates on the Internet.
- E-mail-based collaboration tools.
- High-speed, full-text searching capability for searching your local drive, network drives, and Microsoft® Outlook.
- New drawing and imaging features.

Microsoft Word 2002 includes the following new features:
- Drawing canvas makes it easier to place and arrange graphics in a document.
- Reveal Formatting task pane streamlines the formatting process.
- Send for Review feature integrates reviewing capabilities in Word with Outlook electronic mail features.
- Three-level sorting for tables and lists provides complex sorting capabilities.
- Context-sensitive smart tags give you access to names and addresses stored in Outlook.

Microsoft Excel 2002 includes the following new features:
- Web Query interface links a worksheet to data on the Web.
- Sorting now recognizes data types.
- Border drawing.
- Tab colors for worksheet tabs.
- Password protection for a range or data on a worksheet.

Microsoft PowerPoint 2002 includes the following new features:
- Print Preview lets you view your slides before you print them.
- Slide Design task pane displays all your template, color, and animation options.
- Presenter view and tools let you add speaker notes that are invisible to the audience.
- Built-in diagrams for organization charts and a variety of diagram types.
- Compress Picture feature lets you reduce the file size of a presentation.

Start-up Checklist
HARDWARE
Minimum Configuration
- PC with 90 MHz processor
- 32 MB RAM for Windows 98
- 64 MB RAM for Windows NT or Windows 2000
- 4 MB available space in the registry for Windows NT
- Hard disk with 350 MB free for typical installation
- CD-ROM drive
- VGA monitor with video adapter
- Microsoft Mouse, IntelliMouse, or compatible pointing device
- 28.800 bps or higher modem
- Printer
Recommended Configuration
Pentium PC with greater than 32 MB RAM
Super VGA 256-color monitor
33.600 bps modem
Multimedia capability
For e-mail, Microsoft Mail, Internet SMTP/POP.3, or other MAPI-compliant messaging software
SOFTWARE
Windows 98, Microsoft Windows NT 4 with at least Service Pack 6, Windows 2000, or Windows Millennium Edition, Windows XP
Internet Explorer Browser 5

Before you start to work, please read this introduction. Spending this time before you begin will enhance your learning experience.

Conventions: Different type styles have special meaning. You will save time by recognizing the nature of the text from the type style.

Type Style	Color	Use	Example
Bold Italics	**Black**	Key terms	*word processing*
Bold	**Black**	Action items	Press the **Enter** key
Bold	**Red**	File names	2.2toxls
			3.3pf stylesdoc

ANCILLARIES

Student Data Files: All data files mentioned in the text that are needed to complete the exercises for this book are located on on a separate CD called a Review Pack. They can also be downloaded for each title on www.course.com.

Instructor's Resource Kit (IRK CD-ROM): The Instructor's Resource Kit (IRK) contains a wealth of instructional material you can use to prepare for and aid in your teaching of Office XP. On the CD, you will find:

- Data files for the course.
- Solution files for the course.
- Exercises to supplement those found in the student book.
- Answers to all exercises.
- Lesson plans for each lesson.
- Copies of the figures that appear in the student text, which can be used to prepare transparencies.

- A correlation grid that shows skills required for Microsoft Office User Specialist (MOUS) certification.
- A correlation grid that shows the SCANS workplace competencies skills.
- PowerPoint presentations for each lesson.
- Keyboarding Reinforcement unit.
- Speech recognition unit.

ASSESSMENT

ExamView®

This textbook is accompanied by ExamView, a powerful testing software package that allows instructors to create and administer printed, computer (LAN-based), and Internet exams. ExamView includes hundreds of questions that correspond to the topics covered in this text, enabling students to generate detailed study guides that include page references for further review. The computer-based and Internet testing components allow students to take exams at their computers, and also save the instructor time by grading each exam automatically.

The Rehearsal and Performance phases of each lesson use various companies to demostrate the kinds of documents that a real business might produce. A description of each company used in this text is outlined below. The Performance phase of each unit will identify the company you "work for" by the company logo illustrated. Use these pages as a reference if you need to find information about the company as you complete the project at hand.

Company Name and Contact Information	Description of Company	Logo
Air Land Sea Travel Group *New York* 505 Park Avenue New York, NY 10010 Phone 212-555-5555 Fax: 212-666-6767 E-mail: als@net.com *Boston* One Main Street Boston, MA 02100 Phone: 617-666-6666 Fax: 617-777-7777 E-mail:alsbos@net.com *California* Los Angeles 46 Beverly Drive Beverly Hills, CA 90210 Phone: 310-555-5555 Fax: 310-555-4444 E-mail: alsbh@net.com San Francisco 35 Market Street San Francisco, CA 99876 Phone: 415-888-8888 Fax: 415-222-2222 E-mail: alssf@net.com	The Air Land Sea Travel Group, also known as the ALS Travel Group, has offices in Boston, New York, and two in California. ALS specializes in both corporate and leisure travel packages. The Corporate Travel Department services business clients throughout the country. The company has been in business for over 40 years and is known for its reliable service, great prices, and exclusive offers. The president of the company is Ms. Janice Pierce. The director of the Corporate Travel Department in New York is Mr. Wilson Jones. The director of the Leisure Travel Department is Ms. Robin Byron Byrd.	air land sea travel group
Green Brothers Gardening 32 Braddock Road Fairfax, VA 22030 Phone: 703-555-0005 Fax: 703-555-0015 E-mail: gbg@network.com Web: www.grenbros.com	Green Brothers Gardening, a full-service landscaping and nursery business, has three locations in and around Fairfax, Virginia. Calvin Green, the president and CEO, runs the business with his brother, Ralph Green, the chief financial officer. Maria Torres is their director of Marketing and Sales. They have an office and nursery staff in each store. They also employ workers on a daily basis. The firm handles lawn maintenance programs, tree and shrub planting, pruning, masonry, snow plowing, sanding, and landscape contracting. They carry unique specimen plants and cater to corporate as well as residential markets. They have a reputation for creating natural, lush landscaping.	GREEN BROTHERS GARDENING
Odyssey Travel Gear 445 Michigan Avenue Chicago, IL 60611 Phone: 630-222-8888 Fax: 630-666-8787 E-mail: otg@networld.com Web: www.otg.com	Odyssey Travel Gear offers products that make travel easier, such as luggage and luggage carts, garment bags, rain gear, money belts, sleep sacks, etc. The company has several retail stores, but most of their business comes from catalog and Internet sales. The retail stores are located in Chicago, Miami, Boston, Dallas, and San Diego. The company's headquarters are located in Chicago, Illinois. Ms. Jane McBride is the president and CEO. The Web site features new products, dozens of reduced-priced items from past catalogs, and lots of valuable information.	

Company Name and Contact Information	Description of Company	Logo
Trilogy Productions *California* 101 Sunset Boulevard Beverly Hills, CA 90211 Phone 310-505-0000 Fax 310-606-0000 E-mail tpc@world.com *New York* 350 West 57 Street New York, NY 10106 Phone 212-555-9999 Fax 212-555-8900 E-mail: tpny@world.com	Trilogy Productions is a motion picture and television production company. John Alan, the current CEO (chief executive officer) and president, and Andrew Martin, the current CFO (chief financial officer) formed the company in 1990. Trilogy Productions deals with a number of Hollywood's top talent, including writers, directors, and filmmakers. They have released roughly 50 feature films and numerous Emmy-winning television programs. The Motion Picture and Television Divisions are located in the same building in Beverly Hills, California. Trilogy also maintains a small office in New York, which primarily handles all marketing and sales distribution. The director of Marketing and Sales is Christopher Manning. Ms. Cindy Napster is the manager of the Human Resources department. She handles all employee-related matters for the New York and California offices.	OTG odyssey travel gear
In-Shape Fitness Centers 54 Cactus Drive Phoenix, AZ 85003 Phone: 602-555-1001 Fax: 602-555-1005 E-mail: inshape@net.com	In-Shape Fitness Centers began in Phoenix, Arizona with one location and quickly grew to four other locations within the Phoenix area. In-Shape Fitness is a high-quality health and fitness facility, which offers a wide range of exercise and fitness programs. The company's successful growth over a short time has been the result of its innovative fitness programs, well-trained staff, and dedication to quality and service. Mr. Robert Treadmill, president, retired this year and Ms. Alivea James has replaced him.	TRILOGY PRODUCTIONS 3
Occasions Event Planning *New York* 675 Third Avenue New York, NY 10017 Tel: 212-555-1234 Fax: 212-555-1230 *New Jersey* 1045 Palisades Avenue Fort Lee, NJ 07024 Phone: 201-555-4322 Fax: 201-555-4323 E-mail: oep@world.com	Occasions Event Planning offers full service gourmet catering, DJ's, live bands, recreational rentals, entertainment for children, vending machines, appliance rental, and more. Located in New York City, the Occasions Event Planning Company plans conferences, parties, seminars, and meetings. Recently, it opened a New Jersey office. Jane McBride is the president of the company.	
Four Corners Realty 450 Flora Boulevard Hollywood, FL 33025 Phone: 954-555-4433 Fax: 954-555-4412 E-mail: 4corners@world.net	Four Corners Realty is a real estate company located in Hollywood, Florida. It specializes in the sale and rental of residential and commercial properties. Dennis Halpern is the president and CEO (Chief Executive officer). The company has a large staff of associates servicing the Hollywood, Florida area and has been selling fine properties for more than 25 years.	
Time Out Sporting Goods *Barkely Store* 1412 Barkely Street Chicago, IL 60004 Phone: 847-555-1200 Fax: 847-555-1201 E-mail: tosg@aom.com *Montrose Store* 235 Parsons Boulevard Chicago, IL 60075 Phone: 874-555-1950 Fax: 874-555-1951 Web: www.timeout.com	Time Out Sporting Goods is a family-owned and operated retailer of sporting equipment, sporting apparel, and athletic footwear. Time Out has two stores in the Chicago area. The Barkely store is located in downtown Chicago, while the Montrose store is located in a suburb west of the city.	
Sutton Investment Group 34562 Corona Street Los Angeles, CA 90001 Phone: 213-555-6660 Fax: 213-555-6623 E-mail: sutton@money.com Web: www.sutton.com	Sutton Investment Group is a full-service investment company located in downtown Los Angeles. They service corporate and individual clients and provide investment, financial planning, and brokerage services. They offer their employees a full benefits package and have been in business for ten years.	

UNDERSTANDING MOUS/SCANS

UNDERSTANDING MOUS:
MICROSOFT OFFICE USER SPECIALIST

What is certification?

The logo on the front cover indicates that the Microsoft Corporation has officially certified the book at both the Core and Expert user skill level for Office XP in Word, Excel, Access, PowerPoint, and FrontPage. This certification is part of the **Microsoft Office User Specialist (MOUS)** program that validates your Office skills. For more information about the MOUS program, visit www.mous.net. MOUS skills are identified throughout this book by the MOUS icon ▥. Appendix A provides a chart that lists the Core and Expert MOUS skill sets and activities, and references the page numbers in this text where the skill sets are discussed.

Why would I want to become certified?

- The Microsoft Office User Specialist Program provides an industry-recognized standard for measuring an individual's mastery of Office applications.
- By passing one or more Microsoft Office User Specialist Program certification exams, you demonstrate your proficiency in a given Office application to employers.
- Individuals who pass one or more exams can gain a competitive edge in the job marketplace.

Where does testing take place?

To be certified, you will need to take an exam from a third-party testing company called an Authorization Certification Testing Center. Call **800-933-4493** at Nivo International to find the location of the testing center nearest you. Learn more about the criteria for testing and what is involved. Tests are conducted on different dates throughout the calendar year. Course Technology, a division of Thomson Learning, has developed an entire line of training materials.

Skills Assessment Software

Use SAM XP, our skills assessment software, to gauge students' readiness for the Microsoft Office User Specialist certification exams for Microsoft Office XP. Through predefined MOUS prep exams that map back to skills taught in Course Technology textbooks, your students will have the tools they need to pass the MOUS certification exam with flying colors. For more information, visit www.course.com.

UNDERSTANDING SCANS:
SECRETARY'S COMMISSION ON ACHIEVING NECESSARY SKILLS

The Secretary's Commission on Achieving Necessary Skills (SCANS) from the U.S. Department of Labor was asked to examine the demands of the workplace and whether new learners are capable of meeting those demands. Specifically, the Commission was directed to advise the Secretary on the level of skills required to enter employment. In carrying out this charge, the Commission was asked to do the following:

- Define the skills needed for employment.
- Propose acceptable levels of proficiency.
- Suggest effective ways to assess proficiency.
- Develop a dissemination strategy for the nation's schools, businesses, and homes.

SCANS research verified that what we call workplace know-how defines effective job performance today. This know-how has two elements: competencies and a foundation. The SCANS report defines five competencies and a three-part foundation of skills and personal qualities that lie at the heart of job performance. These eight requirements are essential preparation for all students, whether they are entering the workforce, continuing in a present work environment, or planning further education.

SCANS workplace competencies and foundation skills have been integrated into Microsoft Office XP. The workplace competencies are identified as: 1) ability to use resources, 2) interpersonal skills, 3) ability to work with information, 4) understanding of systems, and 5) knowledge and understanding of technology. The foundation skills are identified as 1) basic communication skills, 2) thinking skills, and 3) personal qualities.

Please refer to the correlation document on the Instructor's Resource Kit CD-ROM for specifics on how the topics in this text meet these requirements.

TABLE OF CONTENTS

PREFACE

INTRODUCTION TO COMPUTERS

PERFORMING WITH EXCEL, INTRODUCTORY UNIT

PERFORMING WITH EXCEL, ADVANCED UNIT

APPENDICES

DIRECTORY OF DOCUMENTS
and
PORTFOLIO WORK SAMPLES

DIRECTORY OF DOCUMENTS

The document types indicated on the left can be found in the Lessons and Pages noted on the right.

PORTFOLIO WORK SAMPLES

You may use the documents that you produce in the Performance Phase of each Lesson as your portfolio work samples. Include all rough (first) copies along with the final document. See Appendix F for Portfolio Basics.

DIRECTORY OF FILES

Note to Learners

Read this section carefully so you have an understanding of the computer, its history, hardware and software applications, the Internet, telecommunications, and related topics.

INTRODUCTION

Thirty-five years ago, few people handled computers. Computer users were limited to specially trained operators and engineers.

No one ever anticipated that today every office worker must work with computers and that most people use computers in their everyday lives—both at home and at school.

Therefore, it is important to learn about the parts of a computer, how a computer operates, some of the tasks a computer can perform, and the many responsibilities of being a computer user. It is also important to understand how the computer you are using today evolved and how this incredible tool can give you access to one of the greatest sources of information—the Internet.

BRIEF HISTORY OF COMPUTERS

Although the microcomputer, or *PC* (personal computer), was developed in the early 1980s, computers have been around for a long time. A major step in computer technology was the development in the early 1800s of machines that could be programmed. The operation was controlled by cards with holes punched in them. In 1886, an electric punch-card machine was developed that could be used with electricity. In 1890, the U.S. Census results were tabulated for the first time with this new electrically driven punch-card tabulator.

In 1944, engineers from IBM and Howard Aiken of Harvard University developed a 50-foot-long, 8-foot-high machine that was able to add, subtract, multiply, divide, and refer to data tables using punched cards.

In 1945, a team from the University of Pennsylvania developed a machine for the U.S. Army's Ballistics Research Lab. This machine could make calculations a thousand times faster than earlier devices. The machine weighed in at approximately 30 tons and covered about 1,000 square feet of floor space.

In 1947, a method was developed for storing programs electronically. This invention of storing programs led the way for the development of today's computers. Before this invention, computers were wired to perform only certain tasks. If you wanted to change the task, the computer had to be rewired.

The first machine to be called a computer was completed in 1948. In 1951, the first commercial computer was completed. Eight of them were sold.

Besides becoming more versatile, computers were becoming faster, cheaper, and smaller. Computers were designed to perform tasks that responded to machine instructions. One of the original IBM computers could perform about 2,000 instructions per second. By the mid-1970s, operating speed had increased by more than 2,000%, to 43,000 instructions per second. By the late 1980s, computers had begun to be rated in *MIPS (millions of instructions per second).* Today's fastest supercomputers can handle well over a billion instructions per second.

The development of tiny silicon chips led the way for desktop microcomputers, or PCs. Microcomputers were first introduced in the mid-1970s. At that time, these small computers had limited memory and storage ability. Two major developments occurred in the early 1970s that led the way for the incredible growth of the computer industry. In 1975, Steve Jobs and Steve Wozniak started Apple Computer in the Jobs family garage and, also in 1975, Paul Allen and Bill Gates established their own company, Microsoft.

Today's modern PC is the direct result of the advancements made by Apple Computer and IBM in hardware and software development, Microsoft in software development, and chip manufacturers such as Motorola and Intel in processor development. These advancements have brought us computers that have thousands of times the capability as those of much larger computer systems of years ago—and at a fraction of the cost.

THE COMPUTER SYSTEM

A *computer* is an electronic device that can perform tasks and calculations based on the instructions that have been given to it.

How a Computer System Works

Although computers amaze us with their apparent "intelligence," all of their functions are based on these three very simple tasks:

- compare numbers or symbols to see if they are the same
- add two numbers together
- subtract one number from another

Computers can perform these tasks with great speed, accuracy, and reliability. Data is entered into the computer; the computer processes the data and displays the desired information. How does the computer know what to do with the data? A *software program,* a detailed set of computer instructions that resides in the computer, tells the computer what to do.

There are two types of computer software programs. One is *system program software,* which controls the way computer parts work together. The other is *application program software,* which tells the computer to perform a specific task. (See later section on software.)

Types of Computers

Computers vary in type, size, speed, and capability. The most common type of computer used in homes, offices, and schools is the *personal computer* (more commonly known as the *PC*), a computer that is small enough to fit on a desk, is relatively inexpensive, and is designed for an individual user. *Laptop computers* (also called *notebooks*), which are portable, also fall into this category.

Other types of computers include the following:

- *Supercomputer*
  The *supercomputer* is the fastest type of computer. It can store data and perform numerous tasks simultaneously at incredible speeds. This type of computer is used for specialized tasks that require vast amounts of mathematical calculations such as weather forecasting and medical and weapons research. Usually comprising many computers working in unison, the supercomputer is used only by government agencies, educational institutions, and large corporations.

- *Mainframe*
  Mainframe computers are less powerful and less expensive than supercomputers, but they are still capable of storing and processing large amounts of data. Several hundred individuals can use a mainframe, with their own terminals, at the same time. These computers are used most often by universities, medical institutions, and large companies such as banks and brokerage houses, where it is necessary to complete millions of daily transactions and save corresponding amounts of data.

- *Minicomputer*
  The *minicomputer*, also called a *server*, is smaller than a mainframe, is larger than a microcomputer, and can support multiple users, with their own terminals, at the same time. Medium-sized companies, such as accounting, advertising, and manufacturing firms, use these computers.

Computer Memory

Computer memory is composed of circuits that are contained in tiny computer chips. The number of memory locations is stated in terms of bytes. A *byte* is a unit of storage capable of holding a single character. A byte is equal to 8 bits. Large amounts of memory are indicated in terms of *kilobytes* (K or KB), *megabytes* (M or MB), and *gigabytes* (G or GB). A *kilobyte* is equal to 1,024 bytes, a *megabyte* is equal to 1,048,576 bytes, and a *gigabyte* is equal to 1,073,741,824 bytes. Twenty megabytes of memory can hold data equivalent to what could be saved on one box of floppy disks.

Every computer comes with a certain amount of physical memory, usually referred to as main memory or *random access memory (RAM)*. Think of main memory as an array of boxes, each of which can hold a single byte of information. A computer that has 1 megabyte of memory, therefore, can hold about 1 million bytes (or characters) of information.

Read-only memory, or *ROM,* is computer memory on which data has been prerecorded.

Data recorded on a ROM chip can only be read; it cannot be deleted. Unlike RAM, ROM preserves its contents even when the computer is shut down. Personal computers contain some ROM memory that stores critical programs, such as those needed for system start-up, for example.

Processing Power

A computer's procesing speed (also known as clock speed) is measured in *megahertz* (mHz) and *gigahertz* (gHz). In 1993, the average computer processing speed was 25 mHz. By the end of 1994, processing speed increased to 66 mHz for the PC. The 486DX2 chip was new, and there was talk about two new revolutionary chips from Motorola and IBM—the PowerPC and Pentium chips.

The PowerPC chip's speed started at 60 mHz and was capable of running at 120 mHz—unheard of in 1996. The Pentium matched these speeds. Within a year, chip speeds increased exponentially. Today, the PowerPC can run up to 733 mHz, and the current speeds for a Pentium 4 run at 1.4 and 1.5 gHz.

Although processor speed is one of the major factors of computer speed, several other significant factors give a computer a greater operating speed. In addition to faster RAM (the memory chips that hold data when the computer is running), computers now take advantage of data buffer called *cache* (pronounced "cash"). Cache is a series of superfast RAM chips that allow the processor to communicate more quickly and efficiently with the rest of the computer.

As for the future, both Motorola and Intel are working on the next-generation processor, again exceeding current processing speeds. These advancements in technology will be a step toward computers 100 billion times as fast as today's most powerful personal computers.

PARTS OF A COMPUTER

A computer system is made up of two principal components: hardware and software.

Computer hardware

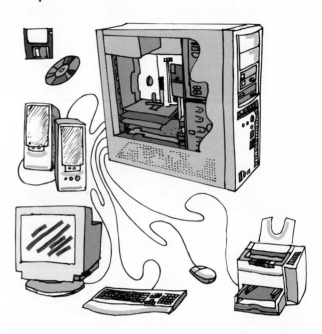

Hardware

Hardware refers to the physical parts of the computer and includes four main components: input devices, processing unit, output devices, and storage devices.

Input Devices *Input devices* transport data into the computer.

- *Keyboard*
  The **keyboard** is the most commonly used input device. It contains typewriterlike keys as well as specialized keys for entering data.

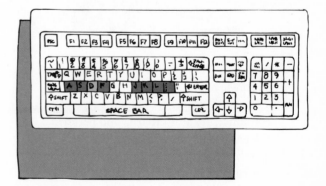

- *Mouse, pointing stick, trackball, light pen, puck, and touchpad*
  These small alternative input devices direct the movement of the insertion point on the screen.

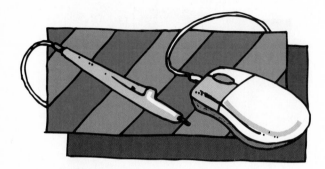

- *Optical character recognition (OCR) system*
  This device scans the printed page and translates characters and images into a computer file that can be edited (by a word processing application, for example).

- *Scanner*
  A *scanner* is a device that can read text or illustrations and transmit them in a digitized format to the computer screen. Scanners can be handheld or as large as a photocopy machine.

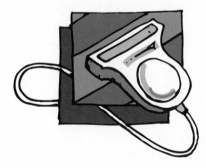

- *Digital camera*
  This is a filmless camera that captures images into memory storage. A *digital camera's* images can be transferred to a computer and edited or inserted into a document.

- *Video input camcorder*
  A *video input camcorder* is a digital video camera that can record live audio and video, which can then be downloaded into a computer for multimedia applications.

- *Microphone*
  A *microphone* accepts voice input to enter data or execute commands.

Processing Unit The processing unit, also referred to as microprocessor or *CPU (central processing unit)*, is the "brains" of the computer. This piece of hardware contains the computer chips and circuits that control and manipulate data to produce information.

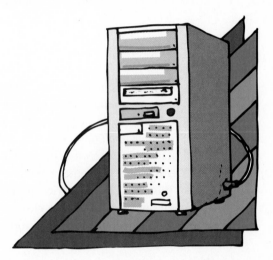

Output Devices Output devices allow the user to see or hear the information the computer compiles.

- *Printers*
  Printers are devices that print text or graphics on paper. Printers come in a variety of types and are categorized as either impact or nonimpact. An *impact printer* uses a device that strikes a ribbon on paper; *nonimpact printers* use laser and inkjet technology. The quality of the print and the printing speed determine the cost of a printer.

- *Speakers*
  Speakers are devices that amplify sound. Speakers can be internal or external to the computer.

- *Monitor*
  A **monitor**, also known as a **display**, **CRT** (cathode ray tube), **VDT** (video display terminal), or simply **computer screen**, allows the user to view computer information. Computer screens vary in size and cost depending on their **resolution**, which is the clarity and sharpness of an on-screen image. If you look closely at a computer screen, you will see that it is made up of a series of **pixels**, which is a series of dots. The more closely packed the pixels, the higher the resolution of the image.

Storage Devices *Storage devices* allow instructions and data to be saved. Some storage devices are housed within the computer; others are removable and thus allow data to be transported from one computer to another.

- *Hard drive*
  A **hard drive**, an internal storage device, is also known as a "fixed" disk. Hard drives can hold huge amounts of information. The size of the drive, that is, how much information it can save, affects the price of the computer. A computer that has one "gig" (gigabyte) of storage capacity can hold 1 billion bytes of information.

- *Floppy disks*
  Floppy disks (often called *diskettes*) are bendable oxide-coated magnetic plastic with a hard cover that can be inserted and removed from a disk drive. The 3½" floppy disk can store 1.4 MB of data.

- *Zip disks*
  Zip disks are larger versions of floppy disks. Each Zip disk holds as much information as 80 floppy disks (about 100 megabytes). Zip disks require a Zip drive, which can be connected inside or outside of the computer.

- *CD-ROM (compact disc—read only memory)*
  These disks can store huge amounts of data (approximately 650 megabytes, or about 500 floppy disks). Because of their large storage capability, **CD-ROMs** are often used to save graphics, video, and audio. CD-ROM discs require a CD-ROM drive.

- *DAT (digital audio tape)*
  Digital audio tape is a standard magnetic tape that resembles basic audiocassettes. DATs have the ability to hold tremendous amounts of information on a tape much smaller than an audiocassette. DAT devices can hold up to 10 separate DAT tapes, each of which can hold up to 26 gigabytes of information.

Software

Software is a set of instructions written by programmers in a machine (or programming) language that tell the computer what to do, how to do it, and how to perform tasks based on input from the user. The numerous **programming languages** include FOR-TRAN, COBOL, BASIC, C, C++, Java, JavaScript, Visual Basic, Visual C++, and RPG.

The words "software", "program", and "application" are used interchangeably. There are two types of software: operating system software and application software. Application software (like Microsoft Office) can run only when operating system software (like Windows 98) is installed and running on a computer. Operating system software can be compared to the foundation of a house; application software can be compared to the rooms within the house.

Operating System Software The basic operation of the computer is controlled by *operating system software.* This type of software manages the computer's files and programs and acts as a graphic interface that translates mouse and keyboard actions into appropriate programming code. There are many types of operating systems, each having different capabilities. Some operating systems can run only a single application at a time; others can multitask and run several at once. The most popular operating systems include Microsoft Windows and Apple Computer's Mac OS. Others include IBM's OS/2 Warp, Microsoft DOS (Disk Operating System), and UNIX, a text-based command-line interface operating system.

Some operating systems were created specifically for use on a network. These include Novell NetWare, AppleShare IP, Microsoft Windows for Workgroups, and Microsoft Windows NT Server.

Application Software Sometimes referred to as "tool" software, *application software* provides the tools needed to complete a task. Tool software is widely used by business, government, schools, and individuals for anything from financial management, Web surfing, and word processing to sound engineering, graphic design, and cooking.

These are the most common types of application software:

- *Word processing*
  Word processing software is used to create and print documents such as letters, memos, and reports. This type of software allows for easy editing of text. Microsoft Word is an example of word processing software.

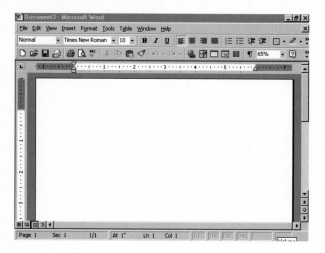

- *Spreadsheet*
  Spreadsheet software is used for analysis and reporting of statistical or numerical data to complete such tasks as preparing budgets, payroll, balance sheets, and profit and loss statements. Spreadsheet software can create charts from statistical information. Microsoft Excel and Lotus 1-2-3 are examples of spreadsheet software.

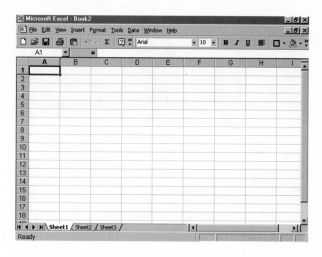

- *Database*
  Database software allows the user to collect, store, organize, modify, and extract data. Microsoft Access is an example of database software.

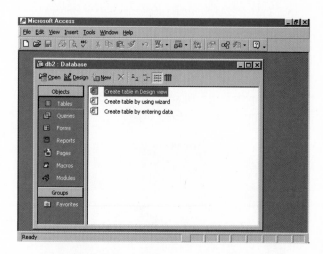

- *Accounting*
  Accounting software is used for organizing and managing money and finances. QuickBooks is an example of this type of software.

- *Groupware*

  Groupware is software that helps groups of users communicate and organize activities, meetings, and events through one common interface. For example, group software is used within corporations so all employees can share the same common screens on their computers. Lotus Notes is an example of groupware.

- *Communication*

  Communication software is used to transmit and receive information from one computer to another. For the transfer to take place, both the receiver and the sender must have the software installed.

- *Internet browsers*

  Internet browser software is used to locate and display Web pages. The most popular Internet browsers are Netscape Navigator and Microsoft Internet Explorer.

- *E-mail programs*

  E-mail programs are used to send and retrieve e-mail from a mail server. Eudora is an example of an e-mail program. Many e-mail programs are now part of other software applications. For example, you can now e-mail from within all Microsoft Office XP applications.

- *Online service*

  Online service software provides subscribers with the ability to communicate with one another, through e-mail, for example, as well as connect with unlimited third-party information providers, such as news, weather, and sports bureaus. America Online and MindSpring are examples of online service software. Access to this information also requires communications equipment. (See section on Telecommunications.)

- *Presentation*

  Presentation software is used to create slides that can be shown while an oral report is given. The slides often summarize report data and emphasize report highlights. Microsoft PowerPoint is an example of presentation software.

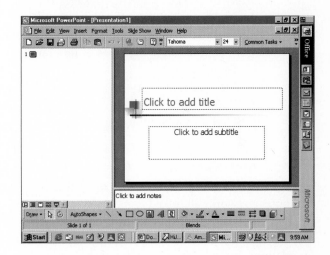

- *Voice recognition*

  Voice recognition software is used to create, edit, and format documents by speaking into a microphone (which is attached to the computer). The dictation is transcribed directly on the computer. Dragon Naturally Speaking and Point and Click are two popular voice recognition software products.

- *Web page*

  Web page software is used to create and manage professional-quality Internet Web sites. Microsoft FrontPage and Adobe PageMill are examples of Web page design software.

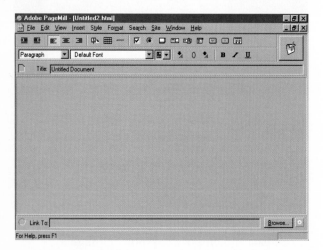

- *Graphics*

  A variety of **graphics** software packages are used to create charts, pictures, illustrations, drawings, and 3D images. Included in this category are the following types of programs:
  - Paint
  - Illustration/design
  - Photo-editing
  - Desktop publishing

THE INTERNET

The **Internet** is a worldwide network of smaller computer networks all linked together by unique **IP (Internet Protocol)** addresses. These computers may be located in businesses, schools, research foundations, hospitals, and/or individuals' homes. The Internet has unlimited uses. Businesses use the Internet to share information and to advertise their services and products. Students use the Internet for research and to share information with fellow students and professors. The Internet can be used to book airline flights, buy movie tickets, check your savings account, buy and sell stocks, order a pizza, shop for a gift, apply to a college, find a job, and buy a home. Internet users can also share personal information about themselves through chat groups, bulletin boards, and e-mail.

To access the Internet, a user must sign up with an **Internet Service Provider (ISP)**, which sells access to the Internet for a monthly charge. Some popular ISPs include the Microsoft Network, America Online, EarthLink, net.com, MindSpring, and AT&T Worldnet. Connecting via modem to an ISP allows a user access to the **World Wide Web,** a service of the Internet on which pages, or *Web sites,* display information. These Web sites are created by companies, individuals, schools, religious institutions, government agencies—just about anybody.

By subscribing to an ISP, a user is offered much more than access to the Web. Other ISP services include e-mail, news on demand, personal Web site hosting, and much more.

Some ISPs offer specific online content such as Dow Jones News Retrieval and Lexis/Nexis. These ISPs provide financial and business news that is updated daily. The cost to use these services depends on how long a user stays online and how much of the information is downloaded.

Information on the Web is created using a programming language called **HTML** (*hypertext markup language*). A Web browser translates HTML into a readable format. The Internet user can choose to use one of several dozen different Web browsers. Some popular Web browsers include Netscape Navigator and Microsoft Internet Explorer. Certain Web sites have a different look when viewed with different Web browsers due to translation inconsistencies. A Web browser can locate a specific site by its **uniform resource locator (URL)**, also known as its Web address. For example, the URL for the Microsoft home page is: www.microsoft.com.

TELECOMMUNICATIONS

To transmit data over a phone line, you need a modem. A **modem** (modulator/demodulator) is a device that connects a computer to a phone line, allowing data to be transmitted from one computer to another. For the transmission to work, both computers must have modems and the appropriate communications software. A modem can be internal (inside the computer in the form of a circuit board) or external.

Modems have various speeds at which they transmit data. Downloading files and transmitting data requires fast modem speeds. Otherwise, tasks can be very time consuming. Modem speeds are defined in terms of **baud rates.** For example, a 57,600-baud modem transmits data at 57.6 bits per second *(bps)*. A *bit* is a single binary unit of measurement.

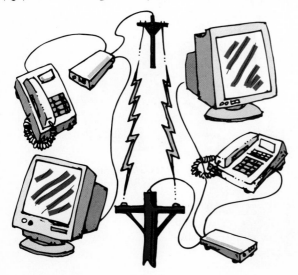

A *fax modem* not only transmits data, but allows graphics and documents to be sent as well. In this respect, the modem is similar to a real facsimile machine; however, the computer, unlike the fax machine, can receive faxes while it is turned off. To transmit faxes via the computer, you need to have the appropriate communications software package installed.

There are various ways to transmit data, sound, and video electronically. Here are some of the more common options:

* *Electronic mail (e-mail)*
  This method of transmitting electronic messages does not necessarily use a telephone line or assistance from an ISP. It may use a *network system* also known as an *intranet*. Users are able to send messages to one or more Internet mailboxes simultaneously. They can also retrieve messages. Access to an electronic mailbox is exclusive and limited. Generally, users of the mailbox must know a *password,* or code, to send or retrieve messages 24 hours a day to anyone around the world who has an e-mail address. E-mail addresses are usually formatted in a specific way: user@domain.com. For example, John Doe works for the Pixie Soda Company. His e-mail address might be john.doe@pixiesoda.com.

* *Fax*
  A term derived from the word "facsimile" (which means "duplicate" or "copy"), a *fax* is a machine connected to a telephone, that scans a document and translates the visual image into electronic impulses. These impulses are then transmitted along telephone lines to another fax machine at a different location. The remote machine receives the electronic impulses, reconstructs the visual image of the document, and prints out an exact copy of the original document.

* *Electronic bulletin board*
  Information on a variety of topics can be placed on or accessed from an *electronic bulletin board.* Through a computer connected to a telephone line, it is possible to "talk" with other users, "discussing" or exchanging information on topics ranging from zoology to taxes, stocks and bonds to medical issues.

Access to some bulletin boards is free; others charge a subscription fee.

- *Teleconferencing*
  Teleconferencing allows persons in different locations to see and hear one another. A videoconference is accomplished by using a television camera and microphone to transmit voice and video signals through satellite networks.

Networks

A computer **network** is a linked group of computers. Networks allow computers to share information, programs, printers, or scanners, or to facilitate communication between people via e-mail. There are two principal kinds of networks: *intra* networks and *inter* networks. An **intranet** refers to an internal network confined within a specific location, usually one particular office or building. An intranet is sometimes referred to as a *LAN (local area network)*. An intranet can also include several interlinked LANs.

The main purpose of an intranet is to share files and records within a company. An intranet can also be used to facilitate group collaboration, and for teleconferences. For example, a law office might set up its own intranet so that every computer in the office can access the same files and case information and every computer prints to the same printer. An intranet can connect users to a common *file server* (minicomputer) that allows all of the computers connected to the network to access the same hard drive or the Internet or to go outside the company to a *WAN* (wide area network).

Regardless of whether you are connected to a LAN or a WAN, you must always enter a password to access, or "log in to," the network. Network connections transmit data at a much faster speed than does a modem or a telephone line.

In addition to networked computers, businesses have the ability to communicate with workers outside the office as well as with overseas co-workers through telecommunication and access to the Internet. Developing computer video and sound technology makes it possible for business meetings to take place entirely through computers (video conferencing). This is known as the "virtual office." Because the Internet provides 24-hour access to information, businesses that operate in multiple locations and time

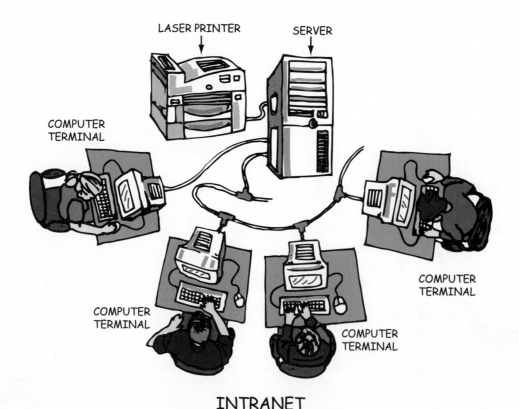

LASER PRINTER   SERVER

COMPUTER TERMINAL

COMPUTER TERMINAL

COMPUTER TERMINAL

COMPUTER TERMINAL

COMPUTER TERMINAL

INTRANET

zones can continue to work even when one workday is ending and another is just beginning. Workers no longer need to share office space or have a networked computer to share important information and accomplish team projects.

WIDE AREA NETWORK

Telecommuting

Telecommuting is a term used to describe employees using technology to perform regular work activities from a remote location. Telecommuting moves the work to the worker instead of vice versa, almost completely eliminating the need for a downtown business office.

The typical telecommuter has a personal computer (usually a laptop) with a fax/cellular modem. Once dialed into the company network as a remote user, the telecommuter has full use of the company's intranet, including the e-mail system, server files, and, in some cases, Internet capability as well.

COMPUTERS AND SOCIETY

At home, computers perform many functions. Application software can be used to calculate an individual's taxes, the household budget, and interest on a personal loan, or to determine an amount owed on a mortgage. More and more banks, through the use of ATMs (automatic teller machines), offer individuals the opportunity to do their banking without ever having to leave their homes. Financial transactions can be performed on one's personal computer, which, through the Internet, can be linked with a bank's computers.

In addition, many home computers have Internet access, and more and more home users are able to use the World Wide Web to shop. Internet credit card purchasing has increased significantly. Now you can book a flight to Walt Disney World; reserve a hotel room, order a pizza; and buy books, clothing, vitamins, or even concert tickets with very little effort.

Tired of television? Then play games! Computer-based video games have become increasingly popular among young and old alike. The types of games available range from traditional games—such as chess, backgammon, and poker, which are adapted to video screens—to more-complex, interactive games, such as flight simulation and strategy games in which the computer is a challenging opponent.

Computers are often present in the household in less visible ways. Home heating thermostats, watches, cars, and even children's toys all contain complicated computer systems. Washing machines, microwave ovens, answering machines, and dishwashers are just a few of the household appliances containing small computers that greatly reduce manual household labor.

Future Technologies

Computer technology is developing at an extraordinary rate. It has been said that the state of technology doubles in efficiency and speed every year. Computer hardware and software become obsolete within months of their initial development, while at the same time new products with extraordinary capabilities become available to the general market. For example, *DVDs (digital versatile discs)* have seven times the storage capacity of CD-ROMs without taking up any more space. In addition, DVD players are backward compatible and thus able to support the soon-to-be-outdated CD-ROM technology. DVD will eventually replace laserdiscs, CD-ROMs, and traditional VHS videotape.

Another example of a rapidly developing technology is virtual reality. *Virtual reality (VR)* software uses three-dimensional graphics and special devices such as a data glove and VR goggles to allow the user to interact with a computing environment in "real space." Although many people are familiar with VR in relation to computer simulation games, the development of VR technology has had a significant impact on many professions and fields of research.

Voice recognition software technology is making incredible advancements in perfecting the computer's ability to carry out voice commands and take dictation. It is now possible to purchase software for as little as $200 that allows the user to speak naturally into the computer up to 160 words per minute without pausing between words. The words appear immediately on the computer's screen.

An up-and-coming technology known as *intercasting* is the merging of the personal computer with the television. Web TV is a television that can be used to surf the Internet. Computer data must still be converted into signals that can be understood by the television. With the development of digital television and cable modems, however, complete intercast, with high-quality resolution, will be a definite reality.

Your Responsibility Using a Computer

In business, workers mostly deal with public information; however, a great deal of private information (e.g., phone numbers, Social Security numbers, tax records, credit card information, medical histories, and legal records) is also stored on computers. Access to this information usually requires knowledge of passwords and/or codes. Therefore, a computer database may be a secure place to keep private, extremely important, or secret records. Computer databases can be a more secure storage medium than a piece of paper. Some of the U.S. government's top secret records and research are entered into computers. In the wrong hands, such information could do great damage.

When irresponsible or unethical individuals, sometimes referred to as *hackers,* discover ways to break codes and hack into classified files, not only personal but also national security may be threatened.

A great deal of responsibility goes along with personal computing. Working in an office allows you to obtain confidential information only when you are authorized to do so. It is a criminal offense to retrieve or view information from a private or limited-access computer or database without permission. It is also illegal to make copies of software programs. In addition, information provided on the World Wide Web is usually copyrighted and protected by the creators and Webmasters of the site. Copying software or duplicating information from the Web for public business is a violation of U.S. copyright infringement regulations. Violators are subject to prosecution and imprisonment. Finally, when using information from the Internet for independent research, cite the Web site, author, and original source where applicable. Not to do so is considered plagiarism.

CARE OF YOUR COMPUTER, PERIPHERALS, AND DATA

To maximize the use of your computer, take steps to maintain its operation. Some maintenance is required periodically; other care is required each time you use your computer. It is also critical to take positive, proactive steps to reduce the risk of data loss.

Care of Computer and Peripherals

System Care The system case should be cleaned, both inside and out, on a regular basis to prevent buildup of dust.

- Wipe the outside case clean with a damp cloth. Never spray liquids directly on the casing.
- The inside of the computer can be cleaned by using a compressed-air can to blow out dust, or by using a small handheld vacuum to remove the dust.
- Check the power supply fan periodically to be sure that it has good ventilation and is free of dirt and dust buildup.

Monitors

- Clean monitors using a soft, damp cloth to remove the dust, which accumulates rather quickly. This should be done at least once a week.

- Be sure to check that the monitor's cooling vents are never blocked.
- Do not keep monitors turned on for extended periods of time, and certainly not overnight. This will minimize safety risks and increase the monitor's life span.

Floppy Disk Drives Unlike hard disk drives, which are sealed within the central processing unit of the computer, floppy drives are exposed to the outside air. The drive's read/write heads should be cleaned every few months using alcohol or special cleaning kits.

Keyboards Keyboards are somewhat resistant to abuse, but over time they will develop keys that stick or repeat if they are not maintained. To avoid these problems, keep food and liquids away from the keyboard.

- Develop a "no eating and drinking" policy while using the computer. Should liquids spill into the keyboard, it is likely you will need to replace it.
- Clean the key caps at least once every six months, and use compressed air to blow out dust from between the keys.

Mice Like keyboards, mice are handled all the time and tend to accumulate a good deal of dirt. If the ball becomes dirty, it will not roll properly and the pointer will not react on the screen's surface. Using a damp cloth, clean the mouse and the rollers inside the mouse unit at least once a month.

Care of Media

Floppy Disks

- Do not subject disks to temperatures above 120°F, because they will warp and all data on them will be lost. Keep disks in a cool, dry place.
- Do not touch the surface of the disk, because fingerprints or dirt can cause problems reading the disk.

- Do not expose disks to moisture or liquid.
- Do not expose disks to magnetic fields (magnets, stereo speakers, home appliances). This too can cause data loss.
- Although disks are called "floppy," the magnetic tape within the jacket should not be bent. Doing so will damage the disk.
- Airport X-ray machines do not affect disks.

Compact Discs (CDs) Compact discs are more durable than floppies and they do not require as much special care.

- CDs should not be subjected to temperatures above 100°F.
- Do not handle the surface of a CD. Doing so causes the surface to become scratched, which will interfere with the disc's being read by the computer.
- Moisture and liquids will not harm a CD. If a CD becomes wet, simply wipe it off with a soft cloth.
- CDs are not affected by magnetic fields.
- CDs can be cleaned using a damp, soft cloth.
- Airport X-ray machines do not affect CDs.

Care of Data

To prevent data loss, perform daily backup of your data from your hard drive to a floppy disk, Zip disk, or tape drive.

To avoid losing data in an unexpected shutdown of your computer, be sure to:

- Save data frequently in all applications.
- Close all open applications.
- Shut down your operating system according to the instructions given to you by the system.

Install a virus-scan program on your computer to protect data from becoming infected.

Delete unwanted files from your hard drive monthly to increase hard drive performance.

PERFORMING WITH EXCEL
INTRODUCTORY UNIT

Excel Basics

In this lesson, you will learn about the Excel screen, including the toolbars, menus, and view preferences. While exploring the screen, you will use navigation techniques, express movements, and learn some basic worksheet concepts. File management will be discussed, and you will learn to store your workbooks in their own folder.

▶ **Upon completion of this lesson, you should have mastered the following skill sets:**

- ✴ Start Excel
- ✴ Explore the Excel workbook
- ✴ Explore menus and toolbars
- ✴ Set view preferences
- ✴ Navigate the worksheet
- ✴ Use scroll bars
- ✴ Use the Go To command Ⓜ
- ✴ Create a folder for saving workbooks Ⓜ

Terms
MOUS-related
Worksheet
Workbook
Status bar
Task pane
Title bar
Menu bar
Toolbar
Formula bar
Active cell
Name box
Column
Row
Cell
Cell address
Active cell reference
Scroll bars
Working folder
Folder

TRYOUT

 GOAL
To practice using the following skill sets:
- ✷ Start Excel
- ✷ Explore the Excel workbook
- ✷ Explore menus and toolbars
- ✷ Set view preferences

TASK 1

WHAT YOU NEED TO KNOW

About Excel

Excel is a powerful spreadsheet tool you can use to analyze, chart, and manage data for personal, business, and financial use. You can also use Excel to produce worksheets, charts, databases, and publish data to the Web.

Start Excel

> To start Excel, on the Windows taskbar, click Start, select Programs, and click Microsoft Excel. If the Office Shortcut Bar is installed on your taskbar, just click the Excel icon.

TRY *it* OUT

1. Click **Start** on the Windows taskbar.
2. Select **Programs.**
3. Click **Microsoft Excel.**

Explore the Excel Workbook

> When you start Excel, a new workbook, called Book1, appears and you are on a *worksheet* entitled Sheet1. The *workbook* contains three worksheets identified by the sheet tabs at the bottom of the workbook. The active sheet is Sheet1, as shown in Figure 1.1, but you can click another sheet tab to make it the active sheet. You can increase the number of sheets in a workbook to 255.

> The bottom of the screen also contains the *status bar,* which displays the condition of worksheet calculations and settings. This bar shows items such as the setting for caps or number lock.

TRY *it* OUT

1. Click **Sheet2.**
2. Click **Sheet3.**
3. Click **Sheet1.**

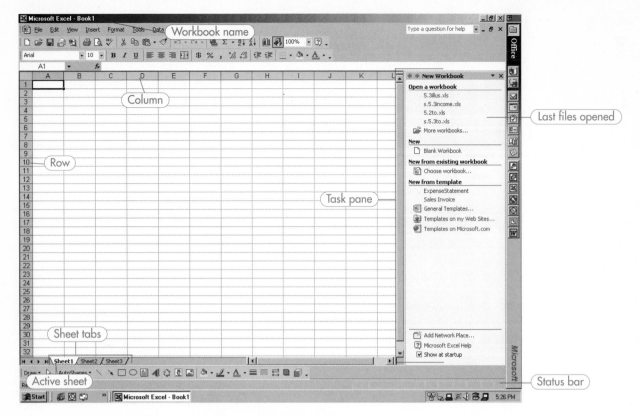

Figure 1.1 Excel workbook screen

> On startup, the *task pane,* on the right side of the screen, appears and shows options for the task at hand. In the New Document task pane, the Open a workbook section shows the last four files opened. In the New section, you can open blank, existing, or template workbooks. Use this pane to select workbook options, or close it as needed. If the task pane does not display, you can set View Preferences to display it discussed on the next page.

Explore Menus and Toolbars

> The top portion of the screen contains the *title bar,* the *menu bar,* and the *toolbar.* Excel also has a *formula bar,* which contains the name box on the left, the Insert Function button, and an area that displays the contents of the active cell. The *active cell* is the location of the worksheet insertion point and shows where you are currently working. The name of the active cell appears in the *name box.*

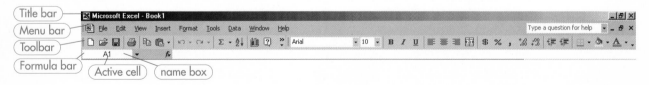

Figure 1.2 Excel title bar, menu bar, toolbar, and formula bar

> The opening screen shows, on one row, the most frequently used toolbar buttons from the Standard and Formatting toolbars. You can select buttons that are not displayed from the list that appears when you click the arrow at the end of the toolbar. However, for ease of use and to correlate your computer screen with the figures in the Excel unit, display both toolbars fully, as shown in Figure 1.3, by selecting the Show Buttons on Two Rows option.

TRY*it* **OUT**

1. Click **File.**

2. Position the mouse pointer over all other menu headings to display the menu items.

3. Click the **Toolbar options** arrow.

4. Click the **Show Buttons on Two Rows** option.

5. Position the mouse pointer over each button to view its function.

Figure 1.3 Standard and Formatting toolbars displayed on two rows

Set View Preferences

> Use the View menu to set display options for your Excel workbook. As shown in Figure 1.4, Task Pane, Formula Bar, and Status Bar are checked on the menu, which means they are displayed. Click the check marks for these features to remove them from the display.

Figure 1.4 View menu

> To further customize view preferences, click Tools, Options, and click the View tab in the Options dialog box, as shown in Figure 1.5. Here, you can deselect multiple windows in the taskbar or show formulas, page breaks, or gridlines in color.

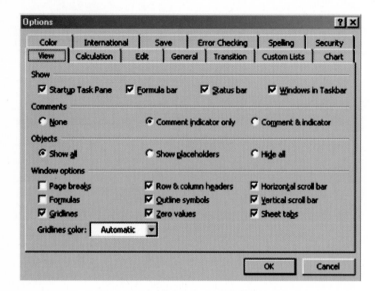

Figure 1.5 Options dialog box

> If you are working on a large worksheet or have difficulty seeing all the data, two View options will help. The Full Screen option on the View menu expands the worksheet to fill the screen and closes the toolbars and the formula bar. The Zoom option on the View menu lets you set the magnification of cells in a worksheet, as shown in Figure 1.6.

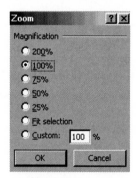

Figure 1.6 Zoom dialog box

TRY *it* **OUT**

1. Click the **View** menu. Notice the checked features.

2. Highlight **Toolbars.** Notice the checked and available toolbars.

3. On the View menu, click **Full Screen.**

4. Click **View, Full Screen** to return to the normal view.

5. Click **View, Zoom** to see the dialog box.

6. Click **Cancel.**

7. Click **Tools, Options.**

8. Deselect the **Status bar** and click **OK.**

9. Restore the status bar using the View menu.

REHEARSAL

 GOAL
To explore the Excel workbook

SETTING THE STAGE/WRAPUP
Start Excel

TASK 1

WHAT YOU NEED TO KNOW

> If you have a shortcut to Excel on your desktop, double-click it to start the application, or click Start, Programs, and Microsoft Excel.

> In this Rehearsal activity, you will explore the Excel workbook, toolbars, and menus. You will use the View menu to set and reset preferences.

▼ DIRECTIONS

1. Click **File.** Notice the menu selections.
2. Click away from the File menu once to close it.
3. Select and view the commands on each remaining menu.
4. Click **Sheet3.**
5. Click **Sheet1.**
6. Rest the mouse pointer on a toolbar button to display its name.
7. Find the toolbar buttons for Bold, Print, and Save.
8. Click **View, Toolbars.**
9. Deselect the **Formatting** and the **Standard** toolbars.
10. Restore the toolbars.
11. Click **View, Zoom.**
12. Select and accept other magnifications to view the effect.
13. Return to 100% magnification.
14. Use the View menu to deselect the Task Pane, Formula Bar, and Status Bar.
15. Use the View menu to reselect the Formula Bar and the Task Pane.
16. Click **Tools, Options** to open the dialog box and make the following changes. In the View tab:
    a. Deselect the vertical and horizontal scroll bars.
    b. Set the gridline color to Red.
17. Restore the vertical and horizontal scroll bars and set the color back to Automatic.

Cues for Reference

Start Excel
- Double-click the **Microsoft Excel** icon on the desktop or shortcut bar.
  or
- Click **Start, Programs, Microsoft Excel.**

Set Zoom
1. Click **View, Zoom.**
2. Select percentage of magnification.
3. Click **OK.**

Select Toolbars
1. Click **View, Toolbars.**
2. Select or deselect toolbars.

Set Options
1. Click **Tools, Options.**
2. Select or deselect options.
3. Click **OK.**

TRYOUT

TASK 2

▶ **GOAL**
To practice using the following skill sets:
✷ Navigate the worksheet
✷ Use scroll bars
✷ Use the Go To command Ⓜ
✷ Create a folder for saving workbooks Ⓜ

WHAT YOU NEED TO KNOW

Navigate the Worksheet

> A worksheet has alphabetical *column* headings and numbered *rows*. The intersection of a column and row is called a *cell*. A worksheet contains 256 columns and 65,536 rows, which means that over 16 million cells are available for data. As you will see after the tryout, only a small part of the worksheet is visible on the screen at one time.

> A cell is referenced (referred to) by its unique *cell address*, which is made up of the column and row number. Cell B2, as shown in Figure 1.7, has a heavy border indicating that it is the active cell. The *active cell* is also identified in the *name box* on the formula bar, which always displays the *active cell reference*, and by the bolded column and row of the active cell. The mouse pointer is a plus sign when on the worksheet, as shown below.

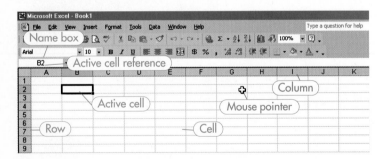

Figure 1.7 Worksheet with active Cell B2 in name box

> To move around the worksheet, press the arrow keys or press both an arrow key and the Ctrl key for express (fast) movements. As you move through the worksheet, the active cell changes, as does the active cell reference in the name box. A table of keystrokes to select cells and to navigate the worksheet is shown on the facing page.

T R Y*it* O U T

Note: As you move through the worksheet, notice the active cell reference in the name box and the rows and columns displayed.

1. Click **Cell D5** to make it active.

2. Press the left arrow key until **Cell B5** is selected.

3. Press the arrow keys to select **Cell H20.**

SELECT WORKSHEET CELLS

Select a cell	Click the cell
Select the worksheet	Ctrl + A, or click corner box
Select a row	Shift + Space
Select a column	Ctrl + Space

NAVIGATE THE WORKSHEET

Move one cell	Use the left, right, up, or down arrow
Move one screen up or down	Page Up or Page Down
First cell in worksheet	Ctrl + Home
First cell in current row	Home
First cell in current column	Ctrl + ↑
Last cell in current row	Ctrl + →
Last cell in current column	Ctrl + ↓

Use Scroll Bars

> To scroll to different areas in a worksheet, use the mouse pointer and the *scroll bars* at the right and bottom of the worksheet window, as shown in Figure 1.8, and summarized in the table below. Scrolling does not change the active cell.

USE SCROLL BARS

One column left or right	Click left or right scroll arrows
One row up or down	Click up or down scroll arrows
Scroll quickly	Click and drag scroll bar, press and hold Shift

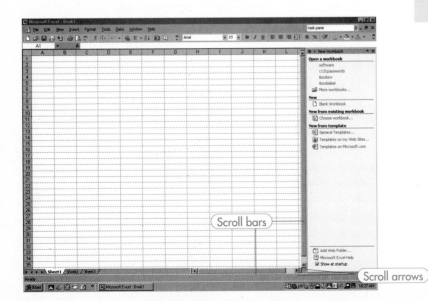

Figure 1.8 Scroll bars

Use the Go To Command

> To move directly to a specific active cell, click Edit, Go To, or press the F5 key. As shown in Figure 1.9, the Go To dialog box, where you enter the cell address, also shows you locations you have selected at least twice previously. If you repeatedly move to the same cell, you can just select it from the list.

> The dollar signs displayed with the cell addresses indicate that the address is an absolute reference (see Lesson 4) to that specific location.

> You can also go directly to a specific cell by entering the cell address in the name box, or by selecting the cell with the mouse pointer.

Figure 1.9 Go To dialog box

TRY it OUT

1. Click **Edit, Go To.**

2. In the Reference text box, enter **J122** and press the **Enter** key.

3. Press the **F5** key and go to **Cell AB321.** Click **OK.**

4. Click the **Name** box on the left side of the formula bar.

5. Enter **E15** and press the **Enter** key.

6. Press the **F5** key and select **Cell J122** from the Go To list.

7. To return to **Cell A1** press the **Ctrl + Home** keys.

Create a Folder for Saving Workbooks

> The *working folder,* or default location for saving your files, is usually the My Documents folder. A *folder* is a location, on a drive, that you create to hold files that are related to each other. In an office or instructional setting, a network administrator may predetermine the folder for saving files. See Appendix C to learn how to organize your files with Windows Explorer.

> Use the Open dialog box to create folders or subfolders to organize your workbook files. Click the Open button on the Standard toolbar and use the working folder provided, or click the down arrow to locate the drive and folder you can use. Click the Create New Folder button, on the Open dialog box toolbar, as shown in Figure 1.10, and name the folder. You can then select this folder so that it is in the Look in box. Use the same procedure to create subfolders within the new folder.

TRY it OUT

1. Click the **Open** button on the Standard toolbar.

2. Click the **Create New Folder** button on the Open dialog box toolbar.

3. Enter the name of the folder: **Excel Workbooks** (Notice that the folder is empty and the folder name is in the Look in box.) Click **OK.**

4. Click **Cancel.**

5. Click the **Save** button on the Standard toolbar. Notice your new working folder.

6. Click **Cancel.**

> Once you have selected a folder for opening and saving, it remains in the Look in box until you turn off the computer.

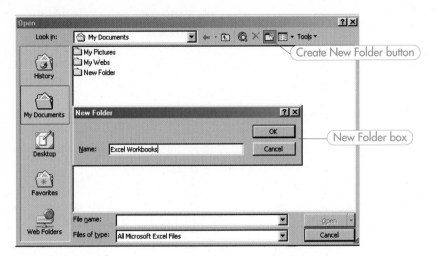

Figure 1.10 Open dialog box, opening a new folder

REHEARSAL

Again

TASK 2

SETTING THE STAGE/WRAPUP
Start Excel

WHAT YOU NEED TO KNOW

> Notice the active cell address in the name box as you move through the worksheet.

> In this Rehearsal activity, you will navigate the worksheet using shortcut keys and express movements. You will also create subfolder in your Excel Workbooks folder.

▼ DIRECTIONS

1. Click **Cell E5** to make it active.

2. Press the arrow keys to select **Cell AA45.**

3. Use express keystrokes to go to the following locations:
   a. Last cell in current row
   b. Last cell in current column
   c. First cell in current row
   d. First cell in worksheet

4. Click the **horizontal** scroll bar, press the **Shift** key, and drag to the right.

5. Click the **horizontal** scroll bar and press the **Shift** key until you can see **Column BZ.**

6. Drag the horizontal scroll bar to the left back to **Column A.**

7. Press the **F5** key to go to **Cell J33.**

8. Repeat Step 7 to go to **Cell BB159** and **Cell J33** again.

9. In the name box, enter: **G5**

10. Press the **Ctrl** key + **space** bar to select **Column J.**

11. Select the entire worksheet.

12. Select any cell.

13. Move one screen down.

14. Press the **Ctrl** + **Home** keys to return to **Cell A1.**

15. Click the **Open** button on the Standard toolbar; then, if Excel Workbooks is not in the Look in box, select it from the list of folders and double-click the folder.

16. Create a new folder and name it **Lesson 2** (for the files in the next lesson).

17. Click **Cancel.**

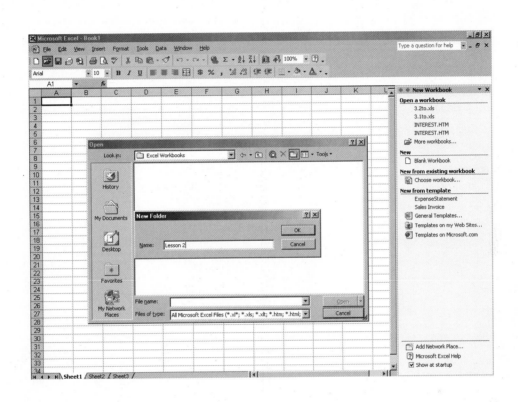

Scroll Through a Worksheet
- Click **scroll bar arrow** to move worksheet view.

  or
- Click **Shift** + **scroll bar arrow** to quickly scroll through worksheet.

Use Go To (Express Navigation)
1. Click **F5.**
2. Enter cell address.
3. Click **OK.**

Use Navigation Shortcuts

Select a row	Shift + spacebar
Select a column	Ctrl + spacebar
Move one cell	Use the left, right, up, or down arrow

Move one screen up or down	Page Up or Page Down
First cell in worksheet	Ctrl + Home
First cell in current row	Home
First cell in current column	Ctrl + ↑
Last cell in current row	Ctrl + →
Last cell in current column	Ctrl + ↓

Create New Folder
1. Click the **Open** button.
2. If necessary, click the list arrow in Look in box, or double-click a listed folder, to select location.
3. Click the **Create New Folder** button.
4. Enter the folder name.
5. Click **OK.**

ENCORE

MULTIPLE CHOICE

Identify the letter of the choice that best completes the statement or answers the question.

1. **The Full Screen option:**
   A. Hides all toolbars.
   B. Is found on the View menu.
   C. Is used when you need more display room.
   D. A and C
   E. A, B, and C

2. **A working folder:**
   A. Is a location where files are saved.
   B. Is found on the scroll bars.
   C. Can contain subfolders.
   D. A and C
   E. A, B, and C

3. **The active sheet:**
   A. Is the sheet with the white tab.
   B. Can be changed by clicking another sheet.
   C. Is shown on the toolbar.

   D. A and B
   E. All of the above

4. **You can navigate the worksheet using:**
   A. The Go To feature.
   B. Arrow(s) and Ctrl.
   C. F5.
   D. All of the above
   E. None of the above

5. **The task pane:**
   A. Displays on startup.
   B. Displays the last four files opened.
   C. Is at the right of the screen.
   D. Can be closed.
   E. All of the above

TRUE/FALSE

Circle **T** if the statement is true or **F** if the statement is false.

T   F   6. The Full Screen option expands the worksheet to fill the screen.

T   F   7. The status bar allows you to scroll to the location you need.

T   F   8. The active cell reference is displayed on the title bar.

T   F   9. The Zoom option lets you magnify the cells.

T   F   10. Go to A1 by pressing the Ctrl + Home keys.

Excel worksheet window

Identify common parts of the worksheet window. Write the number from the worksheet window illustration above next to its name below.

11. Number _____ best identifies the title bar.

12. Number _____ best identifies the name box.

13. Number _____ best identifies the task pane.

14. Number _____ best identifies the menu bar.

15. Number _____ best identifies the Standard toolbar.

16. Number _____ best identifies the worksheet tabs.

17. Number _____ best identifies a column.

18. Number _____ best identifies how to minimize the screen.

19. Number _____ best identifies the formula bar.

20. Number _____ best identifies the scroll bars.

Business Forms

In this lesson, you will learn to use Excel to design business forms and to customize both software and online templates. You will use the Internet to e-mail a form and to access the Microsoft Template Gallery.

Upon completion of this lesson, you should have mastered the following skill sets:

- Enter cell data
  - Enter text, dates, and numbers
  - Enter text beyond cell width
- Format cell data
  - Format dates
  - Format for currency
- Use Save and Save As
- Edit cell data
  - Edit cell contents
  - Align labels
  - Clear cell contents
  - Check spelling
- Use AutoComplete
- Use Print Preview
- Print
- Change print settings
- Work with templates
- Save a file as a template
- View Web templates

Terms

MOUS-related

Label
Left-aligned
Value
Right-aligned
Edit mode
AutoComplete
Template

Document-related

Business form
Transaction
Professional invoice
Purchase order
Vendor
Sales invoice

TRYOUT

TASK 1

GOAL
To practice using the following skill sets:
  ✳ Enter cell data
    ✳ Enter text, dates, and numbers M
    ✳ Enter text beyond cell width
  ✳ Format cell data
    ✳ Format dates M
    ✳ Format for currency M
  ✳ Use Save and Save As M

WHAT YOU NEED TO KNOW

Enter Cell Data

Enter Text, Dates, and Numbers

> When you enter an alphabetic character or symbol (text) as the first character in a cell, the cell contains a *label.* Labels are *left-aligned* in the cell by default.

> When you enter a number or date as the first character in a cell, the cell contains a *value.* Values are *right-aligned* in the cell by default.

> After you enter a label or value in a cell, press the Enter key or the arrow key that points to the location of the next data entry to enter the data. Notice the following in Figure 2.1:

  • Labels are left-aligned.

  • Dates and values are right-aligned.

> The date entry on the formula bar and in the cell memory contains the full year, but the date displayed has the default format of a two–digit year.

T R Y *it* O U T

1. Start Excel.

2. Enter the label in **Cell A1,** as shown in Figure 2.1.

3. Press the **right arrow** key to enter the data.

4. Enter the date in **Cell C1,** as shown on the formula bar.

5. Enter the data in **Row 3** of the illustration.

6. Notice the alignment of data.

7. Do not save or close the file.

Arial ▾ 10 ▾ **B** *I* U ▤ ▤

C1 ▾ *fx* 5/7/2002 — (Formula bar and cell entry)

	A	B	C	D
1	Meeting Costs		5/7/02	
2				
3	Room		650	
4	AV Equipment		200	
5	Coffee		150	
6	Total			
7				
8				

(Right-aligned dates and values)

(Left-aligned labels)

Figure 2.1 Label and value entries

Enter Text Beyond Cell Width

> Although the default cell width displays approximately nine characters, depending on the font, you can enter over 32,000 characters in each cell. If you enter text in a cell that is longer than the default cell width, it appears in the next cell's space as long as no other data is there. However, all the data is still located in the original cell address. Notice in Figure 2.2 that the full label, AV Equipment, is on the formula bar for Cell A4.

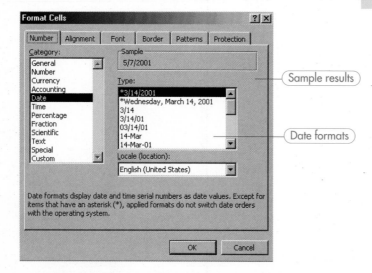

Figure 2.2 Labels beyond cell width.

Format Cell Data

Format Dates

> You can enter a date in any format and reformat it in one of 17 date formats. For example, if you enter the date in the mm/dd/yyyy format, you can change it to mm/dd/yy.

> To format dates, select the date and click Format, Cells. In the Format Cells dialog box, click the Number tab, click Date from the Category list, and click a date format from the Type list, as shown in Figure 2.3.

Figure 2.3 Format Cells dialog box

T R Y *i t* **O U T**

1. Enter the label in **Cell A4,** as shown.

2. Go to **Cell C4.**

3. Enter the value in **Cell C4.**

4. Click **Cell A4.**

5. Click **Cell B4.** Notice that there is no data on the formula bar.

6. Enter data for **Row 5.**

7. Do not close or save the file.

T R Y *i t* **O U T**

1. Click **Cell C1.**

2. Click **Format, Cells.**

3. Click **Date.**

4. Select the **March 14, 2001,** or full date format.

5. Click **OK.**

6. Do not close or save the file.

Format for Currency

> When you enter numbers or values, they are in the General format, which means that decimal places are only shown if there are decimal values. To add a dollar sign and two decimal places (Currency format), click the Currency Style button on the Formatting toolbar.

Use Save and Save As

> Excel workbooks are named Book1, Book2, and so forth, until you save them with your own file names. Click the Save button on the Standard toolbar to save a new file or to overwrite an existing file.

> When you click the Save button to save a new file, the Save As dialog box opens. Naming a file in the Save As dialog box creates an Excel Worksheet file with an .xls extension.

> When you created a new folder for your workbooks in Lesson 1, you created your working folder. If it is listed in the My Documents folder that appears, double-click your folder to make it active. If it is not listed, use the Save in box, in the Save As dialog box, to locate your folder.

> You can save Excel files with different names, in different locations, and in different file formats using the settings in the Save As dialog box. To save a file with any of these changes, click File, Save As, and select the appropriate settings. Notice the Save as type list, as shown in Figure 2.4.

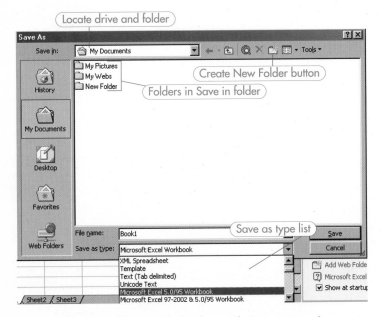

Figure 2.4 Save As dialog box with Save as type list

TRY it OUT

1. Click **Cell C3.**

2. Click the **Currency Style** button.

3. Format **Cells C4** and **C5** for currency.

4. Do not close or save the file.

TRY it OUT

1. Click the **Save** button.

2. Double-click the name of your working folder, if it is listed, or locate your folder using the list arrow in the Save in box.

3. Enter **2.1to** as the file name.

4. Click **Save.** Notice the file name on the title bar.

5. Enter **Total** in **Cell A6.**

6. Click the **Save** button. The new data is saved in that file.

7. Click **File, Save As.**

8. Enter **2.1to2** as the file name, to save the file under a new name.

9. In the Save as type box, click **Excel 5.0/95 Workbook,** for use with the earlier version of the software.

10. Click **Save.**

REHEARSAL

TASK 1

GOAL
To create a professional invoice

SETTING THE STAGE/WRAPUP
File names: 2.1proinv
                2.1solution

WHAT YOU NEED TO KNOW

> A *business form* is a document format that you develop for a business activity that occurs often. Once you create the form, you always use it to record that particular *transaction,* or business event, in a uniform manner. Many business forms are numbered consecutively for reference in records or communications.

> A *professional invoice* is a bill that a company or individual creates for professional services. Generally, consultants and professionals use this type of invoice for fee-based service businesses. You can itemize a professional invoice by the services provided.

> You can use preprinted forms or predesigned Excel worksheets for business forms. You can also create your own forms with Excel.

> In this Rehearsal activity, you will use the model illustration to create a professional invoice for Occasions Event Planning, for planning services.

▼ DIRECTIONS

1. Open a new blank worksheet. In **Cell C1,** enter the label as illustrated on the facing page. (Press the arrow keys to move to **Cell A3.**)

2. Enter the long label in **Cell A3.**

3. Enter the label in **Cell E3** and the date in **Cell F3.**

4. Click **Cell F3** to make it the active cell.

5. Click **Format, Cells,** to set the date format, as illustrated.

6. Enter the remaining data in the exact locations illustrated.

7. Format the date in **Cell B14** using the same date format.

8. In **Cell F16,** enter the value and format for currency.

9. Save the file; name it **2.1proinv.**

10. Resave the file as **2.1solution,** as an Excel 97 file type.

11. Close the file.

	A	B	C	D	E	F
1			INVOICE			
2						
3	Occasions Event Planning				Date:	5-Mar-02
4	675 Third Avenue					
5	New York, NY 10017				212-555-1234	
6						
7						
8	Bill to:		Mr. Martin Meyers			
9			1050 Greenway Street			
10			Brooklyn, NY 12015			
11						
12	Description				Amount	
13	Event:	Training Seminar				
14	Date:	5-Mar-02				
15						
16		Professional event planning services			$ 525.00	

Enter a Label or Value
1. Click cell to receive data.
2. Enter the label or value.
3. Press **Enter** or press an **arrow** key to move to next cell.

Format Dates
1. Select the date.
2. Click **Format, Cells.**
3. In the Number tab, click **Date.**
4. Select a date format.
5. Click **OK.**

Format Currency
1. Select the value to format.
2. Click the **Currency Style** button. 🔲$

Save
- For a new file, click the **Save** 🔲 button, see Save As, Steps 2 through 5, at right.
  or
- To resave an existing file, click the **Save** button. 🔲

Save As
1. Click **File, Save As.**
2. In Save in box, select location.
   or
- Double-click folder in current folder.
3. Enter file name in File name box.
4. Click **Save as type** down arrow, and click file type, if necessary.
5. Click **Save.**

TRYOUT

TASK 2

 GOAL

To practice using the following skill sets:

★ Edit cell data
  ★ Edit cell contents Ⓜ
  ★ Align labels Ⓜ
  ★ Clear cell contents Ⓜ
  ★ Check spelling Ⓜ
★ Use AutoComplete
★ Use Print Preview
★ Print Ⓜ
★ Change print settings

WHAT YOU NEED TO KNOW

Edit Cell Data

Edit Cell Contents

> If you notice an error *before* you complete an entry, press the Backspace key to edit data before you press the Enter key. Once you press the Enter key, the data is entered in the cell.

> If you notice an error *after* you enter the data, you can redo the entry or edit the data. If you redo the entry, the new data overwrites the original data.

> To edit data in Edit mode, press the F2 key or double-click the cell. If you want to add information at the end of the label, press the F2 key and the insertion point appears at the end of the label. However, if you want to insert text at the beginning or in the middle of the cell, double-click the mouse in the edit location.

TRY*it* OUT

1. Open **2.2to** from the Data CD.

2. Change "Legal Pads" to: **Legal Size Paper**
   a. Click **Cell C4.**
   b. Press the **F2** key. The insertion point is at the end of the label.
   c. Press the **Backspace** key to delete "Pads" and enter: **Size Paper**

3. Correct "Envelopes" to:
   #10 Envelopes
   a. Place the mouse pointer at the beginning of **Cell C3** and double-click the cell. You should be in Edit mode with the insertion point at the beginning of the cell.
   b. Enter: **#10** and a space

4. In **Cell A6,** enter: **130**

   Before it is entered, press the **Backspace** key and enter: **135.**

5. In **Cell A7,** enter: **182**
   Then, press the **Enter** key.

6. In **Cell A7,** enter **185:**
   Then, press the **Enter** key.

7. Do not close or save the file.

Align Labels

> As discussed in Task 1, by default, label text is left-aligned, whereas values and dates are right-aligned in the cell, as shown in Figure 2.5.

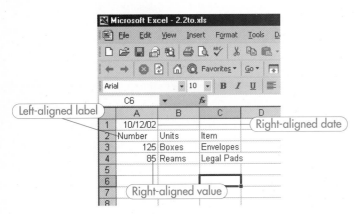

Figure 2.5 Excel workbook with default alignments

> However, you can change the alignment of data to improve the appearance of the worksheet by using the alignment buttons on the Formatting toolbar. You can left-align, center, or right-align data.

> To align labels, select the cell and click the appropriate alignment button. You should have the Formatting toolbar displayed, as shown in Figure 2.6, because in Lesson 1 you selected the Show Buttons on Two Rows option.

Figure 2.6 Alignment buttons on Formatting toolbar

Clear Cell Contents

> If you want to remove data you enter in a cell, select the cell and press the Delete key.

> You can also remove data by clicking Edit, Clear, and Contents.

T R Y *i t* **O U T**

1. Continue working in **2.2to.**

2. Click **Cell A2** and click the **Center** alignment button.

3. Center the label in **Cell B2.**

4. Center the label in **Cell C2.**

5. Left-align the data in **Cell A6.**

6. Right-align the data in **Cell A6.**

7. Do not close the file.

T R Y *i t* **O U T**

1. Continue working in **2.2to.**

2. Click **Cell A6.**

3. Press the **Delete** key.

4. Click **Cell A7.**

5. Click **Edit, Clear,** and **Contents.**

6. Do not close the file.

Check Spelling

> The Spelling feature compares the words in your file to the words in the application's dictionary. In Excel, there is no indication of a spelling error until you use the Spelling feature. Click the Spelling button on the Standard toolbar to check the spelling of worksheet labels.

T R Y *it* **O U T**

1. In **Cell B6,** enter the word: `reem` Then, press the **Enter** key.

2. Click the **Spelling** button.

3. Click **Yes** to start at the beginning of the worksheet.

4. Select **ream** in the Suggestions box and click **Change.**

5. Delete the text in **Cell B6.**

6. Do not save or close the file.

Use AutoComplete

> The *AutoComplete* feature lets you enter labels automatically if you have previously entered them in the same column.

> When you enter the first letter or letters of repeated data, Excel AutoCompletes the label from your previously entered data. If the label is correct, press the Enter key to confirm the entry. If it is not correct, continue entering the new label.

T R Y *it* **O U T**

1. Continue working in **2.2to.** Follow instructions to add **10 Boxes Pencils** in **Row 5.**

   a. In **Cell A5,** enter: `10`

   b. In **Cell B5,** start to enter: `Boxes` The AutoComplete feature will complete the label.

   c. Press the **Enter** key to accept the completed label.

2. In **Cell C5,** enter: `Pencils`

3. Do not close the file.

Use Print Preview

> Before printing, it is advisable to preview the worksheet because worksheets can become too large for one page. Click the Print Preview button on the Standard toolbar to open Print Preview.

> If the preview is satisfactory, as shown in Figure 2.7, you can print the worksheet using the Print button on the Preview screen.

T R Y *it* **O U T**

1. Continue working in **2.2to.**

2. Click the **Print Preview** button.

3. Click the data to get a better view.

4. Click the **Print** button on the Preview toolbar.

5. Click **OK** in the Print dialog box. The worksheet prints as previewed.

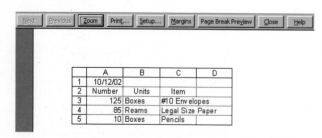

Figure 2.7 Print Preview screen

Print

> Use the Print button on the Standard toolbar to print a worksheet. Printing with the toolbar button prints the worksheet with default settings. The entire worksheet prints in portrait orientation without gridlines or row and column headings. If this is satisfactory, the Print button is the most efficient way to print.

TRY*it*OUT

1. Continue working in **2.2to.**

2. Click the **Print** button on the toolbar.

3. Click **OK** in the Print dialog box. The worksheet prints with default settings.

Change Print Settings

> To customize your printing, you may want to make changes to the default settings.

> To print only part of a worksheet, you must define the print area. With the mouse, select the block of cells you want to print, and click File, Print Area and set Print Area. You can clear the print area by clicking File, Print Area, and Clear Print Area.

> To change other print settings, use the Page Setup dialog box. For example, to set up gridline printing click File, Page Setup, click the Sheet tab, and select Gridlines in the Print section, as shown in Figure 2.8.

TRY*it*OUT

1. Continue working in **2.2to.**

2. Click in **Cell A2,** hold down the mouse button, and drag to select the block of cells from **A2** to **D5.**

3. Click **File, Print Area,** and **Set Print Area.** The area is outlined.

4. Click **File, Page Setup,** and click the **Sheet** tab.

5. Click the **Gridlines** check box in the Print section, and click **OK.**

6. Click the **Print Preview** button.

7. Click the **Print** button on the Preview toolbar.

8. Click **OK.** The worksheet prints as previewed with area and gridline settings.

9. Save the file **2.2to;** close the file.

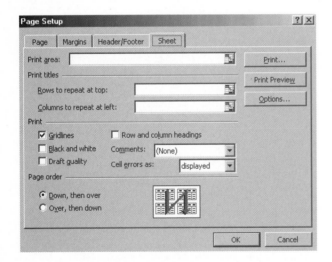

Figure 2.8 Page Setup dialog box with Sheet tab and Gridlines selected

REHEARSAL

TASK 2

GOAL
To create a purchase order

SETTING THE STAGE/WRAPUP
File name: **2.2purord**

WHAT YOU NEED TO KNOW

> A *purchase order* is a business form that a firm completes and sends to a *vendor,* or supplier, when merchandise or supplies are needed.

> The Received column is left blank, because it is used to check the order when it is received. The terms of the purchase define the agreement for payment. You can obtain the stock or item numbers and descriptions for the purchase order from the vendor's catalog, quotations, or Web site.

> When you enter data in a cell containing values and text, such as an address, Excel formats the entry as a label.

> In this Rehearsal activity, you will create a purchase order for supplies for Time Out Sporting Goods. Because you must enter formulas to calculate the purchase order total, you will not complete the purchase order until the next lesson.

DIRECTIONS

1. Open a new blank worksheet. Create the purchase order illustrated on the facing page by entering the values, dates, and labels in the appropriate cell locations. Press the arrow keys to enter the data and move to the cell you need for the next data item.

2. In **Cell B15,** notice the AutoComplete effect as you begin to enter the label.

3. Go to **Cell A13.**

4. Double-click the cell to use Edit mode and change the value to: **3**

5. Center the labels in **Cells A12, B12,** and **C12.**

6. Right-align the labels in **Cells G12** and **H12.**

7. Press the **F2** key to go into Edit mode to edit Cell D15. Change the cell data to: **#2345 Folders – Green**

8. Overwrite data in **Cell H5;** Change "30 days," to: **Check**

9. Set the print area for the range **A1:F6.**

10. Click the **Print** button to print a copy.

11. Clear the print area.

12. Make the setting to print the worksheet with gridlines.

13. Check the Print Preview screen, and print the entire worksheet.

14. Save the file, name it **2.2purord.** Close the file.

	A	B	C	D	E	F	G	H	I
1				PURCHASE ORDER					
2	Time Out Sporting Goods					Date:		10/15/XX	
3	1412 Barkely Street					Order #:		1000	
4	Chicago, IL 60064					Ship Via:		UPS	
5						Terms:		30 days	
6	Phone:	847-555-1200				Ordered by:		Bill	
7									
8	TO:	Supplies Unlimited							
9		545 Industrial Way							
10		Chicago, IL 60064							
11									
12	Quantity	Unit	Received	Description			Price	Amount	
13	5	Boxes		#2343 Folders			10.55		
14	4	Cartons		#654 Copy Paper			23.85		
15	2	Boxes		#2345 Folders			11.95		
16									
17									
18									
19									

Change to: Check

Change to: 3

Change to:
#2345 Folders - Green

Cues for Reference

Enter a Label or Value
1. Click cell to receive data.
2. Enter data.
3. Press **Enter** or press appropriate arrow to move to next cell.

Align Labels
1. Select the cell to align.
2. Click the appropriate alignment button:

Align Left

Center

Align Right   ▤

Edit Data
1. Double-click cell at edit location or press **F2.**
2. Edit data using Backspace, arrows, or other edit keys.

Clear Cell Contents
- Click **Edit, Clear, Contents.**
  or
1. Click the cell.
2. Press **Delete.**

Set Print Area
1. Select area to print.
2. Click **File, Print Area, Set Print Area.**

Clear Print Area
Click **File, Print Area, Clear Print Area.**

Print with Gridlines
1. Click **File, Page Setup,** and **Sheet** tab.
2. Click **Gridlines** check box.
3. Click **Print** in the dialog box.
4. Click **OK.**

TRYOUT

TASK 3

▶ **GOAL**

To practice using the following skill sets:

✴ Create a workbook using a template
✴ Work with templates [M]
✴ Save a file as a template [M]
✴ View Web templates

WHAT YOU NEED TO KNOW

Work with Templates

> Excel provides model worksheet designs, or *templates*, for common business forms. A template contains worksheet settings, such as fonts, formatting, styles, and formulas. Template files have an .xlt extension, and are model worksheets that are not changed or overwritten. You can open the available Excel templates using the New Workbook task pane, New from template section, as shown in Figure 2.9. If the task pane is not displayed, click File, New.

Figure 2.9 New Workbook task pane, New from template section

> Click General Templates to open the Templates dialog box and click the Spreadsheet Solutions tab, as shown in Figure 2.10.

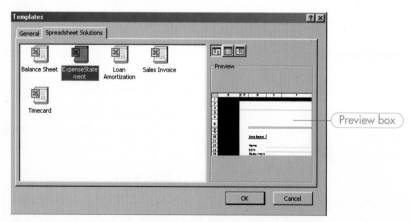

Figure 2.10 Templates dialog box, Spreadsheet Solutions tab

T R Y *it* **O U T**

1. If the New task pane is not displayed, click **File, New.**

2. Click **General Templates** on the New Workbook task pane to open the Templates dialog box.

3. Click the **Spreadsheet Solutions** tab.

4. Click each icon and view a sample in the Preview box.

5. Double-click the **ExpenseStatement** template.

6. Enter your name on the expense statement and press the **Enter** key.

7. Do not save or close the file.

Save a File as a Template

> If you customize a template, save it as a template file so that it will remain intact after each use. When you save a file as a template, Excel automatically saves it in the Templates folder, with an .xlt extension.

> Save a file as a template in the Save As dialog box by clicking Template in the Save as type drop-down list, as shown in Figure 2.11. The new template file is then found in the General tab in the Templates dialog box (see Figure 2.10).

Figure 2.11 Saving a file as a template

View Web Templates

> Additional templates are available at Microsoft.com at Office on the Web or at Web sites you have personally located. You can view, customize, and save them to your computer. If you are online, you can select Templates on Microsoft.com from the New Workbook task pane, which will directly link you to Internet Explorer and the appropriate Web site, as shown in Figure 2.12.

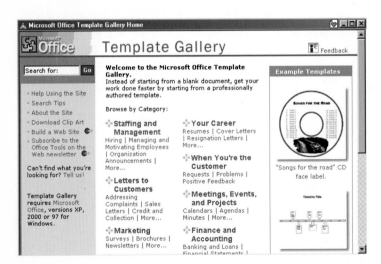

Figure 2.12 Online Template Gallery

TRY*it*OUT

1. Click **File, Save As.**

2. Name the file **myexpenses.**

3. Click the **Save as type** list arrow and click **Template.**

4. Click **Save.**

5. Close the file.

6. Click **General Templates** in the New Workbook task pane and click the **General** tab in the Templates dialog box. Notice the location of your template.

7. Right-click your template's icon and click **Delete.** Click **Yes** to send to Recycle Bin.

8. Close the Templates dialog box.

TRY*it*OUT

Note: You need Internet capabilities for this Try it Out. You may prompted to install and run "Microsoft Office Tool on the Web Control" to open templates. If so, do the install so that you can use Templates on Microsoft.com.

1. Click **File, New** to display the task pane.

2. Click **Templates on Microsoft.com.**

3. Explore the Business Forms, Invoices, and Billing categories.

4. Select and view the **Services Invoice.**

5. Exit the browser.

6. Close Excel.

R E H E A R S A L

TASK 3

 GOAL
To create a customized sales invoice template and then create a sales invoice

SETTING THE STAGE/WRAPUP
File names: **2.3invoice**
2.3timeout

WHAT YOU NEED TO KNOW

> A *sales invoice* is a bill that a seller prepares and sends to a customer to whom the seller supplies goods. It usually contains an itemized list of items sold, as well as shipping and payment information, and may contain the customer's purchase order number.

> Customize the Excel template for the sales invoice for your company and save it as your own template. You can then use this template to prepare all company invoices in the future. Because the template contains formulas, it automatically calculates the total bill.

> In this Rehearsal activity, you will prepare an invoice template, as shown in Figure 2.13, and an invoice for Supplies Unlimited. It has sent supplies ordered by Time Out Sporting Goods and needs to bill Time Out for the goods.

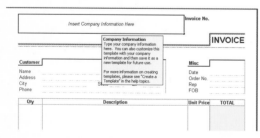

Figure 2.13 Sales Invoice template, company information

▼ D I R E C T I O N S

1. Open the Sales Invoice template in the Spreadsheet Solutions tab of the Templates dialog box.

2. Click in the **Company Information** box at the top of the invoice, double-click and select the **Insert Company Information Here** line.

3. Enter the company information, as illustrated on the facing page.

4. Scroll to the bottom of the invoice to the **Insert Fine Print Here** section.

5. Select the box and text and use the Edit menu to clear the contents of this box.

6. Select the box and text for the **Insert Farewell Statement Here** box and enter the slogan, as illustrated.

7. Save the file as a template; name it **2.3invoice.**

8. Close the file.

9. Open the new **2.3invoice** template file in the General tab of the Templates dialog box.

10. Complete the invoice, as illustrated. Notice that the totals are automatically calculated.

11. Enter shipping charges of: **$10**
Click the **Undo** button and change the amount by entering: **$15**

12. Enter the tax rate of **6.25%** in **Cell L37,** the white box closest to the **Tax Rate** label.

13. Print the invoice.

14. Save the file as an Excel workbook file and name it **2.3timeout.**

Supplies Unlimited * 545 Industrial Way * Chicago, IL 60064 * 847-555-6545

Invoice No.

INVOICE

Customer

Name	Time Out Sporting Goods
Address	1412 Barkely Street
City	Chicago
Phone	847-555-1200

State IL   ZIP 60064

Misc

Date	10/20/xx
Order No.	1000
Rep	Joe
FOB	

Qty	Description	Unit Price		TOTAL	
3	Boxes #2543 Folders	$	10.55	$	31.65
4	Cartons #654 Copy Paper	$	23.85	$	95.40
2	Boxes #2545 Folders	$	11.95	$	23.90

These values will change when shipping charges are added

SubTotal	$		150.95
Shipping			
Tax Rate(s) 6.25%	$		9.43
TOTAL	$		160.38

Payment   Check

Comments	
Name	
CC #	
Expires	

Office Use Only

Enter shipping charges as directed

Your unlimited resource for supplies!

Open Templates Dialog Box
1. Click **File, New** to display the New Workbook task pane.
2. Click **General Templates** in the New Workbook task pane.

Customize Template
1. Select area to customize.
2. Double-click on placeholder text, and drag mouse to select it.
3. Enter in the custom information.

Save File as Template
1. Click **Save.**
2. Enter the file name.
3. Click **Template** in the Save as type box.
4. Click **Save.**

PERFORMANCE

▶ **SETTING THE STAGE/WRAPUP**

Act I: File names: 2.1proinv
                    2p1.bill

Act II: File names: 2p2.otginv
                     2p2.bertle

Act III: File name: 2p3.quote

WHAT YOU NEED TO KNOW

Act I

Wilson Jones, the director of the Corporate Travel Group at Odyssey Travel Gear, has just completed arrangements and travel bookings for a corporate conference in Scottsdale, Arizona. The conference is planned for February 10/13 for Garrison Games, Inc, 342 Third Avenue, New York, NY 10017. You are to prepare a bill for $2200 using a Professional Invoice form to bill for conference-planning services.

※ In the New Workbook task pane, click **New from existing workbook,** and open the file **2.1proinv** from the Data CD. This opens the Professional Invoice file from Task 1 as a new file.

※ Edit the file using the current information. Use today's date on the invoice.

※ Save the file; name it **2p1.bill.**

Act II

You work for Marilyn Healy in the Marketing Department at Odyssey Travel Gear. She has asked you to prepare an invoice using an invoice template for wholesale catalog sales. Odyssey is now beginning to market to hotel boutiques by providing a trade discount price list with the catalog. The sale was made to the Bertleson Hotel, 2356 Lakeview Drive, Chicago, IL 60611, 800-555-8787.

※ Create a new invoice template for Odyssey Travel Gear. Enter the company name and address, and the "Fine Print" and "Farewell Statement" as listed below:

Company Information: Enter the name and address on one line, using asterisks (*) between the company name and address to separate the data.

Fine Print: `For questions, call Customer Service at 630-555-8888, Extension 15.`

Farewell Statement: `Thank you for choosing Odyssey Travel Gear.`

Save the file as a new template; name it **2p2.otginv.**

✯ Complete the invoice using today's date and the data below:

Invoice No. 2000, Order No. BH543, Rep. Marilyn

Qty	Description	Unit Price
12	Leather waist packs #432	1235
6	Collapsible luggage cart #1654	1850
12	Travel alarm clock #211	1450

Shipping is $18.50.

There is no sales tax, because this is a wholesale transaction.

Payment method is Credit.

✯ Save the document; name it **2p2.bertle.**

✯ Attach the invoice to an e-mail to Mr. Mark at the Bertleson Hotel (but send it to your teacher). Tell Mr. Mark that his order is being shipped, that the invoice is attached, and that the invoice will also be included with the shipment.

Act III

You work for the sales manager, Kiley Thompson, in the New York office of Trilogy Productions. A small independent film company has requested a quotation of rates for using the studios and editing facilities. Locate a template for a quotation online using the Microsoft Template Gallery. Either click Templates on Microsoft.com in the New Workbook task pane, or access the Web site at: office.microsoft.com/templategallery/default.asp Find the quotation form by selecting **Business Forms, Invoices and Billing,** and **Price Quotation.**

✯ When you locate the Price Quotation form, select **Edit the form in Excel.** Save the file; name it **2p3.quote** and disconnect from the Internet.

✯ Enter the following information:

Date: 3/10/02, Quotation valid until: 4/10/02, Quotation: 100, Customer ID: 346

Prepared by: Your name

Bill to: Jamal Johnson
Johnson Films, Inc
432 Christopher Street
NY, NY 10012

212-555-4388

2 days	Use of studio for filming short subject	$4200.00
1 day	Use of editing facilities	$1000.00

Customer will provide personnel.

✯ Use Edit mode to edit the line below the total to read: `If you have any questions concerning this quotation, contact Kiley Thompson, Extension 420.`

✯ Save the worksheet as **2p3.quote.**

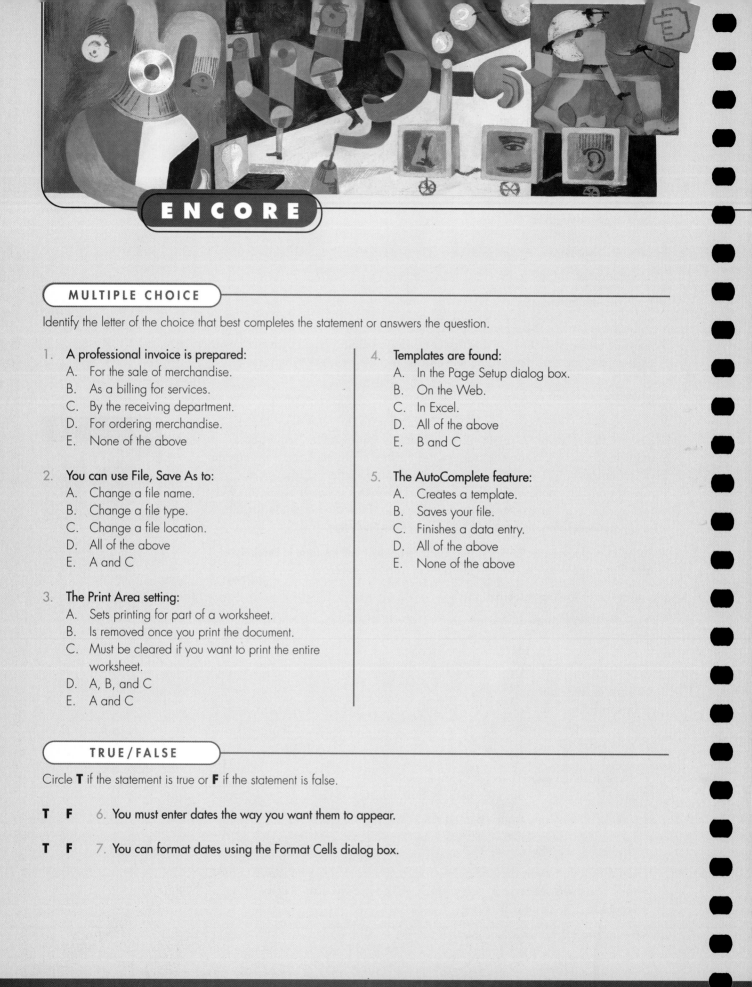

ENCORE

MULTIPLE CHOICE

Identify the letter of the choice that best completes the statement or answers the question.

1. **A professional invoice is prepared:**
    A.   For the sale of merchandise.
    B.   As a billing for services.
    C.   By the receiving department.
    D.   For ordering merchandise.
    E.   None of the above

2. **You can use File, Save As to:**
    A.   Change a file name.
    B.   Change a file type.
    C.   Change a file location.
    D.   All of the above
    E.   A and C

3. **The Print Area setting:**
    A.   Sets printing for part of a worksheet.
    B.   Is removed once you print the document.
    C.   Must be cleared if you want to print the entire worksheet.
    D.   A, B, and C
    E.   A and C

4. **Templates are found:**
    A.   In the Page Setup dialog box.
    B.   On the Web.
    C.   In Excel.
    D.   All of the above
    E.   B and C

5. **The AutoComplete feature:**
    A.   Creates a template.
    B.   Saves your file.
    C.   Finishes a data entry.
    D.   All of the above
    E.   None of the above

TRUE/FALSE

Circle **T** if the statement is true or **F** if the statement is false.

T   F   6. You must enter dates the way you want them to appear.

T   F   7. You can format dates using the Format Cells dialog box.

T F   8. Currency format includes three decimal places and a dollar sign.

T F   9. Templates are files that are created with the AutoComplete feature.

T F   10. Use Print Preview after printing a file.

COMPLETION

Complete each sentence.

11. When you want to save a file and change its file name, use the _____ feature.

12. When you enter labels, the data is aligned to the _____ by default.

13. When you enter values, the data is aligned to the _____ by default.

14. When you enter dates, the date is aligned to the _____ by default.

15. You can go into Edit mode by pressing the _____ key.

16. The AutoComplete feature helps you _____ data.

17. The Spelling feature is used for checking _____.

18. Press the Delete key to _____ the contents of the cell.

19. Use the _____ setting to print only part of the worksheet.

20. Model worksheets that contain formats and formulas are called _____.

LESSON 3

Accounting Records

In this lesson, you will learn to use Excel to create accounting records and statements. You will use formulas, functions, and formatting to complete the tasks. You will use the Internet to locate tax forms and rates.

Upon completion of this lesson, you should have mastered the following skill sets:

- Apply number formats Ⓜ
- Select a range of cells
- Clear number formats Ⓜ
- Use the Office Clipboard to cut, copy, and paste Ⓜ
- Use formula basics Ⓜ
- Use AutoSum to create a formula Ⓜ
- Enter the range in a formula Ⓜ
- Use functions with AutoSum Ⓜ
- Enter functions with the formula bar Ⓜ
- Use AutoFill
- Create a series

- Modify page setup options and page orientation Ⓜ
- Set page margins and centering Ⓜ
- Edit formulas using the formula bar Ⓜ
- Enter functions using Insert Function Ⓜ
- Move data
- Add and edit cell comments Ⓜ
- Apply and modify cell formats with the Format Cells dialog box Ⓜ
- Use the Format Painter Ⓜ

Terms
MOUS-related

Range
Office Clipboard
Formulas
Order of mathematical operations
AutoSum
Function
Insert Function button
Function arguments
AutoFill
Fill handle
Series
Drag-and-drop
Cell comment
Format Painter

Document-related

Account
General ledger
Accounts receivable
Accounts payable
Account Statement
Journal
Sales journal
Tax status
Payroll register
Reimburse
Expense report

TRYOUT

TASK 1

GOAL

To practice using the following skill sets:

* Apply number formats Ⓜ
* Select a range of cells
* Clear number formats Ⓜ
* Use the Office Clipboard to cut, copy, and paste Ⓜ
* Use formula basics

WHAT YOU NEED TO KNOW

Apply Number Formats

> You can format numbers with the Formatting toolbar buttons. To format numbers, select the data to format, and click the appropriate button, as shown in Figure 3.1.

Figure 3.1 Formatting toolbar, number format buttons

> The number format buttons on the Formatting toolbar are listed below:

* Currency Style adds two decimal places and a dollar sign. $

* Percent Style changes the value to a percentage. %

* Comma Style adds commas and two decimal places. ,

* Increase Decimal adds one decimal place.

* Decrease Decimal decreases one decimal place.

Note: Decreasing decimals causes the values to be rounded.

TRY*it*OUT

1. Open **3.1to** from the Data CD.

2. Format the cells in Column B to match the illustration in Figure 3.2.

3. Do not close the file.

	A	B	C	D	E	F
1	Number	Number after format		Format		
2	450	$ 450.00		Currency		
3	1245	1,245.00		Comma		
4	0.75	75%		Percent		
5	12.6	12.60		Increase Decimal		
6	12.6764	12.68		Decrease Decimal (2)		
7						

Figure 3.2 Sample number formats

Select a Range of Cells

> If you want to format a group of numbers, you can select the range by clicking and dragging the mouse over the cells to include. A *range* is a group of cells in a row, column, or block.

> The beginning and ending cell addresses identify a range. For example, B2:B6 is selected in Figure 3.3 and the data for the entire worksheet shown is in the range A1:D6. Click the first cell in the group, hold down the mouse, and drag the selection until all the cells to format are selected. Notice that a dark border outlines the range and, except for the first cell, all cells are selected.

	A	B	C	D	E	F
1	Number	Number after format		Format		
2	450	$ 450.00		Currency		
3	1245	1,245.00		Comma		
4	0.75	75%		Percent		
5	12.6	12.60		Increase Decimal		
B2:B6	12.6764	12.68		Decrease Decimal (2)		
7						

Figure 3.3 Selected cells in a range

Clear Number Formats

To clear number formats without deleting the values, click Edit, Clear, and Formats.

TRY*it*OUT

1. Continue working in **3.1to.**

2. Select the cells in the range **B2:B6.**

3. Click the **Currency Style** button. Do not deselect the range.

TRY*it*OUT

1. Continue working in **3.1to.**

2. With the range **B2:B6** selected, click the **Undo** button to reverse currency format.

3. Clear all formats by clicking **Edit, Clear,** and **Formats.**

4. Click the **Undo** button to reverse the Clear Formats command.

5. Deselect the range by clicking another cell.

6. Do not close the file.

Use the Office Clipboard to Cut, Copy, and Paste

> When you copy data in Excel, it is stored in a memory location called the *Office Clipboard*. You can cut, copy, or paste data using the Cut, Copy, and Paste buttons on the Standard toolbar.

> If you copy more than one group of data and want to view samples of your copied data, click View, Task Pane to display the Clipboard task pane. This is useful if you are reordering or reassigning locations for several items of data, or if you want to paste items several times. As shown in Figure 3.4, after each row is copied the sample appears on the Clipboard, with the last selection shown on top.

TRY*it***OUT**

1. Continue working in **3.1to.**

2. Click **View, Task Pane.**

3. Copy the data in the range **A2:D2.**

4. Copy the data in the range **A3:D3.**

5. Copy the data in the range **A4:D4.**

6. Select **Cell G2** and click the **Comma** data on the Clipboard. The data is pasted.

7. Select **Cell G3** and click the **Currency** data on the Clipboard.

8. Close the file without saving.

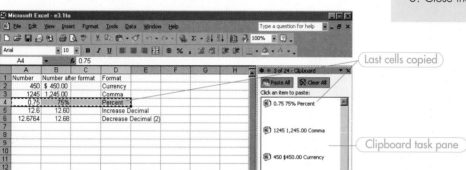

Figure 3.4 Office Clipboard task pane

Use Formula Basics

> *Formulas* are equations or instructions you use to calculate values on the worksheet. All formulas start with an equal sign (=), contain no spaces, and include the cell addresses and mathematical operators necessary to complete the formula. For example, =B5+B6 adds the values in B5 and B6.

> The standard mathematical operators used in formulas are:

+ Addition   - Subtraction   * Multiplication

/ Division   ^ Exponentiation

> To enter formulas correctly, you should understand the way the computer processes an equation. The *order of mathematical operations*, or the order in which a formula is processed, is listed below:

1. Parentheses   ( )

2. Exponents   ^

3. Multiplication *   Division   /

4. Addition   +   Subtraction   -

> Operations enclosed in parentheses have the highest priority, and the computer processes them first; it executes exponential calculations second. Multiplication and division operations have the next priority, and the computer completes them before any addition and subtraction operations. You can remember the order of mathematical operations by using the memory aid "Please Excuse My Dear Aunt Sally" for "Parentheses, Exponents, Multiplication, Division, Addition, and Subtraction."

> The computer executes all operations from left to right, in order of appearance. For example, in the formula =A1*(B1+C1), B1+C1 is calculated first, before the multiplication is performed. If the parentheses were omitted, A1*B1 would be calculated first and C1 would be added to that answer. This would result in a different outcome.

> You can enter a formula directly by entering the symbols and cell addresses. You can also enter the symbols and select the cell addresses as they appear in the formula. Selecting the cell addresses eliminates the possibility of entry errors. As you enter the formula, it appears in the formula bar. After you enter the formula, the answer appears in the cell and you can see the formula in the formula bar.

TRY it OUT

1. Open **2.2purord** from your files or **3.1tob** from the Data CD.

2. In **Cell H13,** enter a formula to multiply the quantity by the price:
   a. Enter = (equal sign).
   b. Click **Cell A13.**
   c. Enter * (asterisk).
   d. Click **Cell G13.**
   e. Press the **Enter** key.

3. Click **Cell H13** and notice the formula on the formula bar.

4. Enter the appropriate formula in **Cell H14.** *(Hint: =A14*G14)*

5. Click **Cell H14,** copy the formula, and paste it to **Cell H15.** Notice that the formula in **Cell H15** copies relative to the new location.

6. Select the range **H14:H15** and add one decimal place.

7. Enter a formula in **Cell H17** to add the three values in Column H. *(Hint: =H13+H14+H15)*

8. Save the file; name it **3.1tob.** Close the file.

REHEARSAL

 GOAL
To create an acount and account statement

SETTING THE STAGE/WRAPUP
File names: 3.1account
3.1statement

WHAT YOU NEED TO KNOW

> An *account* is an accounting record that keeps track of the increases and decreases for one item in a business. It is set up in a bankbook-style arrangement that contains columns for increases, decreases, and balances. You can set up accounts for items such as cash and merchandise, and you can use them to record transactions from journals, as you will learn in Task 2.

> The *general ledger* contains all the accounts of a business. The *accounts receivable (AR)* ledger is a subsidiary ledger that contains records of customers, the people who owe the business money, and the *accounts payable (AP)* ledger contains records of creditors, the people to whom the business owes money.

> Customers' accounts are used to create the *account statements* or bills that are sent out each month.

> In this Rehearsal activity, you will create an account and an account statement for Time Out Sporting Goods. The business has an accounts receivable ledger for its customers where invoices (which increase the account) and credits and returns (which decrease the account) are used to tabulate the account balance. The account statement or bill is sent out at the end of the month to every customer, based on the activity in the account.

DIRECTIONS

1. Open **3.1account** from the Data CD.

2. As shown in Illustration A on the facing page, in **Cell G8**, calculate the balance on 5/3. Because the first invoice is also the balance on 5/3, enter **=E8** in **Cell G8.**

3. Calculate the balance on 5/15 in **Cell G9.** The formula should subtract the return in **Cell F9** from the previous balance in **Cell G8.** *(Hint: =G8-F9)*

4. Enter a formula in **Cell G10** that can be used for any balance calculation in this account. *(Hint: Previous balance+charges−credits =G9+E10-F10)*

5. Format the credit in **Cell F11** by adding two decimal places.

6. Clear all formats in **Cell F11.** Click **Undo** to keep the format.

7. Copy the formula from **Cell G10,** and paste it to **Cell G11.**

8. Select and format the values in **Column G** for commas.

9. Save the file **3.1 account.**

10. As shown in Illustration B on the facing page, copy the following ranges to create the account statement:

    a. **C3:C5** Name and address of customer

    b. **A7:G7** Column headings

    c. **A8:G11** Account data

11. Open **3.1statement** from the Data CD.

12. Paste the following data to the locations listed below:

    a. Name and address to **Cell A9**

    b. Column headings to **Cell A13**

    c. Account data to **Cell A15**

13. Format the final balance in **Cell G18** for currency.

14. Print the account statement without gridlines.

15. Save the file **3.1 statement.** Close both files.

Illustration A

	A	B	C	D	E	F	G	H
1	Accounts Receivable Ledger							
2								
3	Customer:		Central High School - Health Ed. Dept.					
4			2382 Margate Avenue					
5	No. C15		Chicago, IL 60064					
6								
7	Date	Explanation		Reference	Charges	Credits	Balance	
8	5/3/02	Invoice #2325		S5	434.56			
9	5/15/02	Return - #CM450		J9		65.35		
10	5/22/02	Invoice #2336		S5	1045.32			
11	5/25/02	Damaged #CM501		J9		150		
12								
13							Enter formulas here to calculate daily balance	
14								
15								
16								

Illustration A

Illustration B

	A	B	C	D	E	F	G	H	I	J	K
1				STATEMENT OF ACCOUNT							
2											
3	Time Out Sporting Goods										
4	1412 Barkely Street				Date:		May 31, 2002				
5	Chicago, IL 60064										
6											
7	847-555-1200										
8											
9						Paste name and address in A9					
10											
11											
12											
13						Paste column headings in A13					
14		Balance forward					0				
15						Paste account data in A15					
16											
17											
18											
19											
20											
21											
22											
23											
24											
25											
26								Pay the last amount in this column			
27											
28	Time Out Sporting Goods										

Illustration B

Cues for Reference

Apply Number Formats
1. Select cell or range of cells.
2. Click format button:

Percentage Style	%
Currency Style	$
Comma Style	,
Increase Decimal	
Decrease Decimal	

Clear Number Formats
1. Select cell or range of cells.
2. Click **Edit, Clear, Formats.**

Use Office Clipboard Task Pane
1. Click **View, Task Pane.**
2. Select Office location for pasted data.
3. Click data sample on Office Clipboard.

Enter Formulas
1. Enter = (equal sign)
2. Select formula data.
3. Enter a mathematical operator.
4. Select formula data.
5. Repeat Steps 3 and 4 until formula is complete.
6. Press **Enter.**

TRYOUT

TASK 2

To practice using the following skill sets:

- ✴ Use AutoSum to create a formula M
- ✴ Enter the range in a formula M
- ✴ Use functions with AutoSum M
- ✴ Enter functions with the formula bar M

WHAT YOU NEED TO KNOW

Use AutoSum to Create a Formula

> The *AutoSum* feature automatically enters a built-in formula to find the total of a group of cells.

> To add a column of data, make the location of the total the active cell. Then, when you click the AutoSum button on the Standard toolbar, Excel selects the cells it thinks you want to add and surrounds them with a moving dotted line. In the cell where the total is to appear, you see the automatic sum formula to add the cells, =SUM(B4:B47). If the cells selected are the ones you want to add, just press the Enter key; if not, revise the selected range of data, as shown in Figure 3.5.

TRY*it* OUT

1. Open **3.2to** from the Data CD.

2. Go to **Cell B8.**

3. Click the **AutoSum** button. Notice the formula in the cell and on the formula bar.

4. Press the **Enter** key.

5. Find the totals in **Cells C8** and **E8.**

6. Select the range **C8:E8** and decrease decimals to two places.

7. Do not close the file.

Figure 3.5 AutoSum feature

Enter the Range in a Formula

> If the range suggested by AutoSum is not correct, you must enter the correct range. An accurate way to enter a range address in a formula is to drag through the range with the mouse pointer.

Use Functions with AutoSum

> A *function* is a built-in formula that performs a special calculation automatically. Function formulas contain an equal sign, the function name, open parentheses, range or arguments, and then close parentheses. For example, in the SUM function created with AutoSum in the previous Try it Out, the function adds all the values, or arguments, in the range specified.

> At the right of the AutoSum button is a list arrow, as shown in Figure 3.6, that provides other commonly used functions you can select for the range of data. See Task 3 for an explanation of the More Functions selection. The functions available are listed below:

Sum	Calculates the total of numbers in a range
Average	Calculates the average, or mean, of numbers in a range
Count	Counts the number of values in a range
Max	Calculates the highest value in a range
Min	Calculates the lowest value in a range

Figure 3.6 AutoSum options list

TRY*it*OUT

Note: To check the accuracy of the data, add the Sales Tax and Sales totals horizontally to see if they equal the "Due from Customer" total.

1. Continue working in **3.2to.**

2. Go to **Cell F8.**

3. Click the **AutoSum** button. Notice that the range is incorrect.

4. Drag to select the range **B8:C8;** the correct range.

5. Press the **Enter** key.

6. Do not close the file.

TRY*it*OUT

1. Continue working in **3.2to.**

2. Go to **Cell B9.**

3. Click the **AutoSum** list arrow.

4. Click **Average.**

5. Correct the range to **B4:B6.**

6. For the following, be sure to correct the range to **B4:B6:**
   a. In **Cell B10,** find the COUNT, or number of values.
   b. In **Cell B11,** find the MAX, or highest value.
   c. In **Cell B12,** find the MIN, or lowest value.

7. Do not close the file.

Enter Functions with the Formula Bar

> When you press the equal sign, the formula bar provides a drop-down list of commonly used functions, Cancel and Enter buttons, and the *Insert Function* button (the *fx* button), as shown in Figure 3.7. You can use these buttons or press Esc or Enter keys to cancel or enter a formula.

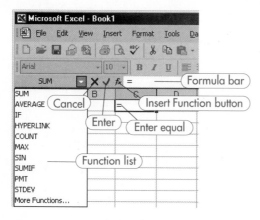

Figure 3.7 Formula bar function list

> If you use the Insert Function button, Excel enters the function name automatically in the formula and prompts you for the function arguments. *Function arguments* are the cell ranges that supply the data for the formula.

> When you select a function from the list, the Function Arguments dialog box opens, as shown in Figure 3.8. This box provides a view of the arguments or range, an explanation of the function, the result of the formula, and Help features.

> The Collapse Dialog Box button, at the right of the range, collapses the dialog box, and the Expand Dialog Box button redisplays the dialog box, to help you select the correct range. When the dialog box is collapsed, it still may obstruct the range. You can move it away by dragging its title bar with the mouse pointer.

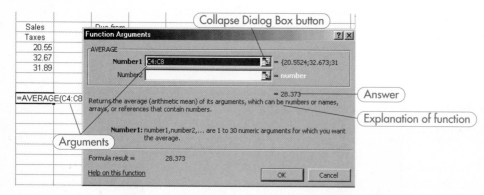

Figure 3.8 Function Arguments dialog box

1. Continue working in **3.2to.**

2. Enter the equal sign = in **Cell C9.**

3. Click **Average** from the drop-down list of functions.

4. Click the **Collapse Dialog Box** button.

5. Drag the dialog box title bar out of the way, if necessary.

6. Select the range **C4:C6.**

7. Click the **Expand Dialog Box** button.

8. Click **OK.**

9. Use the same method to complete the formulas for **Cells C10, C11,** and **C12.**

   Note: If the Count, Max, and Min functions are not visible, click more functions to locate them.

10. Format the value in **C10** for no decimal places and the values in **C11** and **C12** for two decimal places.

11. Copy the formulas from **Cells C9:C12** to **E9.**

12. Save the file **3.2to.** Close the file.

REHEARSAL

 **GOAL**
To create a Sales Journal

SETTING THE STAGE/WRAPUP
File name: 3.2journal

TASK 2

WHAT YOU NEED TO KNOW

> All accounting records keep track of events for money management and decision-making purposes. A *journal* is a chronological record of business events or transactions. One type of journal, a *sales journal*, is a record of the sales made to customers on credit.

> When a salesperson makes a sale on credit, a sales invoice is prepared, which becomes the basis for the entry in the journal. Entries from the journal are then transferred to the accounts for each customer, as discussed in Task 1, to manage accounts receivable. In some businesses, the journal and ledger accounts are generated from the preparation of the invoice, using accounting system software.

> The final (retail) consumer of merchandise pays sales tax; however, wholesale customers who are resellers and nonprofit organizations are tax exempt.

> In this Rehearsal activity, you will prepare a sales journal for Time Out Sporting Goods to record sales for its credit business, which is a small part of its sales.

DIRECTIONS

1. Open **3.2journal** from the Data CD.

2. Select the range **A3:H4** and center the column headings.

3. Enter the additional invoices as follows:
   a. Enter data in columns A, B, C, and H as shown on the illustration. Note that AutoComplete will help you enter the customers' names.
   b. Copy the formulas from columns F and G down for the new invoices.

4. Select the range **F5:H18** and format for two decimal places using the Comma format.

5. Use the AutoSum feature to find the total in **Cell F20.**

6. Use the AutoSum feature to find the average of the range **F5:F18** in **Cell F22,** using the mouse pointer to correct the range.

7. Click the **equal sign** in **Cell F23** and use the formula bar to enter a function to find the highest value (Max). Click the Collapse Dialog Box button to select the range.

8. Use the method you prefer to find the remaining data.

9. Copy the range of summary data: **F20:F25**

10. As illustrated on the facing page, paste the range twice to **Cells G20** and **H20.**

11. Print the journal with gridlines.

12. Save the file **3.2journal.** Close the file.

	A	B	C	D	E	F	G	H
1								
2			SALES JOURNAL					Page 5
3						Accounts	Sales	Sales
4	Date	Invoice #	Customer			Receivable	Taxes	Income
5	5/3/02	2325	Central H.S. Health Ed Dept			434.56		434.56
6	5/4/02	2326	Jason Gym			550.00		550.00
7	5/7/02	2327	Eastern H.S. - Gym			515.00		515.00
8	5/9/02	2328	Fitness King			1,255.00		1,255.00
9	5/11/02	2329	Harry Putter			185.94	10.94	175.00
10	5/14/02	2330	Eastern H.S. - Gym			325.00		325.00
11	5/14/02	2331	Jason Gym			385.00		385.00
12	5/16/02	2332	Fitness King			155.00		155.00
13	5/17/02	2333	Harry Putter			313.44	18.44	295.00
14	5/18/02	2334	Eastern H.S. - Gym			660.00		660.00
15	5/21/02	2335	Kelly Klinger			143.44	8.44	135.00
16	5/22/02	2336	Central H.S. Health Ed Dept			1,045.32		1,045.32
17	5/24/02	2337	Jason Gym			451.56		451.56
18	5/31/02	2340	Kelly Klinger			90.31	5.31	85.00
19								
20			Totals				→	→
21								
22			Averages				→	→
23			Highest				→	→
24			Lowest				→	→
25			Count				→	→
26								
27							Copy F20:F25 to	
28							G20 and to H20	
29								

Cues for Reference

Use Auto Sum
1. Select cell to display answer.
2. Click the **AutoSum** button.
3. If range is correct, press **Enter.**
4. If not, use mouse pointer to reselect the correct range and press **Enter.**

Enter Range in a Formula
1. Place mouse pointer on first cell in range.
2. Click, hold, and drag to last cell in range.

Use Functions and AutoSum
1. Select cell to display answer.
2. Click **AutoSum** list arrow.
3. Select function.
4. Correct the range.
5. Press **Enter.**

Use Functions and the Formula Bar
1. Select cell to display answer.
2. Click **equal (=).**
3. Select function from drop-down list.

4. Click the **Collapse Dialog Box** button.
5. Drag the dialog box title bar out of the way, if necessary.
6. Select the range.
7. Click the **Expand Dialog Box** button.
8. Press **OK.**

TRYOUT

 GOAL

To practice using the following skill sets:
- ✳ Use AutoFill
- ✳ Create a series
- ✳ Modify page setup options and page orientation Ⓜ
- ✳ Set page margins and centering Ⓜ
- ✳ Edit formulas using the formula bar Ⓜ
- ✳ Enter functions using Insert Function Ⓜ

TASK 3

WHAT YOU NEED TO KNOW

Use AutoFill

> You can use the *AutoFill* feature to create sequential lists of values or labels, or to copy labels, values, or formulas in a cell to a range of cells. You can also access this feature by clicking the Edit, Fill commands.

> To use AutoFill, select the cell to be copied and place your insertion point on the *fill handle*, the small square at the bottom right of the cell to copy, as shown in Figure 3.9. The mouse pointer changes from a white plus sign to a thin black plus sign. When this occurs, click and drag the cell border to fill the appropriate range. You will find this to be an easy way to copy formulas.

	A	B	C	D	E	F
1						
2		Gross	Taxes	Union	Net	
3	Employee	Pay		Dues	Pay	
4						
5		280	67	10	337	
6		300	79	10	389	
7		295	72			
8		655	146			
9		432	96	10		
10		425	89			

Fill handle

Figure 3.9 AutoFill activated

Create a Series

> To create a *series* of values or labels, such as check numbers, days of the week, months, years, etc., enter the first two items in the series and use the fill handle to complete the column.

TRY_it_**OUT**

1. Open **3.3to** from the Data CD.

2. AutoFill a value:
   a. Click **Cell D6** and place your mouse pointer on the fill handle.
   b. When the insertion point changes to a black plus sign, click and drag the border down to **Cell D10**.

3. AutoFill a formula: In **Cell E6,** use the fill handle to fill the formula down to **Cell E10.**

4. Fill a formula from **Cells B12** to **E12:**
   a. Select the range **B12:E12**.
   b. Click **Edit, Fill,** and **Right.**

5. Do not close the file.

TRY_it_**OUT**

1. Continue working in **3.3to.**

2. Enter **1000** in **Cell A1** and **1001** in **Cell A2.**

3. Select both values and use the fill handle to create a sequential list to **Cell A10.**

4. Enter **January** in **Cell F1** and **February** in **Cell G1.**

5. Select **both values** and use the fill handle to fill to **Cell K1.**

6. Do not close the file.

Modify Page Setup Options and Page Orientation

> If you discover that the worksheet is wider than a page width when using Print Preview, you must change print settings and orientation. Use landscape orientation to print horizontally on the page for wide worksheets.

> In the Page Setup dialog box with the Page tab selected, as shown in Figure 3.10, you can set page orientation and scaling. Every tab in the Page Setup dialog box has a Print Preview button to view your settings.

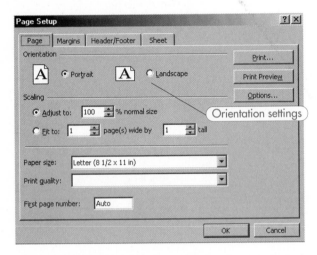

Figure 3.10 File, Page Setup, Page tab seletected

Set Page Margins and Centering

> On the Margins tab, you can center the worksheet on the page and set the margins shown in Figure 3.11. You can also set Margins manually by clicking the Margins button on the Print Preview toolbar.

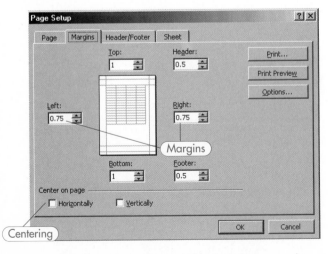

Figure 3.11 Page Setup dialog box, Margins tab

TRY*it* **OUT**

1. Continue working in **3.3to.**

2. Click **File, Page Setup,** and click the **Page** tab.

3. Click the **Print Preview** button. Notice that the worksheet is not completely visible. Click **Close** on the Print Preview toolbar.

4. Click **Landscape** orientation in the Page tab of the Page Setup dialog box.

5. Click the **Print Preview** button.

6. Click **Close** on the Print Preview toolbar.

7. Do not close the file.

TRY*it* **OUT**

1. Continue working in **3.3to.**

2. Click **File, Page Setup,** and click the **Margins** tab.

3. Under **Center on page,** click **Horizontally** and **Vertically.**

4. Click the **Print Preview** button.

5. Click the **Margins** button on the Print Preview toolbar.

6. Drag the margin grids to move the margins closer to the data manually.

7. Click **Close** on the Print Preview toolbar.

8. Do not close the file.

Edit Formulas Using the Formula Bar

> To edit or revise a formula, press the F2 key or double-click the formula to go into Edit mode. In edit mode, Excel highlights the arguments in the formula in the cell and on the formula bar in a color to match a box around the arguments. This clearly identifies each part of the formula and may clarify the errors that need correction. Figure 3.12 shows a range in Edit mode.

> Once you are in Edit mode, you can drag the border of the range or cell, or backspace to correct errors. Figure 3.13 shows how formula arguments appear in Edit mode.

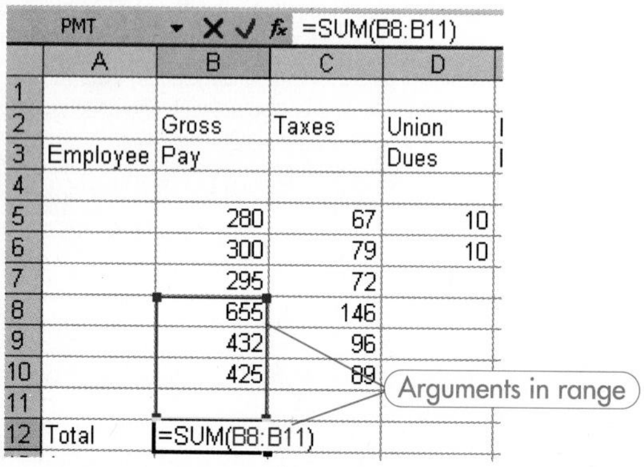

Figure 3.12 Edit mode for arguments in a range

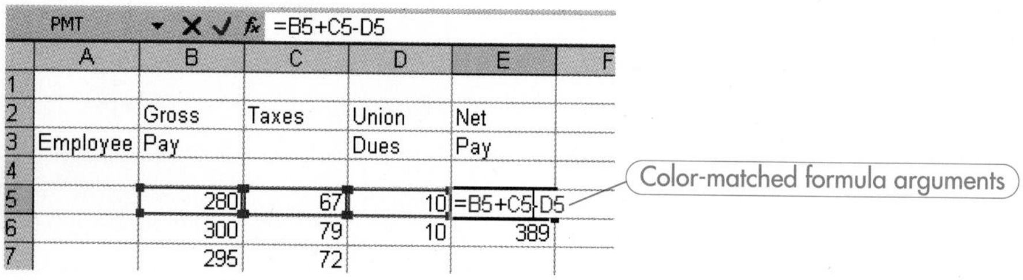

Figure3.13 Edit mode for formula arguments

1. Continue working in **3.3to.**

2. Double-click **Cell E5** to edit the formula.

3. Revise formula to read **=B5-C5-D5** because both the taxes and dues should be subtracted. Press the **left arrow** and the **backspace** keys to change plus to minus.

4. Press the **Enter** key.

5. In **Cell E5,** click the **fill handle** to AutoFill the revised formula down from **Cell E5** down to **E10.**

6. Double-click **Cell B12** and notice the range.

7. Drag the range border to correct it so that it adds the range **B5:B10.**

8. In **Cell B12,** click the **fill handle** to AutoFill the revised formula across from **Cells B12** to **E12.**

9. Do not close the file.

Enter Functions Using Insert Function

> If you want to view all the functions available in Excel, you can use the *Insert Function button* on the formula bar or click the AutoSum list arrow and click More Functions.

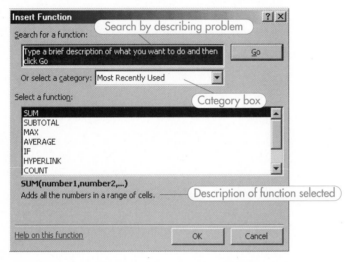

> When you click the button, an equal sign appears and the Insert Function dialog box opens, as shown in Figure 3.14. You can state what you want to accomplish, in the Search for a function box, or find the function you need in the Or select a category box. Once you select the function, use the Function Argument dialog box, as discussed in Task 2.

Figure 3.14 Insert Function dialog box

T R Y *i t* **O U T**

1. Continue working in **3.3to.**

2. In **Cell B13,** click the *fx* button on the formula bar to open the Insert Function dialog box.

3. In the Or select a category box, click the list arrow and select **All.** Scroll to view the functions.

4. Select the **Most Recently Used** category.

5. Scroll and double-click the **AVERAGE** function from the select a function box.

6. Collapse the dialog box to select the range.

7. Expand the dialog box and click **OK.**

8. Click the **Decrease Decimal** button to format the answer with no decimal places.

9. Use the fill handle to copy the formula across to **Cell E13.**

10. Save the file as **3.3to.** Close the file.

GOAL
To create a payroll

SETTING THE STAGE/WRAPUP
File name: 3.3payroll

WHAT YOU NEED TO KNOW

> To complete payroll calculations, you need to know the employee's *tax status* data, i.e. marital status and the number of dependents claimed. You use this data with tables to find the federal withholding tax. State taxes vary with each state having different withholding tax rates, tables, and rules. Social Security and Medicare taxes are deducted from all payrolls at the rates of 6.2% and 1.45%, respectively. You can use a percent in an Excel formula.

> Payrolls are completed by the Accounting Department in a large firm or outside services may prepare them. A *payroll register* is a form used to calculate the salaries, taxes, and net pay due each employee for the pay period. You will calculate gross pay (the salary before taxes), the taxes on gross pay, and the net pay (the salary less all the deductions). Once you complete a payroll register for a firm, you can save the formulas and format as a template for each week's payroll. Internet sites also provide paycheck calculators for small businesses.

> In this Rehearsal activity, you will prepare a weekly payroll for In Shape Fitness Centers, located in Phoenix. You will use 17% of the federal tax deduction for the Arizona state withholding tax.

▼ DIRECTIONS

1. Open **3.3payroll** from the Data CD.

2. *Employee Number:* Select the range **A7:A8** and use the fill handle to drag the series of numbers to every employee.

3. *Gross Pay:* In **Cell G7,** enter a formula to find gross pay. *(Hint: =Regular Earnings+Overtime – use cell addresses in the formula)*

4. Use the fill handle in **Cell G7** to copy the formula down to each employee's payroll.

5. *State Withholding Tax:* In **Cell I7,** enter a formula to find state withholding tax, which is 17% of the federal withholding tax deduction. *(Hint: =Federal W.T.*17%)*

6. *Social Security:* In **Cell J7,** enter a formula to find the social security tax, which is 6.2% of the gross pay. *(Hint: =Gross Pay*6.2%)*

7. *Medicare:* In **Cell K7,** enter a formula to find the medicare tax, which is 1.45% of the gross pay.

8. *Total Deductions:* In **Cell L7,** use AutoSum to enter a formula to find the total of all the payroll deductions from the range **H7:K7.**

9. *Net Pay:* In **Cell M7,** enter a formula to find net pay, which is the gross pay less the total deductions.

10. As shown in the illustration on the facing page, select the range **I7:M7,** and use the fill handle to fill all the formulas for the payroll.

11. In **Cell E15,** use AutoSum to find the total of the column.

12. In **Cell E17,** press **equal (=)** and use the formula bar drop-down function list to enter the formula for the column average. Be sure to correct the range.

13. In **Cell E18,** use the *fx* button to search for the function for median. Notice the definition of the function. Select the range of salaries and enter the function.

14. In **Cell E19,** use the AutoSum drop-down list, to find the count. Be sure to correct the range.

15. Select the range **E15:E19** and use the fill handle to copy the formulas across to all columns.

16. Format payroll data in the range **E7:M18** in comma format.

17. Center column headings for the range **E5:M6.**

18. Use Page Setup to print the payroll in landscape orientation, centered horizontally. Print one copy.

19. Save the file **3.3payroll.** Close the file.

	A	B	C	D	E	F	G	H	I	J	K	L	M
1					PAYROLL REGISTER								
2													
3	For Pay Period Ended:			6/15/xx			Date of Payment:		6/20/xx				
4													
5	Employee				Regular		Gross	Federal	State	Social		Total	Net
6	Number	Status	Name		Earnings	Overtime	Pay	W.T.	W.T.	Security	Medicare	Deductions	Pay
7	225	S1	Bosco, Vince		280	85		39.02					
8	226	M2	Ingram, Sally		800	200		115.24					
9		S2	Josephs, Ted		250			13.7					
10		M2	Lee, Gina		435			30.49					
11		M4	Montez, Maria		475			20.33					
12		S0	Pasternak, Joan		250			29.85					
13		S1	Thompson, John		450	100		66.77					
14													
15			Totals										
16													
17			Average										
18			Median										
19			Count										

Cues for Reference

Edit Formulas

1. Select formula.
2. Press **F2.**
3. Edit range by dragging border, or Edit operators in formula.

Use AutoFill

1. For series, select first two cells in series.
   For formulas, values, and text, select a cell.
2. Point cursor to fill handle in bottom right corner.
3. Drag to fill series.

Modify Page Orientation

1. Click **File, Page Setup,** and click **Page** tab.
2. Click **Landscape.**
3. Click **OK.**

Set Page Margins and Centering

1. Click **Print Preview** button.
2. Click **Margins** button on the Print Preview toolbar.
3. Drag margins to appropriate location.
4. Click **Close** on the Print Preview toolbar.
   or
1. Click **File, Page Setup,** and click **Margins** tab.
2. Set margins or centering.
3. Click **OK.**

Enter Functions Using the Formula Bar

1. Click **fx** on the formula bar.
2. Search for the function, click **Go,** or select the function from the list.
3. Click **Collapse Dialog Box** button.
4. Select the range.
5. Click the **Expand Dialog box** button to redisplay the box.
6. Click **OK.**

T R Y O U T

GOAL
To practice using the following skill sets:

- ✳ Move data
- ✳ Add and edit cell comments
- ✳ Apply and modify cell formats with the Format Cells dialog box Ⓜ
- ✳ Use the Format Painter Ⓜ

TASK 4

WHAT YOU NEED TO KNOW

Move Data

> You can move data by using the Cut and Paste buttons on the Standard toolbar, or by selecting the range and dragging it to the paste location (known as *drag-and-drop*). When you move data, you remove it from the first location and paste it to the new location. This action overwrites existing data in the new location.

> To drag-and-drop data, select the data to move and place the mouse pointer on the edge of the range until it changes to a four-headed arrow. Drag the outline of the range to the first cell in the new location's range. As shown in Figure 3.15, as you drag the data, the curent range or location appears. Data formats move with the data, but you must check that formulas are correct after a move operation.

	A	B	C	D	E	F	G
1		Baltimore	Annapolis	Philadelphia			
2				3/15/xx	3/13/xx	3/12/xx	
3	Hotel			315	132	125	
4	Meals			94	141	54	
5	Air Fare			155	210	195	
6	Car Renta				56		
7	Telephone			8	22	18	
8	Entertain			185		135	
9	Misc.			27	43	17	
10							
11	Totals		B2:B11	804	604	544	
12							

New range address — Select to drag — Outline of range in new location

Figure 3.15 Selected range moved to new location

Add and Edit Cell Comments

> You can attach a text comment in a cell to document formulas or assumptions built into the worksheet, or to comment on data sent to you by someone else. Because this feature is used when sharing workbooks, the user's name will also be on the comment.

T R Y *it* O U T

1. Open **3.4to** from the Data CD.

2. Select the range **E2:E11.**

3. Click the **Cut** button.

4. Select **Cell C2,** and then click the **Paste** button.

5. Select the range **F2:F11.**

6. Place the mouse pointer at the edge of the range until the pointer becomes a four-headed arrow.

7. Click, hold, and drag-and-drop the range to **Cell B2.**

8. Do not close the file.

T R Y *it* O U T

1. Continue working in **3.4to.**

2. In **Cell B1,** click **Insert, Comment.**

3. Enter this name:
   J&R Equipment Supply

Continued on next page

> Enter a comment in the cell by clicking Insert, Comment and entering the comment in the comment box. A red triangle appears in the top corner of the cell to indicate the presence of a *cell comment,* as shown in Figure 3.16. When the mouse moves over that cell, the comment appears. If this does not occur, you must click the Comments indicator only option on the Tools, Options, View tab to view the comment.

> To edit a comment, select the comment cell and click Insert, Edit Comment.

> To print comments, select one of the Comments drop-down list print options on the Sheet tab of the Page Setup dialog box, as shown in Figure 3.17.

4. Click on any cell to come out of Comment mode.

5. In **Cell C1,** insert the following comment: `Sailboat Show and Conference`

6. In **Cell B1,** click **Insert, Edit Comment.**

7. Edit the comment to read: `Meeting with J&R Equipment Supply.`

8. Click on any cell to come out of Comment mode.

9. Use the Page Setup dialog box to print the worksheet. Select **Comments: At end of sheet.**

10. Do not close the file.

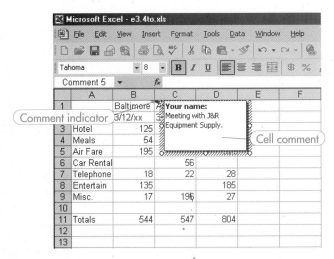

Figure 3.16 Cell comment

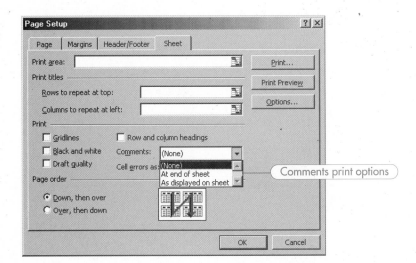

Figure 3.17 Page Setup, Sheet tab, with comments print options

Apply and Modify Cell Formats with the Format Cells Dialog Box

> You have been using the Formatting toolbar buttons to format cells. You can set all formats at once and have additional formatting options if you use the Format Cells dialog box as shown in Figure 3.18. When you click Format, Cells, or the Ctrl + 1 keys, notice the six cell formatting tabs that appear. Format a cell by selecting the appropriate options from any or all tabs and click OK.

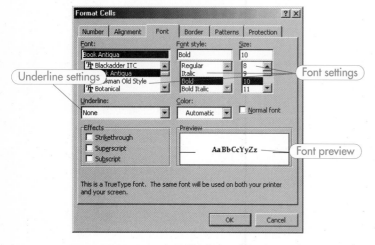

Figure 3.18 Format Cells dialog box, Font tab

Use the Format Painter

> Once you have set formats for text or values, you can copy formats from one cell to another by using the *Format Painter* button on the Formatting toolbar. When you are in Format Painter mode, the mouse pointer includes a paintbrush icon.

> To format more than one area of the worksheet with Format Painter, double-click the button to enable formatting of multiple cells, as shown in Figure 3.19. After formatting is complete, click Format Painter again to release Format Painter mode.

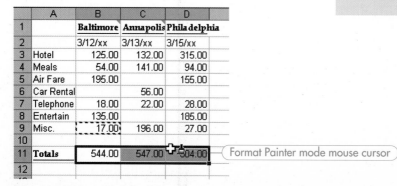

Figure 3.19 Format Painter

TRY *it* OUT

1. Continue working in **3.4to.**

2. Select the range **B1:D1.**

3. Click **Format, Cells,** and click the **Font** tab in the Format Cells dialog box.

4. Format for Book Antiqua font, bold, Single Accounting Underline.

5. Click **OK.**

6. In the number tab, select the range **B2:D9** and press the **Ctrl + 1** keys.

7. Open the Format Cells dialog box again and, in the Number tab, select a number format with two decimals.

8. Click **OK.**

9. Do not close the file.

TRY *it* OUT

1. Continue working in **3.4to.**

2. Select **Cell B9.**

3. Click the **Format Painter** button.

4. Select and apply the format to the range **B11:D11.**

5. Select **B1** and click **Format Painter.**

6. Select and apply the format to **Cell A11.**

7. Save the file **3.4to.** Close the file..

R E H E A R S A L

TASK 4

GOAL
To create an expense report

SETTING THE STAGE/WRAPUP
File name: 3.4expense

WHAT YOU NEED TO KNOW

> When employees travel on company business, the company usually *reimburses,* or refunds, their expenses. They may get a cash advance before the trip, which is then deducted from the total expenses listed on the report. After the trip, they must submit all expenses and receipts for reimbursement with an *expense report.* Business travel expenses are part of the cost of doing business.

> In this Rehearsal activity, you will prepare an expense report for Sara Vickers, an employee of Occasions Event Planning. She made a business trip to Rochester, N.Y. to meet with the hotels, vendors, and co-sponsor of the photography conference she is planning.

DIRECTIONS

1. Open **3.4expense** from the Data CD.

2. Select the range **A1:A3** and use the Format Cells dialog box to format for MS Sans Serif, bold, 12 point.

3. Move the letterhead, using drag-and-drop to **Cell D1.**

4. Use Format Painter to apply the font format from **Cell D1** to the EXPENSE REPORT title.

5. Select the labels in the range **A6:A8** and format them for bold.

6. Double-click the **Format Painter** button and apply bold format to the column headings, as shown on the facing page.

7. Click **Format Painter** to turn off multiple cell format.

8. Center the column headings in the range **D10:I10.**

9. Format the dates as shown in the illustration on the facing page.

10. Select the range **A23:I31** and move the range to **Cell A18.**

11. As illustrated on the facing page, in **Cell D18,** use AutoSum to find the total of the column.

12. Use the fill handle to extend the formula to **Cell I18.**

13. In **Cell I21,** enter a formula to find the amount due Sara Vickers. *(Hint: =Total-Advance)*

14. Select the range **D11:I21** and format for two decimals.

15. Use Format Painter to apply the same format to **Cell I25.**

16. Use Format Painter to apply the bold format from **Cell A10** to the range **A23:I24**

17. Click **Cell I20,** click **Insert, Comment,** and enter the comment:
    `Receipt #86 9/11`

18. Click **Cell I21,** click **Format, Cells,** and click the **Font** tab to add a Double Accounting underline.

19. Edit the comment to add the current year.

20. Print the expense report with the comment displayed at the end of the sheet.

21. Save the file **3.4expense.** Close the file.

	A	B	C	D	E	F	G	H	I
1				Occasions Event Planning					
2				675 Third Avenue					
3				New York, NY 10017					
4	EXPENSE REPORT								
5									
6	Employee:		Sara Vikers						
7	Purpose:		Trip to Rochester, NY to plan Photography Conference						
8	Date (s):		September 12 and 13, 2002						
9									
10	Date	Description		Meals	Travel	Lodging	Phone	Other	Total
11	9/12	Employee		35		96	23	15	169
12	9/12	Entertainment*		137					137
13	9/13	Car Rental Charges			75				75
14	9/13	Fuel			35				35
15	9/13	Tolls			8.5				8.5
16	9/13	Employee		52			21	22	95
17									
18		Totals		☐	→				
19									
20							Less: Advance		250
21							Net due		☐
22									
23									
24	Entertainment Expenses Detail*								
25	Date	Client/Company Entertained		Purpose			Restaurant		Amount
26	9/12	R. Frank, Vision Camera Co.		Conference planning			Blue Hill Restaurant		137

PERFORMANCE

SETTING THE STAGE/WRAPUP

Act I: File name: 3p1.salejour

Act II: File name: 3p2.payroll

Act III: File names: 3p3.expense.xlt

                              3p3.exp1012

Act I

Ralph Green, the CFO of Green Brothers Gardening has asked you to work on the sales journal, which records sales to customers who use a Green Brothers account for goods and services. Although the sales journal normally provides totals at the end of the month, he wants data on June 15th, to help with business decisions. He needs the totals, the number of sales in each category, and the average, highest, and lowest sale for the 15 days. This sales journal for Green Brothers' smallest nursery divides sales into the services provided at that location, i.e., nursery, maintenance contracts, and landscaping. Use 4.5% for the sales tax rate for Virginia and apply it only to nursery sales.

GREEN BROTHERS GARDENING

- Open **3p1.salejour** from the Data CD.
- Sales Income column: Enter formula to add all services.
- Sales Tax column: Enter formula to calculate taxes on nursery sales only.
- Accounts Receivable column: Enter formula to add tax to sales.
- Fill the formulas down the columns.
- Invoice number column: Use AutoFill.
- Find totals and statistics for all columns.
- Format numbers for commas and set appropriate alignments.
- Print the journal using landscape orientation.
- Save and close the file **3p1.salejour**.

Act II

Odyssey Travel Gear has asked you to complete the weekly payroll for the Chicago store for the week ending July 20. The deductions for federal and state income taxes are based on the salary and tax status of the employee and are obtained from tax tables or from online services. The tax status, for example M2, is made up of the marital staus (M = married, S = single) and the number of federal exemptions. Social Security (6.2%) and Medicare (1.45%) taxes are calculated using the current tax rate. Store employees are paid based on an hourly rate.

odyssey travel gear

✴ Open **3p2.payroll** from the Data CD.

✴ The employees' hours for the week are shown below:

Name	Status	Hours	Rate
Miller, Carson	M 2	40	14.50
Vaughn, Tamika	M 1	40	10.95
Sanchez, Linda	S 0	35	9.00
Frommel, Sam	S 2	38	9.00
Witnaur, Mary	M 0	40	8.25

✴ Enter formulas for Gross Pay *(Hint: Hours*Rate)*, Social Security Tax, Medicare Tax, Total Deductions, and Net Pay. Fill the formulas for all employees and format values.

✴ The federal and state taxes are included for the first three employees. Use the Paycheck Calculator on www.paycheckcity.com to look up the federal and state taxes for the last two employees. On the Web site, you will have to enter the State (Illinois), Gross Pay, Pay Frequency (weekly), Married or Single for federal filing status and enter the number of federal exemptions. When you click Calculate, the detailed paycheck will appear. Copy the state and federal taxes and enter them on your worksheet. Use the Fill Color button (Automatic setting) to remove colors that copy with the values.

✴ Find summary values for the payroll, including Totals, Averages, Highest, and Lowest. Format all values for commas.

✴ Print Preview, change the orientation to print the worksheet on one page, print, save, and close the file **3p2.payroll.**

Act III

Carl Westfield, from the Television Division in the California office of Trilogy Productions, has just returned from a business trip to San Diego, California. He needs an expense report for his trip. He made the trip to meet with local stations and writers from October 12 to October 15, 2002.

✴ Open **3p3.expense** from the Data CD, and format font, font size and style, as you want, for the Trilogy Productions heading and the title of the report. Center the column headings and save the file as a template.

✴ Mr. Westfield drove from 1010 Sunset Boulevard in Los Angeles to 1250 Federal Boulevard in San Diego. His mileage expense is reimbursed at $.21 per mile driven.

✴ Mr. Westfield provides you with the following receipts and list of expenses. Enter and place the expense amounts in the appropriate columns.

10/12 Fuel $12.76

10/13 Entertainment: $325.64 – Dinner meeting – Ocean View Restaurant, SDTV Marketing Team

10/14 Entertainment: $114.95 – Luncheon, XY Project – Carson Willers, screenwriter, at LaTavola

10/15 Other expenses: $72.89, Hotel $389.85, Meals $412.65, Telephone $45.89, Fuel $23.54

10/15 Mileage: 300 miles @ $.21 per mile (Enter a formula to multiply the mileage by $.21 in the Transport column to find the expense.)

✴ Because Mr. Westfield just estimated the mileage, you have been asked to check the distance of this trip on the Internet by going to www.MapBlast.com. Use the Directions tab to determine the one-way mileage for this trip. Then, on an unused area of the worksheet, calculate the mileage by doubling the one-way mileage and adding 50 miles for in-town driving. (Edit the formula and the label to show the new mileage figure.)

✴ He has asked you to enter a comment in the Transport calculation cell to note the number of trip miles and the number of in-town miles.

✴ He received an advance of $300 before the trip and would like to be reimbursed for the balance.

✴ Complete formulas to add values across and down and formats, as necessary.

✴ Print the expense report, changing the print settings if necessary. Save the file as an Excel workbook file; name it **3p3.exp1012.**

MULTIPLE CHOICE

Identify the letter of the choice that best completes the statement or answers the question.

1. Numbers with two decimal places and a dollar sign are formatted for:
   A. Percent.
   B. Currency.
   C. General with two decimal places.
   D. Currency with comma.

2. The formula =E6-(F6+G6) directs the worksheet to:
   A. Multiply two numbers first and subtract the first number.
   B. Divide the first number by the sum of the second two numbers.
   C. Add the first number and add the following two numbers.
   D. Add two numbers first and subtract the total from the first number.
   E. None of the above

3. You can enter functions in formulas by:
   A. Clicking the down arrow on the AutoSum button.
   B. Clicking the list on the formula bar.
   C. Clicking the *fx* button.
   D. A and B
   E. A, B and C

4. The Office Clipboard task pane:
   A. Shows formulas and functions.
   B. Displays copied blocks.
   C. Clips boards together.
   D. All of the above
   E. None of the above

5. You can edit formulas by:
   A. Double-clicking the cell.
   B. Using color-coded arguments.
   C. Viewing range indicators.
   D. All of the above
   E. A and B

TRUE/FALSE

Circle **T** if the statement is true or **F** if the statement is false.

T   F   6. Cell addresses are used to develop formulas, not the values themselves.

T   F   7. The formula =MIN(A12:E12) returns the highest value in the range.

T   F   8. To print a wide worksheet, it may be necessary to change page orientation.

T   F   9. Use the Format Cells dialog box to set multiple and advanced formats for cells.

T   F   10. Function arguments are the data used by the function and are shown in parentheses.

Complete each sentence or statement.

11. Use _____ orientation to print a wide worksheet.

12. _____ format consists of two decimal places and a dollar sign.

13. _____ format consists of two decimal places and commas where necessary.

14. To find the highest value in a range, use the _____ function.

15. To find the lowest values in a range, use the _____ function.

16. The _____ button provides automatic entry of the most common functions.

17. A note entered to provide more information about a cell is called a _____.

18. The feature that copies formats from one cell to another is the _____.

19. The feature that copies formulas from a cell down to a range is _____.

20. The range in a function is called the _____.

LESSON 4

Data Analysis

In this lesson, you will learn to use Excel features, functions, and multiple worksheet workbooks to create and complete analyses of business data. Completed worksheets and workbooks will be saved as a Web page.

Upon completion of this lesson, you should have mastered the following skill sets:

- Change row or column size in a worksheet Ⓜ
- Insert a page break Ⓜ
- Apply and modify cell formats Ⓜ
  - Cell borders
  - Decimal place and negative number format
- Filter lists using AutoFilter Ⓜ
- Use numeric labels
- Indent text
- Insert and delete rows and columns Ⓜ
- Use formulas with absolute and relative reference Ⓜ
- Convert workbooks into Web pages Ⓜ
  - Save a workbook as a Web page Ⓜ
  - Use Web Page Preview Ⓜ

- Apply and modify worksheet formats
  - AutoFormat Ⓜ
  - Color buttons (fill color and font color)
- Modify workbooks Ⓜ
  - Insert and delete worksheets Ⓜ
  - Move and copy worksheets Ⓜ
  - Rename and format worksheet tabs Ⓜ
  - Group worksheets
- Enter date format and functions Ⓜ
- Use financial functions Ⓜ
  - The PMT function Ⓜ
  - The FV function Ⓜ
  - The PV function Ⓜ
- Use Paste Special, Values

Terms
MOUS-related
AutoFit
Page break
Border
Negative numbers
AutoFilter
Numeric label
Label prefix
Relative reference
Absolute reference
Web page
Interactivity
AutoFormat
Tab scrolling buttons
Group sheets
Serial value
Financial functions
PMT
Rate
Nper
PV
FV
Paste values
Document-related
Budget
Quarterly
Income statement
Revenue
Principal
Annual interest
Terms
Reciprocal

TRYOUT

 GOAL

To practice using the following skill sets:

✳ Change row or column size in a worksheet [M]

✳ Insert a page break [M]

✳ Apply and modify cell formats [M]

   ✳ Cell borders

   ✳ Decimal place and negative number format

✳ Filter lists using AutoFilter [M]

TASK 1

WHAT YOU NEED TO KNOW

Change Row or Column Size in a Worksheet

> All worksheets columns are set for a standard column width of 8.43, the number of characters displayed using the standard font. When you enter long labels, they appear in the next cell, if it is empty. When you enter long values, Excel fills the cell with number signs (########), or displays the number in scientific notation to indicate the need to widen the column.

> To change the width of a column, click Format, Column, Width, and set the width. Or, place the mouse on the line between the column letter headings and, when the mouse pointer changes to a double-headed arrow, drag the column to size. The width is displayed as you make this adjustment, as shown in Figure 4.1. However, the most efficient way is to double-click the column header line, and the column will *AutoFit,* or widen to fit the data in that column.

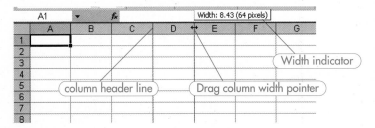

Figure 4.1 Column width indicator display

> Row height is automatically determined by the point size of the typeface used. However, you may change row height by clicking Format, Row, Height, and setting the height, or by dragging the row to size. You may also set the alignment of text in the row by clicking Format, Cells, and clicking the Alignment tab. You can format text so that it appears at the top, middle, or bottom of the row. The default settings set row height appropriate to the font size and align text at the bottom of the row.

T R Y *it* O U T

*Note: The worksheet in **4.1to** is a three-month analysis of a family budget.*

1. Open **4.1to** from the Data CD. Notice the cells with errors due to column width.

2. Double-click the line between **Columns B** and **C** to AutoFit the text in **Column B.**

3. Select **Columns C:F.**

4. Place the insertion point between **Columns F** and **G.**

5. When you see the double-headed arrow, drag to increase the column width to **13.00.**

6. Select **Cell A1** and change the font size to **18.** Notice the change in the row height.

7. Select **Rows 2** and **3,** place the insertion point between **Rows 3** and **4,** and set both row heights to **18.00.**

8. Do not close the file.

Insert a Page Break

> A *page break* is the location on the page where one page ends and another begins. Excel automatically inserts a page break when data goes beyond the bottom and right margins of a page.

> Use the View, Page Break Preview commands to go into Page Break Preview and view the existing page breaks to see if your worksheet will fit on one page, as shown in Figure 4.2. You can adjust the page breaks by dragging the dotted lines that represent the breaks. If you move the page breaks to include more rows, the cell size decreases to fit all rows on the page. Use the View menu to return to normal view.

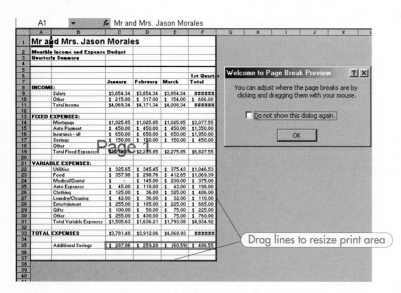

Figure 4.2 Page Break Preview

Apply and Modify Cell Formats

> Excel provides several ways for you to format the cells in a worksheet to create professional-looking documents. You can add a variety of borders and determine how numeric values are displayed.

Cell Borders

> To outline or separate data, you can include a variety of line styles that *border* the edge of a cell or range of cells. You add borders by clicking the Border tab of the Format Cells dialog box or by clicking the Borders button on the Formatting toolbar, as shown in Figure 4.3.

TRY*it*OUT

1. Continue to work in **4.1to.**

2. Click **View, Page Break Preview.**

3. Scroll down and notice the blue horizontal line that breaks the page.

4. Drag the line down so that there are two empty rows beneath the last item.

5. Click **File, Page Setup,** and notice that the worksheet has been scaled to 98%.

6. Print the file and return to Normal on the View menu.

7. Do not close the file.

TRY*it*OUT

1. Continue to work in **4.1to.**

2. Select the range **A4:F4** and click the **Border** button.

3. Select the **Thick Bottom Border** style.

4. Select the range **C35:F35.**

5. Click **Format, Cells,** and click the **Border** tab.

6. Select the **Double Line** style and click the preset **Outline** style. Notice the preview box.

7. Select the range **C35:F35,** and click the **No Border** style on the Border button to clear the borders.

Continue on next page

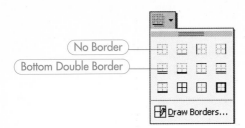

No Border

Bottom Double Border

Draw Borders...

Figure 4.3 Borders button options

8. Click **Undo** to reverse the **No Border** style.

9. Do not close the file.

> The Border tab in the Format Cells dialog box, as shown in Figure 4.4, contains three preset border formats you may select. In addition, there are other border styles illustrated around the preview box. The Line Style and Color boxes allow you to set these features for the selected border style. Your settings are illustrated within the preview box.

> Border formats do not change when you clear cell contents. You must clear border settings separately. Select the No Border option from the Borders button drop-down list, or the None style in the Border tab of the Format Cells dialog box, to clear borders.

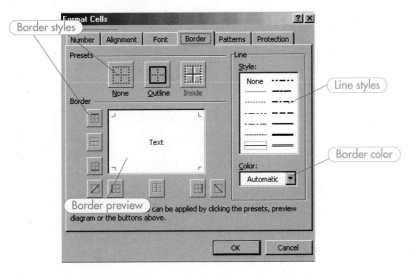

Figure 4.4 Format Cells dialog box, Border tab

Decimal Place and Negative Number Format

> Make settings for decimal places and commas with the toolbar buttons discussed earlier. You can format data for these formats and for negative numbers as well, by clicking the Number tab in the Format Cells dialog box, as shown in Figure 4.5.

> When *negative numbers* are the result of a calculation, the default format displays the value with parentheses. However, to show negative values with a minus sign, in red with parentheses, or both, click Format, Cells, and click the Number tab. You need a color printer to print red numbers.

T R Y *it* O U T

1. Continue to work **4.1to.**

2. Select **Cell E35.**

3. Click **Format, Cells,** and click the **Number** tab.

4. Click **Currency** in the Category list.

5. Select red negative numbers with parentheses.

6. Click **OK.**

7. Save the file **4.1to;** do not close.

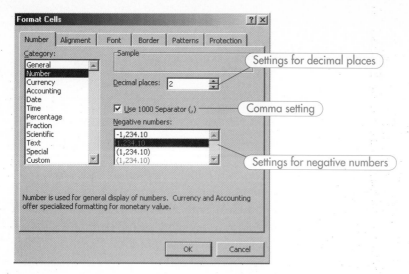

Figure 4.5 Format Cells dialog box, Number tab

Filter Lists Using AutoFilter

> When data is arranged in a list on a worksheet, you can use *AutoFilter,* an Excel data list feature that applies a filter mechanism to the worksheet. The filter hides all items that do not meet the criteria you set and displays only the item(s) you want to see.

> To apply AutoFilter, select any cell in a list and click Data, Filter, AutoFilter. A series of arrows appears at the top of each column. When you select a column and an item from the drop-down list, you are setting a criterion, which will filter the list and show only the items you select.

> For example, in the sales journal shown in Figure 4.6, after you select a customer's name, you see all the sales made to that customer. All others are filtered out.

> To remove the filter, click All on the drop-down list, and deselect AutoFilter on the Data, Filter menu.

Figure 4.6 AutoFilter and drop-down filter list

T R Y *i t* O U T

1. Open **4.1toa** from the Data CD.

2. Select **Cell C4** and click **Data, Filter,** and **AutoFilter.**

3. Click the list arrow in the **Customers** column, and select **Fitness King.** Sales to Fitness King appear.

4. Click the **list arrow,** and select **Eastern H.S.-Gym.**

5. Click the **list arrow** and select **All** to remove the filter.

6. Click **Data, Filter** and **AutoFilter** to remove the filter arrows.

7. Make **4.1to** active.

8. Apply **AutoFilter** in the VARIABLE EXPENSES section.

9. Filter to find the amount of Medical/Dental expenses.

10. Remove the filter and deselect **AutoFilter.**

11. Save the files **4.1to** and **4.1toa.** Close both files.

REHEARSAL

 **GOAL**
To create a budget analysis

SETTING THE STAGE/WRAPUP
File name: 4.1budget

TASK 1

WHAT YOU NEED TO KNOW

> A *budget* is an analysis of the projected income and expenses for a future period. Companies create budgets based on past history and projections of future trends. Budgets are the basis for management decisions and plans for expenditures.

> Businesses analyze data *quarterly,* which is every three months, or four times a year. They may compare budgets for the quarter with the actual expenditures to note the items that created the changes in expected profits. Percentages are used when analyzing data for ease of comparison.

> In this Rehearsal activity, you will create a budget analysis for the quarter ending September 30, 2002, for Time Out Sporting Goods. This company is comparing its budget for the third quarter, prepared earlier, with the actual data for the quarter.

▼ DIRECTIONS

1. Open **4.1budget** from the Data CD.

2. Set the following formats as illustrated on the facing page:
   a. Select **Cell B1** and format for 24 pt, Arial. Notice the change in row height.
   b. Select the range **A3:H3** and apply a Thick Bottom Border for the row.
   c. Add a Thick Bottom Border to the range **A7:H7.**

3. Select **Columns C:F** and drag to change column width to **12.00.**

4. Enter a formula in **Cell E9** to find the Increase/Decrease from Budget. *(Hint: Actual-Budget)*

5. Click **Format, Cells,** and click the **Number** tab in the Format Cells dialog box to format **Cell E9** for red negative numbers with parentheses and for commas with no decimal places. (Set the decimal places, and check the comma separator.)

6. Copy the formula down to **Cell E33.** Delete dashes or zeros where they are not necessary.

7. Enter a formula in **Cell F9** to find the % Increase/Decrease from Budget. *(Hint: E9/Budget)*

8. Format **Cell F9** for percent with two decimal places. (Click the Percent and Increase or Decrease Decimal buttons.)

9. Copy the formula down to **Cell F33.** Delete dashes or zeros where they are not necessary.

10. Click the **Border** button to add a Bottom Border under the values for **Rows 12** and **28.**

11. Click the **Border** button to add a single Top and Double Bottom border under the values for **Row 33.**

12. Use AutoFilter on the Expenses list to find the Rent data.

13. Display all the data and remove the AutoFilter.

14. In Page Break Preview, extend the margins to fit the worksheet on one page.

15. Return to normal view and print the worksheet.

16. Save the file **4.1budget.** Close the file.

Time Out Sporting Goods

← [16pt Arial]

Comparison of Budgeted Income Statement with Actual Income Statement

For Quarter Ended September 30, 2002

[Thick Bottom Border]

[Widen column to AutoFit text]

[Bottom Border]

[Top and Double Bottom Border]

	A	B	C	D	E	F	G	H
4						% of		
5					Increase/	Increase/		
6			Budget	Actual	Decrease	Decrease		
7			3rd Qtr	3rd Qtr	from Budget	from Budget		
8	Revenue:							
9	Net Sales		442,500	443,780				
10								
11	Cost of Goods Sold:							
12	Cost of Goods Sold		287,625	289,675				
13								
14	Gross Profit		154,875	154,105				
15								
16	Expenses:							
17	Advertising/promotions		3,750	3,795				
18	Depreciation		5,625	5,625				
19	Insurance		4,500	4,500				
20	Legal/accounting		4,125	4,075				
21	Loan interest payments		6,375	6,375				
22	Miscellaneous expenses		2,850	2,815				
23	Payroll expenses		3,150	3,165				
24	Rent		56,250	56,250				
25	Repairs/maintenance		1,350	1,858				
26	Salaries/wages		20,738	20,805				
27	Supplies		1,988	1,850				
28	Utilities		1,935	1,925				
29	Total Expenses		112,635	113,038				
30								
31	Net Income before Taxes		42,240	41,067				
32	Taxes		12,672	12,320				
33	Net Income after Taxes		29,568	28,747				

Cues for Reference

Apply Borders

1. Select area to receive border.
2. Click **Border** button.
3. Click border style.

or

1. Click **Format, Cells,** and click **Border** tab.
2. Select line, color, and style.
3. Click **OK.**

Change Row or Column Size

- To AutoFit column data, double-click right edge of column heading.

or

1. Select column(s) or row(s) to change.
2. Place mouse pointer on right edge of last column or bottom edge of row.
3. When mouse pointer changes to a double-headed arrow, drag column or row to appropriate width.

Format Decimals and Negative Numbers

1. Select data to format.
2. Click **Format, Cells,** and click **Number** tab.
3. Click **Number** category.
4. Use list arrows to select decimal settings.
5. Use list arrows to select negative number setting.
6. Select comma indicator, if appropriate.

Correct Page Break

1. Click **View, Page Break Preview.**
2. Drag margin line(s) to correct page break.
3. Click **View, Normal** to return.

Apply AutoFilter

1. Select any cell in the list to filter.
2. Click **Data, Filter, AutoFilter.**
3. Click the list arrow in column to filter.

Show All Data in Filtered List

1. Click the list arrow in filtered column.
2. Select **All.**

End AutoFilter

- Click **Data, Filter,** and **AutoFilter** to deselect the feature.

TRYOUT

TASK 2

 GOAL
To practice using the following skill sets:
- ✶ Use numeric labels
- ✶ Indent text
- ✶ Insert and delete rows and columns Ⓜ
- ✶ Use formulas with absolute and relative reference Ⓜ
- ✶ Convert workbooks into Web pages Ⓜ
  - ✶ Save a workbook as a Web page Ⓜ
  - ✶ Use Web Page Preview Ⓜ

WHAT YOU NEED TO KNOW

Use Numeric Labels

> A *numeric label* is a value or number that is not used for calculations and is treated as a label or text. It is wise to enter numeric column headings as numeric labels so the values are not included in the total by accident.

> To enter a number as a numeric label, begin the entry with an apostrophe ('), which serves as the *label prefix.* For example, to enter the year 2002, you would enter '2002. The label prefix appears only on the formula bar, and the number is left-aligned text, as shown in Figure 4.7.

> You will notice that Excel labels certain types of data with smart tags. Smart tag buttons appear on the worksheet and provide options for actions that you usually would have to open another application to complete. The actions you can take depend on the data that is tagged. The smart tag indicator, a purple triangle, appears in the cell on your worksheet as you enter data, as shown in Figure 4.7. It may also appear when you open a previously saved document. Smart tags are turned off in Excel by default.

TRY it OUT

1. Open **4.2to** from the Data CD.

2. In **Cell B2,** overtype the value with a numeric label: **'2002**

3. Enter a numeric label in Cell C2 for 2001: **'2001**

4. Center the labels.

5. Do not close the file.

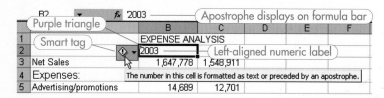

Figure 4.7 Delete dialog box

Indent Text

> Indentation allows you to align text away from the left edge of the cell. On the Formatting toolbar, indent text quickly by clicking the Increase Indent button, and adjust or undo indentation by clicking the Decrease Indent button. Use indentation to set off lists of text from heading labels.

TRY it OUT

1. Continue working in **4.2to.**

2. Select the range **A5:A16.**

3. Click the **Increase Indent** button.

4. Do not close the file.

Insert and Delete Rows and Columns

> You can insert or delete columns or rows to change the structure of a worksheet. Always save a workbook before doing this to avoid deleting data in error.

> When you insert a column or row, you create a blank area. Existing data shifts to allow for the new space. Select the column or row where you want the new space to be and click Insert, Columns or Rows. If you want to insert more than one column or row, select that number of rows or columns, starting with the location where the new column or row begins.

> When you delete a column or row, all data in that space is eliminated and existing data shifts to fill in the space. However, when you select specific cells in a row or column and click Edit, Delete, the Delete dialog box displays, as shown in Figure 4.8, to clarify the deletion request.

Figure 4.8 Delete dialog box

Use Formulas with Absolute and Relative Reference

> When you copy formulas from one cell to another, the cell references change, relative to their new location. This is called *relative reference,* the most commonly used technique of entering and copying formulas.

> However, in some cases a value in a formula must remain constant when copied to other locations. This is called an *absolute reference.* To identify a value as an absolute reference, or constant, a dollar sign ($) must precede the column and row references for that cell.

> For example, you need an absolute reference to find the percentage each value in a list represents of the total, because the total must be a constant in each formula. Therefore, in the formula =B5/$B$17, B17 represents the total and is an absolute reference. When this formula is copied, B17 remains constant in the formula but B5, with no absolute reference code, changes relative to the formula location. You can enter the dollar signs ($) in the formula by keying them in or by pressing the F4 key.

TRY*it*OUT

1. Continue working in **4.2to.**

2. Select **Column C.**

3. Click **Insert, Column.**

4. Select **Row 3.**

5. Click **Edit, Delete.** The row and the data are deleted.

6. Select **Row 2,** and insert a row.

7. Select the range B5:C5, and click **Edit, Delete.** (Notice the Delete dialog box.)

8. Click Cancel.

9. Do not close the file.

TRY*it*OUT

1. Continue to work in **4.2to.**

2. In **Cell B17,** check the formula on the formula bar.

3. Copy the formula to **Cell D17** and check the formula (copied with relative reference).

4. Enter a label in **Cells C3** and **E3:**
   % of Total

5. Enter a formula in **Cell C5** to find the percentage each expense is of the total. *(Hint: =B5/$B$17 Click the **F4** key to enter the dollar signs after entering Cell B17.)*

6. Format the value for percent.

7. Copy the formula down to **Cell C16** for all expenses.

8. Check the formulas for each expense (copied with absolute reference).

Continued on next page

9. Find the total in **Cell C17** and format for percent (100%).

10. Complete the analysis for Column E.

Convert Workbooks into Web Pages

> You may need to publish data you create for employees, customers, interested parties, or stockholders who may be in various locations. You can do this quickly by saving all or part of a workbook as a Web page.

Save a Workbook as a Web Page

> A *Web page* is a location on an Internet server, part of the World Wide Web, which can be reached and identified by a Web address. Web pages have an .htm or .html file extension.

> Before you save an Excel workbook as a Web page, you should carefully edit and check the content, and save the file. Then, click File, Save As Web Page to open the Save As dialog box with Web page settings. There are settings to save the entire workbook or the selected sheet, and a setting to add interactivity. The *Interactivity* setting creates an HTML file that allows the users to work in the workbook and make changes. If you save the workbook as a noninteractive workbook, users cannot make changes in the browser.

> To create a title for your Web page, click the Change Title button. The Set Page Title dialog box opens, as shown in Figure 4.9, and the title you enter appears centered over your worksheet on the Web page.

TRY*it* OUT

1. Continue to work in **4.2to.**

2. Save the file.

3. Click **File, Save as Web Page.**

4. Click **Selection: Sheet.**

5. Click **Change Title.**

6. Enter **Time Out Sporting Goods** and click **OK.**

7. In the File name box, enter the file name: **test**

8. Do not close the file.

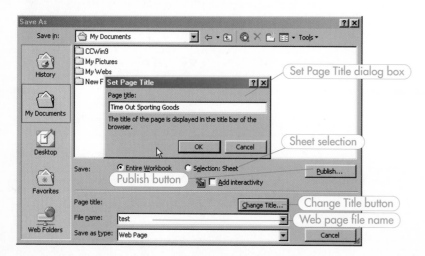

Figure 4.9 Save As Web Page and Set Title dialog box

Use Web Page Preview

> After you name the file and make the save settings, click Publish, and click Browse to select a local disk folder as the publish location. Check Open Published Web Page in Browser, and click Publish. The published page is saved to your local drive and the Web page opens in Internet Explorer or your Web browser for you to preview, as shown in Figure 4.10.

> If you added interactivity, you can now make changes to the workbook in the browser; otherwise, you can go back to the Excel file and make any changes you want. When your edits are complete, you can republish the Web page to your public location.

> Some Web site hosting companies let you publish Web pages directly to the Internet, but you or your facility must sign up for an account. Some accounts are free if you accept advertisements that automatically appear on your site.

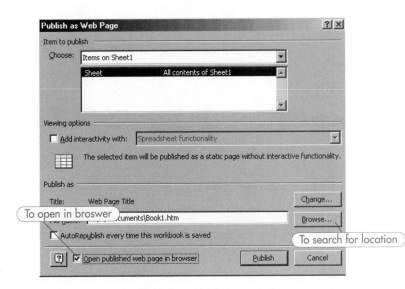

Figure 4.10 Publish as Web Page dialog box

TRY*it***OUT**

1. Continue to work in **4.2to.**

2. Click **Publish.**

3. Click **Browse** and select location for the file.

4. Check **Open published Web page in browser. Click Publish.** (The file will open in Internet Explorer or your default browser.)

5. Review the data and click the **Close** button.

6. In the worksheet, bold the title in **Cell B1.**

7. Format the totals in **Cells B17** and **D17** for currency with no decimal places, adjusting column width as necessary.

8. Republish the worksheet:
   a. Click **File, Save as Web Page.**
   b. Click **test.htm.**
   c. Check **Republish:Sheet.**
   d. Click **Publish** on the Save As dialog box.
   e. Click **Publish** on the Publish as Web Page dialog box.

9. Close the browser.

10. Save the file **4.2to.** Close the file.

REHEARSAL

TASK 2

 GOAL
To use absolute reference formulas to create an income statement analysis and to save the file as a Web page

SETTING THE STAGE/WRAPUP
File name   4.2is

WHAT YOU NEED TO KNOW

> At the end of the year companies prepare an *income statement* to show the income, expenses, and profits for the year. To help analyze the income statement and how it relates to past results, it is compared to the statement for the previous year. This is called a trend analysis.

> Percentages are used to analyze data to make comparisons easier. For example, you can compare the increase in expenses from year to year, even though sales data vary, by determining what percentage expenses are of net sales for that year. Because net sales are used as a constant in every formula for this analysis, it is necessary to use an absolute reference.

> In this Rehearsal activity, you will prepare a comparison of summary income statements for Time Out Sporting Goods for two years, and save it to the Web.

DIRECTIONS

1. Open **4.2is** from the Data CD.

2. Widen Column A to AutoFit the text.

3. Indent text in the range **A6:A7**.

4. Select **Column C** and insert two columns.

5. Insert a row at **Row 5** and create column headings as illustrated on the facing page, using numeric labels where necessary.

6. Enter a formula in **Cell C7,** using an absolute reference, to find the percentage each line is of net sales.

7. Format the result for Percent style. (The answer in **Cell C7** should be 100%, because this is the net sales value.)

8. Copy the formula down for each item.

9. Delete unnecessary formula results.

10. Delete **Row 11.**

11. Enter a formula in **Cell F7** to find the percentage of net sales.

12. Format the result for percent, copy the formula, and clear unwanted results.

13. Add borders as shown in the illustration on the facing page.

14. Check your formats and results.

15. Save the file **4.2is.**

16. Save the file to the Web. Use the same file name and change the title to: **Time Out Sporting Goods**

17. Publish the file to your directory and open the published Web site in your browser.

18. Close the browser and the files.

	A	B	C	D	E	F	G
1		Time Out Sporting Goods					
2		Comparison of Income Statement Summaries					
3		For Years Ended December 31, 2002 and 2001					
4	numeric labels →	2002	→		2001		
5		Amount	% of Sales		Amount	% of Sales	
6	Income:						
7	Net Sales	1,647,778	=B7/$B$7		1,548,911		
8	Less: Cost of Goods Sold	1,045,212			1,002,543		
9							
10	Gross Profit	602,566			546,368		
11			delete row 11				
12							
13	Expenses:	446,049			413,341		
14							
15	Net Income before Taxes	156,517			133,027		
16	Less: Taxes	46,955			39,908		
17	Net Income after Taxes	109,562			93,119		
18							
19							
20							
21			← insert 2 columns →				
22							

Cues for Reference

Indent Text
1. Select cells with data to indent.
2. Click **Increase Indent** button.

Insert Rows or Columns
1. Select row(s) or column(s) at the insertion point.
2. Click **Insert, Column** or **Insert, Row.**

Enter Numeric Label
1. Enter apostrophe (').
2. Enter a value.
3. Press **Enter.**

Delete Rows or Columns
1. Select row(s) or column(s) to delete.
2. Click **Edit, Delete.**

Use Absolute Reference Formulas
1. Enter formula, including absolute reference cell.
2. Press **F4** to insert dollar signs.

Save as Web Page and View in Browser
1. Click **File, Save as Web Page.**
2. Click **Change Title.**
3. Enter Web page title.
4. Click **OK.**
5. Name file.
6. Click selection: **Worksheet**
7. Click **Publish.**
8. Click **Open published web page in browser.**
9. Click **Publish.**

TRYOUT

TASK 3

GOAL

To practice using the following skill sets:

❋ Apply and modify worksheet
formats
  ❋ AutoFormat Ⓜ
  ❋ Color buttons (fill color and
    font color)
❋ Modify workbooks Ⓜ
  ❋ Insert and delete worksheets Ⓜ
  ❋ Move and copy worksheets Ⓜ
  ❋ Rename and format
    worksheet tabs Ⓜ
  ❋ Use group worksheets

WHAT YOU NEED TO KNOW

Apply and Modify Worksheet Formats

> Excel provides built-in formats that you can apply to a
range of data.

AutoFormat

> The *AutoFormat* feature includes automatic formats for
numbers, fonts, borders, patterns, colors, alignments, row
heights, and column widths.

> When you select a range and open the AutoFormat dialog
box, you find a selection of 16 table formats. As shown in
Figure 4.11, all formats include only column headings and
data. When you use AutoFormat, you must format title
rows separately.

TRY*it*OUT

1. Open **4.3to** from the Data CD.

2. Select the range **A4:F17.**

3. Click **Format, AutoFormat.**

4. View the AutoFormat selections.

5. Select the **Classic 3** AutoFormat.

6. Click **OK.**

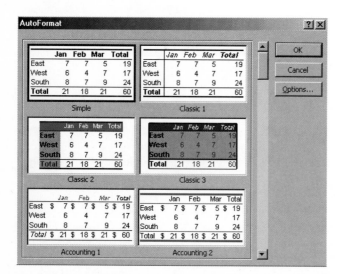

Figure 4.11 AutoFormat dialog box

Color Buttons (Fill Color and Font Color)

> The Color buttons on the Formatting toolbar provide a palette of colors that you can use to set the fill color or the font color in a selected cell or range of cells. You can use them to format sections of an entire worksheet or for titles on an AutoFormat worksheet.

> You can also apply shading or patterns to a selected range by clicking Format, Cells, and the Patterns tab. Select a color from the Cell shading color palette or a pattern from the Pattern palette, as shown in Figure 4.12. If you place your mouse pointer over a pattern or color in the Patterns tab, or over a color on the toolbar palettes, the name of the pattern or color will appear.

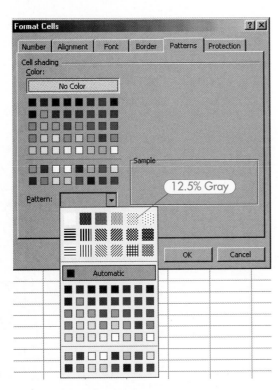

Figure 4.12 Format, Cells dialog box, Patterns tab

Modify Workbooks

> Excel lets you work with sheets in many ways. For example, you can delete, insert, rename, move, copy, and hide sheets.

Insert and Delete Worksheets

> In some cases you will need to use multiple worksheets for data. For example, a chain of stores may have sales data for each store on separate sheets in one workbook.

TRY it OUT

1. Continue to work in **4.3to.**

2. Select the range **A1:F3.**

3. Click **Format, Cells, Patterns** tab, and click the **Pattern** list arrow to select the **12.5% Gray** pattern. Click **OK.**

4. With the range **A1:F3** still selected, use the **Fill Color** button and select **Light Gray.**

5. Do not close the file.

TRY it OUT

1. Continue to work in **4.3to.**

2. Click **Insert, Worksheet.** A new sheet appears.

3. Right-click any sheet tab.

4. Click **Insert** and click **OK** in the Insert dialog box. A new sheet appears.

5. Right-click **Sheet5.** Click **Delete.**

6. Delete **Sheet4.**

7. Do not close the file.

> There are three sheets, labeled Sheet1 through Sheet3 on the sheet tabs. The active sheet tab is white, and the inactive sheets are shaded. The *tab scrolling buttons* allow you to scroll hidden sheets into view.

> To insert sheets, select Insert, Worksheet. You can also insert and delete sheets by using the shortcut menu that appears when you right-click a sheet tab. Right-click a sheet tab and click Insert or Delete on the shortcut menu, as shown in Figure 4.13.

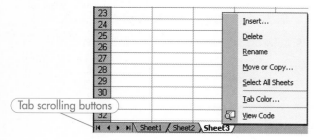

Figure 4.13 Sheet tabs and worksheet shortcut menu

Move and Copy Worksheets

> You can move sheets by using the drag-and-drop method. When you drag the sheet tab, the mouse pointer displays a sheet that you can drop in any location.

> To move or copy a sheet, right-click the sheet tab and select Move or Copy. When the Move or Copy dialog box opens, as shown in Figure 4.14, notice that you have the option of moving or copying the sheet to another workbook, or to a location in the current workbook. When you copy a sheet, it will copy with the same sheet name, identified with a (2) to show it is a second copy.

Figure 4.14 Move or Copy dialog box

Rename and Format Worksheet Tabs

> As seen on the shortcut menu in Figure 4.13, you can select Rename, which brings you into the sheet tab name area for entering a new name. A quick way to rename a sheet is to double-click the sheet tab and enter the new name.

> You can format the color of the sheet tab by clicking Format, Sheet, Tab Color, or clicking Tab Color on the shortcut menu. Then, select the color from the Format Tab Color dialog box, as shown in Figure 4.15.

Figure 4.15 Format Tab Color dialog box

Group Worksheets

> If you are creating a worksheet that you want to copy to one or more worksheets, you can group the sheets and make the entries on all sheets simultaneously. To *group sheets,* click the first sheet, press and hold the Ctrl key, and select all other sheets. If the sheets you want to select are next to one another, you can click the first sheet, press and hold the Shift key, and click the last sheet.

> To print a multiple worksheet file or to make print settings for the entire workbook, first group all sheets. Make print settings with sheets grouped, and click Entire workbook in the Print what section in the Print dialog box, as shown in Figure 4.16.

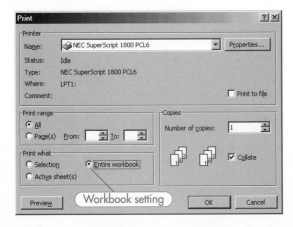

Figure 4.16 Print dialog box

T R Y *i t* **O U T**

1. Continue to work in **4.3to.**

2. Double-click the **JANUARY(2)** sheet and rename it: **FEBRUARY**

3. In **Cell F4,** enter **FEBRUARY** and widen the column.

4. Click **Sheet2,** right-click, and delete the sheet.

5. Click the **JANUARY** sheet, then click **Format, Sheet, Tab Color, Blue.** Click **OK.**

6. Right-click the **FEBRUARY** sheet, and click **Tab Color, Red.** Click **OK.**

7. Do not close the file.

T R Y *i t* **O U T**

1. Continue to work in **4.3to.**

2. Select **JANUARY,** press and hold the **Shift** key, and click **FEBRUARY.** Notice that both sheets are active.

3. In **B3,** enter: `Boston Store` Check both sheets.

4. With sheets still grouped, click **File, Page Setup.**

5. Deselect the **gridlines** setting on the Sheet tab.

6. Click **OK.**

7. Click **File, Print.**

8. Click **Entire workbook, OK.**

9. Click **Sheet3** to clear grouping.

10. Save the file **4.3to.** Close the file.

REHEARSAL

TASK 3

GOAL
To create a revenue analysis on multiple worksheets

SETTING THE STAGE
File name: 4.3revenue

WHAT YOU NEED TO KNOW

> In a year, *revenue* (income) will vary depending on the season, economy, or other factors. Business owners analyze revenue figures to note economic trends and warning signs and use this data to make management decisions.

> In this Rehearsal activity, you will create a revenue analysis workbook by formatting a quarterly analysis on multiple worksheets. Occasions Event Planning plans conferences, parties, seminars, meetings, etc. The company makes arrangements with vendors such as hotels, food caterers, printers, etc., to plan clients' events. Its revenues come from charges for consultation hours and a charge of 18% of all contract vendor bills.

DIRECTIONS

1. Open **4.3revenue** from the Data CD.
2. Insert an additional worksheet at the end of the workbook.
3. Copy Column A from Sheet1 to remaining sheets:
   a. Copy Column A on Sheet 1.
   b. Group Sheets 2-4 by clicking **Sheet2,** press and hold the **Shift** key, and click **Sheet4.**
   c. Paste data to **Cell A1** on Sheet2. (Column A data will be on all sheets.)
   d. Widen Column A by double-clicking the column edge.
4. Rename Sheets 1-4: 1ˢᵗ Qtr., 2ⁿᵈ Qtr., 3ʳᵈ Qtr., and 4ᵗʰ Qtr.
5. Cut and paste April, May, and June data as illustrated on the facing page, from 1ˢᵗ Qtr. sheet to 2ⁿᵈ Qtr. sheet in **Cell B3.**
6. Group all sheets. (Select **1st Qtr.,** press and hold the **Shift** key, and click **4th Qtr.**)
7. Enter the following labels, formats, and formulas on all grouped sheets:
   a. In **Cell E3,** enter a column heading: **Total**
   b. In **Cell E5,** enter a formula to add the values for the three months.
   c. AutoFill the formula down to **Cell E18.**
   d. In **Cell B13,** enter a formula to add the values for the month.
   e. AutoFill the formula for all months.
   f. In **Cell B16,** enter a formula to find Fees on Contracts. (18% of total billings for the month: =Total*18%) AutoFill across for all months.
   g. In **Cell B18,** enter a formula to find Total Revenue by adding Fees and Consultation Revenues. AutoFill across for all months.
   h. Clear unwanted zeros and format for commas with no decimal places.
   i. Select the range **A3:E18** and AutoFormat the sheets using the List 1 format.
   j. Select the range and **A1:E2,** and Fill Color the range using a light turquoise.
8. Ungroup sheets by clicking the **3ʳᵈ Qtr.** sheet tab.
9. Group 3ʳᵈ and 4ᵗʰ Qtr. sheets and widen Columns B:E to **8.00.** (These sheets have no data yet.)
10. Color sheet tabs as you prefer.
11. Group all sheets and print workbook by clicking **Entire workbook** in the Print dialog box in the Print what section.
12. Save the file **4.3revenue.** Close the workbook.

	A	B	C	D	E	F	G	H	I
1	OCCASIONS EVENT PLANNING						Cut and paste to new sheet		
2	Revenue and Billings Analysis								
3		January	February	March	Total		April	May	June
4	Billings for Contract Vendors:								
5	Food/Catering	53,445	43,766	33,232			56,433	49,876	65,876
6	Hotels/Venues	87,543	65,888	73,455			98,665	82,565	98,665
7	Printing/Advertising	13,232	10,533	8,564			11,654	10,112	14,323
8	Music/Entertainment	45,865	45,865	45,865			45,865	45,865	45,865
9	Personnel/Speakers/Security	56,454	43,566	44,345			53,888	48,975	57,645
10	Audio/Visual	17,654	15,433	13,245			16,543	14,987	17,909
11	Computers/Special Equipment	54,333	54,678	32,122			50,323	42,945	44,567
12	Miscellaneous	11,342	9,453	6,590			7,645	6,588	9,856
13	Total								
14									
15	Revenue:								
16	Fees on Contracts								
17	Consultation Revenues	10,540	11,450	11,340			12,500	12,600	11,800
18	Total Revenue								
19									
20		AutoFormat all worksheets							
21		using List 1 format							
22									

Cues for Reference

AutoFormat Data
1. Select worksheet data beginning with column headers.
2. Click **Format, AutoFormat.**
3. Click **AutoFormat style.**
4. Click **OK.**

Group Consecutive Sheets
1. Click the first sheet to group.
2. Press and hold **Shift.**
3. Click last sheet to group.

Delete Sheet
1. Click sheet to delete.
2. Right-click sheet tab.
3. Click **Delete.**
4. Click **OK.**

Insert Sheet
1. Right-click any sheet tab.
2. Click **Insert.**
3. Click **OK.**

Rename Sheet
1. Double-click sheet and type new name or right-click sheet to rename.
2. Click **Rename.**
3. Enter new name.

Format Tab Color
1. Right-click sheet to format.
2. Click **Tab Color.**
3. Click color.
4. Click **OK.**

TRYOUT

TASK 4

GOAL

To practice using the following skill sets:

* Enter date format and functions M
* Use financial functions M
  * The PMT function M
  * The FV function M
  * The PV function M
* Use Paste Special, Values

WHAT YOU NEED TO KNOW

Enter Date Format and Functions

> You can use the date function, =DATE(year, month, day), to enter a date as a numeric value. Usually it is not necessary to do so, because entering a date automatically creates a *serial value*. The serial, or numeric, value allows you to use dates in formulas and represents the number of days from January 1, 1900 to the date entered. To view a date's serial value, format the date as a number using the General format, as shown in Figure 4.17.

	A	B	C	D	E
1		Dates	1/1/1900	1/30/1900	12/24/2000
2	General number format				
3	produces serial values		1	30	36884
4					

Figure 4.17 Dates formatted to show serial values

> Once you enter a date, you can change the format, as discussed in Lesson 1, by clicking Format, Cells, the Number tab, and then clicking Date from the Category list. The format of the date does not affect or change its serial value.

> You can enter the current date, based on the computer's clock, on any worksheet by pressing the Ctrl + ; (semicolon) keys, or you can enter the current date and time by using =NOW().

TRY*it*OUT

1. Open **4.4to** from the Data CD.

2. Notice the test dates and select the range **C1:E1.**

3. Click **Format, Cells,** and the **Number** tab. Select **General** to format the dates as numbers. (These are the serial values.)

4. Reformat the range **C1:E1** as dates in a format that shows a four-digit year.

5. In **Cell C2,** press the **Ctrl + ;** keys.

6. Enter =Now( ) in **Cell D2.**

7. In **Cell B7,** enter a formula to calculate 15 days after the date in **Cell B5.** (Hint: =B5+15)

8. In **Cells B8, B9,** and **B10,** enter formulas to calculate the dates for 30, 45, and 90 days after the purchase date in B5.

9. If dates did not appear as the answers in the range B7:B10, format the serial values in a date format.

10. Do not close the file.

Use Financial Functions

> *Financial functions* are used to analyze loans, calculate payments, and compute depreciation on assets. The financial functions most frequently used for analyzing loans are the PMT, FV, and PV functions.

The PMT Function

> The *PMT* (payment) function is used to calculate a loan payment based on the *principal* (present value of loan), interest rate, and number of payments. The function and arguments are =PMT(Rate, Nper, Pv, Fv, Type). (*Note: The last two arguments are optional here and in all the other functions shown below.*)

> *Rate* =interest rate per period. Because rates are generally stated as *annual interest* rates, when calculating a monthly payment you must divide the annual interest rate by 12. For example, you would enter 10% annual interest rate as 10%/12.

> *Nper* =number of payments.

> *Pv* = present value or principal of loan.

> To enter financial functions, click the Insert Function button on the Standard toolbar, select a financial function, as shown in Figure 4.18, and use the Collapse dialog boxes to select the function arguments, as shown in Figure 4.19. You may have to enter absolute reference codes or divide the annual interest rate after you select the appropriate argument.

TRY *it* **OUT**

1. Continue to work in **4.4to.**

2. In **Cell E13,** click the **fx** button on the formula bar, and click **PMT,** under Select a function.

3. For Rate, collapse the dialog box and click **Cell A13.** Restore the dialog box.

4. Next to **A13** in the Rate box, enter **/12** next to A13 to divide the annual rate into a monthly rate.

5. For Nper, number of payments, click **A15.**

6. For Pv, the principal, select **Cell A14,** and click F4 to make it absolute. (For practice, not necessary here.)

7. Click **OK.** (The negative answer shows the payment as a reduction of the loan.)

8. Do not close the file.

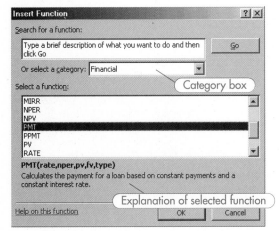

Figure 4.18 Insert Function dialog box, PMT function

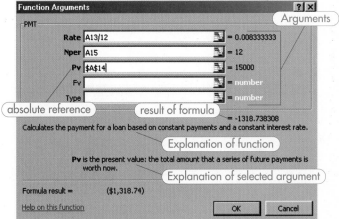

Figure 4.19 PMT Function Arguments dialog box

The FV Function

> The *FV* (future value) function is used to calculate the future value of a series of equal payments, at a fixed interest rate, for a specific number of payments. You can use this function to calculate the value of equal savings deposits at the end of a period. The function and arguments are =FV(Rate,Nper,Pmt,Pv,Type), as shown in Figure 4.20.

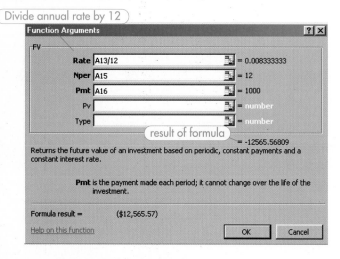

Figure 4.20 FV Function Arguments dialog box

The PV Function

> The *PV* (present value) function is used to calculate the present value of a series of equal payments, at a fixed interest rate, for a specific number of payments. You can calculate the principal, or money needed now, to generate equal payments in the future. The function and arguments are =PV(Rate,Nper,Pmt,Fv,Type), as shown in Figure 4.21.

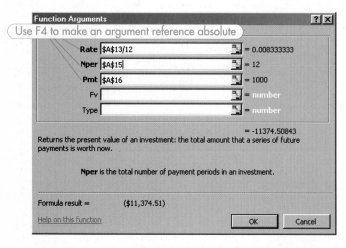

Figure 4.21 PV Function Arguments dialog box

T R Y *i t* **O U T**

1. Continue to work in **4.4to.**

2. In **Cell E14,** enter the FV function as follows:
   a. Click the **fx** button and select the **Financial category** and **FV** function.
   b. The Rate, in **Cell A13,** is an annual rate, and should be divided by 12.
   c. The Nper, in **Cell A15,** is 12 months.
   d. The Pmt in **Cell A16** is $1000.

3. Click **OK.**

4. Do not close the file.

T R Y *i t* **O U T**

1. Continue to work in **4.4to.**

2. In **Cell E15,** enter the PV function to find the present value of 12, $1000 payments, at 10%. (Divide the annual rate by 12.)

3. Check your formulas and answers against the Check column. (Absolute references, as shown in figure 4.21, would be necessary if the formulas were to be copied.)

4. Do not close the file.

Use Paste Special, Values

> When you used copy and paste in previous tasks, you copied the entire contents of a cell. If you want to copy and paste specific cell content, use the Paste Options button, which is a smart tag that appears on the worksheet, or use the Paste button options list on the Formatting toolbar, as shown in Figure 4.22.

Formulas
Values
No Borders
Transpose
Paste Link
Paste Special...

Figure 4.22 Paste button options list on the Formatting toolbar

> One of the special paste operations is to paste only the values from a cell, not the formula. *Paste Values* will paste the numeric value or answer without including the formula in cases where the formula will not work in the new location. You can select the Values option from the Paste button options list on the Formatting toolbar, as shown in Figure 4.22. Or, you can select Values Only from the Paste Options button list on the worksheet, as shown in Figure 4.23.

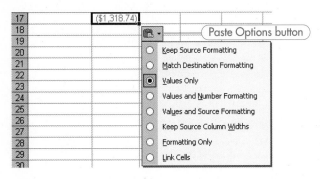

Figure 4.23 Paste Options button, options list

1. Continue to work in **4.4to.**

2. Click **Cell E13,** which includes a formula and answer, and click **Copy.**

3. Click **Cell B19** and click **Paste.** (Zeros or a #REF error appears.)

4. Click the list arrow on the **Paste** button, and click **Values.** (The answer appears.)

5. Check the formula bar for **Cells B19** and **E13.** Notice the difference.

6. Click **Cell E14,** which includes a formula and an answer, and click **Copy.**

7. Click **Cell B20,** click the list arrow on the **Paste** button, and click **Values.**

8. Use the Paste Options button on the worksheet to copy and paste (Values Only) the answer from **Cell E15** into **Cell B21.**

9. Save the file **4.4to.** Close the file.

REHEARSAL

TASK 4

GOAL
To use financial and date functions to analyze the options for the purchase of equipment

SETTING THE STAGE/WRAPUP
File name: 4.4loan

WHAT YOU NEED TO KNOW

> When making a large purchase, individuals and businesses should analyze all the options for payment. Because this involves loan time and interest calculations, you use financial functions to calculate the cost of the money.

> Sellers often give buyers credit *terms* that involve discounts for early payment. Thus, the notation 2/20, 1/45, n/60 means that the buyer will get 2% off the bill if paid in 20 days, 1% if paid in 45 days, or the full amount is due in 60 days.

> When calculating the amount due after a 2% discount is taken, you can use the *reciprocal,* the difference from 100%, or 98%, to calculate the discounted payment.

> In this Rehearsal activity, you will prepare an analysis to help In-Shape Fitness Centers consider payment options for additional equipment for the gym. The options include paying cash, taking a loan, or saving for the purchase.

DIRECTIONS

1. Open **4.4loan** from the Data CD.

2. Format the title and Column A section labels as illustrated on the facing page.

3. In **Cell C8,** find the total loan principal; the amount of the purchase.

4. In **Cell C12, C13,** and **C14,** enter formulas to calculate the dates for each discount and for full payment.

5. In **Cell C16,** enter a formula to find the purchase price after a 2% discount. *(Hint: Total Loan Principal*98%)*

6. In **Cell C17,** enter a formula to find the purchase price after a 1% discount.

7. Click **Paste Special, Values** to copy **Cell C16** to **Cell C20, Cell C17** to **Cell D20,** and **Cell C8** to **Cell E20.**

8. All loan calculations are for 12 months. In **Cell C21,** enter a financial function to find the monthly payment (PMT), using the annual interest rate in **Cell B21** divided by 12, 12 payments, and the principal in **Cell C20** with an absolute reference.

9. Copy the formula down for all interest rate choices to **Cell C25.**

10. Repeat Steps 8 and 9 for the 60-day and 90-day loan amounts.

    Note: Use absolute reference for the loan amounts and in De20 and E20, and divide the annual rate by 12.

11. In **Cell C32,** enter a formula to calculate the Total Payments if you make 12 payments of $1100.

12. In Cell C34, enter a financial function to calculate the future value (FV) of the annual interest in **Cell B34** divided by 12, for 12 payments (absolute reference), for the payment in **Cell C30** (absolute reference).

13. Copy the formula down for all interest rates.

14. Click Print Preview and print the report.

15. Save the file **4.4loan.** Close the file.

	A	B	C	D	E	F
1	16 point Bold →	**In-Shape Fitness Centers**				
2		**Equipment Purchase Options**				
3						
4	**Equipment**	**Equipment Order**				
5		QXR All Weight Trainer	10,765.00			
6		HiClimb Stair Climber	1,525.00			
7		Pacer Treadmill W14	1,450.00			
8		**Total Loan Principal**				
9						
10	**Cash Terms**	**Purchase Date**	**4/23/02**			
11		**Terms: 2/30, 1/60, n/90**				
12	Format using	2% discount date - 30 days				
13	bold, thick	1% discount date - 60 days				
14	border, and	90 days full payment date				
15	green					
16	shading	**Loan Principal less 2%**				
17		**Loan Principal less 1%**				
18						
19			**30 days**	**60 days**	**90 days**	
20	**Loan Options**	**Annual Interest Rate**				**Principal**
21	Loan for 12 months to	10%				
22	pay amount due.	10.50%				
23		11%				
24		11.50%				
25		12%				
26						
27						
28						
29	**Fund Options**	**Fund for Purchase**				-
30		Monthly Savings	$ 1,100.00			
31		Months	12			
32		Total Payments				
33		**Value of Savings in One Year**				
34		6%				
35		6.50%				
36		7%				

Cues for Reference

Paste Special, Values
1. Select item to copy.
2. Click **Copy** button.
3. Select paste location.
4. Click **Paste** button.
5. Click list arrow on **Paste** or **Paste Options** button.
6. Select **Values** option.

Insert a Financial Function
1. Click **fx** button on formula bar.
2. Click list arrow to select **Financial** category.
3. Select **Function.**
4. Click **OK.**

5. Click the **Collapse Dialog Box** button to select each argument from the worksheet.
6. Add any additional formula items, as necessary (absolute reference or division of annual interest rates by 12).
7. Click **OK.**

 PERFORMANCE

▶ **SETTING THE STAGE/WRAPUP**
Act I File name: 4p1.budget
Act II File name: 4p2.incomebk
Act III File name: 4p3.loanoptions

WHAT YOU NEED TO KNOW

Act I

You prepare accounting data for the Boston office of the Air Land Sea Travel Group. The office manager has asked you to develop an analysis of expenses for the last two years and has provided his estimate of expenses for the year 2003. This report will be e-mailed to the other offices in California and New York, so that they can complete similar analyses for consolidation into one report.

Follow these guidelines:

✶ Open **4p1.budget** from the Data CD.

✶ Create title lines for the report that include the company name, report name "Expense Budget Analysis", and "Boston Office". Insert rows if necessary, and format text using any desired font and font size.

✶ Re-enter year column headings as numeric labels.

✶ Adjust column widths as necessary.

✶ Enter and fill formulas to complete Projected Change and % Change columns, and Totals row.

✶ The Projected Change column shows the change the 2003 budget is from the 2002 actual numbers.

✶ The % Change is the percentage the Projected Change is of the 2002 Actual data. To get the % Change for the Totals line, include the Totals line when you copy down the formula in Cell F5.

✶ Format numbers and percentages as appropriate.

✶ AutoFormat the column headings and data in one of the styles provided.

✶ Use color buttons to format the area above the column headings to match the AutoFormat selected.

✶ Check your work and save the file.

✶ Attach the worksheet to an e-mail to the other offices (using an address provided by your instructor). Write a note to accounting personnel requesting that they complete a similar analysis for their office so that all the reports can be consolidated.

✶ Save the file **4p1.budget.** Close the file.

Act II

You work in the company headquarters of Odyssey Travel Gear. All the retail stores have sent in income statement data over the last year. You have been asked to format the existing raw data and to add an analysis for each store on a separate worksheet to determine what percentage each item represents of sales for the annual total. The resulting workbook will be saved as a Web page to provide corporate information.

Follow these guidelines:

✴ Use the file **4p2.incomebk** from the Data CD.

✴ Format the June 30 and December 31 worksheets as you want, using font styles, indents, borders, etc. Include totals in Column G.

✴ Add additional worksheets to create one for each store; rename and color the tabs accordingly.

✴ Use grouping to paste the heading and Column A data to all the individual store worksheets. Create columns named "Totals" and "% of Sales" on the store worksheets for June 30 and December 31.

✴ Copy the data to the appropriate columns on each sheet and group them to complete the Totals and % of Sales columns. You will need to use an absolute reference formula to find % of Sales.

✴ Format all store worksheets as a group and print a copy of the entire workbook.

✴ Save the file **4p2.incomebk** and save the workbook as a Web page with an appropriate title. Preview the workbook on your browser.

Act III

Trilogy Productions is contemplating the purchase or lease of warehouse space in Brooklyn, New York, to service its New York distribution center. The price of the building has been negotiated at $550,000. The company has researched loan costs and have determined that for 10-year loans, the interest rate varies, depending on the amount of the down payment provided. As an alternative, Trilogy could also sign a 10-year lease for the property. The company has asked you to develop an analysis of the options to help it make this decision.

Follow these guidelines:

✴ Use the file **4p3.loanoptions** from the Data CD.

✴ Calculate the Down Payment and Net Principal columns.

✴ Use Paste Options to copy the range D7:D9 to Cell A13.

✴ Calculate the monthly payments beginning in Cell D13 for each set of loan terms using the PMT function.

✴ To realize the cost of the lease payments, calculate the present and future value of the lease payments at a rate of 10%.

✦ *Optional:* Find the future value (FV) of each down payment, beginning in Cell F7, to show what the funds could do if they were invested in the business and not spent on the building. Use 10% for Rate, 10 (years) for Nper, omit the Pmt argument, and use the down payment as the Pv.

✦ Format the worksheet using color, border, and font settings.

✦ Preview and print a copy of the worksheet.

✦ Save the file **4p3.loanoptions.**

MULTIPLE CHOICE

Identify the letter of the choice that best completes the statement or answers the question.

1. When entering a formula you expect to copy, you can make an argument into a constant by using:
   A. Relative reference.
   B. Cell reference.
   C. Absolute reference.
   D. Active reference.
   E. All of the above

2. Page Break View in Excel:
   A. Displays page number.
   B. Displays break lines.
   C. Displays formulas.
   D. None of the above
   E. A and B

3. When saving your worksheet to the Web:
   A. First carefully check your data.
   B. It becomes an .htm file.
   C. Preview the page in your browser.
   D. All of the above
   E. None of the above

4. When using financial functions:
   A. Click the Collapse Dialog Box button to select formula arguments.
   B. PV means positive value.
   C. The interest rate must be expressed in months if the payments are monthly.
   D. A and C
   E. A, B, and C

5. The feature that automatically widens columns to the widest label is called:
   A. AutoFormat.
   B. AutoFit.
   C. AutoFilter.
   D. AutoFill.
   E. All of the above

TRUE/FALSE

Circle **T** if the statement is true or **F** if the statement is false.

T   F   6. When hatch marks or number signs (###), or asterisks (***) appear in a cell, it means the cell is empty.

T   F   7. A workbook contains numerous sheets, called worksheets.

T   F   8. Cell references change relative to their new location during the copying process.

T   F   9. An explanation of each financial function appears in the Insert Function dialog box.

T   F   10. Dates have serial values that you can use in formulas.

Complete each sentence or statement.

11. _____ is a feature that allows you to widen a column to the width of the widest data item.

12. When formulas are copied, they generally copy using _____.

13. If a cell address in a formula must remain constant, you must use _____.

14. When you want to enter data on three sheets at once, you must _____ the sheets.

15. You can determine if a worksheet fits on the page by using _____ view.

16. Worksheets can be formatted with colors, lines, and alignments using _____.

17. Financial functions can be entered using the _____ button.

18. _____ is a feature that allows you to sort out unwanted data from a list.

19. _____ is a feature that allows you to copy and paste the answer in a cell without the formula.

20. The extension for a file saved to the Web is _____.

LESSON 5

Financial Reports

In this lesson, you will learn to use logical functions, 3-D formulas, print settings, and the linking and formatting features in Excel to prepare financial reports.

Upon completion of this lesson, you should have mastered the following skill sets:

- Merge, center, and split cells 🔳
- Arrange multiple workbooks
- Paste link between workbooks 🔳
- Work with hyperlinks 🔳
  - Insert a hyperlink
  - Use a hyperlink
  - Edit a hyperlink
- Hide and unhide rows and columns 🔳
- Freeze and unfreeze rows and columns 🔳
- Modify page set up options
  - Print nonadjacent sections of a worksheet
  - Print titles

- Use logical functions in formulas 🔳
- Add headers and footers to worksheets 🔳
  - Add customized headers and footers
- Enter 3-D references 🔳
- Apply a style 🔳
- Define a new style 🔳
- Modify a style 🔳
- Remove a style 🔳
- Find and replace cell data and formats 🔳
  - Find cell data
  - Find and replace data and formats

Terms
MOUS-related
- Merge and Center button
- Split cells
- Paste Link option
- Hyperlink
- Freeze Panes
- Print Titles
- IF statement
- Headers and footers
- 3-D references
- Styles
- Find and Replace

Document-related
- Schedule of accounts receivable
- Schedule of accounts payable
- Trial balance
- Worksheet
- Consolidated income statement
- Balance sheet

 T R Y O U T

TASK 1

 GOAL
To practice using the following skill sets:
- ✷ Merge, center, and split cells 🅜
- ✷ Arrange multiple workbooks
- ✷ Paste link between workbooks 🅜
- ✷ Work with hyperlinks 🅜
  - ✷ Insert a hyperlink
  - ✷ Use a hyperlink
  - ✷ Edit a hyperlink

WHAT YOU NEED TO KNOW

Merge, Center, and Split Cells

> The *Merge and Center* button on the Formatting toolbar centers text over a selected range by merging the cells. Returning the cells to their normal width is called *splitting* the cells. You can set these features in the Alignment tab of the Format Cells dialog box, as shown in Figure 5.1.

> To center a title across the top of a worksheet, enter the title in Column A, select the title and the range over which to center it, and click the Merge and Center button. The title is still in Column A, but it is centered in one large cell you created by merging the cells across the range. You can merge only one line at a time.

> To remove the settings, reselect the range and click the Merge and Center button to split the cells, or deselect Merge Cells in the Alignment tab of the Format Cells dialog box.

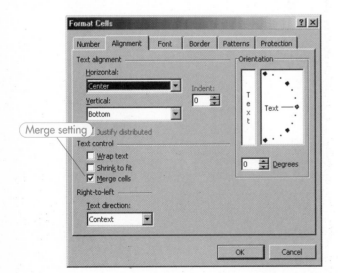

Figure 5.1 Format Cells dialog box, Alignment tab, Merge setting

T R Y *it* O U T

1. Open **5.1to** from the Data CD.

2. Select the range **A1:E1**.

3. Click the **Merge and Center** button to merge the cells and center the text.

4. Click the **Merge and Center** button again to split the cells.

5. Click the **Undo** button to keep the merge and center setting.

6. Select the range **A2:E2** and merge and center the text.

7. Select **Cell A2** and click **Format, Cells, and Alignment.**

8. Deselect **Merge cells** and click **OK.**

9. Click the **Undo** button to keep the center setting.

10. Do not close the file.

Arrange Multiple Workbooks

> When working with more than one workbook, you can switch between workbooks using the file buttons on the taskbar or by selecting the file name from the list of open files on the Windows menu, as shown in Figure 5.2.

> You can arrange the files on the screen by using the Window, Arrange command. The Arrange Windows dialog box, shown in Figure 5.3, provides options for arranging multiple files as well as for viewing windows of the active workbook.

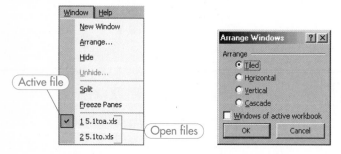

Figure 5.2 Windows menu with list of open files

Figure 5.3 Arrange Windows dialog box

> When multiple files are arranged on the screen, as shown in Figure 5.4, the active file is indicated by the blue title bar. Click any cell in a worksheet to make the worksheet the active file.

5.1toa

	A	B	C	D	E
1	Carriage Leather Goods				
2	Trial Balance				
3				Debits	Credits
4	Cash			13,434.98	
5	Accounts Receivable				
6	Merchandise Inventory			56,787.56	
7	Supplies			3,256.98	
8	Equipment			45,656.98	
9	Allowance for Depreciation				12,343.87
10	Accounts Payable				
11	Val Roamer, Capital				125,812.13
12	Purchases			132,333.54	
13	Sales Income				312,345.65
14	Salaries Expense			86,545.54	
15	Rent Expense			75,433.00	
16	Insurance Expense			12,500.00	
17	Advertising Expense			11,580.00	
18	Payroll Tax Expense			9,765.90	
19					
20	Totals			447,294.48	450,501.65

Sheet1 / Sheet2 / Sheet3

5.1to

	A	B	C	D	E
1		Carriage Leather Goods			
2		Schedule of Accounts Receivable			
3					
4		Altona, Dara		1,647.80	
5		Cainter, Mary		2,311.55	
6		MacPherson, Alan		1,420.13	
7		Ramshorn, Alisa		2,041.40	
8		Warneke, Michael		1,427.72	
9		Wunder, Carl		2,145.55	
10		Total		10,994.15	
11					
12					
13					
14					
15					
16					
17					
18					
19					
20					

AR / AP / Sheet3

Figure 5.4 Files arranged vertically

TRY*it* OUT

1. Continue to work in **5.1to.**
2. Open **5.1toa** from the Data CD and notice the totals.
3. Switch to **5.1to** using the Windows menu.
4. To arrange both files on the screen, click **Window, Arrange,** and **Vertical.**
5. Do not close the files.

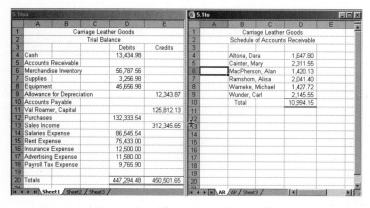

Paste Link Between Workbooks

> In the last lesson, you used the Paste Special, Values feature to copy and paste only the values in a formula cell. Another Paste Special feature is the *Paste Link* option. This option links cells to another worksheet or workbook so that if you change the original data, it changes in the linked location as well.

> This feature is invaluable when combining schedules or data from various workbooks into a summary workbook, because any corrections to the schedule or source data are reflected in the summary worksheet.

> To link a cell or cells, copy the cell(s), go to the location to link, (which may be in another workbook) and click Edit, Paste Special, and Paste Link. You can also click the Paste button on the Standard toolbar and click Paste Link from the drop-down list or use the Paste Options button on the worksheet, and click Link Cells from the drop-down list.

> On the formula bar of a linked cell you will see a reference to the original file, for example, =[5.1to.xls]Sheet1$D$10, which means that the cell is linked to Cell D10 on Sheet1 of the 5.1to file.

> Links between files are saved when you save and close the files. If you change the linked data in the original file, the linked file may display a prompt when you open it, as shown in Figure 5.5, requesting permission to update the file. The file updates automatically, without a prompt, if you select that option in the Tools, Options menu.

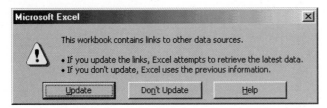

Figure 5.5 Prompt to update linked files

TRY*it* **OUT**

1. Continue to work in **5.1to** and **5.1toa.** Make sure they are arranged vertically on the screen.

2. In **5.1to**, copy the total in **Cell D10.**

3. In **5.1toa** in **Cell D5**, click **Edit, Paste Special,** and **Paste Link.**

4. Click **Cell D5** and notice the paste link reference on the formula bar.

5. In **5.1to**, select the **AP** sheet and copy **Cell E8.**

6. In **5.1toa** in **Cell E10**, click **Paste,** click the list arrow, and click **Paste Link** to link the data. Notice the totals now.

7. In **5.1to**, correct Mary Cainter's balance on the AR sheet (Cell D5) to: **$1311.55**

8. Notice the updated AR total on both worksheets and the grand totals in **5.1toa.**

9. Do not close the files.

Work with Hyperlinks

Insert a Hyperlink

> A *hyperlink* is a shortcut that allows you to jump to another location. When you click a hyperlink, it can open another workbook, a file on your hard drive or network, or an Internet address. A hyperlink sends the user to a location that provides additional supporting background or related information.

> To insert a hyperlink, first enter the text that will become the linking area. Then, click the Insert Hyperlink button on the Standard toolbar, and the Insert Hyperlink dialog box opens. As you can see in Figure 5.6, in the Link to pane on the left side of the dialog box you can select the location to hyperlink to, and select the file or location in the Look in box.

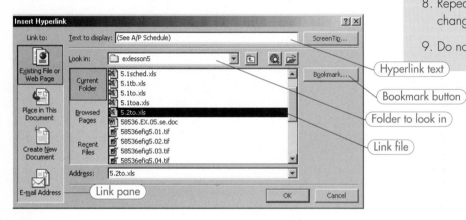

Figure 5.6 Insert Hyperlink dialog box

> To link to a specific location in a workbook, click the Bookmark button to open the Select Place in Document dialog box. There, you can identify where you will go when you activate the link. Figure 5.7 shows the dialog box and the sheet names in the file, as well as any other defined names.

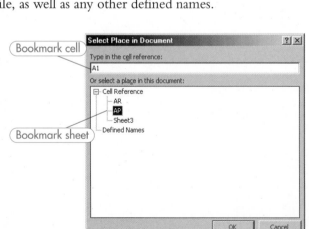

Figure 5.7 Bookmark dialog box

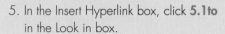

1. Continue to work in **5.1to** and **5.1toa.**

2. In **Cells C5** and **C10** of **5.1toa,** enter: **(See Schedule)**

3. Widen **Column C** to fit the widest entry.

4. In **Cell C5,** click the **Insert Hyperlink** button.

5. In the Insert Hyperlink box, click **5.1to** in the Look in box.

6. Click **Bookmark** and click the **AR** sheet.

7. Click **OK** twice.

8. Repeat Steps 4–7 for **Cell C10,** except change Step 6 to select the **AP** sheet.

9. Do not close the files.

Use a Hyperlink

> When you point to text or a graphic that contains a hyperlink, the mouse pointer becomes a hand to indicate that they are links. A ScreenTip also appears, stating the link reference and instructions for using a hyperlink, as shown in Figure 5.8. You can click once to follow the link or click and hold to select and edit the cell.

> After you view and close the file referenced by the hyperlink, you return to the original location.

Figure 5.8 ScreenTip display for a hyperlink

Edit a Hyperlink

> To edit only the hyperlink text, click the hyperlink, hold the mouse button down until the hand pointer changes to a plus sign, as shown in Figure 5.9, then, edit the text on the formula bar.

Figure 5.9 Hold mouse pointer down for Edit mode

> To edit any part of the hyperlink, right-click the hyperlink and click Edit Hyperlink from the shortcut menu. Use the Edit Hyperlink dialog box to edit any hyperlink settings. The dialog box shown in Figure 5.10 is almost identical to the Insert Hyperlink dialog box, except that it has a Remove Link button.

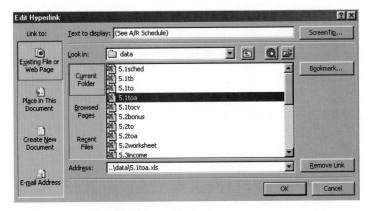

Figure 5.10 Edit Hyperlink dialog box

T R Y *i t* **O U T**

1. Continue to work in **5.1to** and **5.1toa**.

2. In **5.1toa,** move your mouse pointer near **Cell C5** to view the ScreenTip.

3. Click **Cell C5** to jump to the AR sheet in **5.1to**.

4. Close the file **5.1to**.

5. In **5.1toa**, click **Cell C10** to jump to the AP sheet in **5.1to**.

6. Close the file **5.1to**.

7. Do not close the file **5.1toa**.

T R Y *i t* **O U T**

1. Continue to work in **5.1toa**.

2. Click and hold the mouse pointer on the hyperlink text in **Cell C5** until it changes to a plus sign.

3. In the formula bar, edit the hyperlink text to read: **(See AR Schedule)**

4. Right-click the hyperlink text in **Cell C10** and click **Edit Hyperlink**.

5. In the Text to display box, edit the text to read: **(See AP Schedule)**

6. Click **OK**.

7. Save the **5.1to** and **5.1toa** files. Close the files.

REHEARSAL

TASK 1

 GOAL
To create accounts receivable and payable schedules and a trial balance with hyperlinks and paste linked totals

SETTING THE STAGE/WRAPUP
File names: 5.1sched
5.1tb

WHAT YOU NEED TO KNOW

> Schedules and trial balances are lists of account balances that a business prepares at the end of each month to check the accuracy of its accounts.

> The *schedule of accounts receivable* (AR) is a list of all the customers that owe the business money. The *schedule of accounts payable* (AP) is a list of all the business's creditors, or vendors that it must pay.

> The *trial balance* is a list of all the accounts in a business ledger and their balances for the end of the month. Accounts either have debit (left side) or credit (right side) balances, depending on the type of account. For example, Accounts Receivable and Cash have debit balances and Accounts Payable and Sales have credit balances. In a trial balance, the debit and credit balances must be equal to prove the accuracy of the ledger, or book of accounts.

> In this rehearsal activity, Green Brothers Gardening wants to check its schedules and trial balance for the year ended December 31, 2002. You will merge and center the headings, paste link the schedule totals, correct the schedules, and create and edit hyperlinks on the trial balance.

DIRECTIONS

1. Open **5.1sched** from the Data CD.

2. Group both the AR schedule and the AP schedule sheets.

3. Merge and center each of the three title rows over **Columns A** to **E**.

4. Click **Sheet3** to ungroup the sheets and check the titles on both sheets.

5. Use AutoSum to find the totals on each schedule and format for currency.

6. Open **5.1tb** from the Data CD.

7. Merge and center each of the three title rows over **Columns A** to **E**.

8. Practice splitting the cells for **Row1** to return to the original settings.

9. Merge and center **Row1** again.

10. Use AutoSum to find the total of all the debits in **Column D** and all the credits in **Column E.**

11. Arrange both worksheets on the screen vertically.

12. Copy the total of the AR schedule (**5.1sched, Cell D22**) and paste link it to **Cell D7** on the trial balance, as illustrated on the facing page.

13. Copy the total of the AP schedule (**5.1sched, Cell D14**) and paste link it to **Cell E15** on the trial balance, as illustrated on the facing page.

14. Check to see if the trial balance actually balances; debits should equal credits.

15. To find the error, the bookkeeper first checked the schedule accounts and found an error in the Miller Plant Supply AP account. The business owes $950, not $1950. Make the correction on the AP schedule sheet and notice the automatic update to the trial balance.

Continued on p.108

	A	B	C	D	E	F
1			Green Brothers Gardening		Merge and Center each	
2			Trial Balance		title over columns A:E	
3			For the Year Ended December 31, 2002			
4						
5	**Account No.**	**Account**		**Debit**	**Credit**	
6	110	Cash		12,807.67		
7	120	Accounts Receivable	(see Schedule of AR)	21,372.89		AR and AP
8	150	Nursery Inventory		22,876.90		values linked to
9	155	Merchandise Inventory		18,765.89		schedules
10	160	Supplies	Hyperlinks to	3,915.89		
11	180	Equipment	**5.1sched**	28,650.00		
12	181	Accumulated Depreciation			1,640.30	
13	190	Buildings		535,000.00		
14	191	Accumulated Depreciation			56,565.00	
15	200	Accounts Payable	(see Schedule of AP)		11,723.05	
16	210	Payroll Taxes Payable			82,765.96	
17	230	Mortgage Payable			422,000.00	
18	300	Calvin Green, Capital			80,610.40	
19	350	Raph Green, Capital			80,610.40	
20	400	Sales Income			586,000.00	
21	510	Purchases - Nursery		196,879.93		
22	520	Purchases - Mdse		97,876.76		
23	610	Advertising Expense		36,788.00		
24	620	Lease Expenses		16,755.00		
25	630	Insurance Expense		8,986.00		
26	640	Salary Expense		290,876.78		
27	650	Supplies Expense		3,657.87		
28	660	Miscellaneous Expense		1,876.98		
29	670	Payroll Taxes Expense		24,828.55		
30						
31				1,321,915.11	1,321,915.11	

	A	B	C	D	E	F
1			Green Brothers Gardening			
2			Schedule of Accounts Receivable			
3			For the Year Ended December 31, 2002			
4						
5		Abermarle, Kelly		2144.65		
6		Capital Bank		5434.54		
7		Drury, David		1232.87		
8		Engle, Dr. Carrie		346.87		
9		Fairfax Water Co		1124.75		
10		Grinder, Sam		769.76		
11		Harrison Tools Co		2212.77		
12		Johnson, Linda		435.87		
13		Logan, Harry		909.56		
14		Loomis, Bart		212.87		
15		Samson, Peter		543.98		
16		Samuels, Larry		634.87		
17		Souten, Willem G.		540.00		
18		Toomey, Martin		563.55		
19		United Cars		2389.00		
20		Whiticomb, Roger		1876.98	Copy total and	
21					paste link to Trial	
22				21372.89	Balance	
23						

	A	B	C	D	E	F
1			Green Brothers Gardening			
2			Schedule of Accounts Payable			
3			For the Year Ended December 31, 2002			
4						
5		Bulbs Unlimited		1439.55		
6		Nursery Supply Inc		976.65		
7		Varsity Nurseries		3426.98		
8		Grollier Farms		1549.75		
9		KCG Supply Co		549.45		
10		Pride Farms		1290.67		
11		Miller Plant Supply		950.00	Correct	
12		Jay's Perrenials		1540.00	value	
13						
14				11723.05	Copy total and	
15					paste link to	
16					Trial Balance	

16. Enter hyperlink text in **Column C** of the Trial Balance to refer users to the schedules, as illustrated.

17. In **Cell C7,** enter: **(see Schedule of AR)**

18. In **Cell C15,** enter: **(see Schedule of AP)**

19. Create hyperlinks for each text string, using bookmarks to send the user to the correct sheet.

20. Check the hyperlinks.

21. Edit the hyperlink text to delete the word "see" on both hyperlinks.

22. Print a copy of the Trial Balance.

23. Save the **5.1sched** and **5.1tb** files. Close both files.

Cues for Reference

Merge and Center Cells
1. Select cells to merge.
2. Click **Merge and Center** button.

Split Cells
1. Select merged cells to split.
2. Click **Merge and Center** button.

Arrange Workbooks
1. Open workbooks.
2. Click **Windows, Arrange,** and select an arrangement.
3. Click **OK.**

Paste Link Cells
1. Copy the cell to link.
2. Select link location.
3. Click **Paste** button list arrow.
4. Click **Paste Link.**

Insert a Hyperlink
1. Enter hyperlink text.
2. Click **Hyperlink** button.
3. Select location in the Look in box.
4. Click **Bookmark**, if a specific location is necessary.
5. Select a bookmark.

6. Click **OK.**
7. Click **OK.**

Edit a Hyperlink
1. Right-click hyperlink text.
2. Click **Edit Hyperlink.**
3. Make corrections as necessary.
4. Click **OK.**

TRYOUT

TASK 2

GOAL
To practice using the following skill sets:
* Hide and unhide rows and columns [M]
* Freeze and unfreeze rows and columns [M]
* Modify page setup options [M]
  * Print nonadjacent sections of a worksheet
  * Print titles
* Use logical functions in formulas

WHAT YOU NEED TO KNOW

Hide and Unhide Rows and Columns

> You can hide detail columns and rows on the screen display to simplify a complicated worksheet, or for security purposes. Hidden columns and rows do not print.

> To hide columns or rows, select the rows or columns to hide, click Format, Column or Row, and click Hide. You can also drag the border of the row or column to hide it. When you hide a column or row, the worksheet border does not display the column letter or row number.

> You can display hidden columns by selecting the columns or rows before and after the hidden area and dragging right for columns or down for rows, as shown in Figure 5.11. You can also click Format, Columns or Rows, and select Unhide.

Figure 5.11 Display hidden column—drag to right

Freeze and Unfreeze Rows and Columns

> When you work with a large worksheet that requires scrolling across or down, you may find that the column headings or row labels that identify the data scroll out of view. You can keep them in view by freezing them. Select the row below or the column to the right of the data to freeze, and click Window, Freeze Panes.

> The *Freeze Panes* command locks the pane, a group of rows or columns above or to the left of the cell you select, so that area does not move during scrolling. To remove the freeze, click Windows, Unfreeze.

TRY*it*OUT

1. Open **5.2to** from the Data CD.

2. Click **No** at the update prompt.

3. Select **Column B.**

4. Click **Format, Column,** and **Hide.**

5. Click **Format, Column,** and **Unhide.**

6. Select **Rows 23:28.**

7. Click **Format, Row,** and **Hide.**

8. Select **Rows 22** and **29,** and drag down to unhide the rows.

   Note: Be sure to return rows to normal height.

9. Click at the right edge of **Column B** and drag to the left to hide the column.

10. Do not close the file.

TRY*it*OUT

1. Continue to work in **5.2to.**

2. Click in **Cell A6** and click **Window, Freeze Panes.**

3. Use the vertical scroll bar to scroll down the page and notice the frozen rows at the top of the screen.

4. Click **Window, Unfreeze Panes.**

5. Click in **Cell D6** and freeze the columns.

6. Use the horizontal scroll bar to scroll to the right to view the entire worksheet.

7. Clear the freeze.

8. Do not close the file.

Modify Page Setup Options

Print Nonadjacent Sections of a Worksheet

> If you want to print sections of a worksheet that are not adjacent, you can hide the columns or rows that are not needed and print the data as displayed.

> If a worksheet is wider or longer than the width of the page, you can adjust the page break lines, or you can use the Page Setup dialog box and click the Page tab, to select the Fit to 1 page wide by 1 page tall scaling option, as shown in Figure 5.12.

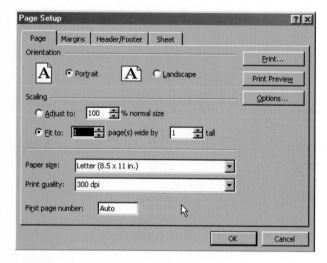

Figure 5.12 Scaling options in Page Setup dialog box

Print Titles

> The *Print Titles* feature allows you to print column or row titles on subsequent pages of a worksheet that prints on more than one page. For example, the worksheet in 5.2to would require two pages to print, if it were fully displayed. You can set column titles to repeat at the left of the second page so that you can identify the values on each page.

> To print titles, click File, Page Setup, click the Sheet tab, and use the Collapse Dialog Box button to select the rows or columns to repeat in the Print titles section. If you have merged cells for the title rows, you must undo the merge so that you can select the columns you need rather than the merged selection. Notice the setting for column titles in Figure 5.13.

TRY*it*OUT

1. Continue to work in **5.2to.**

2. Hide **Columns C:F.**

3. Click **View, Page Break Preview.** (Notice that the worksheet is wider than the page.)

4. Click **View, Normal.**

5. Click **File, Page Setup.**

6. On the Page tab, with the Scaling option displayed, click **Fit to 1 page wide.**

7. Print the worksheet as displayed. Only Columns A, G, H, I, J, K, and L will print.

8. Select **Columns A** and **G** and unhide the columns. (Keep Column B hidden.)

9. Click **File, Page Setup.** Click **Adjust to,** and change the size back to **100%** normal size.

TRY*it*OUT

1. Continue to work in **5.2to.**

2. Click each merged title row and click the **Merge and Center** button to undo the merge.

3. Click **File, Page Setup,** and click the **Sheet** tab.

4. Click the **Collapse Dialog Box** button for columns to repeat at left.

5. Click **Column A** and click the **Restore Dialog Box** button.

6. Click **OK.**

7. Click the **Print Preview** button.

8. Click **Next** on the preview screen to see Page 2.

9. Click **Close** to close the preview.

10. Save the **5.2to** file. Close the file.

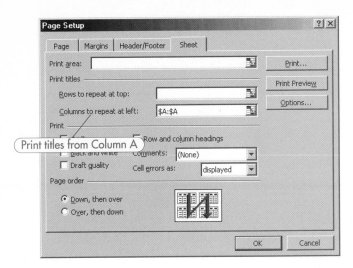

Figure 5.13 Page Setup dialog box, Sheet tab, Print titles setting

Use Logical Functions in Formulas

> You can use an **IF** *statement* in a formula to test a situation and determine a value based on the outcome of the test. An IF statement is a function in the Logical Functions category. The format for an IF statement is:

=IF(CONDITION,X,Y)

If a condition you are testing for is true, then the result is X. If the condition is false, then the result is Y.

> For example, suppose salespeople get a 1% bonus on sales when they make sales over $30,000. In other words, if sales are greater than $30,000, then the bonus equals sales multiplied by 1%, else the bonus equals zero. Suppose the sales amount resides in Cell C2. The IF statement would read:

=IF(C2>30000,C2*1%,0)

The following table shows how to translate this statement:

Formula	Function	Condition	X	Y
English	If	sales are greater than $30,000	then multiply sales by 1% to calculate the bonus	else the bonus equals 0
Excel	=IF	(C2>30000,	C2*1%,	0)

TRYi*t* **OUT**

1. Open **5.2toa** from the Data CD. Notice the sales in Column C.

2. In **Cell E2,** enter an IF statement to calculate the bonus.
   a. Click the **fx (Insert function)** button.
   b. Select the **Logical** category and the **IF** function.
   c. In Logical test, enter: **C2>30000**
   d. In the Value_if_ true, enter: **C2*1%**
   e. In the Value_if_false, enter: **0**
   f. Click **OK.**

3. In **Cell E2,** view the resulting formula on the formula bar.

4. Use the fill handle to copy the formula for all salespeople. Notice how the bonuses were applied.

5. Do not close the file.

> IF statements use the following conditional operators to state the conditional question:

= Equal

> Greater than

< Less than

<> Not equal to

<= Less than or equal to

>= Greater than or equal to

> To enter an IF statement, click the Insert Function button on the formula bar and select IF from the Logical category. There are Collapse Dialog Box buttons in the Insert Function dialog box so that you can select cells from the worksheet, or you can enter the function directly into the cell. Notice the entries in the dialog box in Figure 5.14.

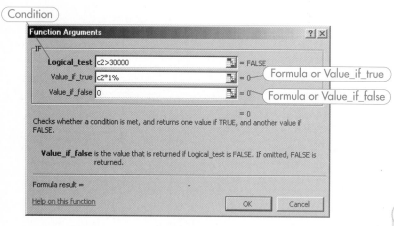

Figure 5.14 Function arguments for IF statement

> You can use an IF statement to insert text depending on a condition. For example, if the sales are greater than a certain amount, you can insert "Great work;" if not, you can insert "Sales seminar on Thursday." When you use an IF statement to enter text, the text must be placed within quotation marks. Excel automatically inserts quotation marks if you use the Insert Function dialog box; however, you must enter them if you enter the formula directly into the cell. Notice the formula bar and the Sales and Note columns in Figure 5.14.

If statement to enter text

H2		fx =IF(C2>30000,"Great work!","Sales Seminar on Thursday.")						
	A	B	C	D	E	F	G	H	I
1	SALES STAFF		SALES	COMMISSION	BONUS	SALARY	EARNINGS	NOTE	
2	Acosta, Sam		29,921.22	598.42	-	1,500.00	2,696.85	Sales Seminar on Thursday.	
3	Billings, Mary		28,321.32	566.43	-	1,500.00	2,632.85	Sales Seminar on Thursday.	
4	Camino, Juan		18,545.77	370.92	-	1,500.00	2,241.83	Sales Seminar on Thursday.	
5	Kelly, Joe		51,567.54	1,031.35	515.68	1,500.00	4,078.38	Great work!	
6	Lincoln, Terry		32,598.09	651.96	325.98	1,500.00	3,129.90	Great work!	
7	Parson, Alice		35,325.78	706.52	353.26	1,500.00	3,266.29	Great work!	
8	Sulfa, Sally		55,896.95	1,117.94	558.97	1,500.00	4,294.85	Great work!	
9									

Figure 5.14 IF statement to enter text

TRY*it*OUT

1. Continue to work in **5.2toa.**

2. In **Cell H2,** enter an IF statement to generate the notes.
   a. Click the **fx (Insert function)** button.
   b. Select the **Logical** category and **IF** function.
   c. In the Logical_test box, enter:
      C2>30000
   d. In the Value_if_true box, enter:
      Great work!
   e. In the Value_if_false box, enter:
      Sales seminar on Thursday
   f. Click **OK.**

3. In **Cell H2,** view the resulting formula on the formula bar.

4. Use the fill handle to copy the formula for all salespeople.

5. Save the **5.2toa** file. Close the file.

REHEARSAL

TASK 2

GOAL
To create a sales and commissions schedule and to use the data in a worksheet

SETTING THE STAGE/WRAPUP
File names: 5.2bonus
              5.2worksheet
Format: All values should be
             formatted for commas with
             no decimal places

WHAT YOU NEED TO KNOW

> In Excel, the spreadsheets are called worksheets. In accounting terminology, however, a *worksheet* is a form used to gather trial balance and adjustments information at the end of an accounting period to plan the preparation of the income statement and balance sheet.

> The worksheet adjustments, usually prepared by the accountant, are corrections that are made at the end of the period so that the accounts will reflect their true balances. The net income is calculated and the income statement and balance sheet are planned on the worksheet using the adjusted trial balance data. Many corporations round numbers on financial reports, as noted in the Setting the Stage directions above.

> The sales and commission schedule calculates the sales, commissions, and bonuses for the period. IF statements are used to calculate the commissions and bonus for each salesperson. The commission expense for the period is linked to the appropriate location on the worksheet.

DIRECTIONS

1. Open **5.2bonus** from the Data CD.

2. Set font sizes for titles, as indicated in Illustration A on the next page, and merge and center the title rows.

3. Bold all column headings and center headings in **Columns C:F,** as illustrated.

4. Enter a formula in **Cell D6** to calculate a 1.5% commission on sales.
   (Hint: Sales*1.5%)

5. Enter an IF statement in **Cell E6** to calculate a .5% bonus on sales greater than $2,000,000.

   (Hint: Condition: Sales>2000000 If True: Sales*.5% If False: 0)

6. Enter a formula in **Cell F6** to calculate the total paid to the employee.

7. Enter an IF statement in **Cell G6** to enter an asterisk (*) if the sales were over $2,500,000 and nothing if they were not.
   (Hint: Use quotation marks around the asterisk and around the blank, i.e., "*" or " ".)

8. Copy formulas down for ad salespersons and total the columns.

9. Save the file **5.2bonus.**

10. Copy the total in **Cell F19.**

11. Open **5.2worksheet** from the Data CD.

12. Paste link the total to the Commissions Expense location in **Cell B22.**

13. Format titles and column headings, as shown in Illustration B on page 115.

14. Insert a column after Column A.

15. In **Cell B22,** enter a hyperlink to **5.2bonus** using "(See Schedule)" as the hyperlink text.

Continued on next page

> In this Rehearsal activity, Sutton Investment Group wants you to prepare and format the quarterly Sales and Commissions Schedule (Illustration A) and link the data to the worksheet (Illustration B). On the worksheet, you will format and complete totals, modify the columns and rows, and print part of the worksheet.

16. Freeze panes in **Cell B7** and find totals for **Columns C:L.**

    Note: Columns C and D, E and F, and G and H should match or balance with each other.

17. In a blank area below the worksheet, subtract the Income Statement totals, Column I from Column J (J-I). This value, the net income, should be placed in **Cells I31** and **L31.**

18. In **Cell I32,** add **Cells I30** and **I31.** Copy this formula to **Columns J:L.**

    Note: Columns I and J and K and L should balance with each other.

19. Include borders and lines, as shown in Illustration B.

20. Hide **Columns B:F** and print the worksheet to fit on one page.

21. Unhide the columns and print the worksheet on two pages with column titles.

22. Save the file **5.2worksheet.** Close the file.

	A	B	C	D	E	F	G	H	I
1	**Sutton Investment Group**			←	Arial 14				
2	Sales and Commission Schedule			←	Arial 12				
3	For the quarter ended March 31, 2002			←					
4									
5	Salesperson		Sales	Commission	Bonus	Total	President's Club		
6	Abrams, Sally		2,465,739						
7	Baer, Buddy		1,543,849						
8	Gomez, John		1,995,975	Enter formula to calculate 1.5% commission	Enter IF statement to caculate bonus	Enter formula to find total compensation	Enter IF statement to enter asterisk for high sales employees		
9	Jackson, Rob		2,543,766						
10	Keyes, Tracy		1,234,945						
11	Lee, Randy		2,256,789						
12	Martino, Jack		2,087,654						
13	Nunez, Debra		1,544,856						
14	Okowski, Bill		1,098,557						
15	Ringold, Diane		2,368,523						
16	Sullivan, Tara		2,877,078						
17	Watson, George		2,245,876						
18									
19	Totals								
20									
21									
22									
23									
24									
25									
26									
27									
28									
29									
30									
31									
32									
33									
34									

Illustration A

	A	B	C	D	E	F	G	H	I	J	K
1						**Sutton Investment Group** `Arial 14`					
2						**Worksheet**					
3		`Arial 12`				For the quarter ended March 31, 2002					
4											
5	`Merged and Centered`	**Trial Balance**		**Adjustments**		**Adjusted Trial Balance**		**Income Statement**		**Balance Sheet**	
6		Debit	Credit	Debit	Credit	Debit	Credit	Debit	Credit	Debit	Credit
7	Cash	36,470				36,470				36,470	
8	Securities borrowed	75,437				75,437				75,437	
9	Accounts Receivable	1,288,145				1,288,145				1,288,145	
10	Securities Inventory	100,514				100,514				100,514	
11	Equipment	103,065			17,588	85,477				85,477	
12	Investments	67,218				67,218				67,218	
13	Insurance	4,356			3,865	491				491	
14	Supplies	6,445			5,045	1,400				1,400	
15	Notes Payable		141,219				141,219				141,219
16	Accounts Payable		304,856				304,856				304,856
17	Securities Loaned		443,255				443,255				443,255
18	John Sutton, Capital		710,540				710,540				710,540
19	Commission Revenue		349,955				349,955		349,955		
20	Management Fees		166,256				166,256		166,256		
21	Interest Income		95,885				95,885		95,885		
22	Commissons Expense					448,181		448,181			
23	Rent	24,856				24,856		24,856			
24	Equipment Expense			17,588		17,588		17,588			
25	Communications	23,611				23,611		23,611			
26	Brokerage 5,849					5,849		5,849			
27	Interest Expense	27,819				27,819		27,819			
28	Insurance Expense			3,865		3,865		3,865			
29	Supplies Expense			5,045		5,045		5,045			
30	Totals										
31	Net Income										
32											
33											
34											
35											
36											
37											

Annotation (near A31): Insert a column here and enter hyperlink to schedule

Annotation (near H31/J31): Calculate difference between Income Statement totals on Row 30 and place on Net Income line in two locations

Illustration B

Cues for Reference

Hide Columns or Rows
1. Select row(s) or column(s) to hide.
2. Click **Format, Row** or **Column,** and **Hide.**

Unhide Columns or Rows
1. Select rows or columns on either side of hidden area.
2. Click **Format, Row** or **Column,** and **Unhide.**

Freeze Columns or Rows
1. Place insertion point after column(s) or row(s) to freeze.
2. Click **Window, Freeze Panes.**

Unfreeze Columns or Rows
- Click **Window, Unfreeze Panes.**

Enter IF Statement
1. Click **fx (Insert Function)** button.
2. Click **Logical** category and **IF** function.
3. In Logical test, enter or select condition.
4. In Value_if_true, enter or select data or formula.
5. In Value_if_false, enter or select data or formula.
6. Click **OK.**

Print Nonadjacent Sections of a Worksheet
1. Hide columns or rows that are not needed.
2. Click **Print** button.

Fit Worksheet to One Page
1. Click **File, Page Setup.**
2. On Page tab, click **Fit to one page wide.**

Print Titles
1. Clear merged cells, if necessary.
2. Click **File, Page Setup,** and click **Page** tab.
3. Select row or column titles to repeat.
4. Click **OK.**

TASK 3

> **GOAL**
> **To practice using the following skill sets:**
> * Add headers and footers to
>   worksheets
>   * Add customized headers and
>   footers
> * Enter 3-D references

WHAT YOU NEED TO KNOW

Add Headers and Footers to Worksheets

> *Headers and footers* allow you to repeat the same information at the top (header) or bottom (footer) of every page. You use this feature to enter a company name, date, file name, sheet name, etc. You can select from built-in headers or footers, or you can customize your own.

> To add a header or footer, click View, Header and Footer to display the Header/Footer page of the Page Setup dialog box. You can select built-in header and footer text from the drop-down lists in each section. In Figure 5.15, notice the built-in footers that are displayed.

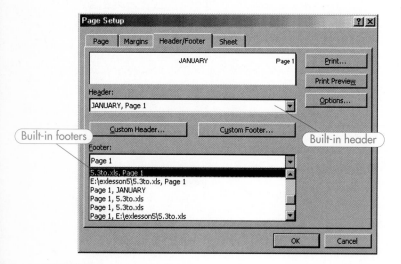

Figure 5.15 Header and Footer dialog box displaying built-in footers

TRY*it* OUT

1. Open **5.3to** from the Data CD.

2. Click **View, Header and Footer.**

3. Click the list arrow in the Header section, and select the **JANUARY, Page 1** header.

4. Click the list arrow in the Footer section and select the file name or the **5.3to** footer.

5. Click **OK.**

6. Click the **Print Preview** button. Notice the headers and footers.

7. Click **Close** to close the preview screen.

8. Do not close the file.

Add Customized Headers and Footers

> To enter a customized header or footer, click the Custom Header or Custom Footer button on the Header/Footer page, (see Figure 5.15), and the Header or Footer custom dialog box opens.

> As shown in Figure 5.16, text entered into the left, center, and right sections is aligned in that section. You may click the appropriate button to include the date, time, page number, tab name, file name, or picture. There is also a Format Picture button that you can use once the picture is in place. You can also use this feature to insert logos on every page.

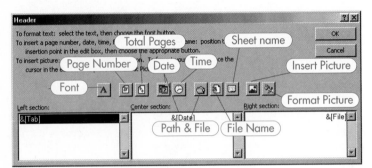

Figure 5.16 Custom Header dialog box

T R Y *i t* **O U T**

1. Continue to work in **5.3to.**

2. Click **View, Header and Footer,** and **Custom Header.**

3. In the left section, click the **Sheet Name** button; in the center section, click the **Date** button; in the right section, click the **File Name** button.

4. Click **OK.**

5. Click **Custom Footer,** and in the left section, click the **Insert Picture** button.

6. From your data folder, open the **clipartlogo** and click **Insert.**

7. Click the **Format Picture** button.

8. Set picture height to **.78"** and click **OK.**

9. Enter **Trainor's Department Store** in the left section after the picture code.

10. Click **OK.**

11. Click the **Print Preview** button.

12. Click **Close** to close the preview screen.

13. Do not close the file.

Enter 3-D References

> If you want to summarize data from several sheets onto a totals sheet within a workbook, you can use a formula with the *3-D reference* style. The style is called three dimensional because it is used in formulas that calculate values through the sheets of a workbook to a summary worksheet at the end of the workbook.

> A 3-D reference includes the range of sheet names, an exclamation point, and the cell or range reference.

EXAMPLE OF 3-D REFERENCES	EXPLANATIONS
=SUM(Sheet1:Sheet3!D7)	Adds the values in D7 from Sheets 1 to 3
=AVERAGE(Sheet3:Sheet5!D7:D12)	Averages values in D7:D12 from Sheets 3 to 5
=January!D8+February!D8	Adds the values in D8 from the January and February sheets

> To enter a 3-D reference, either enter the reference in the formula, or select the sheets and cells involved, and enter the mathematical operators, as necessary. You will practice both in the Try it Out section. Notice the formula in Figure 5.17, which was entered by selection. When 3-D references are copied, the cell references change, relative to the new location, but the sheet names remain constant.

Figure 5.17 3-D formula entered by selection

TRY*it*OUT

1. Continue to work in **5.3to.**

2. Rename Sheet3: **TOTALS**

3. In **Cell D7,** use the selection method to enter a 3-D reference to add the values in **Cell D7** from the JANUARY and FEBRUARY sheets:

   a. Enter: **=**
   b. Click **Cell D7** on the JANUARY sheet.
   c. Enter: **+**
   d. Click **Cell D7** on the FEBRUARY sheet.
   e. Press the **Enter** key and go to **Cell D7** to view the formula.

4. In **Cell E7,** enter in a 3-D reference to add the values in **Cell E7** from the JANUARY and FEBRUARY sheets. *(Hint: =Sum(January:February!E7)*

5. Use AutoFill to copy **Cell E7** to **Cell F7,** and copy all three formulas down to, and including the TOTALS, **Row 14.**

6. Adjust color and line formats.

7. Save the **5.3to** file. Close the file.

REHEARSAL

TASK 3

 GOAL
To create a consolidated income statement using 3-D references and a custom footer

SETTING THE STAGE/WRAPUP

File name: 5.3income

Format: All values should be formatted for commas with no decimal places

WHAT YOU NEED TO KNOW

> Corporations must report their financial data to their stockholders quarterly and annually. If a company has branches or divisions in various parts of the country, they need to combine income statement data into one financial report. A *consolidated income statement* combines data from various divisions into one report.

> An income statement is prepared at the end of a financial period using income, cost, and expense accounts from the trial balance. It calculates gross profit, the markup on your product or service, and net profit, the final profits for the period after deducting expenses. It is a valuable source of information for stockholders or owners and for potential investors or lenders.

> In this Rehearsal activity, you will create a consolidated income statement for Time Out Sporting Goods. You will combine the numbers from the Barkely and Montrose stores into one income statement using 3-D references, and add a custom footer to the report.

DIRECTIONS

1. Open **5.3income** from the Data CD.

2. Group the Barkely and Montrose sheets and format as shown in the illustration on the facing page. (Font and bold settings, borders and lines, fill color, and values in comma format with no decimals.)

3. With the sheets still grouped, enter formulas in the cells listed below to calculate the following income statements items. (Hints for some formulas provide guidance as to how to use the values in the formulas.)

   D9:   Net Sales *(Hint: Sales - Sales Returns)*

   D13: Gross Profit *(Hint: Net Sales - Cost of Goods Sold)*

   D25: Total Expenses

   D27: Net Income before Taxes *(Hint: Gross Profit - Total Expenses)*

   D29: Net Income after Taxes

4. Ungroup the sheets using the worksheet tab shortcut menu.

5. Copy the entire Barkely worksheet.

6. Use the worksheet tab shortcut menu to insert a new sheet.

7. Paste the Barkely worksheet to **Cell A1** on the new sheet.

8. Move the new sheet to the last position; rename it:
   `Consolidated Income Statement`

9. Adjust column widths as necessary and change the second title to read: `Consolidated Income Statement`

10. Delete the values in **Column C** on the Consolidated Income Statement sheet.

11. Group the sheets and freeze panes in **Cell A4** so that you can view the length of the report without losing the title. Ungroup the sheets using the shortcut menu.

12. In **Cell C7,** on the Consolidated Income Statement sheet, enter a 3-D formula to add the values from the Barkely sheet and the Montrose sheet in **Cell C7.** *(Hint: =Barkely!C7+Montrose!C7)*

Continued on next page

13. Use AutoFill to copy the formula down to **Cell C28.** Delete all zeros or dashes where the formula did not find values.

14. Check your work by looking at a value on the consolidated sheet to see if it totals the two sheets correctly.

15. Format the worksheet tabs with colors, as appropriate.

16. Group the sheets and set a custom footer to print the sheet name, date, and file name.

17. Save the file, **5.3income,** and print a copy of all worksheets.

18. Close the file.

	A	B	C	D	E	F	G	H
1	**Time Out Sporting Goods**				◄ 24 Point Bold			
2	Income Statement - Barkely Store				◄ 14 Point Bold			
3	For Year Ended December 31, 2002							
4								
5								
6	**Income:**							
7	Sales Income		1,086,567					
8	Less: Sales Returns		140,691					
9	Net Sales				◄ Calculate Net Sales			
10								
11	Less: Cost of Goods Sold		589,765	589,765				
12								
13	**Gross Profit**				◄ Calculate Gross Profit.			
14								
15	Expenses:							
16	Advertising Expense		8,100					
17	Credit Card Fees		5,433					
18	Insurance Expense		5,876					
19	Miscellaneous Expense		4,532					
20	Payroll Taxes Expense		15,463					
21	Rent Expense		63,668					
22	Salary Expense		164,500					
23	Supplies Expense		5,543					
24	Utilities Expense		7,650					
25	Total Expenses				◄ Calculate Total Expenses.			
26								
27	Net Income before Taxes				◄ Calculate Net Income before Taxes			
28	Less: Taxes		22,604	22,604				
29	**Net Income after Taxes**				◄ Calculate Net Income after Taxes			
30								
31								

Cues for Reference

Add Headers and Footers
1. Click **View, Header/Footer.**
2. To select a built-in header or footer:
   - Click **Header** and **Footer** drop-down list.
   - Select header/footer.

Add Customized Headers and Footers
1. Click **View, Header and Footer.**
2. Click **Custom Header** or **Custom Footer.**
3. Click in section.
4. Enter text or insert header or footer code.
5. Repeat as necessary.
6. Click **OK.**
7. Click **OK.**

Enter 3-D References
- Enter the reference.
   or
   Use the mouse:
1. Enter equal sign, function, and parentheses, if necessary.
2. Select sheet and cell to reference.
3. Enter mathematical operator.
4. Repeat Steps 2 and 3 and close parentheses, if necessary.
5. Press **Enter.**

TRYOUT

TASK 4

* Apply a style 🖾
* Define a new style 🖾
* Modify a style 🖾
* Remove a style 🖾
* Find and replace cell data and formats 🖾
  * Find cell data
  * Find and replace data and formats

WHAT YOU NEED TO KNOW

Apply a Style

> A *style* is a defined collection of data formats such as font, font size, indentation, number formats, alignments, etc., that you name and store so that you can apply all those formats at once.

> Excel provides basic styles for numbers, as listed in the Style dialog box. To apply a basic style, select the cells to format, click Format, Style, and click the style from the Style name list. When you apply a style, you apply all the defined formats. Notice the Normal, or default, style formats for data, as shown in Figure 5.18.

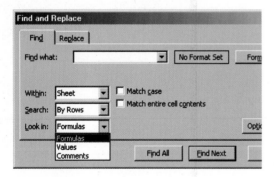

Figure 5.18 Style dialog box, Normal style

TRY*it* OUT

1. Open **5.4to** from the Data CD.

2. Select the range **C6:C10** and click **Format, Style.** Notice the settings for Comma style.

3. Click the **Style name** list arrow and select the **Normal** style. Notice the settings for Normal style.

4. Click **OK.** Notice the changes in the numbers.

5. Click **Format, Style,** and apply the Comma [0] style (commas with no decimal places).

6. Click **OK.**

7. Use the Format Painter feature to copy the style to **Cell D11.**

8. Do not close the file.

Define a New Style

If you find that you need a combination of formats in your work, you can define a new style. You can specify the formats in the Style dialog box. However, an easier way is to select a cell with the formats you want and name it in the Style dialog box. Once you name the style, the cell formats appear in the dialog box. Notice the "title" style in the Style dialog box in Figure 5.19.

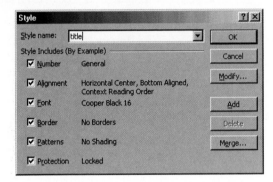

Figure 5.19 Style dialog box, title style

Modify a Style

> Use the Style dialog box to modify existing formats or to set formats for new styles. To modify a style, open a style that you want to change, or, to set formats for a new style, enter a new style name. Then, click the format to change and click Modify. In the Format cells dialog box that opens, click a tab to select the format you want and click OK. Repeat this procedure as necessary, and click OK to return to the Style dialog box. Click OK to apply the style or, if you just want to add the style to your styles list without applying it, click Add.

> If you modify a style, all the data using that style automatically changes. The Style feature provides consistency and saves reformatting the entire worksheet for a format modification.

TRY*it* **OUT**

1. Continue to work in **5.4to.**

2. In **Cell A1,** change the font to Cooper Black, 22 point. (If this font is not installed, use another heavy, dark font.)

3. Click **Format, Style.**

4. Enter **title** in the Style name box, and notice the settings.

5. Click **OK.**

6. Click **Cell A2** and apply the **title** style setting.

7. Do not close the file.

TRY*it* **OUT**

1. Continue to work in **5.4to.**

2. In **Cell A2,** click **Format, Style.**

3. Change "title" to read **title2** in the Style name box.

4. Click **Font, Modify.**

5. In the Format Cells dialog box, with the **Font** tab selected, click **16 point.**

6. Click **OK** to set the format.

7. Click **OK** to apply.

8. Do not close the file.

Remove a Style

> You can remove a style from selected cells by clicking Format, Style, and click Normal style.

> You can remove a style from the Style name list by clicking the style and clicking the Delete button. Any cells set with that style revert to the Normal style setting.

Find and Replace Cell Data and Formats

> If you want to review or edit specific text or numbers, you can search for the data and replace it, if necessary. This is called the *Find and Replace* feature. You can also find cells that match a format of a cell you specify. This feature is helpful if you want to change a format on selected cells, because you can replace all occurrences as you find them.

Find Cell Data

> To find data, click Edit, Find and the Find and Replace dialog box opens in the Find tab. If you click the Options button, you notice, as shown in Figure 5.20, that you can define your search by looking in the sheet, in the workbook, searching by columns or rows, and looking for formulas, values, or comments. In addition, you can select options to match the case or the contents of the entire cell, and you can search for specific formats.

> Once you set your options, you can click Find All or Find Next. When you click Find All, you get a list of all the cell addresses that contain a match. When you click Find Next, you go to each location as it appears in the worksheet.

TRY *it* **OUT**

1. Continue to work in **5.4to**.

2. In **Cell D11**, click **Format, Style,** and **Normal.**

3. Click **OK.**

4. In **Cell D11**, click **Format, Style,** and **Currency [0].**

5. Click **OK.**

6. Click **Format, Style,** and **title2.**

7. Click **Delete.**

8. Click **OK.**

9. Apply the **title** style to **Cell A2.**

10. Save the **5.4to** file. Close the file.

TRY *it* **OUT**

1. Open **5.4toa** from the Data CD.

2. Click **Edit, Find,** and **Options.**

3. Enter `Miscellaneous` in the Find what box.

4. Set the search for the Workbook and click the **Match case** check box.

5. Click **Find Next** and keep clicking it until you find all occurrences.

6. Click **Find All** to see a list of all the locations.

7. Click the **Close** button in the dialog box.

8. Do not close the file.

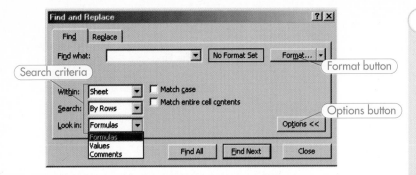

Figure 5.20 Find and Replace dialog box, Find tab, Look in list

Find and Replace Data and Formats

> In the last Try it Out, you only found specific data.
However, if you want to find the data and replace it, click
Edit, Replace, and the Find and Replace dialog box opens
in the Replace tab. Figure 5.21 shows the dialog box with
options selected and the Format button list arrow active.

> To search for a certain format, you can select a cell with
the format you want, click the Format list arrow, click
Choose Format From Cell, and that format becomes the
search criteria. You can then change the format on the
Replace with line by clicking Format, to set the new
format.

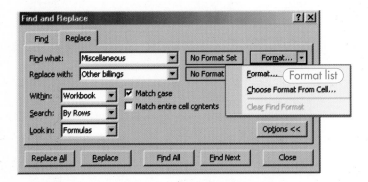

Figure 5.21 Find and Repace dialog box, Replace tab, Format list

> After entering the Find and Replace information, you can
click Replace All or just Replace. Clicking Replace All
replaces all occurrences without giving you a chance to
view each change. Clicking Replace lets you view each
replacement before it is made so you can be sure you want
to replace it. You can undo a Find and Replace operation.

T R Y _i t_ O U T

1. Continue to work in **5.4toa.**

2. Click **Edit, Replace,** and **Options.**

3. Enter the information as shown in
Figure 5.21, but do not click the
Format button.

4. Click **Replace All** and notice the
changes.

5. Click the **Undo** button and
click the **Redo** button.

6. Select and delete the text in
the **Find what** and **Replace with** boxes.

7. Click the **Format** button list arrow on
the Find what line and click **Choose
Format From Cell.**

8. With the Choose cell pointer, click
Cell B3.

9. Click **Format** on the Replace with line.

10. In the Font tab, set the format for **Arial,
10 point, bold, Dark Blue** color, and
click **OK.** Notice the preview.

11. Click **Replace** each time to view the
corrections.

12. Save the **5.4toa** file. Close the file.

R E H E A R S A L

TASK 4

 GOAL
To create a balance sheet using styles
and the Find and Replace features

SETTING THE STAGE/WRAPUP
File name: 5.4balsheet

WHAT YOU NEED TO KNOW

> A business prepares a *balance sheet*,
which is a financial report that
shows the value of the firm's assets
and liabilities, owner's worth, or
stockholder's equity on a certain
date. The balance sheet is based
on the basic accounting equation
assets = liabilities + capital (owner's
worth).

> The information for the balance
sheet comes from the accounts and
the worksheet. The owner's worth
includes the profit for the period
and shows the owner's share of the
business. According to the formula,
the creditors, or liabilities listed,
and the owner, share in the
ownership of the assets. The
proportion of ownership and the
types of assets and liabilities listed
are valuable information for a
stockholder or the owner, and for
potential investors or lenders.

> In this Rehearsal activity, you will
complete a balance sheet for Sutton
Investment Group, set styles for
enhancing the report, and find and
replace data and formats.

▼ DIRECTIONS

1. Open **5.4balsheet** from the Data CD.

2. Using the illustration on the facing page as a guide, enter the
formulas to complete the balance sheet. The Total Assets, in
Cell F21, and the Total Liabilities and Owner's Equity, in
Cell F38, should balance or equal.

3. Include lines under the numbers to indicate the additions, as
illustrated.

4. In **Cell A1,** merge and center the title, and set the font for **Photina
Casual Black, 16 point, bold.** (If this font is not installed, select a
font similar to that shown in the illustration.)

5. Use Format Painter to format **Cell A2** with the same formats.

6. In **Cell A2,** change the font size to **14 point.**

7. Click **Cell A2** and define a style using that format; name it:
header2.

8. Apply the **header2** format to **Cells A6, A23,** and **A33.** *(Hint: You
can select each of these cells while pressing and holding the **Ctrl**
key so that you can apply the style all at once.)*

9. Format **Cell B7** for **Arial, 12 point, bold,** and define it as a style
named: header3.

10. Apply the **header3** format to **Cells B16, B24, B29,** and **B38.**

11. As shown in the illustration, indent labels that have not been
formatted.

12. Select all the values in **Columns D, E,** and **F,** and format for
commas with no decimal places.

13. Modify the **header2** style so that it includes a double-accounting
underline. (All cells formatted with the header2 style will change.)

14. Use the Find and Replace feature to find the word "Capital" and
replace it with the word **Equity** in all occurrences.

Continued on next page

15. Use the Find and Replace feature to choose the format in **Cell F21,** and replace it with Currency format, no decimals, and bold font. (Cells F21 and F38 formats should change.)

16. Select the entire report, the range **A1:F38,** and use Fill Color to shade it a light green.

17. Enter a footer that contains the file name and date.

18. Center the report vertically and horizontally using the Page Setup dialog box.

19. Print one copy.

20. Save the **5.4balsheet** file. Close the file.

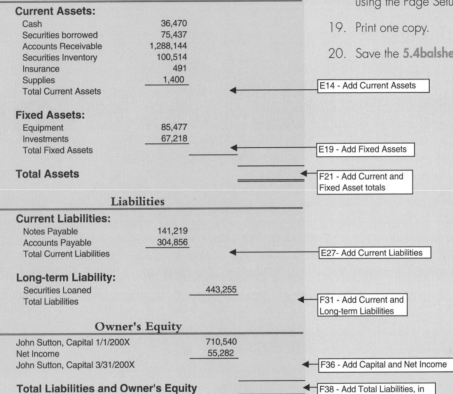

Sutton Investment Group
Balance Sheet
For the quarter ended March 31, 200X

Assets

Current Assets:
Cash	36,470
Securities borrowed	75,437
Accounts Receivable	1,288,144
Securities Inventory	100,514
Insurance	491
Supplies	1,400
Total Current Assets	

E14 - Add Current Assets

Fixed Assets:
Equipment	85,477
Investments	67,218
Total Fixed Assets	

E19 - Add Fixed Assets

Total Assets

F21 - Add Current and Fixed Asset totals

Liabilities

Current Liabilities:
Notes Payable	141,219
Accounts Payable	304,856
Total Current Liabilities	

E27- Add Current Liabilities

Long-term Liability:
Securities Loaned	443,255
Total Liabilities	

F31 - Add Current and Long-term Liabilities

Owner's Equity
John Sutton, Capital 1/1/200X	710,540
Net Income	55,282
John Sutton, Capital 3/31/200X	

F36 - Add Capital and Net Income

Total Liabilities and Owner's Equity

F38 - Add Total Liabilities, in F31, and Capital in F36

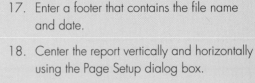

Cues for Reference

Define a New Style
1. Click a cell that contains the style you want.
2. Click **Format, Style.**
3. Enter a name for the style in the Style name box.
4. Click **OK.**

Apply a Style
1. Select cell(s) to receive style.
2. Click **Format, Style.**
3. Click the **Style** list arrow and click style to apply.
4. Click **OK.**

Modify a Style
1. Click **Format, Style.**
2. Click the **Style** list arrow and click style to modify.
3. Click format item and click **Modify.**
4. In the Format Cells dialog box, set the format.
5. Click **OK** twice.

Find and Replace Data
1. Click **Edit, Replace.**
2. Enter data in Find what box.
3. Enter data in Replace with box.
4. Click Options and set, if appropriate.
5. Click **Replace** to do one at a time.

or
• Click **Replace All** to replace all occurrences.

Find and Replace Formats
1. Click **Edit, Replace.**
2. Clear text in Find and Replace boxes.
3. On the Find what line, click **Format, Choose Format From Cell.**
4. Select cell with format to find.
5. On Replace with line, click **Format** and select **Format.**
6. Set the new format.
7. Click **Replace** or **Replace All.**

PERFORMANCE

 SETTING THE STAGE/WRAPUP

Act I File names: 5p1.sched
                         5p1.trialbal

Act II File name: 5p2.cis3d

Act III File names: 5p3.worksheet
                         5p3.balsheet

WHAT YOU NEED TO KNOW

Act I

You work in the Accounting Department of Odyssey Travel Gear in Chicago, and at the end of the year your department combines accounts from all stores and outlets into one Trial Balance. You have been asked to prepare the Schedules of Accounts Receivable and Accounts Payable and use the Paste Link and Hyperlink features to link the data to the Trial Balance.

Odyssey Travel Gear has thousands of customers, or accounts receivable, that are billed on a 20-day cycle. The business organizes the accounts alphabetically into billing groups; for example, customers with names from Aa to Be, are billed on the first day of the cycle. Therefore, the Schedule of Accounts Receivable is arranged by billing groups, and the total due from each group is listed.

Follow these guidelines:

> Open the files **5p1.sched** (two worksheets) and **5p1.trialbal** from the Data CD. In both files, group sheets where possible, format the titles and column headings using Merge and Center, bold and font formats, lines or borders, and format workbook values for commas with no decimal places.

> In the schedules file, rename and color the tabs. Find the total on each schedule, and add single and double lines.

> Copy the Accounts Receivable and Accounts Payable totals from the schedules and paste link them to the proper location on the Trial Balance. Link the totals next to the account title, in the Debit column for Accounts Receivable and in the Credit column for Accounts Payable.

> Total the Trial Balance and include a single line for adding and double lines under totals. The Debits and Credits should balance. Add a column to the right of the account titles. Insert hyperlinks to the appropriate schedule sheet in the file **5p1.sched**, using appropriate hyperlink text.

> Enter appropriate footers, save both files, print a copy of the Trial Balance and both schedules, and close the files.

> Attach both files to an e-mail to the managers of the five retail stores. (You can use the Internet addresses of other students in your class or addresses provided by your instructor.) Inform them that you are sending the trial balance and schedule data for the year ending December 31, 2002, for their records.

Act II

The Air Land Sea Travel Group has agencies in Boston, New York, Los Angeles and San Francisco. Each agency has sent in its quarterly income statement data, which has been copied into one worksheet. Ms. Janice Pierce, the president of the company, is looking forward to seeing a consolidated report along with the supporting agency reports.

Follow these guidelines:

> The reports need formatting, headers and footers, and formulas. Combine them, using 3-D references, to prepare a Consolidated Income Statement.

> Open the file **5p2.cis3d** from the Data CD.

> Copy any sheet and place it at the end of the worksheets. Rename and color-format each tab using the city name, and name the last tab: `Consolidated Income Statement`

> Group sheets to enter formulas for calculating Total Income (F11), Total Expenses (F25), and Net Income (F27). Include lines for adding and double lines for totals, where necessary.

> On the last sheet, clear the data from Column E, which belonged to one of the agencies, leaving the formulas in Column F. Correct the title to read: `Consolidated Income Statement` Use 3-D references in Column E to combine all the data from the four agencies onto the Consolidated Income Statement sheet. Clear any unnecessary formulas, and check to make sure the existing formulas in Column F are working correctly.

> Group the sheets to format values for commas with no decimals, use color buttons to format the Income Statements, format the Net Income value for currency with no decimals, include headers and/or footers, and include the sheet name, date, file name, and company logo.

> Save the workbook, print copies of all sheets, and close the file.

> Optional: Insert another sheet and create an Income Analysis comparing the total and net income from the agency in each city. Calculate what percentage the net income is of total income so you can compare the results.

Act III

Green Brothers Gardening's chief financial officer, Ralph Green, has started to prepare the worksheet and Balance Sheet for the year. He has asked you to complete and format the reports. Ralph Green needs the Balance Sheet for meetings with bankers and the president, Calvin Green, because Green Brothers is contemplating an expansion and requires additional funding.

Follow these guidelines:

> Open the files **5p3.worksheet** and **5.p3balsheet** from the Data CD.

> Format worksheet titles and column headings with fonts, merge and center, and bold. Format worksheet values for commas with no decimal places.

> Freeze panes to be able to work in the worksheet. In Cell H33, find Net Income by subtracting the total in Cell H32 from Cell I32. The yellow areas show where you should place formulas. Find totals where indicated, and Place the Net Income value in Cell K33 and find the totals in the range H33:K33. The values in each set of debit and credit columns, beginning with Columns B and C, should be equal. After formulas are completed, remove the color.

> On the Balance Sheet, format the titles and values and establish styles for the headings in Cells A6, A21, and A29, and for the section headings in Cells B7, B14, B19, B22, B25, B27, B37, and B39.

> Subtract the Allowance for Depreciation from the Equipment account balance. Divide the Net Income from the worksheet in half, and place it under each partner's equity to calculate the new equity. Enter all formulas necessary to complete the Balance Sheet.

> Find and replace all occurrences of the word "Equity" with "Capital."

> Ralph Green needs the following printouts:

  Balance sheet

  Partial worksheet with the Trial Balance and Adjustments columns hidden

  Full worksheet on two pages using the Print Titles feature

> Save and close all files.

> Search the www.entrepreneurmag.com site to develop a list of the "best banks for small businesses" for the state of Virginia.

> Group Project: Use the same Web site to research the characteristics, problems, and advantages of organizing a business as a partnership (as in this family business) or as a corporation. The Green brothers are discussing incorporation and would like more information about this type of business organization.

> Write an essay that summarizes the aspects of organizing a business as a partnership, as compared to a corporate form of organization.

MULTIPLE CHOICE

Identify the letter of the choice that best completes the statement or answers the question.

1. The Merge and Center feature:
   A. Centers text over a selected range.
   B. Can merge and center several rows at once.
   C. Leaves the text in its original cell.
   D. All of the above
   E. A and C

2. The Hyperlink feature:
   A. Creates a shortcut to move to another location.
   B. Can be used to connect to an Internet address.
   C. Is used with hyperlink text.
   D. All of the above
   E. A and C

3. In the IF statement =IF(C2>100,D2*3%,0):
   A. C2>100 is the condition.
   B. 0 is the true value.
   C. > means less than.
   D. All of the above
   E. A and C

4. Custom headers and footers can include:
   A. Date and time.
   B. Graphics.
   C. Sheet name.
   D. All of the above
   E. A and C

5. Using styles allows you to:
   A. Maintain consistent format styles throughout a document.
   B. Modify the style rather than change the formats for formatted data.
   C. Select a formatted cell as the basis for a style.
   D. A and C
   E. All of the above

TRUE/FALSE

Circle **T** if the statement is true or **F** if the statement is false.

T F 6. You can remove a style by selecting the cells and applying the Normal style.

T F 7. Use logical functions to calculate worksheet totals.

T F 8. Freezing titles is useful when the worksheet is small.

T F 9. You can create hyperlinks with the Paste Link feature.

T F 10. Excel provides built-in headers and footers you can select.

Complete each sentence or statement.

11. When you modify a _____, all those formats change automatically.

12. In the IF statement =IF(F3>34000,"Sales Award","See Mr. Jones"), if the sales were $48,000, _____ would print.

13. In the IF statement =IF(F3>34000,"Sales Award","See Mr. Jones"), if the sales were $33,000, _____ would print.

14. You can _____ rows so that the headings are visible when scrolling.

15. You can _____ to print several pages of worksheets with the same headings.

16. Use a(n) _____ to calculate different answers, depending on a condition.

17. Use a(n) _____ to separate sheet names from cell addresses in a 3-D reference.

18. You can _____ columns to print nonadjacent sections of a worksheet.

19. You can drag columns to the left to _____ them.

20. Use a(n) _____ to find the total of several worksheets in one workbook.

CLOSE
> Review, discuss and answer questions on the material covered in the lesson.

ASSESS
> Administer the lesson test.

CD-ROM
> Answers to Encore questions are also in the related Test Bank in ExamView.

LESSON 6

Charts

In this lesson, you will learn to use features in Excel to create, modify, print, and position sales and profit charts, expense analysis charts, portfolio analysis charts, and graphics.

Upon completion of this lesson, you should have mastered the following skill sets:

- Explore chart basics
- Create charts M
- Create column, line, and pie charts M
- Apply chart options
- Position a chart M
- Print charts M
- Format charts M
- Size embedded charts
- Modify charts M
- Copy and paste charts
- Change orientation of data
- Use custom chart types
- Create graphics M
- Position graphics M
- Modify graphics M
- Insert and download graphics and clip art
- Create stock charts

Terms
MOUS-related
- Charts
- Nonadjacent selection
- Series labels
- Legend
- Y=axis or value axis
- X=axis or category axis
- Category labels
- Data series
- Chart Wizard
- Embedded chart
- Chart sheet
- Column chart
- Line chart
- Pie chart
- Orientation
- Combination chart
- Graphics
- AutoShapes

Document-related
- Portfolio
- S&P 500

 GOAL
To practice using the following skill sets:
- ✹ Explore chart basics
- ✹ Create charts Ⓜ
- ✹ Create column, line, and pie charts Ⓜ
- ✹ Apply chart options
- ✹ Position a chart Ⓜ
- ✹ Print charts Ⓜ

T R Y O U T

TASK 1

WHAT YOU NEED TO KNOW

Explore Chart Basics

> *Charts* present and compare data in a graphic format so that you can compare information visually.

> To create a chart, you must first select the data to plot. Figure 6.1 shows two selections of data; each selection produces the chart shown in Figure 6.2. The list of guidelines and definitions below refer to the selection of chart data:

- The selection should be rectangular.

- The selection should not contain blank or unrelated columns or rows. (See Selection A in Figure 6.1.)

- Use a *nonadjacent selection* when data is not contiguous (see Selection B in Figure 6.1). Select data while pressing and holding the Ctrl key to eliminate blanks or unrelated data. You can also hide columns you do not want to select.

- There should be a blank cell in the upper left corner of a selection to indicate that the data to the right and below are series and category labels for the values.

- The *series labels* identify the charted values and appear in the chart legend. The *legend* shows the color and name of the charted values.

- The *category labels* identify each value in the data series, as shown on the horizontal or x-axis.

T R Y *it* O U T

1. Open **6.1to** from the Data CD.

2. Select the range **A4:C8.** This is the charted data.

3. Select the range **A11:A15,** press and hold the **Ctrl** key, and select the range **C11:D15.** This is also the charted data, using a nonadjacent selection.

4. Move the mouse pointer over all the chart objects to locate each ScreenTip, as shown in Figure 6.2.

5. Close the file. Do not save.

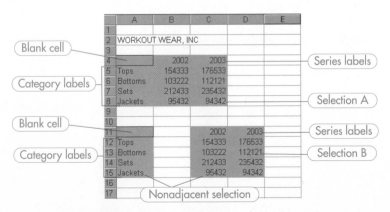

Figure 6.1 Data selections for a chart

> The chart in Figure 6.2 is a column chart produced from either selection in Figure 6.1 (because the same data is selected). Move the mouse pointer over the parts of a chart and ScreenTips display the name of the chart object. The objects in the column chart are labeled on Figure 6.2 and defined below:

- The chart title identifies—the data in the chart and is entered using the Chartp 136 Wizard.

- The y-axis or value axis—typically represents the vertical scale. The scale values are entered automatically by Excel.

- The y-axis or value axis title—identifies the values and is entered using the Chart Wizard.

- The x-axis or category axis—typically represents the horizontal scale and the data series categories.

- The category labels—identify each category and are obtained from the selected data (see Figure 6.1).

- The x-axis or category axis title—identifies the category and is entered using the Chart Wizard.

- The series labels-legend—identifies each data series and is obtained from the selected data (see Figure 6.1).

- The data series—groups of values identified by a label, such as 2002 data in the illustration.

- The plot area—the space where the values are charted.

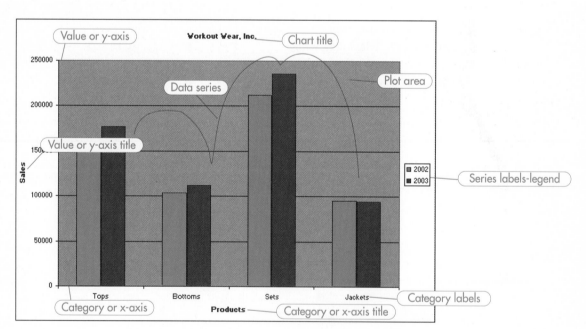

Figure 6.2 Column chart objects

Create Charts

> The **Chart Wizard** makes creating charts easy by providing step-by-step instructions.

> The basic steps to create a chart are:

  • Select the worksheet data to chart.

  • Click the Chart Wizard button.

  • Follow the Chart Wizard prompts:

    Step 1. Select chart type.

    Step 2. Check chart source data range.

    Step 3. Select chart options.

    Step 4. Select chart location.

> The Chart Wizard takes you through the four steps to create a chart. Each step consists of tabbed dialog boxes that allow you to select and format all the objects in your chart. As you make selections, the Chart Wizard shows you exactly how the chart looks so you can select the format that is best for presenting your data.

> In Step 4, when you select the chart location, you create either an *embedded chart,* which exists as an object on your worksheet, or a *chart sheet,* which exists on a separate sheet within the workbook. Excel names chart sheets as Chart1, Chart2, etc. Figure 6.3 shows the Step 4 screen displaying the chart placement options.

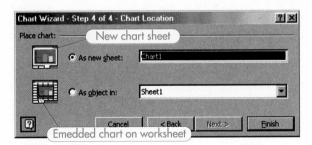

Figure 6.3 Chart Wizard, Step 4 screen

> If you select As new sheet as the placement, you can name the chart sheet in the text box to describe the chart better. If you click As object in as the placement, you can indicate the worksheet to receive the chart.

1. Open **6.1toa** from the Data CD.

2. Select the range **A3:E5.** This is the data range to chart.

3. Click the **Chart Wizard** button.

4. Click **Next** to accept the Column chart type.

5. Click **Next** to accept the data range.

6. In the Step 3 dialog box, enter **Occasions Event Planning** as the chart title.

7. Click **Next** to accept the title.

8. Select **As new sheet** for the chart location.

9. Enter **Column Chart** as the sheet name.

10. Click **Finish** to complete the chart. The chart appears on Column Chart, a new sheet.

11. Do not close the file.

Create Column, Line, and Pie Charts

> The *column chart* (see Figure 6.2) compares individual or sets of values. The height of each bar is proportional to its corresponding value in the worksheet.

> Fourteen standard chart types are available in the Chart Wizard. Each of these types offers at least two subtypes. The subtypes for the Column chart are shown in Figure 6.4.

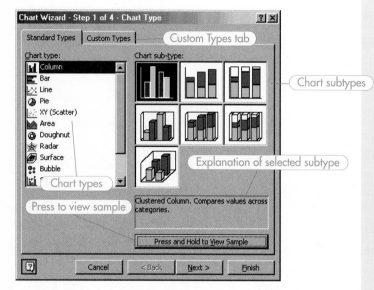

Figure 6.4 Chart Wizard, Step 1, Chart type

> A *line chart,* shown in Figure 6.5, is like a column chart because it compares individual sets of values, but lines connect the points of data. This is useful if you want to show a progression over time.

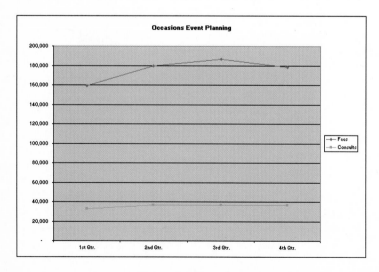

Figure 6.5 Line chart

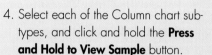

1. Continue to work in **6.1toa,** on the Quarterly Revenues sheet.

2. Select the range **A8:A10,** press and hold the **Ctrl** key, and select the range **C8:F10.**

3. Click the **Chart Wizard** button.

4. Select each of the Column chart sub-types, and click and hold the **Press and Hold to View Sample** button.

5. Switch to Bar and Line charts and test the subtypes as described in Step 4 above.

6. Click **Cancel.**

   Note: Only one numerical range is selected.

7. Select the range **A3:B5** and click the **Chart Wizard** button.

8. Switch to Pie charts and test the chart subtypes as described in Step 4 above.

9. Click **Cancel.**

10. Do not close the file.

> The *pie chart,* as shown in Figure 6.6, is a circular graph
you can use to show the relationship of each value in a data
range to the entire range. The size of each slice of the pie
represents the percentage each value contributes to the total.
You can use only one numeric data range in a pie chart.

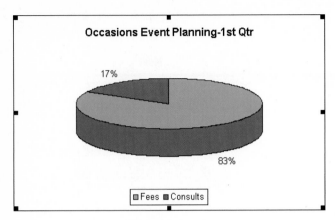

Figure 6.6 Pie chart

Apply Chart Options

> The Step 3 screen of the Chart Wizard allows you to set
chart options on six tabs. You can change or enter chart
titles, axes, gridlines, legends, data labels, and a data table
for most charts. The number of tabs and options vary with
the type of chart selected. For example, pie charts only
have three option tabs.

> In Figure 6.7, you can see the Step 3 screen on the Titles
tab for the column chart you completed earlier. You can set
and view each option on your chart in the preview
window as you add the option.

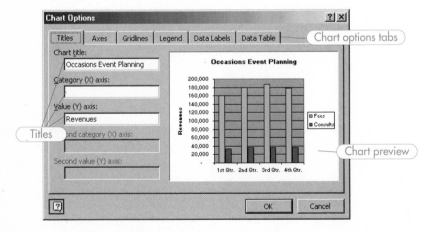

Figure 6.7 Chart Wizard, Step 3, Titles tab

Position a Chart

> The last step in the Chart Wizard asks you to determine whether you want to embed the chart on the worksheet or on a new sheet. You previously placed a chart on a new sheet; however, when you place a chart on a worksheet, it often does not fall where you want it to be.

> To position, size, edit, move, and copy a chart on a worksheet, click the chart once to select it. Handles appear around the chart border, as shown in Figure 6.8, which indicate that the chart is selected and in Edit mode. Notice that Excel highlights the charted data as well.

> To move a chart, you must select the chart, click it, and drag it to its new location. The mouse pointer changes to a four-headed arrow during the move.

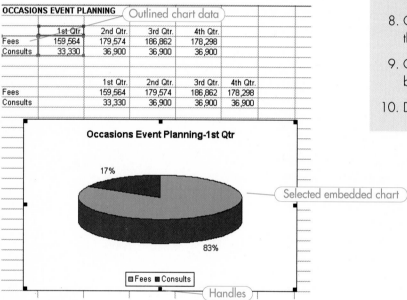

Figure 6.8 Selected embedded chart

1. Continue to work in **6.1toa.**

2. Select the range **A3:B5** and click the **Chart Wizard** button.

3. Select **Pie** chart, **second** sub-type, **3-D Visual Effect,** and click **Next.**

4. Click **Next** to accept the data range.

5. On the Titles tab, enter: `Occasions Event Planning — 1st Qtr`

6. On the Legend tab, select **Bottom** placement for the legend.

7. On the Data Labels tab, select **Percentage.**

8. Click **Finish.** The pie chart appears on the worksheet, as shown in Figure 6.8.

9. Click and drag the chart to **A12,** a blank location on the worksheet.

10. Do not close the file.

Print Charts

> You can print charts with the worksheet, or on a separate sheet. If you print the chart with the worksheet, use Print Preview to be sure both fit on the page.

> If you select an embedded chart on a worksheet or a chart sheet, it will print on a separate sheet to fit one page. Use Print Preview to see how the chart will print. Excel selects the page orientation (portrait or landscape) that matches the shape of the chart. On the Page Setup dialog box, to provide options for a chart, the Chart tab replaces the Sheet tab, as shown in Figure 6.9. Chart setup options include chart size and printing quality.

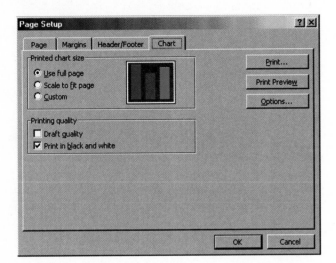

Figure 6.9 Page Setup dialog box, Chart tab

TRY*it* **OUT**

1. Continue to work in **6.1toa.**

2. Select the **Colum Chart** sheet.

3. Click the **Print Preview** button.

4. Click **Print** and **OK.**

5. On the Quarterly Revenues sheet, click the chart.

6. Click the **Print Preview** button.

7. Click **Setup** and click the **Chart** tab.

8. Click **Print in black and white** and click **OK.**

9. Click **Print, OK.**

10. Select the range **A1:G30,** and click the **Print Preview** button.

11. Close the preview screen.

12. Save the file **6.1toa.** Close the file.

REHEARSAL

TASK 1

 GOAL
To create charts to analyze sales and income data

SETTING THE STAGE/WRAPUP
File name: 6.1salechart

WHAT YOU NEED TO KNOW

> Although detailed data is found on financial reports and analysis worksheets, businesses frequently use charts to convey an overview of data for meetings, presentations, and annual reports. The chart type you select often determines the impression the data makes.

> Column and bar charts are similar, except that the data markers are vertical in column charts and horizontal in bar charts.

> In this Rehearsal activity, you will create charts using various chart types on chart sheets, and you will embed them in the workbook for Time Out Sporting Goods. They are testing chart types to determine which chart makes the best impression.

DIRECTIONS

1. Open **6.1salechart** from the Data CD.

2. On the chart data sheet, use a nonadjacent selection to select the ranges **A3:A6** and **C3:E6**.

3. Create a column chart with the following options on the Chart Wizard screens:

   Step 1: Click **Column** chart. Use the Clustered column with a 3-D visual effect subtype (Row 2, Column 1); click **Next**.

   Step 2: Check the data range and, if correct, click **Next**.

   Step 3: In the Titles tab, enter **Time Out Sporting Goods** for the chart title. Enter **Stores** for the X-Axis title. On the Legend tab, place the legend at the bottom of the chart.

   Step 4: Place the chart as a new sheet and enter **Column Chart** as the chart name.

4. Using the same datat, create a bar chart with the following options on the Chart Wizard screens:

   Step 1: Click **Bar** chart. Use the Clustered bar with a 3-D visual effect subtype (Row 2, Column 1); click **Next**.

   Step 2: Check the data range and, if correct, click **Next**.

   Step 3: In the Titles tab, enter **Time Out Sporting Goods** for the chart title. Enter **Stores** for the X-Axis title. On the Legend tab, place the legend at the bottom of the chart.

   Step 4: Place the chart as a new sheet and enter **Bar Chart** as the chart name.

5. Create a line chart using the same procedures.

6. Use a nonadjacent selection to select ranges **A3:D3** and **A6:D6**.

Continued on next page

7. Create a pie chart with the following options on the Chart Wizard screens:

Step 1: Click **Pie** chart. Use the Pie with a 3-D visual effect subtype (Row 1, Column 2); click **Next**.

Step 2: Check the data range and, if correct, click **Next**.

Step 3: In the Titles tab enter `Time Out Sporting Goods – Net Income` for the chart title. On the Legend tab, place the legend at the bottom of the chart.

Step 4: Place the chart as an object in Chart Data.

8. Drag the pie chart to **Cell A11**.

9. Select and print column chart, bar chart, and chart data sheets.

10. Delete the line chart sheet, because it was not the best way to present the data.

11. Save the file **6.1salechart**. Close the file.

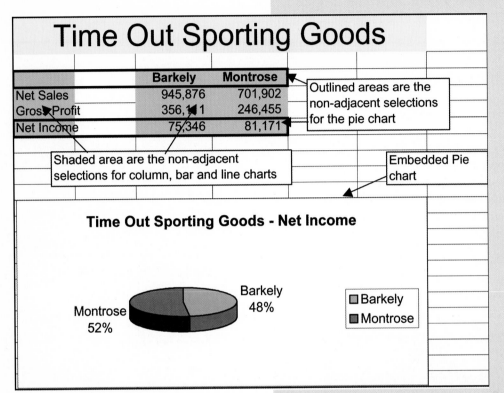

Time Out Sporting Goods

	Barkely	Montrose
Net Sales	945,876	701,902
Gross Profit	356,1 1	246,455
Net Income	75,346	81,171

Outlined areas are the non-adjacent selections for the pie chart

Shaded area are the non-adjacent selections for column, bar and line charts

Embedded Pie chart

Time Out Sporting Goods - Net Income

Barkely 48%
Montrose 52%

☐ Barkely
☐ Montrose

Cues for Reference

Select Chart Data
1. Always keep a blank cell in top left corner.
2. Select rectangular data to chart.
   or
• Press and hold **Ctrl** while selecting nonadjacent data.

Create a Chart
1. Select chart data.
2. Click **Chart Wizard** button.
3. Select chart type and subtype.
4. Click **Next**.
5. Check data range and reenter if incorrect.
6. Click **Next**.
7. Click appropriate tab and set chart options.

8. Click **Next**.
9. Select placement: Click **As new sheet** and enter sheet name in text box.
   or
• Click As object in, accept option offered, or enter sheet name.
10. Click **Finish**.

Select Chart
Embedded Chart
• Click chart. (A border with handles surrounds the chart.)
Chart Sheet
• Select sheet

Position Chart
1. Select chart or chart sheet.
2. Drag to new location. (Mouse pointer changes to four-headed arrow.)

Print Charts
Chart Sheet
1. Select sheet.
2. Click the **Print** button.

Embeded Chart on a Full Sheet
1. Select chart.
2. Click the **Print** button.

Embeded Chart on the Worksheet
1. Select worksheet range including chart.
2. Click **Print**.

TRYOUT

TASK 2

GOAL
To practice using the following skill sets:
* Format charts
* Size embedded charts
* Modify charts
* Copy and paste charts
* Change orientation of data
* Use custom chart types

WHAT YOU NEED TO KNOW

Format Charts

> You can format every object on a chart using the Format Chart dialog box. You can open the dialog box, as shown in Figure 6.10, by double-clicking a chart or any object in a chart. When you double-click a chart object, Excel marks it with a border and handles and displays the name of the object in the name box.

> The Format Chart dialog box varies, depending on which chart object you want to format. Figure 6.10 shows the Format Chart Area dialog box.

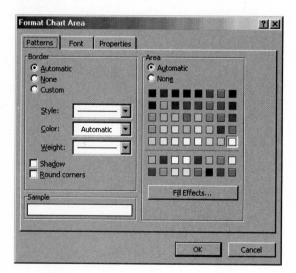

Figure 6.10 Format Chart Area dialog box

TRY*it* OUT

1. Open **6.2to** from the Data CD and display the Pie Chart sheet.

2. Double-click the chart title. The title is bordered and the Format Chart Title dialog box appears.

3. In the Font tab, change the font to **Garamond, 36 point, bold, dark blue.**

4. Click **OK.**

5. Right-click the **pie** chart and click **Format Data Series.**

6. In the Data Labels tab, click **Percentage** and click **OK.**

7. If the Chart toolbar is not displayed, click **View, Toolbars,** and **Chart.**

8. Select **Legend** from the dropdown list in the Chart Object box and click the **Format Legend** button.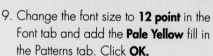

9. Change the font size to **12 point** in the Font tab and add the **Pale Yellow** fill in the Patterns tab. Click **OK.**

10. Do not close the file.

> You can also use the Chart toolbar to format chart objects. Click View, Toolbars, and Chart to display the Chart toolbar, as shown in Figure 6.11, and click the Format Chart button to display the dialog box. In addition, you can right-click any object on a chart and select the Format command from the shortcut menu.

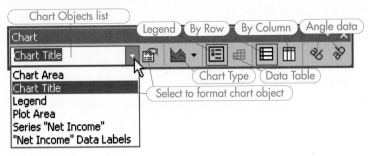

Figure 6.11 Chart toolbar

Size Embedded Charts

> Once you select an embedded chart, you can move it, as you practiced earlier, and make it larger for a better view of the data. Position your mouse pointer over the appropriate handle on the border of the chart and drag it to size the chart. The mouse pointer changes to a double-headed arrow when you position it properly. If you want to make all sides of the chart bigger proportionally, drag the corner handle, as shown in Figure 6.12.

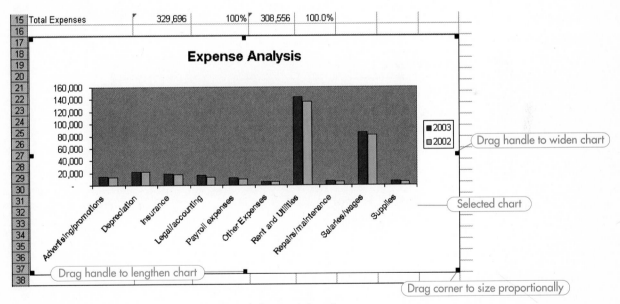

Figure 6.12 Selected chart with handles

Modify Charts

> All modifications of a chart must be made with the chart selected. Use the Chart menu, which appears when you select a chart, to modify or edit your chart settings. The Chart menu, as shown in Figure 6.13, lists commands to revisit each of the steps in the Chart Wizard, where you can change your settings as necessary. You can also use the Chart menu to add data to the chart.

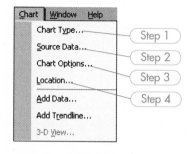

Figure 6.13 Chart menu

> In addition, every object in a chart has a shortcut menu that lets you change the chart type and the source data, format the object, or use other commands relevant to the object. Figure 6.14 shows the shortcut menu for the data series in a chart.

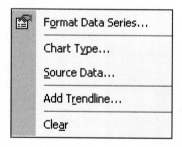

Figure 6.14 Data series shortcut menu

Copy and Paste Charts

> Once you select a chart, you can copy and paste it. Use the Copy and Paste buttons as you do with any other data.

TRY it OUT

1. Continue to work in **6.2to,** and switch to Sheet1.

2. Select the ranges **A4:B14** and **D4:D14** using nonadjacent selection.

3. Create a column chart, first subtype. Enter **Expense Analysis** as the title and place it on Sheet1.

4. Select and drag the chart to **Cell A17.**

5. Use the bottom right corner handle to enlarge the chart over and down to **Cell H37.**

6. Right-click the **Category Labels,** click **Format Axis** to modify to **8 point** font, and click **OK.**

7. Right-click the **Value Labels,** click **Format Axis** to modify to **8 point** font, and click **OK.**

8. Click **Chart, Chart Type,** and change the type to **Bar.**

9. Do not close the file.

Change Orientation of Data

> For all charts except pie charts, Excel automatically determines the chart *orientation* (whether the chart plots the selected data range by row or by column layout). In the second step of the Chart Wizard, as shown in Figure 6.15, Excel lets you change the orientation of the data series.

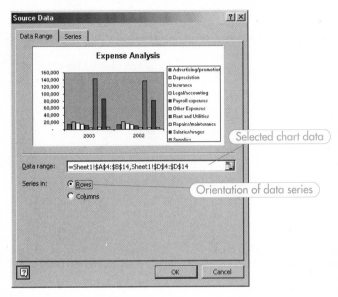

Figure 6.15 Chart Wizard, Step 2 screen, source data

> You can view each orientation selection and decide which best conveys the data for your purposes. You can also change the orientation after you create the chart, by clicking Source Data on the Chart menu.

> You can also change the orientation of chart text in the Format dialog box in the Alignment tab or by using the Angle buttons on the Chart toolbar. The axis labels or titles can be arranged vertically in the Format Axis dialog box, rotated to any angle, or arranged horizontally. In Figure 6.16, notice the rotation box, where you can drag the line to the angle of rotation or set the degree of rotation.

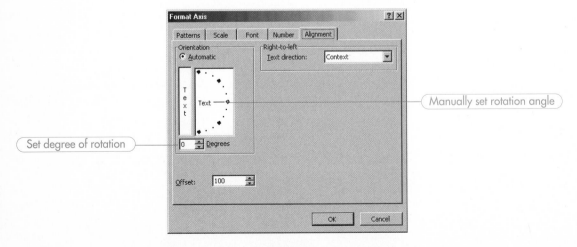

Figure 6.16 Format Axis dialog box, Alignment tab

TRY *it* **OUT**

1. Continue to work in **6.2to,** on Sheet1.

2. Select the **embedded chart** and right-click the **y-axis** labels on the left.

3. On the shortcut menu, click **Format Axis** and click the **Alignment** tab.

4. Set the text alignment to **16 degrees** rotation. Click **OK.**

5. Copy the chart and paste it in **Cell A39.** A second chart, selected, appears.

6. Click **Chart, Source Data,** and change the orientation to Series in **Rows.** orientation. Click **OK.**

7. Format the legend text to **8 points** and a gray background color. Notice the new perspective on the data.

8. Right-click the **y-axis** labels and return them to 0 degrees rotation. (See Steps 2–4.)

9. Do not close the file.

Use Custom Chart Types

> You can create customized chart types by clicking the Custom Types tab in the Chart Type dialog box. As shown in Figure 6.17, Excel plots your data with the custom chart selection. The *combination chart* is a custom chart that plots each data series as a different chart type.

For example, the line-column chart plots 2002 data as a line chart type and 2003 data as a column chart type. This chart provides a clear comparison for presentation purposes. The comparison between the current year in column format and the prior year in line format is clear because each category value is plotted at the same point on the chart, rather than side-by-side as they would be on a column chart.

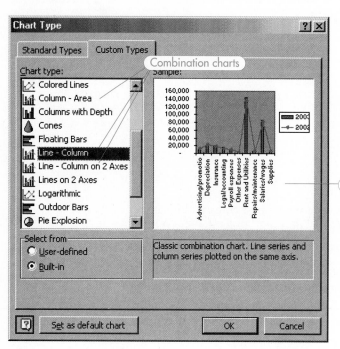

Figure 6.17 Chart Type dialog box, Custom Types tab

TRYit**OUT**

1. Continue to work in **6.2to,** on Sheet1.

2. Select the first embedded chart and click **Chart, Chart Type.**

3. On the Custom Types tab, select the **Line - Column** type.

4. Click **OK.** Notice that the title is cleared.

5. Click **Chart, Chart Options.**

6. In the Titles tab, enter **Expense Analysis** as the title.

7. Click **OK.**

8. Save the file **6.2to.** Close the file.

REHEARSAL

TASK 2

WHAT YOU NEED TO KNOW

> When you change the orientation of data from rows to columns, you reverse the categories and values, which gives you a different perspective on the data.

> In this Rehearsal activity, you will create, format, and modify charts using various chart types on chart sheets and embedded in the worksheet for the Sutton Investment Group. This company is comparing expenses for the past three years to see the developing trends and to determine where it can make changes.

DIRECTIONS

1. Open **6.2expchart** from the Data CD.

2. Use nonadjacent selection to select the labels and data in the ranges **A4:A11** and **C4:E11,** as shown in Illustration D.

3. Create a column chart, as shown in Illustration A. Include the following:

   a. 3-D visual effect subtype

   b. Enter the chart title: **Sutton Investment Group**

   c. X-axis title: **Expenses**

   d. Legend – Place at the top of the chart

   e. Place the chart on a chart sheet named: **Expense Column Chart**

4. Modify the X-Axis data series labels to an **8 point** font.

5. Modify the chart title to a **16 point** font. Select the title area and add – **Expense Analysis** so that the title reads: **Sutton Investment Group – Expense Analysis**

6. Copy the chart and place it in **Cell A1** on **Sheet2.**

7. Click the **Chart, Source Data** option, and change the orientation to rows, as shown in Illustration B.

8. Rename Sheet2 as **Yearly Column Chart** and set Page Setup to Fit on one page for printing purposes.

9. Use the same selection of data and the same chart title to create a custom chart using the Line - Column type. Place it on a chart sheet named: **Line and Column Expenses** as shown in Illustration C.

Continued on next page

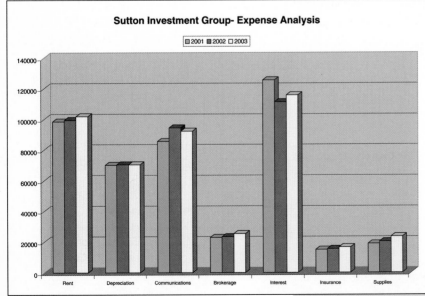

Illustration A: Expense column chart

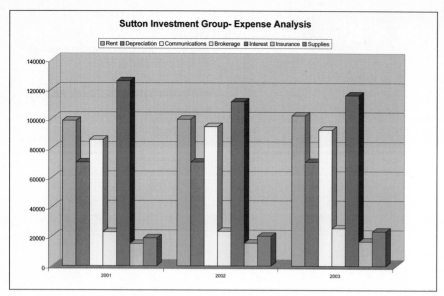

Illustration B: Yearly column chart

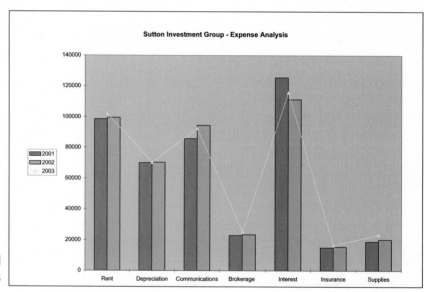

Illustration C: Line and column expenses

Format Charts
1. Double-click the chart object to format.
2. Click the appropriate Format dialog box tab.
3. Set the format.
4. Click **OK.**

Size Embedded Charts
1. Select chart.
2. Place mouse pointer on the handle on side of border to size. Use corner to size proportionally. The mouse pointer becomes a double-headed arrow when positioned correctly.

3. Drag border outline until you reach the required size.

Modify Charts
1. Select chart.
2. Click **Chart** and chart step to modify.
   or
• Right-click chart and select chart step to modify.
3. Make modification.
4. Click **OK.**

Change Orientation of Data
1. Select chart.
2. Click **Chart, Source Data.**
3. Click **Rows.**

4. Click **OK.**

Copy and Paste Charts
1. Select chart.
2. Click **Copy** button.
3. Select location for new copy.
4. Click **Paste** button.

Create Custom Chart
1. Select data to plot.
2. Click **Chart Wizard** button.
3. On Step 1 screen, click **Custom Types** tab.
4. Select custom chart type.
5. Click **Next.**
6. Complete Chart Wizard steps.

10. Select the data labels in the range **A4:A11** and the data in **Column E** to create a pie chart for 2003 data. Use the following options:

  a. Apply the 3-D Visual Effect subtype.

  b. Enter the chart title: `Sutton Investment Group 2003 Expense Dollar`

  c. Place the legend at the bottom of the chart.

  d. Set data labels to show percentages.

  e. Place the chart as an object on Sheet1.

11. Drag and size the chart so it fits in the range **A13:I41.**

12. Select the chart title and press the **Enter** key so that the title is arranged on two lines, as shown in the illustration below.

13. Modify the legend so that it has a light yellow background.

14. Use the Patterns tab of the Format Chart Area dialog box to modify the color of the chart background and the border color to a light green.

15. Merge and center worksheet titles as shown.

16. Select the range **A1:I41** and change the background to a light green.

17. Rename Sheet1 as **Expense Data and Pie Chart** and drag it to the first tab position.

18. Delete **Sheet3.**

19. Group all the sheets and print the entire workbook.

20. Ungroup the sheets.

21. Save the file **6.2expchart** and close the file.

Sutton Investment Group Expense Analysis

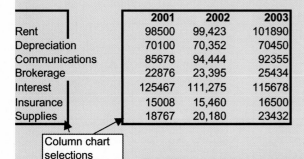

	2001	2002	2003
Rent	98500	99,423	101890
Depreciation	70100	70,352	70450
Communications	85678	94,444	92355
Brokerage	22876	23,395	25434
Interest	125467	111,275	115678
Insurance	15008	15,460	16500
Supplies	18767	20,180	23432

Column chart selections

Chart border color changed to match backgrounds

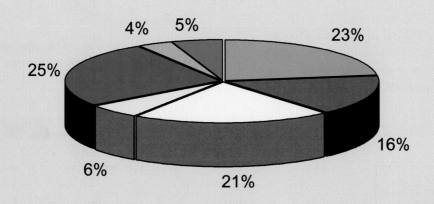

Sutton Investment Group 2003 Expense Dollar

■ Rent ■ Depreciation ☐ Communications
☐ Brokerage ■ Interest ■ Insurance
■ Supplies

Illustration D: Expense Data and Pie Chart

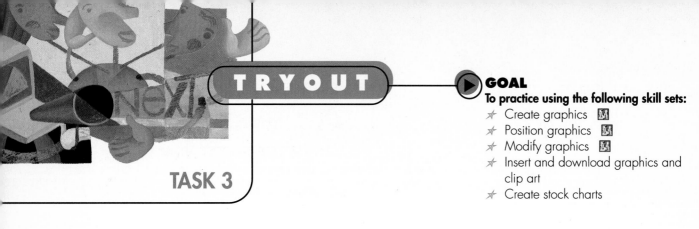

TRYOUT

TASK 3

▶ **GOAL**
To practice using the following skill sets:
✳ Create graphics 🅼
✳ Position graphics 🅼
✳ Modify graphics 🅼
✳ Insert and download graphics and clip art
✳ Create stock charts

WHAT YOU NEED TO KNOW

Create Graphics

> There are two types of *graphics*, or graphical images, that you can create or insert into your worksheets: drawing objects and pictures. If you want to add drawing objects to a worksheet or to a chart, you can create a customized object by using the tools available on the Drawing toolbar. You can draw lines, arcs, arrows, rectangles, polygons, and a selection of shapes or freehand graphics on any area of a worksheet or chart.

> Click View, Toolbars, and Drawing to display the Drawing toolbar. You can dock the toolbar, as shown in Figure 6.18, anywhere on the screen.

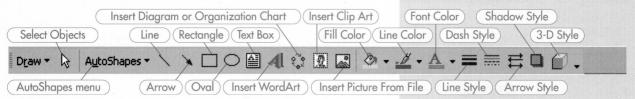

Figure 6.18 Drawing toolbar

> *AutoShapes* are predefined graphical images that you can place and size. When you place your mouse pointer over an AutoShape, the name of the shape appears as a ScreenTip, as shown in Figure 6.19.

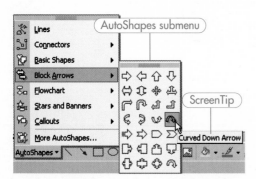

Figure 6.19 AutoShapes menu

TRY*it*OUT

1. Open **6.3to** from the Data CD.

2. Click **View, Toolbars,** and **Drawing.**

3. On the Drawing toolbar, click the **Text Box** button.

4. Draw a text box on the chart, as shown in Figure 6.20, and enter the text shown. (Do not select the chart.)

5. On the Drawing toolbar, click the **Arrow** button.

6. Draw a single arrow as shown, starting at the text box and dragging to the area where the arrow should point.

7. On the Drawing toolbar, click the **AutoShapes** button, select **Lines,** and click the **Double Arrow.** Place as shown.

8. On the Drawing toolbar, click the **AutoShapes** button, select **Block Arrows,** and click the **Curved Down Arrow.** Place it starting in **Cell D7,** as shown in Figure 6.20.

9. Do not close the file.

> Select a button to draw or format an object. The Line, Arrow, Rectangle, Text Box, and Oval buttons enable the mouse pointer to draw those objects as you drag them to the appropriate size. Figure 6.20 shows some of the graphic objects you can create with the Drawing toolbar.

> You can place graphics or drawing objects anywhere on a worksheet, as well as on charts. However, notice that when you select the chart, the graphics disappear. To display, create, and modify graphics, click outside the chart to deselect it.

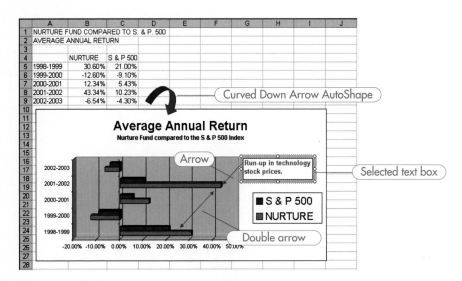

Figure 6.20   Chart with drawing objects

Position Graphics

> A selected graphic has small square white boxes at the ends or on the border of the graphic, as seen in the text box graphic selected in Figure 6.20. Click a graphic to select it. However, notice that to select a graphic you do not select the chart.

> When you attempt to move a selected graphic, place the mouse pointer over the graphic until you see a four-headed arrow, thenS click and drag down to the new position. As with handles on charts, you can use the white boxes to size the object.

Modify Graphics

> To modify or change a graphic, select it and press the Ctrl + 1 keys, or right-click and select the Format option. The Format dialog box, appropriate to the type of graphic selected, appears. For example, Figure 6.21 shows the Format AutoShape dialog box. You can modify all the items indicated in the tabs, including the properties, which let you set the object to move and size proportionally with the chart.

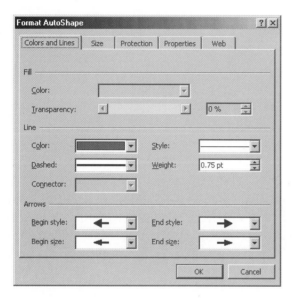

Figure 6.21 Format AutoShape dialog box

TRY*it***OUT**

1. Continue to work in **6.3to.**

2. Click the **Curved Down Arrow** to select it.

3. Press the **Ctrl + 1** keys and make the following changes:
   a. Change Fill Color to **Plum.**
   b. Change Line Color to **Navy.**
   c. In the Size tab, change Rotation to **30 degrees.**
   d. Click **OK.**

4. Position the graphic by dragging it so that the graphic starts in **Cell D9** and the arrow is on the chart.

5. Right-click each graphic arrow on the chart and change the Line Color to **Plum.**

6. Select the text in the text box. Resize the font, if necessary, and change the color to **Plum** using the Font Color button.

7. Save the file **6.3to.** Close the file.

Insert and Download Graphics and Clip Art

> You have practiced using drawing objects. The second type of graphical image is a picture. You can use the Insert menu to insert pictures from clip art, files, scanners or cameras, organization charts, AutoShapes, or WordArt. You can use the Picture, From File option to insert your company logo. Notice the Picture options on the Insert menu, as shown in Figure 6.22, and refer to Figure 6.18 to see the corresponding buttons on the Drawing toolbar.

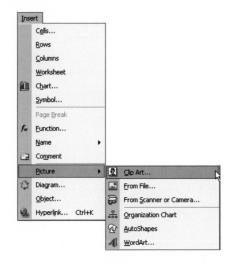

Figure 6.22 Insert menu

> When you click Insert, Picture, Clip Art, the Insert Clip Art task pane appears with search options for clip art, as shown in Figure 6.23.

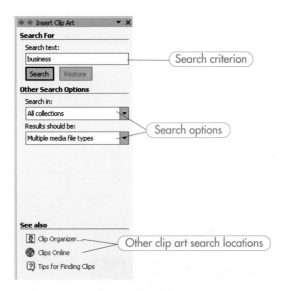

Figure 6.23 Insert Clip Art task pane

1. Open **6.3toa** from the Data CD.

2. Click **Insert, Picture,** and **Clip Art.**

3. In the Insert Clip Art task pane, enter **Business** as the search text.

4. Click **Search** and locate the clip art, as shown in Figure 6.24.

5. Click the **list arrow** on the Clip Art menu and click **Insert.**

6. Place the clip art to the right of the data in the range G:I:I11.

7. On the Picture toolbar, click the **Less Brightness** button several times to darken the graphic.

8. If you have an Internet connection, view some of the graphics available on Clips Online:
   a. Click **Insert, Picture,** and **Clip Art** in the task pane; click **Clips Online.**
   b. Enter a search criterion for **Business** and view available clip art.
   c. Close Clips Online.

9. Do not close the file.

> You also have the option to view the collections directly by clicking Clip Organizer or Clips Online. If you have an Internet connection, you can click Clips Online and connect to the Online Gallery, where you can select graphics to download from the Web.

> Each clip art graphic that appears in the task pane contains an arrow that displays a menu of options. Insert is the first option, and you must click it to place the clip art on your worksheet. Notice the Clip Art list arrow menu in Figure 6.24.

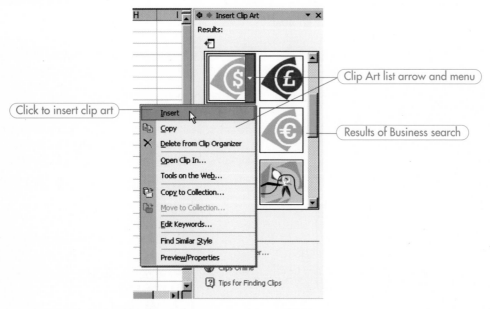

Figure 6.24 Clip Art list arrow menu

> Once you select a picture from the collections and insert it, use the set of handles that appear to position and size the object. The Picture toolbar, as shown in Figure 6.25, appears when you select a picture and contains buttons to modify all aspects of the picture.

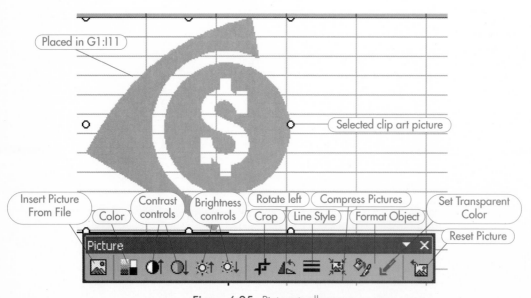

Figure 6.25 Picture toolbar

Create Stock Charts

> Excel provides four chart subtypes for stock market and price analysis, as shown in Figure 6.26. The High-Low-Close, Open-High-Low-Close, Volume-High-Low-Close, and Volume-Open-High-Low-Close charts can track the changes in stock data during a specific period.

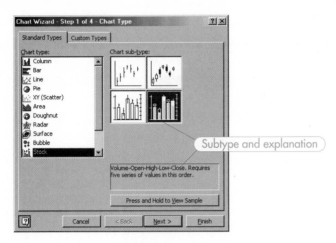

Figure 6.26   Stock chart subtypes

> The Volume value is the sales volume for the stock for the day. The Open value is the opening price of the stock. The High and Low values are the highest and lowest prices for the day. The closing price of the stock is the Close value. As shown in Figure 6.27, a white bar indicates a close that is up in price and a black bar indicates a close that is down in price.

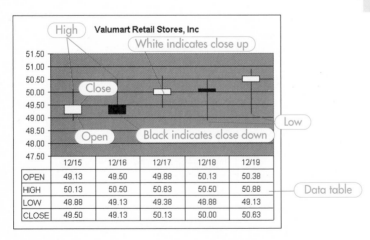

Figure 6.27   Open-High-Low-Close chart subtype

> The data table, as shown in Figure 6.27, is a chart option that you can add to show the charted data. Click the Data Table tab on the Step 3 Chart Options screen and select the Show data table option to display the table.

TRY*it***OUT**

1. Continue to work in **6.3toa**.

2. Use nonadjacent selection to select the ranges **A5:A10** and **C5:F10**.

3. Click the **Chart Wizard** button and create a stock chart as follows:

   Step 1: Click **Stock Chart Subtype: Open-High-Low-Close** as the chart type.

   Step 2: Check data series.

   Step 3: Enter: `Valumart Retail Stores, Inc` as the chart title. Click **Show Data Table**.

   Step 4: Locate the chart as an object on Sheet1.

4. Place the chart in the range **A12:H35**.

5. Create a Volume-Open-High-Low-Close chart using all the data in the range **A5:F10**. In Step 2, change the source data so that the data orientation is by columns. Enter an appropriate chart title and place it on a chart sheet.

6. Save the file **6.3toa**. Close the file.

REHEARSAL

TASK 3

 GOAL
To create charts to analyze investment portfolio performance for stocks and fund investments

SETTING THE STAGE/WRAPUP
File name: 6.3portfolio

WHAT YOU NEED TO KNOW

> Individuals who invest in stocks and mutual funds, and businesses, whose stocks are traded publicly, are interested in tracking the performance of their stocks. The stocks or investments that people and businesses own are said to be in an investment *portfolio.* Stocks are compared to the Standard & Poor's (S&P) 500 index and to the performance of other stocks in the same industry or sector. The sector average shows the growth of all the stocks in that industry.

> The *S&P 500* is a market index, made up of 500 blue–chip stocks, that is used to predict the general trend of U.S. stocks. If the S&P 500 index increases, it is generally a sign that the market is in a positive mode.

> In this Rehearsal activity, you will create and format charts to analyze investment returns for Ms. Alivea James, the president of In–Shape Fitness Centers. She owns several funds, or groups of stocks, in the health sector and is also tracking the stock price for a specific stock, Jackson Laboratories, to make a purchase decision.

DIRECTIONS

1. Open **6.3portfolio** from the Data CD.

2. On the Fund Analysis sheet, create a bar chart to show the comparison between both health funds, the sector average, and the S&P 500 average.
   a. Use a 3-D visual effect bar chart.
   b. Data orientation should be by columns.
   c. Chart title: **Investment Returns for Health Funds**
   d. X-axis title: **Years Held**
   e. Place on the Fund Analysis sheet.

3. Place the chart under the worksheet and size it appropriately.

4. Format the axis labels and legend to **8 point** font.

5. Create the following graphics as shown in Illustration A on the facing page:
   a. Block arrow to point to TR Health value. Color to match TR Health bar.
   b. Text box.
   c. Establish an Internet connection and find a stock market graphic from Clips Online.

6. Format the worksheet and place and size the graphics.

7. On the Stock Analysis sheet for Jackson Laboratories, create a Volume-Open-High-Low-Close chart with a data table. Be sure to plot the data by columns.

8. Place and modify the chart as needed to view data clearly, including formatting the data table and axis labels for **8 point** font.

9. Enter the graphics, as shown in Illustration B on the facing page, and search for clip art in Medical, Health, or Science categories.

10. Print one copy of each worksheet.

11. Save the file **6.3portfolio.** Close the file.

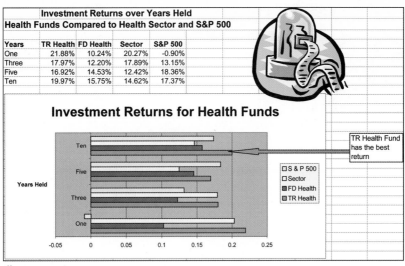

Investment Returns over Years Held Health Funds Compared to Health Sector and S&P 500				
Years	TR Health	FD Health	Sector	S&P 500
One	21.88%	10.24%	20.27%	-0.90%
Three	17.97%	12.20%	17.89%	13.15%
Five	16.92%	14.53%	12.42%	18.36%
Ten	19.97%	15.75%	14.62%	17.37%

Illustration A

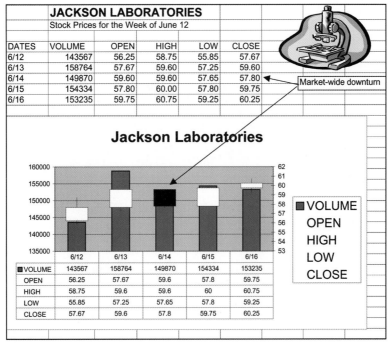

JACKSON LABORATORIES					
Stock Prices for the Week of June 12					
DATES	VOLUME	OPEN	HIGH	LOW	CLOSE
6/12	143567	56.25	58.75	55.85	57.67
6/13	158764	57.67	59.60	57.25	59.60
6/14	149870	59.60	59.60	57.65	57.80
6/15	154334	57.80	60.00	57.80	59.75
6/16	153235	59.75	60.75	59.25	60.25

Illustration B

Cues for Reference

Create Graphics
1. Click **View, Toolbars,** and **Drawing.**
2. Click graphic button.
3. Drag to size.

Modify Graphics
1. Right-click graphic.
2. Click **Format** (graphic name).
3. Select formatting changes.
4. Click **OK.**

Size and Place Graphics
1. Click graphic.
2. Use handles to drag to size.
3. Place mouse pointer on graphic until it becomes a four-headed arrow, and drag to location.

Insert Pictures
1. Click **Insert, Pictures, Clip Art.**
2. In task pane, enter search criteria.
3. Click **Search.**
4. Locate required graphic.
5. Click down arrow and click **Insert.**

6. Size and place graphic.

Download Pictures
1. Establish your Internet connection.
2. Click **Insert, Pictures, Clip Art.**
3. In task pane, click **Clips Online.**
4. Enter search criteria.
5. Click selection box on required clip.
6. Click **Download 1 clip, Download Now.**
7. Right-click clip art in your gallery and click **Insert.**

PERFORMANCE

SETTING THE STAGE/WRAPUP
Act I File name: 6p1.income
Act II File name: 6p2.expense
Act III File name: 6p3.stock

WHAT YOU NEED TO KNOW

Act I

You work in the Finance Department of the Air Land Sea Travel Group. Your department has been asked to create charts for a branch manager meeting about the income and profit figures for the quarter.

Follow these guidelines:

✴ Open **6p1.income,** the Optional Analysis sheet, for your chart data. Use a nonadjacent selection of data.

✴ Create column and bar charts on chart sheets to compare Total Income and Net Income. Format the chart titles, axis labels, and tab names so that the data is easy to read. Change orientation of data to get a different perspective for the bar chart, and use data labels.

✴ Create a pie chart for Total Income and one for Net Income data and place both on the Optional Analysis sheet. Use percentages as labels on the pie sections, and color the charts and chart borders to match the worksheet.

✴ Add graphics, if necessary, to point out important information, or add the company logo to the charts or worksheet. Download a travel graphic, if possible, to add to the blank area on the bar chart.

✴ Print the charts and the Optional Analysis sheet.

✴ Save your work.

Act II

Odyssey Travel Gear has prepared income statements for June 30 and December 31, 2002 by combining data from all its stores. The president is interested in reducing expenses and has asked you to prepare charts to analyze and compare the expenses for the stores for each semiannual report.

Follow these guidelines:

✴ Open **6p2.expense,** the December 31 and June 30 sheets, for your chart data. Use a nonadjacent selection of data, including titles in the range A5:F5 and expense data in the range A12:F14

✴ Create a line chart of the December 31 expense data and place it on the December 31 sheet. Format the axis label and legend fonts. Copy the chart and place it below the line chart. Change the type to a bar chart, so that there are two charts on the worksheet.

* Repeat this analysis for the June 30 sheet.

* Insert a new sheet and name it: **Expense Dollar** Create two pie charts to show the total expense dollar for December 31 and June 30. Select the Expenses labels in Column A and the Totals in Column G on each sheet and place the pie charts on the Expense Dollar sheet. Be sure to indicate the date in the chart title and add percentage labels.

* Use drawing objects to point out the area of increased expenses and add other graphics, if necessary. Color the background of the pie charts.

* Print the sheets that contain charts and save and close the file.

Act III

Trilogy Productions is a public corporation whose stock is traded daily on the stock exchange. The management of the company tracks the open, high, low, and close prices of the stock and the volume of shares traded each day. Management also wants to compare the investment value of owning a share in the company to the average return of other companies in their sector, and to the general market or to the S&P 500. The company is in the Media or Entertainment sector.

You have been asked to prepare charts from the stock data provided for the next meeting of the board of directors. Also, you will research the Media sector on the Internet.

Follow these guidelines:

* Use the file **6p3.stock.**

* On the Investment Analysis sheet, create a column chart to compare the investment growth of the stock as compared to that of the S&P 500 and the Media sector. Begin your data selection in Cell A6. On a separate Price History chart sheet, create a line chart of the prices for 1999–2003. Use a data table to show the stock prices.

* On the Stock Price Analysis sheet, create an Open-High-Low-Close chart. Also use the data to create a Volume-Open-High-Low-Close chart on a separate sheet.

* Format charts and font sizes on titles and axis labels so that they present well. Add a company logo to the charts and/or worksheets. Add drawing objects to point out the increase in the stock price on 11/17 because of a favorable announcement about a new production.

* Research the Media sector and print a list of the companies in the Motion Picture and Video Production and Distribution sector. Also, print a company capsule on one or more media companies, such as Dreamworks, Disney, or Pixar. Compare the annual revenue of several such companies on a worksheet or in a report.

* Use a search engine to look up the sector or find it on the www.hooversonline.com Web site. In the Companies and Industries area, find the master list of sectors, select the sector, and complete your research.

* Print a copy of all worksheets in the file. Save your work.

ENCORE

Identify the letter of the choice that best completes the statement or answers the question.

1. Rules for selecting chart data include the following:
   A. Selection should be rectangular.
   B. Hide unnecessary columns or rows.
   C. Use nonadjacent selection to omit unnecessary data.
   D. All of the above
   E. A and C

2. The labels for the y-axis or value axis:
   A. Are from the worksheet.
   B. Are created automatically.
   C. Are in the legend.
   D. All of the above
   E. A and C

3. An embedded chart is:
   A. On a chart sheet.
   B. Automatically placed and sized correctly.
   C. On a worksheet.
   D. All of the above
   E. None of the above

4. Charts must be selected to be:
   A. Edited.
   B. Sized.
   C. Positioned.
   D. All of the above
   E. A and C

5. Changing the orientation of data on a chart:
   A. Affects the chart title.
   B. Plots data in a pie chart.
   C. Plots data by columns instead of rows.
   D. All of the above
   E. None of the above

Circle **T** if the statement is true or **F** if the statement is false.

T   F   6. You should not include blank rows or columns in chart data selection.

T   F   7. The Chart Wizard moves you through three screens to create a chart.

T   F   8. You need to position and size a chart on a chart sheet.

T   F   9. A Volume-Open-High-Low-Close chart requires four sets of data.

T   F   10. The Chart menu appears when a chart is selected.

Complete each statement.

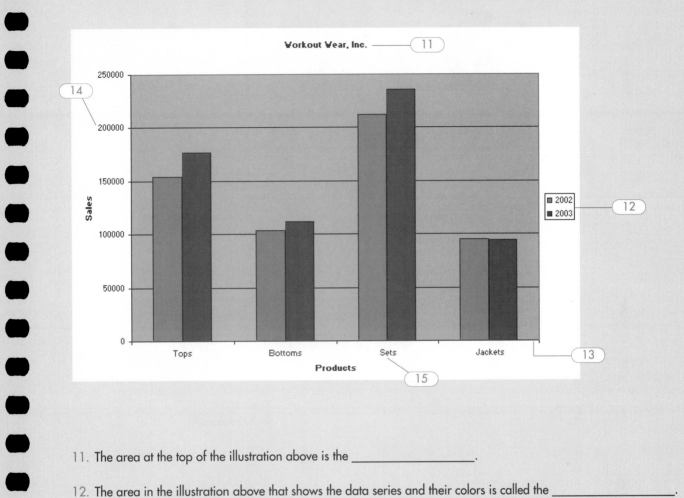

11. The area at the top of the illustration above is the _____.

12. The area in the illustration above that shows the data series and their colors is called the _____.

13. The horizontal data axis of the illustration above is called the _____.

14. The vertical data axis of the illustration above is called the _____.

15. The labels defining the information on the horizontal part of the illustration above are the _____.

16. Charts that are placed on a worksheet are called _____.

17. A chart that can show a progression of data over time is the _____.

18. A chart that must use only one data series is the _____.

19. When you add a textbox to a worksheet, you are adding a _____.

20. Charting data by rows or columns defines the _____ of the data.

LESSON 7

Integration

In this lesson, you will learn to use Excel features to integrate worksheets, charts, and Internet elements into Word documents. You will create a benefit statement, an integrated letter, a travel guide, and a quarterly report.

▶ **Upon completion of this lesson, you should have mastered the following skill sets:**

✴ Understand integration basics
✴ Copy and paste data between applications
  ✴ Drag-and-drop data between applications
✴ Embed worksheets or charts
  ✴ Edit an embedded object
✴ Insert a worksheet in Word
✴ Link data between applications
  ✴ Edit a linked object
✴ Display and use the Web toolbar
  ✴ Paste Web data
✴ Create and respond to discussion comments

Terms
MOUS-related
  Integration
  Source file
  Destination file
  Embedded file
  Linked file
Document-related
  Benefits statement

GOAL
To practice using the following skill sets:
* Understand integration basics
* Copy and paste data between applications
    * Drag-and-drop data between applications
* Embed worksheets and charts
    * Edit an embedded object
* Insert a worksheet in Word

TASK 1

WHAT YOU NEED TO KNOW

Understand Integration Basics

> *Integration* is the sharing or combining of data between Office applications. The source file provides the data, and the destination file receives the data and integrates it into the file. For example, an Excel chart or worksheet (the *source file*) can provide supporting or visual documentation of material for a Word document (the *destination file*), as shown in Figure 7.1. You can paste, embed, or link data into the destination file; the choice depends on the features you require for the file.

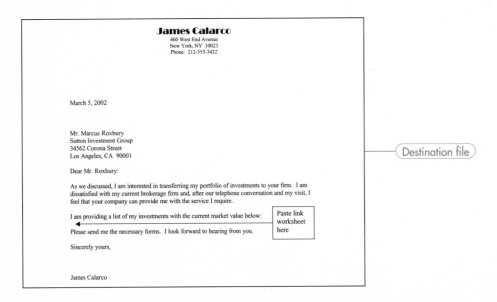

Figure 7.1 Source and destination files

Copy and Paste Data Between Applications

> To copy and paste data between applications, the source and destination files should both be open. You can open either file in its application and click Start, Open Office Document, to open the other file and application, as shown in Figure 7.2. Use the taskbar buttons to switch between applications, as shown in Figure 7.3.

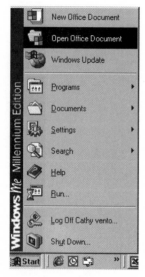

Figure 7.2 Start menu, Open Office Document option

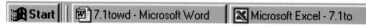

Figure 7.3 Taskbar application buttons

> To paste Excel data into a Word document, go to the Excel file and copy the data you need from the worksheet. Then, switch to the Word document and paste it to the location you want in the document.

> You can edit a worksheet that you paste into a Word document. However, there is no connection to the original worksheet or to Excel, and you cannot view or change the formulas. Use this method only when updated or linked data is not necessary or when formulas do not need editing.

TRY*it*OUT

1. In Excel, open **7.1to.xls** from the Data CD.

2. Click **Start, Open Office Document,** and open **7.1towd.doc** from the Data CD. (Word opens with the Word file.)

3. Switch to the Excel source file using the taskbar button.

4. Select the worksheet data in the Excel file.

5. Click the **Copy** button.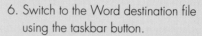

6. Switch to the Word destination file using the taskbar button.

7. Place the insertion point between the second and third paragraphs of the letter, as shown in Figure 7.1.

8. Click the **Paste** button. The worksheet is integrated into the Word document.

9. Change the price of the first condo to: **144,999**

10. Switch back to the Excel file and notice that the change did not affect the worksheet.

11. Close the files without saving them.

Drag-and-Drop Data Between Applications

> You can also use the drag-and-drop technique to copy and paste the data if you make both the source and destination documents visible using window options.

> To see both files, right-click the taskbar to display the shortcut menu, as shown in Figure 7.4. Click Tile Windows Vertically; both files become visible on the screen, arranged vertically.

Figure 7.4 Taskbar shortcut menu

> To drag-and-drop the data between files, select the data, point the mouse at the selection until you see the selection arrow, and press and hold the Ctrl key to copy (rather than move) the data.

Embed Worksheets or Charts

> To edit an integrated worksheet or chart in a Word document while in Excel mode, use the embedding technique to integrate the data. An *embedded file* is an object placed in a destination file that becomes part of that file, and that you can edit in its source application.

> To embed a worksheet or a worksheet and chart, click Insert, Object, Create from File and click Browse. You can then look for the file and select it from the appropriate folder. When you select the file, the path and file name display in the File name box, as shown in Figure 7.5.

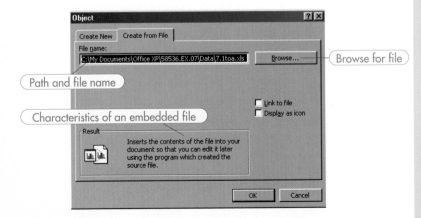

Figure 7.5 Object dialog box, Create from File tab

Tryout Task 1

TRY *it* **OUT**

1. Open **7.1towd.doc** and **7.1to.xls** from the Data CD as you did in the last TryitOut.

2. Right-click the **taskbar** and click **Tile Windows Vertically** from the shortcut menu.

3. In the Excel source file, select the worksheet data.

4. Point the mouse at the selection until the pointer becomes a four head selection arrow, and press and hold the **Ctrl** key.

5. Drag-and-drop the worksheet data in the space between the second and third paragraphs of the Word document.

6. Change the price of the first condo to **144,999** in the Word document.

7. Notice that the change did not affect the worksheet.

8. Save and close the files.

TRY *it* **OUT**

1. Open **7.1toawd.doc** and **7.1toa.xls** from the Data CD.

2. Switch to the Word document and place the insertion point below the last line of text.

3. Click **Insert, Object, Create from File,** and click **Browse.**

4. Locate **7.1toa.xls** and click **Insert.**

5. Click **OK** and the file is embedded. Size the object frame so that only the worksheet is displayed.

6. Switch to the Excel worksheet and select the chart. Click the **Copy** button.

7. Switch to the Word document and place the insertion point below the last line of text.

8. Click **Edit, Paste Special,** and click **Microsoft Excel Chart Object.**

9. Click **OK** and the chart is embedded.

10. Do not close the files.

> Another method you can use to embed a worksheet is to copy the worksheet in Excel, and in the Word application, click Edit, Paste Special, and click Microsoft Excel Worksheet Object. Notice the source file in the Paste Special dialog box, as shown in Figure 7.6, and the Result text in both Figures 7.5 and 7.6.

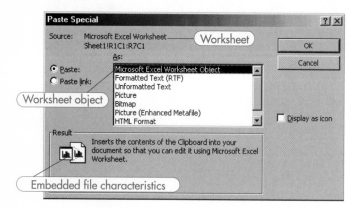

Figure 7.6 Paste Special dialog box for worksheet

> To embed only a chart, copy the chart in Excel, and click Edit, Paste Special in the Word application. When the Paste Special dialog box opens, as shown in Figure 7.7, with Microsoft Excel Chart Object selected, click OK.

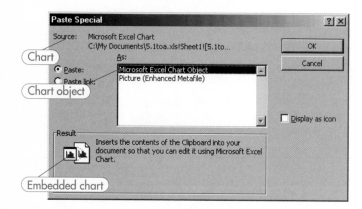

Figure 7.7 Paste Special dialog box for chart

Edit an Embedded Object

> To edit an embedded worksheet or chart, double-click it. You are then in the source application, Excel; however, your edits change only the destination (Word) file, not the source (Excel) file.

Insert a Worksheet in Word

> On the Standard toolbar in Word, there is an Insert Microsoft Excel Worksheet button that allows you to create a new embedded Excel worksheet. When you click this button, you can select the number of cells for the width and length of the new worksheet, as shown in Figure 7.8. You will be in Excel mode, with Excel menus, and can then create a worksheet with the number of rows and columns you specified.

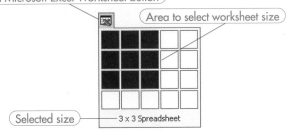

Figure 7.8 Insert Microsoft Excel Worksheet button

TRY *it* **OUT**

1. Continue to work in Word in **7.1toawd.doc** with **7.1toa.xls** active in Excel.

2. In Word, click the embedded worksheet once to select it, and click **Delete.**

3. In Excel, copy only the worksheet data and switch to Word.

4. Click **Edit, Paste Special,** and select **Microsoft Excel Worksheet Object.** Click **OK.**

5. Double-click the embedded worksheet.

6. Format the values in the ranges **B4:B5** and **C8:C10** for currency.

7. Click on the document page to leave Excel Edit mode. (Notice the edits.)

8. Switch to **7.1toa.xls** and notice that the source file did not change.

9. Save the files. Close both files.

TRY *it* **OUT**

1. Open **7.1tobwd.doc** from the Data CD.

2. In the space under the first paragraph, click the **Microsoft Excel Worksheet** button.

3. Select an Excel worksheet that is four cells wide by five cells high.

4. Enter the following data:

REIMBURSEMENT CALCULATION			
Dental bill	$350		
First	100	100%	$100.00
101-500	250	80%	
Reimbursement			

5. Enter a formula in **Cell D4** to calculate 80% of 250.

6. Enter a formula in **Cell D5** to add the contents of the range **D3:D4.**

7. Click the Word document page.

8. Save and close the file.

REHEARSAL

TASK 1

 GOAL
To create a benefits statement and correspondence that include worksheets and a chart

SETTING THE STAGE/WRAPUP

Margins:	1" left and right
Start line:	At 2.5"
File names:	7.1benefits.doc
	7.1rates.xls
	7.1calcmemo.doc

WHAT YOU NEED TO KNOW

> New employees are often given an employee manual containing company procedures, policies, and benefits. A *benefits statement* generally describes insurance and other benefit plans available to employees. The employer may provide the benefits; however, in most cases the employee pays a weekly or monthly premium. Employees get a group rate and pay lower premiums than they would for private insurance coverage.

> When you integrate Excel worksheets and charts into a Word document, you can size the data and you can move the margins to align worksheets to the center of the page.

> In this Rehearsal activity, you will integrate worksheets and charts from an Excel workbook to enhance the Sutton Investment Group Benefits Program, which is a Word document.

DIRECTIONS

1. Open **7.1benefits.doc** and **7.1rates.xls** from the Data CD in the appropriate application.

2. On Page 4 of the Benefits Program, at the end of the Dental section, enter the text below, as illustrated on the facing page:
   Dental Plan Rates and Benefits

3. Use Format Painter to copy the format from the paragraph headers to the new text.

4. Switch to the worksheet to copy the data on the Dental sheet and paste it to the Benefits Program.

5. Move the margin manually so that the worksheet is centered horizontally.

6. Use Find and Replace to change the word "Covered" to:
   100%

7. Switch to the Education sheet in the Excel workbook.

8. Copy the worksheet in the range **A1:G22** and use Paste Special to embed the data on Page 6 of the Benefits Program, the last page.

9. Double-click the worksheet in the Word document and edit the title as illustrated; use **Forte** font, **18 point.**

10. Change the annual contribution by employee to $1,200, as illustrated. (Notice the changes in the growth data.)

11. Switch to the Education sheet in the Excel workbook.

12. Select the chart, and use Copy and Paste Special to embed the chart under the worksheet on the last page of the Benefits Program.

13. Print a copy of the Benefits Program.

14. Save both files. Close both files.

Continued on page 172

Page 1

Introduction

THE SUTTON INVESTMENT GROUP BENEFITS PROGRAM

YOUR ENROLLMENT KIT

This enrollment kit provides you with the information you will need to enroll for the Sutton Investment Group Benefits Program. Here are all the pieces that make up your Benefits enrollment kit:

✓ Booklets about all the benefit plans available through this program;

✓ Your personalized enrollment worksheet; and

This general information booklet describing how Benefits works, eligibility rules, tax information, and how to enroll over the telephone through the Sutton Investment Group Benefits Enrollment Line.

THE BENEFITS OF THE SUTTON INVESTMENT GROUP BENEFITS PROGRAM

The Benefits program offers six major categories of benefits coverage. Within each category are several different benefit options. You select the option(s) from each category that you believe are right for you. The categories of coverage, discussed in detail in the booklets in the enrollment kit are:

✓ Medical

✓ Dental

✓ Life Insurance

✓ Education Incentive Plan

✓ Vision Care

✓ Property and Casualty Insurance

WHO IS ELIGIBLE FOR BENEFITS?

Regular employees on the domestic payroll of Sutton Investment Group, who have completed at least one calendar month of service as a regular employee and

▲*Sutton Investment Group*▲

Page 1

Page 2

who work at least 20 hours each week are eligible to participate in the benefit options available through Sutton Investment Group Benefits.

You can also enroll your eligible dependents for Medical, Dental and Life Insurance coverage. For Sutton Investment Group Benefits, your eligible dependents are your:

✓ Spouse, and

✓ Unmarried children who are under age 19 (or age 23 if they are full-time students).

Children include natural and legally adopted children, stepchildren living in your home and any other child who is supported solely by you and living in your home. Coverage may be continued beyond age 23 under certain circumstances.

Dependents are not eligible for any benefits under the Benefits Program if they are in military service and may not be eligible if they live permanently outside the United States and Canada.

▲*Sutton Investment Group*▲

Page 2

Page 3

Dental

As you read this booklet describing your dental coverage options through the Sutton Investment Group Benefits Program, you should ask yourself when you want from your dental coverage:

1. Do you want the freedom to choose any dentist regardless of cost?

2. Do you want to have lower costs in exchange for receiving dental care from a limited selection of dentists?

3. Would you rather have no dental coverage at all?

WHO IS ELIGIBLE FOR DENTAL BENEFITS?

Regular employees on the domestic payroll of Sutton Investment Group, who have completed at least one calendar month of service as a regular employee and who work at least 20 hours each week are eligible to participate in the benefit options available through Sutton Investment Group Benefits.

You can also enroll your eligible dependents for Medical, Dental and Life Insurance coverage. For Sutton Investment Group Benefits, your eligible dependents are your:

✓ Spouse, and
✓ Unmarried children who are under age 19 (or age 23 if they are full-time students).

Children include natural and legally adopted children, stepchildren living in your home and any other child who is supported solely by you and living in your home. Coverage may be continued beyond age 23 under certain circumstances.

Dependents are not eligible for any benefits under the Benefits Program if they are in military service and may not be eligible if they live permanently outside the United States and Canada.

TRADITIONAL DENTAL PLAN

If you answered, "yes" to the first question, you may want to elect the Traditional Dental Plan. Under the Traditional Dental Plan, you have the freedom to choose any licensed dentist. You also have the option of utilizing the Preferred Dentist Program offered with the Traditional Dental Plan to help control Plan expenses and help lower your out-of-pocket costs.

▲*Sutton Investment Group*▲

Page 3

Page 4

PLEASE NOTE THE FOLLOWING:

This brochure is not a complete description of the Dental Plan offered through Sutton Investment Group Benefits Program. This is only a summary and is not a substitute for the official Plan documents.

The provisions of the official Plan documents and of applicable law will govern in the event of any inconsistency between those provisions and the provisions of this brochure.

Dental Plan Rates and Benefits

Sutton Investment Group
Dental Plan Monthly Premium

Type of Coverage	Employee	Each Dependent
Traditional Dental Plan	27	22
Preferred Dentist Plan	20	15

Dental Plan Benefits

Service		
Examination	100%	
X-Rays	100%	
Cleaning	100%	
Restorative		80%
Endodontists	75%	
Oral surgeons		75%
Periodontists	60%	
Orthodontics	50%	

▲*Sutton Investment Group*▲

Page 4

15. Open **7.1calcmemo.doc** from the Data CD, as shown on the facing page.

16. Insert a worksheet two lines below the last line of the memo and enter the following data:

	Billed	Coverage Payment
Exam	$80	100%
X-Rays	$120	100%
Oral Surgeon	$950	75%
Reimbursement		

17. Calculate the payment for each item and the total reimbursement.

18. Print a copy of the letter.

19 Save the file **7.1calcmemo.doc.** Close the file.

5

Education
••

EDUCATION INCENTIVE PLAN

The Sutton Investment Group's Benefits Program will help you pay for your children's education. The Education Incentive Plan helps you plan ahead for the day tuition bills begin to arrive.

WHO IS ELIGIBLE FOR EDUCATION BENEFITS?

Regular employees on the domestic payroll of Sutton Investment Group, who have completed at least one calendar month of service as a regular employee and who work at least 20 hours each week are eligible to participate in the benefit options available through Sutton Investment Group Benefits.

The Education Incentive Plan is designed to help you save from $5,000 to $40,000 (over a five-to-fifteen year period) toward the education costs you anticipate for each of your dependent children. You may choose to set aside an amount needed to reach your savings goal for one or more dependent children in the selected time period as follows:

✓ **The maximum goal is $40,000 per child; the minimum is $5,000.**

✓ **You may have a maximum of four plan accounts per child.**

✓ **The Company contributes 15% of the amount of your payroll deduction toward Education Benefits.**

The funds will accumulate over a period of five to fifteen years, but not beyond your child's 25th birthday. When a plan reaches the level of money you desire, the funds are paid to you. You can request that the account be cancelled and paid out earlier.

HOW TO GET THE MOST OUT OF THE EDUCATION PLAN

The matching contributions from Sutton Investment Group are reported as ordinary income on your W-2 tax form. That means that any money you earn through our investment, are subject to taxes until all the proceeds are paid out to you.

Your savings and the company matching contributions are invested in stocks and bonds. The full amount of your account will automatically be paid to you upon cancellation of this plan.

▲*Sutton Investment Group*▲

Page 5

6

▲*Sutton Investment Group*▲
Education Plan Sample Growth Chart

Year	Contribution by Employee	Contribution by Sutton	6% Growth*	Annual Total	Cumulative Total
1	1,200.00	180.00	82.80	1,462.80	1,462.80
2	1,200.00	180.00	170.57	1,550.57	3,013.37
3	1,200.00	180.00	263.60	1,643.60	4,656.97
4	1,200.00	180.00	362.22	1,742.22	6,399.19
5	1,200.00	180.00	466.75	1,846.75	8,245.94
6	1,200.00	180.00	577.56	1,957.56	10,203.50
7	1,200.00	180.00	695.01	2,075.01	12,278.51
8	1,200.00	180.00	819.51	2,199.51	14,478.02
9	1,200.00	180.00	951.48	2,331.48	16,809.50
10	1,200.00	180.00	1,091.37	2,471.37	19,280.87
	12,000.00	1,800.00	5,480.87	19,280.87	96,828.65

*Education Plan funds are invested in four mutual funds. The projected growth rate of 6% is a conservative estimate that may be exceeded or not met by the funds. The funds have averaged a 12.5% growth rate for the last five years, however, past performance is no guarantee of future results.

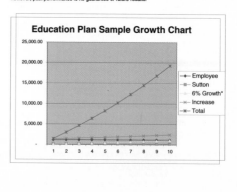

Education Plan Sample Growth Chart

▲*Sutton Investment Group*▲

Page 6

▲*Sutton Investment Group*▲

MEMORANDUM

To: Michael Jasko, Brokerage Department

From: Lynn Goodwin, Human Resources

Date: November 15, 2002

Re: Dental coverage

In response to your call regarding the coverage for your dental bills listed below, please note the calculations that will be applied by our Dental Plan administrators. You should be receiving a check shortly.

Dental bill as per your telephone call:
Exam	$ 80
X-Rays	$120
Oral Surgeon	$950

← Insert worksheet here

Open Office Files from Multiple Applications
1. Start the first application.
2. Open the file.
3. Click **Start, Open Office Document.**
4. Click the file to open. The second application opens automatically.

Switch Between Applications and Files
• Click the **File** button.

Copy Files Between Applications
1. In the first application, select the data you want to copy.
2. Click the **Copy** button.
3. Click the **File** button to switch between files and applications.
4. Place the insertion point in the location you want.
5. Click the **Paste** button.

Embed a Worksheet/Chart in a Word Document
1. In Excel, select the worksheet/chart you want to embed.
2. Click the **Copy** button.

3. Click the **File** button to switch between files and applications.
4. Place the insertion point in the location you want.
5. Click **Edit, Paste Special.**
6. Click **Microsoft Excel Worksheet Object** or **Microsoft Excel Chart Object.**
7. Click **OK.**

Edit an Embedded Worksheet/Chart
• Double-click worksheet/chart to work in Excel mode.

TRYOUT

▶

TASK 2

GOAL

To practice using the following skill sets:
✴ Link data between applications
  ✴ Edit a linked object
✴ Display and use the Web toolbar
  ✴ Paste Web data
✴ Create and respond to discussion comments

WHAT YOU NEED TO KNOW

Link Data Between Applications

> In Lesson 5, you used the Paste Link feature to link data between different workbooks or worksheets. When working with different applications, you can use paste link to create a *linked file* so that if the source data changes, it will change in the destination document as well. The Link feature differs from embedding and copying, because a link is a shortcut to the source file; therefore, the data is not actually located in the destination file.

> There are three advantages to linking integrated data:

- When you double-click a linked Excel worksheet in a Word destination file, you are brought into Excel to make edits and view formulas.

- Any change you make to the worksheet in the source or destination documents appears in both places.

- The destination file is smaller in size than a copied or embedded file because the data remains stored in the source file.

TRY*it*OUT

1. Open **7.2towd.doc** and **7.2to.xls** from the Data CD in the appropriate application.

2. On **7.2to,** the worksheet, select and copy the data in the range **A1:D9.**

3. Switch to **7.2towd,** the document, and place the insertion point several lines below the last line of text.

4. Click **Edit, Paste Special,** and click **Microsoft Excel Worksheet Object.**

5. Click **Paste Link** and **OK.** (The worksheet is linked to the document.)

6. Switch to the worksheet and select and copy the chart.

7. Place the insertion point several lines below the linked worksheet.

8. Click **Edit, Paste Special,** and click **Microsoft Excel Chart Object.**

9. Click **Paste Link** and **OK.** (The chart is linked to the document.)

10. Do not close the file.

> To paste link data between applications, copy the data from the source file, switch to the destination file, click Edit, Paste Special, select the object type, and the Paste Link button from the dialog box, as shown in Figure 7.9. You can use this method to link worksheet or chart data to another application.

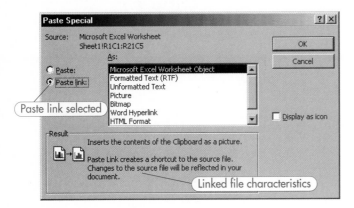

Figure 7.9 Paste Special dialog box with paste link selected

Edit a Linked Object

> To edit a linked Excel object in a destination file, double-click the object. You will be in Excel, in the source file, and able to use Excel menus to make changes. All changes you make are saved to the original source file and, therefore, automatically update in both locations.

> If you edit information in the source file, it also automatically updates in the linked location.

TRY it OUT

1. Continue to work in **7.2towd.doc** and **7.2to.xls**.

2. In **7.2towd.doc**, double-click the worksheet data.

3. In Excel mode, select the graphic and delete it.

4. Switch to the Word document, using the taskbar button and notice the edit.

5. Switch to the Excel workbook and change the value in **Cell B9** to 6.54%, a positive value. Notice the change in the chart.

6. Switch to the Word document and notice the updates.

7. Save both files. Close both files.

Display and Use the Web Toolbar

> The Internet provides access to countless Web sites, many of which contain information you can use to enhance your presentation, provide documentation, or provide current data for worksheets and other Office applications.

> Every Office application has a Web toolbar that allows you to use Internet features seamlessly with your application. Click View, Toolbars, and Web to display the toolbar, as shown in Figure 7.10. You must have an Internet Service Provider (ISP) to use the Web toolbar.

Figure 7.10 Web toolbar

Paste Web Data

> You can copy Web data using Edit, Copy, while in the Web browser. Sometimes you must copy an entire block of data even though you only need part of it. When you switch back to Excel, you can click Paste and use the Paste Options button to select one of three options: Keep Source Formatting, Match Destination Formatting, or Create Refreshable Web Query, as shown in Figure 7.11.

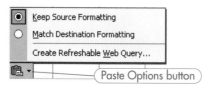

Figure 7.11 Paste options for Web paste

T R Y *it* O U T

1. Open **7.2toa.xls** from the Data CD.

2. Click **View, Toolbars,** and **Web.**

3. Click the **Search the Web** button on the Web toolbar. (Your Internet connection is established, and you are shown a selection of search engines.)

4. You can search for "currency conversion" or
   a. Switch back to Excel.

   b. In the address box of the Web toolbar, enter:
      finance.yahoo.com/m3

5. View the currency conversion Web site.

6. Read the next paragraph and continue to work on this Web site.

T R Y *it* O U T

1. Continue to work in **7.2toa.xls** and on a currency conversion Web site or on finance.yahoo.com/m3

2. On the Web site, select the table provided, click **Edit, Copy,** or right-click and click **Copy.**

3. Switch to Excel and paste the table to the bottom of the workbook.

4. Click the **Paste Options** button on the screen and click **Match Destination Formatting.**

5. Move the data from the US$ column (B) to the appropriate currency, as listed on the worksheet.

6. Include today's date in **Cell D4.**

7. Delete the currency table from the bottom of the worksheet.

8. Save the file. Close the file.

Create and Respond to Discussion Comments

> Another way to integrate data is to have several people collaborate in creating a workbook or document. The Discussions feature lets a group of reviewers collaborate online by attaching comments to a Web page or any document that can be opened with a browser. The discussion comments and messages are stored in a database on a discussion server in a file where replies are nested under the original remarks. You can then incorporate changes to your worksheet based on the feedback you receive.

> Previously, if a group had to comment on a file, the originator of the file had to consolidate comments on various copies of the file. The advantage of this feature is that all the remarks are in one online file and are easily implemented. Each collaborator can view the discussion comments at any time from his or her computer.

> To use this feature, you must save the worksheet as a Web page (so that you open it in a browser), you must have an Internet connection, and your windows NT system administrator must create a Discussion Server during the installation of Office Server Extensions.

> If you do not have a Discussion Server to specify for this feature, you cannot practice using it. Figure 7.12 shows the dialog box in which to specify a server.

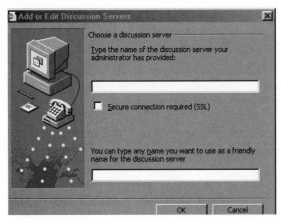

Figure 7.12 Add or Edit Discussions Servers dialog box

> You can start a discussion from your browser or from your Office application. Most browsers have a Discuss feature, as shown on the Internet Explorer toolbar in Figure 7.13.

Figure 7.13 Browser toolbar, Discuss button

> When you click the Discuss button, the Discussion toolbar appears in the browser, as shown in Figure 7.14. (If the Add or Edit Discussions dialog box opens, select a discussion server).

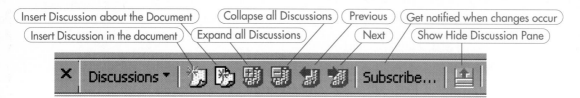

Figure 7.14 Discussions toolbar in Internet Explorer

> Open the Web page on which you want to comment. On the Discussions toolbar that appears, click the Insert Discussion in Document button. Notice that there are two insert buttons, the Insert Discussion *in* the Document button and Insert Discussion *about* the Document button. The Insert Discussion about the Document button creates a general comment about the document. The Insert Discussion in the Document button lets you insert comments at specific locations in the document. A discussion insertion icon (⬚) appears at the end of every paragraph or table cell on your Web page. Click the icon at the appropriate location, enter a name for the discussion subject, and enter your comments. Click OK and your discussion text appears below the icon.

> If the Discuss feature is not present on your browser toolbar, you can open a discussion in Excel by clicking Tools, Online Collaboration, and Web Discussions. The Discussions toolbar appears, as shown in Figure 7.15. (If the Add or Edit Discussions dialog box opens, select a Discussion Server.)

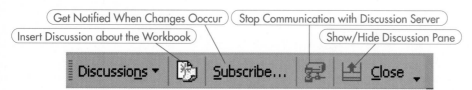

Figure 7.15 Discussions toolbar in Excel

> To reply to a discussion remark that appears on a Web page, go to the Web page that contains the remark and click the Discuss button. Click the Show/Hide Discussion button next to the text you want to respond to, and click the Reply button on the Discussions toolbar. Enter your reply. You can edit or delete only those discussion comments that you have written; you can reply, however, to any comment.

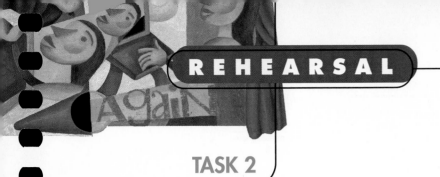

REHEARSAL

GOAL
To create a letter with a worksheet that includes current portfolio values

TASK 2

SETTING THE STAGE/WRAPUP

Margins: Default

Start line: At 1"

File names: 7.2stocks.xls
7.2broker.doc

WHAT YOU NEED TO KNOW

> Investment or brokerage firms can manage your stock or equity holdings. Most brokerage firms now also have online brokerage Web sites so that you can buy or sell stocks directly in your account.

> Stocks represent your ownership certificates in publicly traded companies. The current prices of stocks vary with the economy and market conditions, and can be obtained on your investment firm's Web site or on other "quote" sites.

> In this Rehearsal activity, you will update James Calarco's portfolio worksheet with current stock prices from the Internet. You will integrate the worksheet into a letter to the Sutton Investment Group, stating his interest in transferring his account.

▼ DIRECTIONS

1. Open **7.2stocks.xls** from the Data CD and view the names and symbols of the stocks in the portfolio.

2. Display the Web toolbar and search for a site that shows stock quotes, or go to: www.stockquotes.com.

3. Use the stock symbol for each stock on the worksheet and look up the current market price.

4. Copy and paste the prices to the Excel worksheet, matching the destination format.

5. Disconnect your Internet connection.

6. Enter a formula, multiplying market price by shares owned, to find the market value of the shares in **Column G,** as illustrated on the next page.

7. Find the total market value.

8. Correct formatting, if necessary.

9. Open **7.2broker.doc** from the Data CD.

10. Copy and paste link the Excel worksheet from **7.2stocks.xls** to the Word letter in the second paragraph, as illustrated on the next page.

11. Switch back to the Excel worksheet and check the formula for the cost total in **Column E.**

12. Edit and correct the formula.

13. Switch back to the Word document to check if the changes updated to the linked file.

14. Print a copy of the letter.

15. Save both files. Close both files.

JAMES CALARCO
Investment Record

COMPANY NAME	SYMBOL	SHARES	DATE BOUGHT	COST	MARKET PRICE	MARKET VALUE
Nike Inc	NKE	300	03/09/97	20,550.00		
General Electric	GE	200	06/06/98	6,567.15		
ATT	T	200	01/05/99	8,656.45		
Ford Motor Co	F	100	02/18/01	2,760.00		
Intel	INTC	100	07/07/00	6,966.00		
TOTALS				24,949.60		

Find current market prices for stocks on the Internet

Enter formulas to find total market value for each stock

Calculate total

James Calarco
460 West End Avenue
New York, NY 10023
Phone: 212-555-3432

March 5, 2002

Mr. Marcus Roxbury
Sutton Investment Group
34562 Corona Street
Los Angeles, CA 90001

Dear Mr. Roxbury:

As we discussed, I am interested in transferring my portfolio of investments to your firm. I am dissatisfied with my current brokerage firm and, after our telephone conversation and my visit, I feel that your company can provide me with the service I require.

I am providing a list of my investments with the current market value below:

Please send me the necessary forms. I look forward to hearing from you.

Paste link worksheet here

Sincerely yours,

James Calarco

Cues for Reference

View Web Toolbar
- Click **View, Toolbars,** and **Web.**

Paste Link Between Applications
1. Open files you want to link.
2. In source file, select data to link.
3. Click the **Copy** button.
4. Switch to desination file.
5. Click **Edit, Paste Special.**

6. Click **Paste Link** and select object to link.
7. Click **OK.**

Edit a Linked File
- Edit data in either the source or destination files. (The data will change in both locations.)

Copy and Paste from the Web
1. Locate data you need from Web site.

2. Select data.
3. Click **Edit, Copy,** or right-click and click **Copy** button.
4. Switch back to Excel.
5. Click **Paste** button.
6. Click **Paste Options** list arrow.
7. Select appropriate Paste option.

PERFORMANCE

SETTING THE STAGE/WRAPUP

Act I File names:　7p1.travel guide.doc
　　　　　　　　　7p1.tips.doc
　　　　　　　　　7p1.euro.xls

Act II File names:　7p2.income.xls
　　　　　　　　　7p2.quarterly.doc

WHAT YOU NEED TO KNOW

Act I

You work in the Marketing Department of the Air Land Sea Travel Group. Your company has developed Travel Guide 2003, a handbook that contains practical information for the traveler. Your supervisor would like to add several pages on currency conversion tips, including information about the euro and the latest exchange rate for the U.S. dollar to the euro.

Follow these guidelines:

✶ Open 7p1.tips.doc, 7p1.euro.xls, and 7p1.travel guide.doc from the Data CD.

✶ In 7p1.tips.doc:

　✶ Use Clips Online to insert a clip art object in the first paragraph representing "foreign currencies."

　✶ Integrate the worksheet data from 7p1.euro.xls into the appropriate location.

　✶ Add a sentence stating the current conversion rate of the U.S. dollar to the euro. Use the Internet to find the current rate. You can search for currency conversion or look at the www.xe.com Web site.

✶ Select the entire document and copy and paste it to 7p1.travel guide.doc, before the References page.

✶ In 7p1.travel guide.doc, check that the new information copied correctly and that the pagination is appropriate.

✶ Save all files and print a copy of the new guide.

Act II

You work in the Accounting Department of the Air Land Sea Travel Group. Your department has developed an income workbook for the second quarter consisting of income statements for all offices, a consolidated income statement, an income analysis, and two charts. The chief financial officer, Tyler Willem, has prepared a document explaining the quarterly results and would like the worksheet data integrated into one report. The report will be sent electronically to all managers, officers, and interested parties, and a printed copy will be kept on file.

Follow these guidelines:

✴ Open **7p2.income.xls** and **7p2.quarterly.doc** from the Data CD.

✴ Link the worksheets and chart data where appropriate, as indicated in the document.

  ✴ Remove the parenthetical insert instructions from the document.

  ✴ Remove the text box from the Net Income pie chart.

  ✴ Create a hyperlink with appropriate text to the worksheet.

  ✴ Adjust the size of the objects so that the pages do not have large blank areas, and center the objects horizontally on the page.

✴ Research the current outlook for the travel industry on the Internet. Summarize your findings in several sentences. (If you quote or copy data from a Web site, be sure to indicate your source.)

✴ Write an e-mail, addressed to managers and officers, that includes the following:

  ✴ Announce that the quarterly report and income data are attached.

  ✴ Report on the current outlook for the travel industry, as per your research.

  ✴ Attach the quarterly report and income files to the e-mail.

✴ Optional: If you have a Web server using the Microsoft Office Server Extension feature with a Discussions folder, save the report to the Web server and have various students in the class discuss the report, your presentation, the results for the quarter, etc. Incorporate any suggestions into your final report.

✴ Print a copy of the quarterly report. Save and close all files.

ENCORE

Identify the letter of the choice that best completes the statement or answers the question.

1. When you integrate data:
   A. The source file provides the data.
   B. You combine more than one application's data.
   C. The destination file receives the data.
   D. All of the above
   E. A and C

2. You can switch between open applications by using the:
   A. Menu.
   B. Status bar.
   C. Taskbar.
   D. Windows menu.
   E. A and C

3. When you copy and paste data from one application to another:
   A. It links to the source file.
   B. It has no connection to the source file.
   C. You can edit the data.
   D. None of the above
   E. B and C

4. To use the drag and drop technique to copy and paste data between applications:
   A. Have both files open.
   B. Use the taskbar shortcut menu to display both files.
   C. Select the data to copy while pressing and holding the Ctrl key.
   D. All of the above
   E. None of the above

5. An embedded file:
   A. Is an object that becomes part of the file.
   B. Can be double-clicked to edit it.
   C. Is edited in the source application.
   D. All of the above
   E. A and B

6. A linked file:
   A. Is a shortcut to the source file.
   B. Can be double-clicked to edit it.
   C. Allows changes to update in the source and destination files.
   D. All of the above
   E. A and C

7. You can insert a worksheet in a Word document by using:
   A. Copy and Paste.
   B. Copy and Paste Special.
   C. Insert, Object.
   D. Microsoft Excel Worksheet button.
   E. All of the above

8. The Web toolbar is:
   A. Your link to the Internet.
   B. Available in all Office applications.
   C. Always displayed by default in all applications.
   D. All of the above
   E. A and B

9. You can integrate information from the Internet into your document by:
   A. Clicking the Integrate button.
   B. Copying and pasting the information.
   C. Double-clicking the data.
   D. All of the above
   E. None of the above

10. The Discussions feature:
   A. Provides an opportunity for collaboration.
   B. Requires a Web server.
   C. Allows several people to discuss a Web page.
   E. All of the above
   D. None of the above

TRUE/FALSE

Circle the **T** if the statement is true or **F** if the statement is false.

T F 1. The destination file is the file that provides the information you will integrate into another file.

T F 2. You integrate data from the source file to the destination file.

T F 3. You can edit data that was copied and pasted from one application to another.

T F 4. Editing an embedded file will change both the source and destination files.

T F 5. If you wish to edit integrated data in its source application, you must embed or link the file.

T F 6. You cannot embed, link, or copy a chart into a destination file.

T F 7. When you click an action button on the Web toolbar, you connect to your Internet Service Provider (ISP).

T F 8. Linked data is really just a shortcut to the source file.

T F 9. Destination files that have linked data need more memory than those with embedded data.

T F 10. You can display the Discussions toolbar in your browser.

PERFORMING WITH EXCEL
ADVANCED UNIT

LESSON 8

Budgets and Templates

In this lesson, you will learn to use Excel features to combine information across worksheets and workbooks. You will also learn to create and edit a workbook template to display a budget.

Upon completion of this lesson, you should have mastered the following skill sets:

✴ Create a workspace consisting of two or more workbooks M
✴ Consolidate data from two or more worksheets M
✴ Link consolidated data
✴ Create a workbook template M
✴ Create a new workbook based on a user-created template M
✴ Edit a workbook template M

Terms
MOUS-related
> Workspace
> Data consolidation
> Template

Document-related
> Consolidated budget
> Quarterly budget

T R Y O U T

GOAL

To practice using the following skill sets:

✴ Create a workspace consisting of two or more workbooks Ⓜ

✴ Consolidate data from two or more worksheets Ⓜ

✴ Link consolidated data

TASK 1

WHAT YOU NEED TO KNOW

About Advanced Excel

> Excel is a powerful spreadsheet tool that you can use to analyze, chart, and manage data for personal, business, and financial purposes. Using Excel, you can produce worksheets, charts, databases, and you can publish data to the Web.

> Advanced Excel allows you to build on your basic knowledge of Excel in order to conduct analyses of financial data, manage and share data with other users, and customize records and reports.

> As discussed in Introductory Excel, the default Excel screen shows the most frequently used toolbar buttons from the Standard and Formatting toolbars on one row. To correlate your computer screen with the text figures, display both toolbars fully, as shown in Figure 8.1, by clicking the Toolbar Options arrow and selecting the Show Buttons on Two Rows option.

Figure 8.1 Standard and Formatting toolbars displayed on two rows

Create a Workspace Consisting of Two or More Workbooks

> A convenient way to access two or more workbooks on the same screen is to create a workspace. A *workspace* is a shared location in which you store several workbooks.

> To create a workspace, first open each workbook. Size and place the workbooks so that they are displayed in the position you want.

> Click File, Save Workspace, as shown in Figure 8.2.

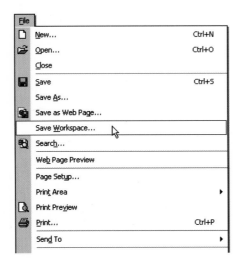

Figure 8.2 Save Workspace

> Enter the name of the workspace in the Save Workspace dialog box.

Note: Workspaces have .xlw as the file extension.

> You can close each workbook individually, or you can press the Shift key while you click File, Close All to close them simultaneously.

> The next time you open the workspace, all of the workbooks in it are available on your screen. They appear in the same format in which you saved them. A workspace file is identified in the Open dialog box by the file type, Microsoft Excel Workspace , and by an enhanced file icon.

> Save any changes that you make to the individual workbooks.

T R Y *i t* **O U T**

1. Open **8.1BUDGET1** from the Data CD.

2. Open **8.1BUDGET2** from the Data CD.

3. Arrange the files on your screen by clicking **Window, Arrange.** Select **Cascade.**

4. Click **File, Save Workspace.** Name the workspace: **8.1FCRBudgets**

5. Select a location in which to save the workspace. Click **Save.**

6. Press the **Shift** key and click **File, Close All.**

7. Open the workspace by clicking **File, Open,** and click the name of the workspace. Keep it open.

8. Click **Window** on the menu bar. Then click **Arrange, Vertical.** Click **OK.**

9. Click **File, Save Workspace** and accept the same workspace file name.

10. Press the **Shift** key and click **File, Close All** to close both files.

11. Click **File, Open,** and select the name of the workspace. Click **Open.**

12. Close the workspace.

Consolidate Data from Two or More Worksheets

> *Data consolidation* is a way to combine the information from different workbooks or worksheets and store it in another workbook or worksheet. This function is useful when different departments or companies have budgets, financial statements, or other business documents that contain data that they need to combine or summarize.

> If you are consolidating data from different workbooks, you can make the workbooks more accessible and easier to work on by creating a workspace that contains them.

> To consolidate data, open all workbooks with the data you want to consolidate. If you are combining data from several worksheets that are contained in one workbook, open that file.

> Create a new workbook (or worksheet) that contains the labels for the consolidated data. You can copy and paste them from one of the worksheets to the consolidated worksheet or enter them manually. Then select a range for the destination of the consolidated numeric data.

Note: If you select the top left cell of the consolidation table range, the data is filled in starting from that location.

> Click Data, Consolidate. The Consolidate dialog box opens, as shown in Figure 8.3.

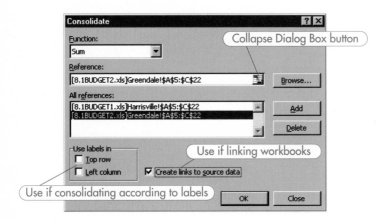

Figure 8.3 Consolidate dialog box

1. Open **8.1BUDGET1** and **8.1BUDGET2** from the Data CD. (Or you can open the workspace **8.1FCRBudgets** that you created in the previous Try it Out.)

2. Click **File, New,** and select **Blank workbook** in the task pane.

3. Go back to the file **8.1BUDGET1** and select the range **A5:A21.**

4. Copy and paste the information in these cells to the blank workbook, starting at **Cell A5.**

5. Click **Cell C6** in the blank workbook.

6. Click **Data, Consolidate.**

7. In the Consolidate dialog box, leave the Function as **SUM.**

8. Click the **Collapse Dialog Box** button.

9. Go to the file **8.1BUDGET1** and select the range **C6:C21.**

10. Click the **Expand Dialog Box**  button. Click **Add.**

11. Repeat Steps 8, 9, and 10 for the **8.1BUDGET2** file.

12. Do not click OK or close the Consolidate dialog box.

> The Function drop–down list contains several operations including Sum, Count, Product, and statistical functions such as Average. Select the function from the list that should be applied during the consolidation process. To designate the range of the data you want to consolidate, you can enter the cell references in the Reference box. Or, you can click the Collapse Dialog Box button (see Figure 8.3), then go to the first worksheet and select the cells containing the data you want to consolidate. When you click the Expand Dialog Box button, as shown in Figure 8.4, you see the selected range in the Reference box. Click Add.

Figure 8.4 Consolidate-Reference box

> Continue to select all of the data you want to combine, moving across worksheets or workbooks and clicking Add for each range of cells you select. When you have completed the data selection, the All references box in the Consolidate dialog box lists the data that you combined. If there are any errors in this list, select the incorrect reference and click Delete.

Link Consolidated Data

> If you check the box Create links to source data, any changes you make in an original data file are updated in the consolidation table.

> The new workbook with consolidated data has a series of plus signs in the left column, labeled Column 1, as shown in Figure 8.5. These plus signs indicate data you have combined. Clicking a plus sign gives you the separate elements that constitute the consolidated data. Notice the details that appear for Insurance expense in Cells C17 and C18 and the consolidated Insurance value in Cell C19. Clicking the minus sign consolidates that data again. Notice the Columns 1 and 2 buttons above the plus signs. If you click the Column 2 button at the top left of the worksheet, all details for each item appear. You can return to the consolidated sheet by clicking Column 1.

Figure 8.5 Consolidated worksheet

> It is easiest to consolidate data if you arrange information in each of the worksheets in the same format. If you arrange information in a different layout on each worksheet, you can consolidate data according to its labels. If you check the boxes Top row and Left column in the Consolidate dialog box, Excel can match up the data according to the labels.

Note: Continue to work in the Consolidate dialog box from the previous Try it Out, which combines data from 8.1BUDGET1 and 8.1BUDGET2, or in workspace 8.1FCRBudgets.

1. Check the box **Create links to source data.**

2. Click **OK.**

3. Copy the headings in **Rows 1:3** from the **8.1BUDGET2** worksheet to the top of the new worksheet. Change **Row 2** to:
   Budget: Consolidated

4. Name the blank workbook **8.1FCRCONSL** and save it. Close the **8.1BUDGET2** file. Leave **8.1FCRCONSL** and **8.1BUDGET1** open.

5. Click **Window, Arrange, Vertical,** and **OK** so that **8.1FCRCONSL** and **8.1BUDGET1** are both displayed on the screen.

6. Go to **8.1BUDGET1** and change the value in **Cell C9** to:
   7000

7. Click outside **Cell C9** and notice what happens to the Advertising line in the **8.1FCRCONSL** file. Undo the change.

8. In the **8.1FCRCONSL** file, click the **Plus sign** to the left of Net Sales.

9. Click the **Minus sign** to the left of Net Sales.

10. Close both files.

REHEARSAL

TASK 1

SETTING THE STAGE/WRAPUP

File names: 8.1Sutton1
8.1Sutton2
8.1CBws
8.1SuttonCB

WHAT YOU NEED TO KNOW

> Consolidated financial statements combine corresponding financial information from two or more sources. These can be separate departments within a company or within affiliated companies owned by a larger corporation. A *consolidated budget* combines the planned or actual income and expenses from several departments or companies.

> A *quarterly budget* is prepared four times a year to reflect income and expense activity up to the end of each three-month period. These statements are usually dated the last day of March, June, September, and December. Quarterly budgets are often used to compare proposed income and expenditures with actual income and expenditures.

> In this Rehearsal activity, you will create a consolidated quarterly budget to show the accumulated activity for two departments that are part of the Sutton Investment Group. You combine departmental data for the proposed and actual budgets for the second quarter.

DIRECTIONS

1. Open **8.1Sutton1** and **8.1Sutton2** from the Data CD.

2. Enter formulas to calculate the Total Expenses and the Net Income for the Budget and Actual columns on both worksheets, as shown in Illustration A on the next page.

3. Size and position the two files according to your preference.

4. Create a shared workspace for these two files.

5. Save the workspace as **8.1CBws** and, when prompted, save **8.1Sutton1** and **8.1Sutton2**.

6. Copy the labels for each budget line from one of the files to a new workbook.

7. Consolidate the data from each of the two departments for the columns labeled Budget and Actual, as shown in Illustration B on the next page.

8. Enter and format titles on the new sheet to indicate it is a consolidated budget for the second quarter. Include the company name, report title, and quarter ending date.

9. Print a copy of the consolidated budget.

10. Save the file as **8.1SuttonCB** and close it.

Illustration A

	A	B	C	D	E	F	G
1	**Sutton Investment Group**						
2		Mutual Funds Division					
3		For Quarter Ended June 30, 2002					
4			Budget	Actual			
5	Revenue						
6	Net Sales/Fees		120,000	132,450			
7							
8	Expenses:						
9	Advertising		4,500	3,475			
10	Depreciation	7,500		7,500			
11	Interest		13,000	13,909			
12	Miscellaneous Expenses		600	625			
13	Rent		10,500	10,500			
14	Salaries/Commissions	60,000		65,090			
15	Supplies	2,300		2,532			
16	Travel		5,000	5,200			
17	Total Expenses						
18							
19	Net Income						
20							

> Enter formulas to calculate Total Expenses and Net Income on both Division worksheets

Illustration A

Illustration B

	A	B	C	D	E	F	G
1	**Sutton Investment Group**						
2		Consolidated Budget					
3		For Quarter Ended June 30, 2002					
4			Budget	Actual			
5	Revenue						
8	Net Sales/Fees						
9							
10	**Expenses:**						
13	Advertising						
16	Depreciation						
19	Miscellaneous Expenses						
22	Salaries/Commissions						
25	Supplies						
28	Travel						
31	Total Expenses						
32							
35	Net Income						
36							
37							
38							
39							

> Add correct label for Consolidated Budget statement

> Use data consolidation to obtain all of the sums

> Copy and paste labels from one of the Division Budgets

Illustration B

Cues for Reference

Create a Workspace
1. Open each workbook.
2. Size and position each file on screen.
3. Click **File, Save Workspace.**
4. Enter name of new workspace and click **Save.**

Consolidate Data
1. Open a new workbook.
2. Copy and paste, or enter, any labels you want in new worksheet.
3. Select cell where consolidated table will begin.
4. Click **Data, Consolidate.**
5. Select function you want to use.
6. Add references for each worksheet from which you are consolidating data. Click **Add** after each one.
7. Check box **Create links to source data,** if you want to link files.
8. Click **OK.**

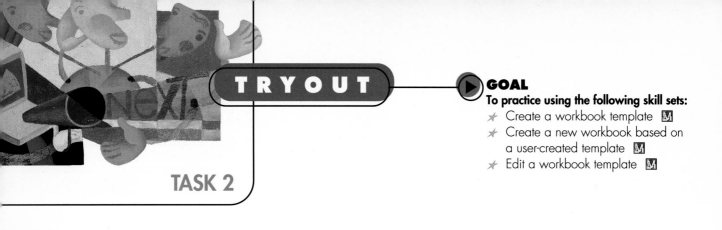

GOAL

To practice using the following skill sets:

* Create a workbook template Ⓜ
* Create a new workbook based on a user-created template Ⓜ
* Edit a workbook template Ⓜ

WHAT YOU NEED TO KNOW

Create a Workbook Template

> A *template* is a workbook that has settings such as fonts, formatting styles, graphics, formulas, and labels, but no data. It serves as an outline or guide into which you can enter data. A template is convenient to use when a business utilizes the same forms, documents, or reports repeatedly. You can simply enter data into the appropriate locations on the form. For example, you can easily produce expense forms, invoices, and budget reports by using templates. By creating a template, you can produce the report or form in a customized layout to suit the specific needs of a business. In addition, templates facilitate data consolidation because the data you want to summarize is in the same layout across worksheets.

> You have already learned that Excel provides some standard templates, both in the Templates folder and on the www.microsoft.com Web site. In this section you create your own templates.

> To create a template, enter all of the information you want to appear on the worksheet, including labels, fonts, formatting, and formulas. Click File, Save As. In the Save As dialog box, as shown in Figure 8.6, name the file and select Template from the Save as type drop-down list. Saved templates, by default, are located in the Templates folder; however, you can change the file location.

Note: Templates have the file extension .xlt.

TRY it OUT

1. Open **8.2TOTEMP** from the Data CD.

2. Format **Rows 4** through **7** so that the labels are **Bold** and the cell background color is **Gray.**

3. Click **File, Save As.**

4. Name the file:
   8.2bgttemp

5. Select **Template** as the file type.

6. Click **Save.**

7. Close the file.

Figure 8.6 Save As dialog box

Create a New Workbook Based on a User-Created Template

> Once you have created a template, you can use it to create workbooks containing data. When you want to use your template, click File, New. Select General Templates in the task pane. Your saved template should appear in the General tab. Double-click the template file to open it.

> When you open a template file, Excel adds a 1 to the file name so that if you save the file, it does not overwrite the template. Once the template is open, enter the data and save the file as a workbook with its own name (that is, the file should have the .xls file extension). When you close the newly named file created from the template, the template stays in its original form.

	Budget	Actual		Budget	Actual
Net Sales	10000	11000	Salaries/Wages	3000	3100
Cost of Goods Sold	5000	5400	Supplies	400	500
Advertising/Promotions	500	600	Taxes	300	400

Edit a Workbook Template

> To edit a workbook template, open the file containing the template. Make any changes in the style, formatting, labels, or graphics that are necessary.

> If you want to replace the original template, save the file with its original file name and as a Template file type. If you want to save your revisions as a new file, assign a new name and save it as a Template file type.

TRY _it_ OUT

1. Open the file you created containing the template **8.2bgttemp.** Click **File, New,** and click **General Templates** in the task pane. Double-click the file name **8.2bgttemp** in the General tab. Notice that the file opens as **8.2bgttemp1.**

2. Enter the following in **Row 3:**
   For the period ending
   March 31, 2002

3. Enter the following data in the appropriate cells as follows:

4. Click **File, Save As.** Name the file:
   8.2bgt0302

5. In Save as type list, select **Microsoft Excel Workbook.**

6. Click **Save.**

7. Print and close the file.

8. Open **8.2bgttemp** using the procedure in Step 1 and notice that the template is intact.

9. Do not close the file.

TRY _it_ OUT

Note: Continue to work in **8.2bgttemp.**

1. Insert a row below **Row 17.** Enter:
   Rent

2. Enter the following formula in **Cell E18:**
   =D18-C18

3. Enter the following formula in **Cell F18:**
   =E18/C18

4. Click **File, Save As.**

5. Select **Template** as the file type. The file name should be **8.2bgttemp.**

6. Click **Save.**

7. Close the file. Reopen it to view the saved changes in the template.

8. Close the file.

REHEARSAL

TASK 2

GOAL
To create a budget template

SETTING THE STAGE/WRAPUP
File names: 8.2FCQB
8.2FCQBudget

WHAT YOU NEED TO KNOW

> When you enter a formula in a template with blank data cells, the formula will result in zeros, an error message, or a dash, until you enter data.

> In this Rehearsal activity, you will create a template for a quarterly budget that the different branches of the Four Corners Realty Company will use as a standard form.

> The template includes the proposed budget, the actual budget, and the analysis of the percent of increase/decrease.

> Once you create and save the template, you then create a workbook for one of the branches based on the template, enter the data, and save the file as a workbook.

> You will also edit the template to include items that you need to add to the original template.

▼ DIRECTIONS

1. Open **8.2FCQB** from the Data CD.

2. Format **Columns C, D,** and **E** to use the Accounting format for numbers, and **Column F** to use Percentage format, as shown in the illustration on the next page.

   *(Hint: Click **Format, Cells,** click the **Number** tab, and select the appropriate formats.)*

3. Insert the formulas to compute Total Expenses, Net Income, Increase/Decrease, and %Increase/Decrease, as follows:
   a. In **Cell C20,** enter a formula to find the Total Expenses.
   b. Use the fill handle to drag this formula to **Column D.**
   c. In **Cell C22,** enter a formula to find the Net Income.
   d. Use the fill handle to drag this formula to **Column D.**
   e. In **Cell E7,** enter a formula to find the Increase/Decrease of the Actual over the budgeted items *(Hint: D7-C7).*
   f. Use the fill handle to drag this formula down **Column E** to **Cell E22.**
   g. In **Cell F7,** enter a formula to find the percent Increase/Decrease *(Hint: E7/C7).*
   h. Use the fill handle to drag this formula down **Column F** to **Cell F22.**
   i. Clear the formulas from **Rows 8, 9,** and **21.**
   j. Adjust lines and borders, if necessary.

4. Save it as a Template file type and name it:
   `8.2FCQBudget`

5. Close the file.

6. Open the template file **8.2FCQBudget.**

7. In **Row 2,** enter:
   `Greendale`

8. In **Row 3,** enter:
   `June 30, 2002`

Continued on next page

9. Enter the following data for the Budget and Actual columns:

	Budget	Actual
Net Sales	100,000	150,000
Advertising	6,000	6,500
Depreciation	1,000	900
Insurance	700	700
Legal/Accounting	6,000	6,200
Miscellaneous Expenses	500	700
Rent	8,200	8,200
Repairs/Maintenance	600	750
Salaries/Commissions	50,000	75,000
Supplies	500	400
Utilities	800	950

10. Save the file as a workbook and name it: **8.2FCQB**

11. Print one copy of the budget.

12. Open the template file and add the following expense item, in alphabetical order, in the Expenses list:
Educational

13. Use the fill handle to copy the appropriate formulas to the Educational expenses line.

14. Save the revised template and name the file:
8.2FCQBudget

15. Close all files.

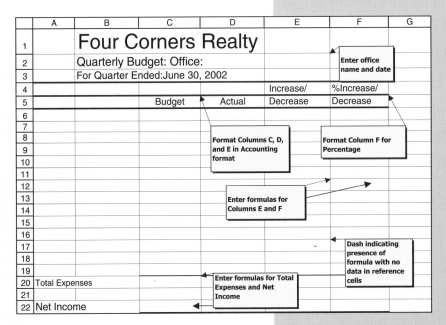

Cues for Reference

Create a Workbook Template
1. Create and format worksheet with appropriate labels, fonts, formulas, etc.
2. Click **File, Save As.**
3. Name file.
4. Click list arrow in **Save as type** box. Select **Template** as file type.
5. Click **Save.**

Create a New Workbook Based On a User-Created Template
1. Click **File, New, General Templates** in task pane.
2. In General tab, double-click appropriate template.
3. Enter values for appropriate locations in template.
4. Click **File, Save As.**
5. Name workbook and save it as a workbook file.

Edit a Workbook Template
1. Click **File, Open,** and locate file containing template.
2. Make changes to items contained in template.
3. Click **File, Save As.**
4. Use same template name or rename it and save as a Template file type.

PERFORMANCE

▶ **SETTING THE STAGE/WRAPUP**

Act I File names: 8p1.budget
8p1budtemp
8p1budgroup

Act II File names: 8p2.boston
8p2.sandiego
8p2consolbud

WHAT YOU NEED TO KNOW

Act I

The Air Land Sea Travel Group would like each department in the organization to use the same quarterly budget form to facilitate financial planning. Prepare a template for the quarterly budget, using **8p1.budget** on the Data CD as a starting point. You are also asked to prepare the budget for the Group Travel Department for the quarter ending September 30, 2002 and to revise the template.

Follow these guidelines:

✴ Change the fonts for the text so that the following labels are larger and set apart from the other text: Air Land Sea Travel, Office, Quarterly Budget for:, Income, Expenses, Net Income.

✴ Enter the formulas necessary to complete the budget template.

✴ Apply the appropriate number formats to each column and adjust column width as necessary.

✴ Apply borders to the appropriate cells to follow accounting styles.

✴ Save the form as a template in the Templates folder and name it: `8p1.budtemp`

✴ Use the template to create the Group Travel Department budget, using the data below, and print a copy of the report.

	Budget	Actual
Net Sales	30,000	40,000
Advertising	1,200	1,375
Rent	3,000	3,000
Salaries	20,000	18,000
Supplies	500	675

✴ Save it as a workbook and name it: `8p1.budgroup`

✴ Add a budget line for Utilities to the template. Resave the template as `8p1.budtemp`.

Act II

In order to conduct a financial analysis, Odyssey Travel Gear is planning to consolidate the budget statements from its Boston and San Diego operations. Open the files **8p2.boston** and **8p2.sandiego** from the Data CD. Enter formulas where appropriate to complete these statements. Create a shared workspace for these two files. Then consolidate the data for both the proposed and actual budgets onto a new worksheet. Print the consolidated budget and save the file.

Follow these guidelines:

⭐ Find the Gross Income for both Boston and San Diego by subtracting Cost of Goods Sold from Net Sales. Calculate Total Expenses and Net Income for both worksheets. (Use Gross Income less Expenses to find Net Income.) Save both files.

⭐ Name the consolidated budget:
8p2.consolbud

⭐ Make sure you copy the list of budget line items to the Consolidated Budget sheet. Consolidate the data from both columns from the Boston and San Diego sheets to the new workbook.

⭐ Enter and format appropriate titles on the Consolidated Budget.

ENCORE

Circle **T** if the statement is true or **F** if the statement is false.

T F 1. When you open a saved workspace, all of the workbooks in it appear in the same size and position as they did when you saved them.

T F 2. When you consolidate data, labels from the original worksheets are automatically pasted to the worksheet containing the consolidated material.

T F 3. Quarterly budgets are usually dated the first day of March, June, September, and December.

T F 4. When you add data to a template, you do not make changes to the template as long as you store the data in a workbook file type.

T F 5. You cannot edit templates once they are saved.

MULTIPLE CHOICE

Identify the letter of the choice that best completes the statement or answers the question.

6. **A workspace is:**
   A. A shared location in which several workbooks are stored.
   B. Another name for a workbook.
   C. Another name for a worksheet.
   D. What you see on a computer screen.

7. **The first step in creating a workspace is to:**
   A. Click File, New.
   B. Open a blank workbook.
   C. Open each workbook that will be in it.
   D. Find the correct template for it.

8. **The advantage of using a workspace is:**
   A. It provides a template for frequently used forms.
   B. You can open all workbooks in it at once.
   C. You can store changes in the data directly in the workspace.
   D. None of the above

9. **Workspaces have the file extension:**
   A. .xlt.
   B. .xls.
   C. .xlw.
   D. .xld.

10. Combining numerical information from several worksheets is called:
    A. Data consolidation.
    B. Data merging.
    C. Summation.
    D. A function.

11. The first step in consolidating data is to:
    A. Open each worksheet that contains data to consolidate.
    B. Create a new worksheet into which the consolidated data is placed.
    C. Click Data, Consolidate.
    D. Fill in the Function drop-down box.

12. If you want to link the consolidated data to the original source data, you should:
    A. Save it all as a workspace.
    B. Select the function Sum in the Consolidate dialog box.
    C. Check All references in the Consolidate dialog box.
    D. Check Create links to source data in the Consolidate dialog box.

13. A workbook that contains settings, fonts, formatting styles, and labels but no data is called a:
    A. Macro.
    B. Worksheet guide.
    C. Budget.
    D. Template.

14. Templates have the file format:
    A. .xlw.
    B. .xls.
    C. .xlt.
    D. .xlb.

15. Once you have entered numerical data to complete a template, you should save it as:
    A. A workbook.
    B. A workspace.
    C. A template.
    D. A .xlw file.

COMPLETION

Complete each sentence or statement.

16. A shared location in which several workbooks are stored is called a _____.

17. A _____ combines the planned or actual income and expenses from several departments or companies.

18. A _____ is a statement of estimated and actual income and expenses prepared four times a year.

19. A workbook that has fonts, formatting styles, graphics, formulas, and labels but no data is called a _____.

20. Templates have the file extension _____.

L E S S O N   9

Data Tables

In this lesson, you will learn how to customize and highlight the display of numerical information in a data table. You will apply these skills to the creation of a sales commission analysis and a regional sales analysis. You will also learn how to name and use ranges in formulas, use the LOOKUP functions in Excel, and examine formulas for errors. You will use these features to create a bonus table and a currency conversion table.

Upon completion of this lesson, you should have mastered the following skill sets:

✷ Create and apply custom number formats Ⓜ
✷ Use conditional formats Ⓜ
✷ Name a range Ⓜ
✷ Use a named range reference in a formula Ⓜ
✷ Use HLOOKUP and VLOOKUP Ⓜ
✷ Audit formulas Ⓜ
　✷ Trace dependents
　✷ Trace precedents
✷ Locate and resolve errors in formulas Ⓜ
✷ Identify dependencies in formulas Ⓜ
　✷ Locate dependencies in formulas
　✷ Remove tracer arrows

Terms
MOUS-related
　Custom number format
　Conditional formats
　Named range
　HLOOKUP
　VLOOKUP
　Dependents
　Precedents
　Tracer arrows
Document-related
　Sales commission analysis
　Listing agent
　Selling agent
　Regional sales analysis
　Bonus table
　Currency conversion table

TRYOUT

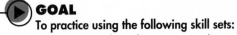

GOAL
To practice using the following skill sets:
- ✶ Create and apply custom number formats M
- ✶ Use conditional formats M

TASK 1

WHAT YOU NEED TO KNOW

Create and Apply Custom Number Formats

> Excel provides several ways to display numbers in a format that suits your needs and makes the information in a worksheet clear and readable. A *custom number format* is a user-created format that specifies how Excel displays numbers within a cell. It can format the number of decimal places, the position of commas, or it can modify Excel's options for representing scientific notation, currency, percents, dates, and times.

> To create a custom number format, select the cells you want to format. Click Format, Cells or press the Ctrl + 1 keys. This opens the Format Cells dialog box. Click the Number tab and click Custom in the Category box, as shown in Figure 9.1.

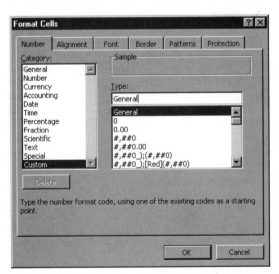

Figure 9.1 Format Cells dialog box

TRY *it* OUT

1. Open **9.1MemberSales** from the Data CD.

2. Select **Cells C6:C18.**

3. Click **Format, Cells,** and click the **Number** tab.

4. Select **Custom** in the Category box.

5. Select **mmm-yy** in the box under Type.

6. In the Type box, add **dd–** between the month and year symbols so that the entry looks like: mmm-dd-yy

7. Click **OK.**

8. Leave the file open.

> To create a custom number format that does not appear in the dialog box, scroll down under Type and select the custom format closest to the format you want to use as a starting point. Click in the Type box and modify its contents with your own format codes. Alternatively, select the contents of the Type box and replace it with your own format codes. Click OK.

> The table below gives some of the symbols that are used in custom number formats.

Number Format Codes	Instruction
#	Display a digit in a particular decimal place; do not put in a value if the number has fewer digits
0	Display a digit in a particular decimal place; put a zero in that location if the number has fewer digits
,	Place a comma at the location to indicate thousands
.	Place a decimal point at the location
$	Place a dollar sign at the location
%	Place a percent sign at the location
E+	Put the numbers to the right in scientific notation
M or m	Months for dates and minutes for time
D or d	Days
Y or y	Years
H or h	Hours
S or s	Seconds

> When you create a custom number format, Excel saves it with the workbook. Your new custom number format appears at the bottom of the Type list in the Format Cells dialog box.

> You can delete custom number formats from the Type box. Locate your custom format in the list and click Delete.

Use Conditional Formats

> *Conditional formats* allow you to apply specific formats to the content of a cell or range of cells if it meets certain criteria. Conditional formatting is a convenient way to make relevant or important data in a table stand out. For example, you might want to highlight data that exceeds or falls below a certain value in a different color or font style.

> To create a conditional format, click Format, Conditional Formatting. The Conditional Formatting dialog box opens, as shown in Figure 9.2.

Figure 9.2 Conditional Formatting dialog box

> In the first box, use the drop-down list to apply the conditional formatting to either a cell or a formula. In the second box, select the relative condition you want to apply from the drop-down list; for example, between or greater than. If you select between, or not between, in the second box, then two boxes will appear to the right. Enter the parameters that the condition should be between (for example, 1 and 100) in the third and fourth boxes, respectively. If you select an absolute condition like greater than, only one box will appear where you can enter the appropriate value. When you click the Format button in the Conditional Formatting dialog box, you can specify the formatting features you want to apply to any data that meets the conditions. The preview window shows how the data looks if the condition is true.

> If you want to apply another conditional format, click Add. You can apply up to three conditional formats. Click OK when you are done.

> Click Delete to remove any conditional formats you no longer need. The Delete Conditional Format dialog box opens, as shown in Figure 9.3. Check the boxes for any of the conditional formats you want to remove. Click OK when you are done.

Figure 9.3 Delete Conditional Format dialog box

Note: To locate any conditional formats you have applied in a worksheet, click Edit, Go To, and Special. Click Conditional formats, click OK, and Excel highlights the cells to which you have applied conditional formatting.

Note: Continue to work in **9.1MemberSales.**

1. Select **Cells G6:G19.**

2. Click **Format, Conditional Formatting.**

3. In the left box, leave the selection as **Cell Value Is.** In the next box, click the list arrow and select **greater than.** In the right box, enter: **100**

4. Click the **Format** button. Select **Bold** and select the color **Red.** Click **OK.**

5. Click **Add.** Condition 2 selection boxes should appear.

6. In the left box, leave the selection as **Cell Value Is.** In the next box, click the list arrow and select **less than.** In the right box, enter: **50**

7. Click **Format.** Select **Bold** and select the color **Blue.** Click **OK.**

8. Click **OK.** Notice the conditional formats.

9. Close and save the file.

REHEARSAL

TASK 1

WHAT YOU NEED TO KNOW

> Some businesses pay employees with commissions, which are compensations based on a percentage of the selling price of a product or service. A business may examine employees' sales performance over a specified period of time by doing a *sales commission analysis.* The business may conduct the study to see if there are notable patterns or to identify individuals who meet, or fall below, sales goals or other criteria important to the business.

> A real estate broker who signs up the homeowner or "lists" the home for sale is called the *listing agent.* The real estate broker who finds a buyer for the home is called the *selling agent.* The real estate agency provides office services to the brokers. The brokers and the agency generally share a commission on a home that averages 6% of the selling price.

> In this Rehearsal activity, you will conduct a sales commission analysis for Four Corners Realty in order to calculate commissions and to identify real estate brokers to honor for exceeding quarterly sales goals. Those who had commissions in excess of $20,000 will be named to the Gold Circle and those who had commissions in excess of $10,000 will be named to the Silver Circle. In addition, you will complete an analysis of agency revenues on another sheet in the same workbook.

▼ DIRECTIONS

1. Open **9.1HomeSales** from the Data CD.

2. Format the dates in **Column C** so that they appear as mmm/yy, as shown in Illustration A on the next page.

3. Using the information in the sales list below, calculate a 2.5% commission for the listing of a property and a 2% commission for the sale of a property for the agents listed. The sales list shows that, in some cases, the agents receive one or both of these commissions.

Broker	Price of Home	Closing	Listing	Selling
Arnold, John	$120,000.00	Apr/02	X	
Butler, Jean	$137,000.00	Apr/02	X	
Freeman, Marilyn	$172,500.00	Apr/02	X	X
Wreston, David	$175,000.00	Apr/02		X
Arnold, John	$199,250.00	May/02	X	X
Butler, Jean	$189,500.00	May/02	X	
Cisco, Michael	$89,000.00	May/02	X	X
Arnold, John	$140,000.00	Jun/02		X
Freeman, Marilyn	$195,600.00	Jun/02	X	X
Freeman, Marilyn	$187,500.00	Jun/02	X	

   a. Enter formulas in **Column D** to calculate a 2.5% commission on the price of each home.

   b. Delete the formulas in the blank areas and where they do not apply in the Listing column, as per the monthly sales table above.

   c. Enter formulas in **Column E** to calculate a 2% commission on the price of each home.

   d. Delete the formulas in the blank areas and where they do not apply in the Selling column, as per the monthly sales table above.

4. Calculate each broker's total commissions for the quarter in **Column F,** in the locations shown in the illustration.

5. Format the Total Commission column so that the data for any realtor who has more than $20,000 in commissions appears in red and bold.

Continued on next page

6. Format the Total Commission column so that the data for any realtor who has more than $10,000 in commissions appears in blue and bold.

7. Name the worksheet tab: **Sales Commissions**

8. Copy the worksheet to Sheet2 to begin to create an analysis of agency fees for the quarter.

9. Delete columns that are not needed and add new column headings so that your worksheet headings look like Illustration B below.

10. In the Agency Listing .5% column in **Cell F6,** enter an IF statement to multiply the Price of Home Sold column by .5% if the value in the Listing Agent column is greater than 1; otherwise, there should be no entry.
    Hint: =IF(D6>1,.5%*B6, 0)

11. Copy the formula for all homes and delete any zero entries.

12. In the Agency Sales 1% column, enter an IF statement to multiply the Price of Home Sold column by 1% if the value in the Selling Agent column is greater than 1; otherwise, there should be no entry.

	A	B	C	D	E	F
1			FOUR CORNERS REALTY (Greendale Office)			
2			Sales Commissions/Quarter Ending June 30, 2002			
3						
4				Listing Agent	Selling Agent	Total
5	Broker	Price of Home Sold	Closing Date	2% Commission	2.5% Commission	Commission
6	Arnold, John	$120,000.00	15-Apr-02			
7		$199,250.00	2-May-02			
8			6-Jun-02			
9						
10	Butler, Jean		2-Apr-02			
11		$189,500.00	14-May-02			
12						
13	Cisco, Michael	$89,000.00	5-May-02			
14						
15	Freeman, Marilyn	$172,500.00	27-Apr-02			
16		$195,600.00	10-Jun-02			
17		$187,500.00	2-Jun-02			
18						
19	Wreston, David	$175,000.00	11-Apr-02			
20						
21						

Callouts in Illustration A: "Format dates so they appear as mmm/yy"; "Calculate commissions for each broker based on whether they listed or sold the house or both"; "Compute the total commission for each broker for the quarter and apply conditional formatting"

Illustration A

	A	B	C	D	E	F	G
1			FOUR CORNERS REALTY (Greendale Office)				
2			Agency Commissions/Quarter Ending June 30, 2002				
3							
4				Listing Agent	Selling Agent	Agency	Agency
5		Price of Home Sold	Closing Date	2.5% Commission	2% Commission	Listing .5%	Sales 1%

Illustration B

13. Copy the formula for all homes and delete any zero entries.

14. Total the Agency Listing and Agency Sales columns.

15. Name the worksheet tab: **Agency Commissions**

16. Print a copy of both the Sales Commissions and the Agency Commissions report.

17. Save the file.

T R Y O U T

TASK 2

GOAL
To practice using the following skill sets:
- Name a range
- Use a named range reference in a formula
- Use HLOOKUP and VLOOKUP

WHAT YOU NEED TO KNOW

Name a Range

> A *named range* is a label that Excel assigns to a specified range of cells. For example, the Cells A2:A10 might be named TotalSales. When they are used in formulas, named range references can make it easier to follow the logic behind a computation.

> To create a named range, select the cells you want to name. Click the Name Box to the left of the Insert Function button, as shown in Figure 9.4. Enter the name of the range and press the Enter key.

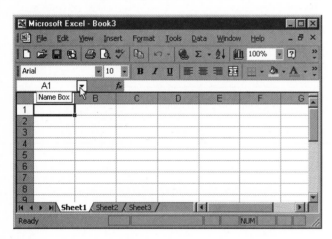

Figure 9.4 Name Box

Note: Remember to press the Enter key or Excel will not name the range.

> Naming ranges makes it easy to select a range. When you click the list arrow next to the Name box and click the name of the range you have created, Excel selects all of the cells on the worksheet to which the name refers.

T R Y *it* O U T

1. Open **9.2RegSales** from the Data CD.

2. Select **Cells C6:F6.**

3. Click in the **Name** box and enter:
   Northeast
   Press the **Enter** key. Click a cell outside of the table.

4. Click the list arrow in the **Name** box. Select **Northeast.** Notice which cells Excel highlights.

5. Select the data from each of the other regions and name them appropriately.

6. Select **Cells E14:F20.**

7. Click in the **Name** box and enter:
   BonusTable

8. Press the **Enter** key.

9. Leave the file open.

> The first character of the name of a named range must be a letter. Names cannot have spaces. Use the underscore character (_) or period (.) to designate a space. For example, Total_Sales is a valid name.

Note: You cannot use a cell reference within a name, e.g., A2B2.

> You can create a three-dimensional named range to refer to the same range on several sheets in a workbook by selecting the range of sheets and then selecting the range of cells.

> If you want to modify a named range, click Insert, select Name, and click Define. The Define Name dialog box opens, as shown in Figure 9.5. Select the name you want to modify from the list. Enter the new name under Names in workbook and click Add. To delete a name, select it from the list and click Delete.

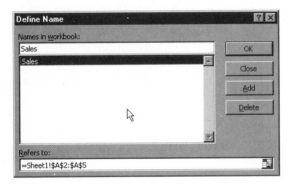

Figure 9.5 Define Name dialog box

Use a Named Range Reference in a Formula

> You can use named ranges in the same ways that you use cell ranges. For example, when you write a formula, simply enter the name of the range that you want to include in a mathematical function.

> If the range is named and you use the AutoSum button, the range will automatically appear in the Sum formula.

> If you are using the Insert Function button to perform a mathematical operation, you can enter the name of the range in the appropriate place in the dialog box.

TRY*it* OUT

Note: Continue to work in 9.2RegSales.

1. Click **Cell G6** and enter:
   =SUM(Northeast)
   Press the **Enter** key.

2. Copy the formula to **Cell G7.** Notice that the name of the range does not change and the result is incorrect and the same as **G6.** Delete the results in **Cell G7.**

3. Place the mouse pointer in **Cell G7** and click the **AutoSum** button. Excel places the correct range name in the Sum function. Press the **Enter** key to accept the formula.

4. Repeat Step 3 for each cell in the Total Sales column.

5. Leave the file open.

Use HLOOKUP and VLOOKUP

> Excel provides two LOOKUP functions, HLOOKUP and VLOOKUP, that check data values against a table and enter a resulting data point in a specified location on a worksheet. Some examples of the ways you can use these functions include looking up taxes to create a payroll, locating postage rates to complete a bill of sale, and finding bonuses based on sales figures for sales personnel.

> Use *HLOOKUP* (horizontal LOOKUP) when the data you are looking up is arranged in rows.

> Use *VLOOKUP* (Vertical LOOKUP) when the data you are looking up is arranged in columns.

> To use the LOOKUP functions, you must first create the table containing the data you are looking up. This table must appear in a separate location on the worksheet or on a separate worksheet.

> Click the Insert Function button.

> The Insert Function dialog box opens, as shown in Figure 9.6. In the box that says Or select a category, scroll down and click Lookup & Reference. In the box that says Select a function, scroll down and click either HLOOKUP or VLOOKUP, depending on how you have arranged your lookup table. Click OK.

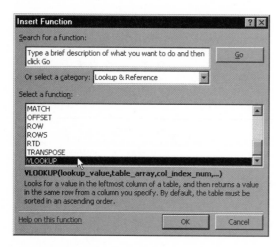

Figure 9.6 Insert Function dialog box

TRY*it*OUT

Note: You will enter a lookup formula to enter the appropriate bonus based on the sales made for the quarter. Continue to work in 9.2RegSales.

1. Click **Cell H6.**

2. Click the **Insert Function** button.

3. In the second box, select **Lookup & Reference.**

4. In the third box, select **VLOOKUP,** since data is arranged in the BonusTable vertically. Click **OK.**

5. In the Function Arguments dialog box, click in the box **Lookup_value** and enter **G6** (or you can click that cell in the worksheet) to LOOKUP the sales on the table.

6. Click in the box **Table_array** and enter **BonusTable** to direct Excel to the range of the data table.

7. Click in the box **Col_index_num** and enter: **2**
   This is because you want the bonus data which is in **Column 2** of the BonusTable.

8. Click **OK.** Check that the correct bonus was entered.

9. Copy the lookup formula to the other cells in the column. (BonusTable stays in each formula as a constant.)

10. Print, save, and close the file.

> The Function Arguments dialog box opens, as shown in Figure 9.7. Lookup_value refers to the value you want Excel to use when it goes to the lookup table. Table_array refers to the lookup table that contains the values against which Excel checks. Col_index_num refers to the column number in the lookup table that contains the data you want to enter in your worksheet. Notice the labeled worksheet in Figure 9.8 that shows all the parts of this formula. When you have entered all of these values, click OK. You should name the lookup table so that when the lookup formula is copied, the table range does not change.

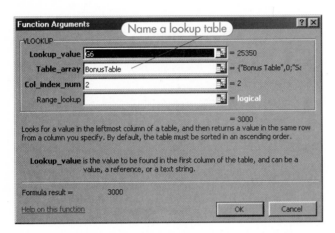

Figure 9.7 Function Arguments dialog box

> The resulting data or information appears in the worksheet cell you originally designated, as shown in Figure 9.8.

		TIME OUT SPORTING GOODS				Lookup Value; Look up sales on BonusTable	
		Regional Sales Summary, 2001					
	Region	**Quarter1**	**Quarter2**	**Quarter3**	**Quarter4**	**Total Sales**	**Bonus**
	Northeast	$7,000.00	$6,450.00	$8,400.00	$3,500.00	$25,350.00	
	Southeast	$6,000.00	$5,500.00	$7,500.00	$4,500.00	Enter VLOOKUP formula here to lookup bonus from table	
	Central	$4,600.00	$5,500.00	$8,900.00	$4,300.0		
	Northwest	$2,500.00	$4,500.00	$6,700.00	$5,600.0		
	Southwest	$3,400.00	$4,600.00	$7,600.00	$6,500.0		
					BonusTable		Lookup table named BonusTable; Data arranged vertically
					Sales	**Bonus**	
					$15,000.00	$1,000.00	
					$20,000.00	$2,000.00	
					$25,000.00	$3,000.00	
					$30,000.00	$4,000.00	
					$35,000.00	$5,000.00	
					Column 1 of BonusTable	Column 2 of BonusTable	

Figure 9.8 Worksheet with lookup table

REHEARSAL

TASK 2

 GOAL
To conduct a regional sales analysis
and use a bonus table

SETTING THE STAGE/WRAPUP
File names: 9.2ne
9.2se
9.2nw
9.2sw
9.2SuttonSales
9.2regionws

WHAT YOU NEED TO KNOW

> Businesses that sell products or services often have regional sales offices that are responsible for different parts of the country or the world. They may want to conduct a *regional sales analysis* to determine their sales figures for different areas of their sales territory. This analysis might be useful in planning where to promote particular products or services, or where to allocate sales efforts.

> Businesses that sell products or services might also want to reward employees who meet or exceed certain sales goals. You can create a *bonus table* to define the extra money awarded to sales personnel, based on their performance.

> For a report where details are not necessary, companies that are reporting large amounts of money often round the values to thousands rather than showing all the detail. For example, $564,678 expressed in thousands would be shown as 565, with a notation that values are in thousands.

DIRECTIONS

1. Open all the regional report files, **9.2ne, 9.2nw, 9.2sw,** and **9.2se,** from the Data CD.

2. Notice that the numbers are expressed in thousands.

3. Find the totals for each region in **Row 9** of the individual worksheets.

4. Include a single line above and double lines below the totals.

5. Arrange the worksheets on the screen so that the totals are visible and save them as a workspace, **9.2regionws.** (Try a tiled arrangement.)

6. Open **9.2SuttonSales** from the Data CD.

7. Copy and paste link the totals from each report to the appropriate location on the Regional Summary report. *(Hint: Copy the totals from a region, place the insertion point in an appropriate location on the summary, click **Edit, Paste, Paste Special,** and **Paste Link.** Be careful to place the totals on the correct line.)*

8. Close the individual regional reports.

9. On the summary report, name the range for each region.

10. Calculate the Total Sales for each region by entering:
    `=SUM(named range reference)`

11. Format values for commas with no decimal places.

12. Create a bonus table starting in **Cell C13.** List the bonuses as follows:

SALES	
(thousands)	*Bonus*
3,000	$ 50,000
4,000	$ 60,000
5,000	$ 70,000
6,000	$ 80,000
7,000	$ 90,000
8,000	$ 100,000
9,000	$ 110,000
10,000	$ 120,000

> In this Rehearsal activity, you will conduct a regional sales analysis for the Sutton Investment Group. You will create a workspace and paste link the data from four regional reports into one report. You will create and apply a bonus table that allocates rewards to high-performing regional offices. The corporate officers have decided to let each regional office distribute the bonuses as they deem appropriate. Use the illustration below for reference.

13. Format the Sales numbers for commas, the Bonus values for currency, and both for no decimal places.

14. Format the bonus table in light green to set it apart from the other data in the table.

15. Name the range of cells that contains the bonus table: **BonusTable**

16. Find the bonus amounts for each sales region by using VLOOKUP.

   Note: Once you obtain the value for the first cell in the bonus column, you can use the fill-handle to fill in the rest of the values in that column.

17. Apply conditional formatting to **Column G** so that the sales figures in any region that exceed 9,000 (nine million dollars), are highlighted in blue. Highlight any region where total sales fell below 4,000 (four million dollars), in red. *(Hint: Select the values from the BonusTable.)*

18. Print and save the **9.2SuttonSales** file and close it.

	A	B	C	D	E	F	G	H
1								
2			SUTTON INVESTMENT GROUP					
3			Regional Sales Summary, 2002					
4								
5		Region	Quarter1	Quarter2	Quarter3	Quarter4	Total Sales	Bonus
6		Northeast						
7		Southeast						
8		Northwest						
9		Southwest						
10								
11								
12								
13								
14								
15								
16								
17								
18								
19								
20								

Paste link the regional data from the individual reports

Compute the bonuses by using VLOOKUP

Name the ranges for the data associated with each region

Compute the total sales for each region by using the named ranges; apply the conditional formatting specified

Create and format the bonus table and place it here on the worksheet

Cues for Reference

Name a Range
1. Select cells you want to name.
2. Click in **Name** box and enter name. Press **Enter.**

Use a Named Range Reference in a Formula
1. Enter formula, but instead of entering cell ranges, enter name you gave to range.

2. If you are using **Insert Function** button, enter name of range in appropriate box.

Use HLOOKUP and VLOOKUP
1. Click cell where outcome of lookup function will go.
2. Click **Insert Function** button.
3. Select **Lookup & Reference.**

4. If data in lookup table is arranged in rows, select **HLOOKUP;** if data is arranged in columns, select **VLOOKUP.**
5. In **Lookup_value,** enter cell reference you are evaluating.
6. In **Table-array,** enter location or named range of lookup table.
7. In **Col_index_num,** enter row or column in lookup table that contains result.

TRYOUT

TASK 3

GOAL

To practice using the following skill sets:

* Audit formulas Ⓜ
    * Trace dependents
    * Trace precedents
* Locate and resolve errors in formulas Ⓜ
* Identify dependencies in formulas Ⓜ
    * Locate dependencies in formulas
    * Remove tracer arrows

WHAT YOU NEED TO KNOW

Audit Formulas

> If you have an error in a formula, you can trace the cells that are connected to the formula to try to resolve the error. This procedure is especially helpful when you are using a worksheet created by someone else.

> Excel provides several new features to assist you as you track down errors in formulas. These include the Evaluate Formula function and the Formula Auditing mode.

Trace Dependents

> *Dependents* are cells containing formulas that reference the cell you are auditing. If you click a cell, you can see all of the other cells that use it in a formula.

> To locate dependents, first click the cell you are auditing, then click Tools, select Formula Auditing, and click Trace Dependents, as shown in Figure 9.9.

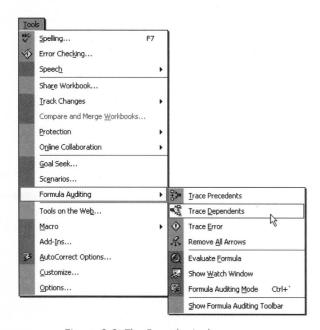

Figure 9.9 The Formula Auditing menu

T R Y *it* O U T

1. Open the file **9.3TOBagSales** from the Data CD.

2. Click **Cell F4.**

3. Click **Tools,** select **Formula Auditing,** and click **Trace Dependents.**

4. Notice the arrows going from **Cell F4** to **Cells E8, E9, E10,** and **E12.** Each of these cells contains **F4** in a formula.

5. Click the **Remove Dependent Arrows** button.

6. Keep the file open.

> Excel draws a line to each cell in which a formula includes that specific cell, as shown in Figure 9.10.

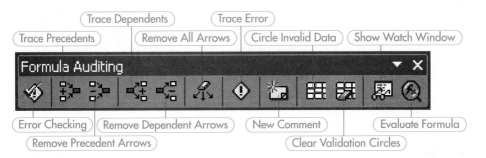

	A	B	C	D	E	F	G	H
1								
2				TIME OUT SPORTING GOODS				
3			Item:			Duffle bag		
4			Current price per item:			$ 12.95		
5								
6				CONVERSION FACTOR			GROSS SALES	
7	COUNTRY		CURRENCY	Per U.S.$	FOREIGN PRICE PER ITEM	# ITEMS SOLD	(Foreign Currency)	
8	Canada		Dollar	1.521	19.70	100	1969.695	
9	France		Franc	7.134	92.39	50	4619.265	
10	Italy		Lira	2106	27272.70	45	1227271.5	
11	Japan		Yen	116.7	#VALUE!	30	#VALUE!	
12	Spain		Peseta	180.9	2342.66	50	117132.75	
13	European Union		Euro	1.161	15.03	25	375.87375	
14								
15								
16								

Figure 9.10 Example of tracing dependents

> Another way to trace dependents is to use the Formula Auditing toolbar, as shown in Figure 9.11. Click Tools, select Formula Auditing, and click Show Formula Auditing Toolbar. Click the Trace Dependents button to locate a cell's dependents. The next button to the right, the Remove Dependent Arrows button, removes the dependent arrows.

Figure 9.11 The Formula Auditing toolbar

Trace Precedents

> *Precedents* are cells that are referenced in a formula. If you click a cell containing a formula, you can trace all of the cells that contribute to that formula.

> To locate precedents, first click the cell containing the formula you want to audit, then click Tools, select Formula Auditing, and click Trace Precedents. Excel draws lines to the audited cell from each cell that contributes to the formula, as shown in Figure 9.12.

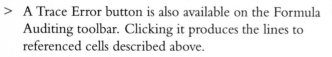

Figure 9.12 Example of tracing precedents

> Another way to trace precedents is to use the Formula Auditing toolbar discussed above. Click the Trace Precedents button. To remove precedent arrows, click the button to its right, the Remove Precedent Arrows button.

Locate and Resolve Errors in Formulas

> Suppose you write a formula and you get one of Excel's error messages such as #VALUE!, #NAME?, or #DIV/0!. You can begin to resolve the error by using the Trace Error function on the Formula Auditing menu. Click the cell with the error and click Tools, select Formula Auditing, and click Trace Error. Excel draws lines from all of the cells that are referenced in the formula. Red lines are drawn from the cells in which there are errors.

> A Trace Error button is also available on the Formula Auditing toolbar. Clicking it produces the lines to referenced cells described above.

> When a cell contains an error, it will have a small triangle in the top left corner. New to this version of Excel is the Error button that appears when you click the cell with the error. The button offers several options to help you resolve the problem in your formula. These options vary with the type of error in the cell. The options might include a link to the Help file, the Trace Error button, or the option to ignore the error.

TRY_it_**OUT**

Note: Continue to work in **9.3TOBagSales.**

1. Click **Cell E12.**

2. Click **Tools,** select **Formula Auditing,** and click **Trace Precedents.**

3. Notice the arrows going from **Cells D12** and **F4** to **Cell E12.** These cells are referenced in the formula in **E12.**

4. Click **Tools,** select **Formula Auditing,** and click **Show Formula Auditing Toolbar.**

5. Click the **Remove Precedent Arrows** button.

6. Keep the file open.

TRY_it_**OUT**

Note: Continue to work in **9.3TOBagSales.**

1. Click **Cell G11.**

2. Click **Tools,** select **Formula Auditing,** and click **Trace Error.**

3. The lines point from the cells that contribute to the formula. The red line indicates that **Cell E11** contains an error.

4. Correct the formula in **Cell E11** so that it says: **=F4*D11**

5. Keep the file open.

> A new function in Excel is Evaluate Formula. This function allows you to see the step-by-step calculations that a formula performs. Often, observing this step-by-step procedure can help you track down an error. To use this function, click the cell you are auditing and click Tools, select Formula Auditing, and click Evaluate Formula. The Evaluate Formula dialog box opens, as shown in Figure 9.13. Click Evaluate. Excel conducts the first step of the computation. Each time you click Evaluate, Excel executes the next step in the computation. When you have finished looking at the steps, click Close.

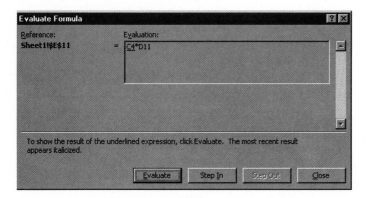

Figure 9.13 Evaluate Formula dialog box

> You can also access the Evaluate Formula function by clicking the Evaluate Formula button on the Formula Auditing toolbar.

> You can keep track of the formulas contained in all cells of your worksheet by using Formula Auditing mode. Click Tools, select Formula Auditing, and click Formula Auditing Mode. Each cell containing a formula now shows that formula directly in the cell. When you click a cell with a formula, all of the cells that it references are highlighted in color codes that match the cell reference itself.

> To exit Formula Auditing mode, press the Ctrl key and the ` (accent) key, which is found to the left of the number 1 key at the top of your keyboard.

TRY_it_ **OUT**

Note: Continue to work in
9.3TOBagSales.

1. Click **Cell E8.**

2. Click **Tools,** select **Formula Auditing,** and click **Evaluate Formula.**

3. Click **Evaluate** three times. Notice the result in the Evaluation box each time you click.

4. Click **Close.**

5. Leave **Cell E8** selected. Click **Tools,** select **Formula Auditing,** and click **Formula Auditing Mode.** Notice the contents of **Cell E8,** as well as the selected cells that are referenced in Cell E8.

6. Press the **Ctrl + `** (accent) keys.

7. Close the file. Do not save.

Identify Dependencies in Formulas

Locate Dependencies in Formulas

> To display both the precedents and dependents in formulas, click Tools, Options, and the View tab. Select Show all under Objects. You can then follow the procedures to trace dependents and precedents. All of the tracer arrows will show on your worksheet.

Remove Tracer Arrows

> The lines that Excel creates to identify dependents and precedents of audited cells are called *tracer arrows.* When you have located and resolved your errors, you can remove the tracer arrows by clicking Tools, selecting Formula Auditing, and clicking Remove All Arrows.

> Another way to remove all tracer arrows is to click the Remove All Arrows button on the Formula Auditing toolbar.

TRY*it*OUT

1. Reopen **9.3TOBagSales** from the Data CD.

2. Click **Cell E11.**

3. Click **Tools, Options,** and the **View** tab.

4. Under Objects, click **Show all.**

5. Click **OK.**

6. Click **Tools,** select **Formula Auditing,** and click **Trace Precedents.**

7. Click **Tools,** select **Formula Auditing,** and click **Trace Dependents.**

8. Click **Tools,** select **Formula Auditing,** and click **Remove All Arrows.**

9. Close the file. Do not save.

REHEARSAL

TASK 3

WHAT YOU NEED TO KNOW

> For companies that engage in international business, it is important to use a *currency conversion table* that identifies the current exchange rate for U.S. dollars. The table can contain the U.S. dollar value of the foreign currency, the foreign currency equivalent of a U.S. dollar, or both. It can also contain computations based on these exchange rates.

> A good source for daily foreign currency exchange rates is: http://moneycentral.msn.com/investor/market/rates.asp

> In this Rehearsal activity, you will work with a currency conversion table for another product that the Time Out Sporting Goods Company sells on the world market. The table has several errors in it. You will locate the sources of the errors, using the auditing tools you learned about, and correct those errors.

DIRECTIONS

1. Open the file **9.3TOWatchSales** from the Data CD.

2. Audit the errors in **Column H,** illustrated on the next page. Locate all dependencies in the cells that have errors.

3. Locate the cells that contain the source of the errors and correct them.

4. Remove all tracer arrows.

5. Print the worksheet.

6. Save the file.

	A	B	C	D	E	F	G	H	I
1									
2					TIME OUT SPORTING GOODS				
3			Item:			SportsWatch			
4			Current price per item:			$	79.99		
5									
6				CONVERSION FACTOR	CONVERSION FACTOR			GROSS SALES	
7	COUNTRY		CURRENCY	(in U.S.$)	(Per U.S.$)	FOREIGN PRICE PER ITEM	# ITEMS SOLD	(Foreign Currency)	
8	Brazil		Real	0.50445	1.98200	158.54	75	11890.5135	
9	Canada		Dollar	0.65764	1.521	121.66	125	15208.09875	
10	European Union		Euro	0.86133	1.161	92.87	75	6965.12925	
11	France		Franc	0.14018	7.134	#DIV/0!	50	#DIV/0!	
12	Germany		Mark	0.47023	2.127	#VALUE!	100	#VALUE!	
13	Italy		Lira	0.00047	2106	168458.94	55	9265241.7	
14	Japan		Yen	0.00857	116.7	9334.83	130	1213528.29	
15	Spain		Peseta	0.00553	180.9	14470.19	75	1085264.325	
16									
17									
18									
19									
20									

Locate the sources of the errors on this worksheet starting with this column

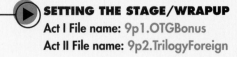

WHAT YOU NEED TO KNOW

Act I

The Odyssey Travel Gear Company would like to conduct a sales commission analysis in order to give its top salespeople end-of-the-year bonuses. Open the file 9p1.OTGBonus from the Data CD. The quarterly sales figures for the sales staff appear in the table. The bonus amount for each level of total sales is given below:

Sales	Bonus
$15,000	$1,000
$20,000	$2,000
$25,000	$3,000
$30,000	$4,000
$40,000	$5,000

Compute the bonus (if any) that each salesperson should receive. Format any total sales figures for individual salespeople that exceed $25,000 in bold and red, and any total sales figures that exceed $15,000 in bold and green.

Follow these guidelines:

✴ Format all currency figures in a custom number format in which there is a dollar sign but no comma to indicate thousands.

✴ Whenever possible, name the ranges that you will use in formulas and dialog boxes.

✴ When you create the bonus table, put it in a separate place on the worksheet and format it in pale yellow.

✴ Use the correct LOOKUP function to derive the bonus figures.

✴ Save the file.

Act II

Trilogy Productions has just finished filming scenes from "The Last Dragon" in several foreign locations, including Japan, India, and Taiwan. The production team has submitted a list of expenses to the accounting office. The information now needs to be converted to U.S. currency and the expense figures totaled.

Open the file **9p2.TrilogyForeign** from the Data CD. Each sheet contains the expenses for each country. The table includes the currency conversion factors to convert the figures to U.S. dollars, as well as the computations to translate the figures to U.S. dollars. However, there are errors in the tables on each worksheet.

Use Excel's formula auditing tools to locate the sources of the errors. Make all necessary corrections and remove all tracer arrows. Then consolidate the data from each of the three worksheets into a new worksheet.

Follow these guidelines:

✶ Start tracing errors in cells that contain totals, e.g., **Cell F15** on each of the three worksheets.

✶ Put the consolidated expense statement on a new worksheet.

- Label the tab on the worksheet: `ConsolExpenses`

- Copy the company information in **Cells D2** and **D3** from one of the country worksheets to the new worksheet. Change the label of the worksheet to:
  `Consolidated Expenses`

- Copy the labels in **Cells C8:C13** and **F6:F7** to the new worksheet.

- Compute the total expenses in U.S. dollars for all three countries.

✶ Use the Internet to research the current conversion rates for these worksheets. Enter the date of your research on the report and change the rates as necessary.

✶ Save and print the file.

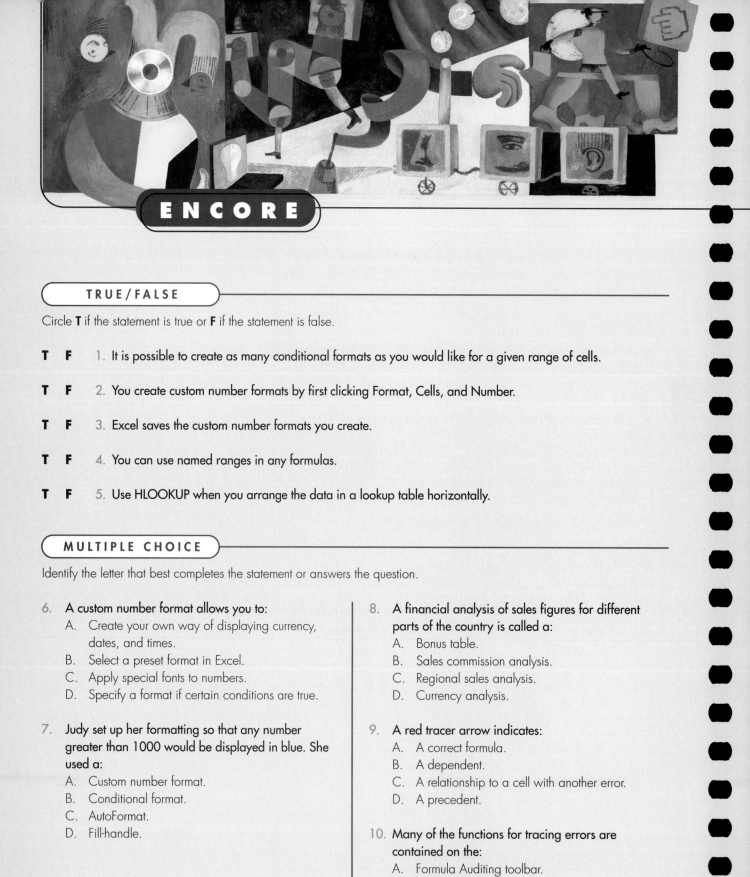

ENCORE

Circle **T** if the statement is true or **F** if the statement is false.

T   F   1. It is possible to create as many conditional formats as you would like for a given range of cells.

T   F   2. You create custom number formats by first clicking Format, Cells, and Number.

T   F   3. Excel saves the custom number formats you create.

T   F   4. You can use named ranges in any formulas.

T   F   5. Use HLOOKUP when you arrange the data in a lookup table horizontally.

MULTIPLE CHOICE

Identify the letter that best completes the statement or answers the question.

6. A custom number format allows you to:
   A. Create your own way of displaying currency, dates, and times.
   B. Select a preset format in Excel.
   C. Apply special fonts to numbers.
   D. Specify a format if certain conditions are true.

7. Judy set up her formatting so that any number greater than 1000 would be displayed in blue. She used a:
   A. Custom number format.
   B. Conditional format.
   C. AutoFormat.
   D. Fill-handle.

8. A financial analysis of sales figures for different parts of the country is called a:
   A. Bonus table.
   B. Sales commission analysis.
   C. Regional sales analysis.
   D. Currency analysis.

9. A red tracer arrow indicates:
   A. A correct formula.
   B. A dependent.
   C. A relationship to a cell with another error.
   D. A precedent.

10. Many of the functions for tracing errors are contained on the:
   A. Formula Auditing toolbar.
   B. Main Excel toolbar.
   C. Drawing toolbar.
   D. Formatting dialog box.

Complete each sentence or statement.

11. If you want to see which formulas a given cell maps on to, you should trace _____.

12. A _____ analysis looks at employees' sales performance over a specified period of time and calculates compensation based on a percentage of the selling price.

13. _____ applies a specific format to data in cells that meet certain specified conditions.

14. When you want to check data against a table of values and enter a resulting data point in the worksheet, you should use _____ or _____.

15. The _____ toolbar contains several functions that are useful in checking errors in formulas.

16. The lines drawn by Excel to show dependents and precedents are called _____.

17. _____ are cells that are referenced in a formula.

18. A _____ is a label applied to a specified range of cells.

19. A data table that contains foreign exchange rates for the money of different countries is called a _____.

20. A user-created format to specify how numbers will display is called a _____.

LESSON 10

Accounting Records

In this lesson, you will learn to customize Excel so that you can create accounting records for accounts receivable more efficiently. You will learn to create customized groups of commands in menus and toolbars. You will also learn to incorporate a series of commands into a few keystrokes, a process called creating a macro.

 Upon completion of this lesson, you should have mastered the following skill sets:

✴ Customize toolbars and menus
  ✶ Add custom menus 𝗠
  ✶ Delete custom menus
  ✶ Add and remove buttons from toolbars 𝗠
✴ Create, edit, and run macros 𝗠
  ✶ Create macros
  ✶ Use relative reference macros
  ✶ Run macros
  ✶ Edit macros using the Visual Basic Editor
  ✶ Delete a macro

Terms
MOUS-related
  Custom menu
  Macro
  Visual Basic Editor
Document-related
  Accounts receivable
  Accounts receivable aging report

 T R Y O U T

GOAL
To practice using the following skill sets:
- ✳ Customize toolbars and menus
  - ✳ Add custom menus Ⓜ
  - ✳ Delete custom menus
  - ✳ Add and remove buttons from toolbars Ⓜ

TASK 1

WHAT YOU NEED TO KNOW

Customize Toolbars and Menus

> When you repeat the same tasks in Excel, you may find it useful to create your own customized drop-down menu that contains the buttons and commands you use frequently. Or, you can modify one of the pre-existing toolbars in Excel so that it contains the buttons that you use most often.

Add Custom Menus

> A *custom menu* is a set of buttons and commands Excel groups into a user-created drop-down menu. You can take buttons and commands from anywhere in Excel and place them in one convenient location with its own name.

> To create a custom menu, click Tools, Customize. The Customize dialog box opens, as shown in Figure 10.1. Click the Commands tab. Scroll down the Categories box and select New Menu. In the Commands box, click New Menu and drag it to the toolbar on which you want the custom menu to appear. A bar, shaped like the letter "I," indicates where Excel will place the menu.

T R Y _it_ O U T

1. Open a new worksheet.

2. Click **Tools, Customize,** and the **Commands** tab.

3. Scroll down the Categories box and click **New Menu.**

4. In the Commands box, click and drag **New Menu** to the Standard toolbar.

5. Right-click **New Menu** and enter the following in the Name box:
   My Menu
   Press the **Enter** key.

6. Click **My Menu** so that you see a blank box under it.

7. In Categories, click **Format.**

8. In Commands, click and drag **Font Format** to the blank box under **My Menu.**

9. In Categories, click **Insert.**

10. In Commands, click and drag **Rows** to the blank box under **My Menu.**

11. Click **Close** in the Customize dialog box.

12. Click the list arrow next to **My Menu** to see the commands on your customized menu.

13. Do not close the worksheet.

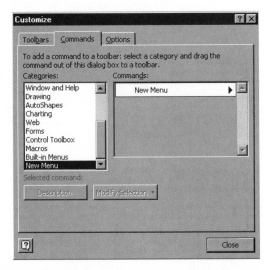

Figure 10.1 Customize dialog box

> To name your menu, keep the Customize dialog box open and right-click New Menu on the toolbar. On the shortcut menu that appears, select New Menu in the Name box and enter the name of your menu. Press the Enter key.

> To add commands to the custom menu, click the menu name you have created. An empty box that holds the drop-down menu items appears, as shown in Figure 10.2. Go to the Customize dialog box and click the category that contains the command you want to put on your custom menu. Drag the command from the Commands box to the empty box for your custom menu. When you are done, close the Customize dialog box.

Figure 10.2 Empty custom drop-down menu

Note: If you are not sure what a command does, select it and click Description in the Customize dialog box.

Delete Custom Menus

> To delete a command from your custom menu, make sure the Customize dialog box is open. Click the command you want to delete. Click Modify Selection in the Customize dialog box and click Delete.

> Another way to delete a command from your custom menu is to open the Customize dialog box by clicking Tools, Customize. Click the list arrow next to your custom menu. Click and drag the command you want to delete off the toolbar.

> To delete the entire custom menu from a toolbar, open the Customize dialog box by clicking Tools, Customize. Click and drag the custom menu off the toolbar.

T R Y _it_ O U T

Note: Continue to work on the sheet for which you have created the custom menu, My Menu.

1. Click **Tools, Customize,** and the **Commands** tab.

2. Click the list arrow next to **My Menu.**

3. Click and drag **Rows** off the toolbar.

4. Click the list arrow next to **My Menu.** Notice that the Rows command is gone.

5. Click and drag **My Menu** off the toolbar.

6. Close the Customize dialog box.

7. Do not close the worksheet.

Add and Remove Buttons from Toolbars

> Excel toolbars are flexible in layout. You can add, remove, or rearrange buttons on Excel's pre-set toolbars to suit the tasks you work on frequently.

> There are several ways to add buttons to toolbars:

- When toolbars are arranged side by side, some of the buttons on each toolbar are not visible. When you click the Toolbar Options arrow at the end of the toolbar, you can view those buttons and click the button you want to use. The button appears on the toolbar for future use.

- You can also click the Toolbar Options arrow and then click Add or Remove Buttons, as shown in Figure 10.3. Check off the buttons you want on the toolbar.

- If you want to add buttons from another toolbar, click Tools, Customize, and the Commands tab. Locate the menu that contains the command you want in the Categories box. Find the button you want in the Commands box. Click and drag it to the toolbar on which you want it to appear. When you are done, close the Customize dialog box.

> There are several ways to remove buttons from toolbars:

- Open the Customize dialog box by clicking Tools, Customize, and the Commands tab. Click the button you want to remove and drag it off the toolbar. Close the Customize dialog box.

- Hold down the Alt key. Click and drag the button off the toolbar.

- Click the Toolbar Options arrow at the end of the toolbar. Click Add or Remove buttons, as shown in Figure 10.3, then uncheck the buttons you do not want on the toolbar menu.

> If you want a toolbar to revert to its original settings, click Tools, Customize, and the Toolbars tab. Click the Reset button. Close the Customize dialog box.

Note: Continue to work on the blank worksheet.

1. Click **Tools, Customize,** and the **Commands** tab.

2. Click **Format** in the Categories box.

3. Click **Double Underline** in the Commands box and drag it to the formatting toolbar.

4. Close the **Customize dialog** box.

5. Press the **Alt** key, click the **Double Underline** button, and drag it off the toolbar.

6. Close the worksheet without saving it.

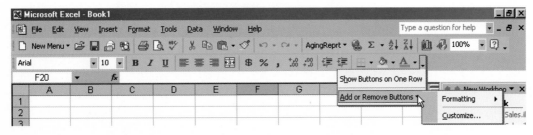

Figure 10.3 Toolbar Options arrow

REHEARSAL

TASK 1

WHAT YOU NEED TO KNOW

> *Accounts receivable* are assets of a business and represent customers who owe the business money. Customers who are sold services or merchandise on credit are required to pay the bill within the time specified on the invoice. Accounts are reviewed monthly to determine which invoices are outstanding or unpaid.

> An *accounts receivable aging report* provides an analysis of how many days payments from customers are overdue. Many businesses expect payment within 30 days of the purchase or transaction. Based on the analysis, a company can identify delinquent customers, or may assess finance charges or late fees. These charges may vary, depending on the number of days an account is overdue, and are imposed to enforce payment.

> In this Rehearsal activity, you will prepare a workbook that you will use later in this lesson to create an accounts receivable aging report for Occasions Event Planning. You create a custom menu and add specific buttons to one of the toolbars in Excel to make the task easier and more efficient. Occasions Event Planning usually collects payment on the day of the planned event. However, if they are not paid at that time, they expect full payment for their services within 10 days of the invoice.

DIRECTIONS

1. Open **10.1OEPAgingReport** from the Data CD.

2. Create a custom menu called **AgingReprt**, as shown in the illustration on the next page, that contains the following commands:
   Format, Apply Outline Borders
   Format, Fill Color
   Insert, Page Break
   File, Page Setup
   Tools, Trace Error

3. Add the following buttons to the Standard toolbar:
   Insert, Rows
   Insert, Columns
   Edit, Delete Rows
   Tools, Macros
   Tools, Record New Macro
   Data, AutoFilter

4. Remove the AutoFilter button from the toolbar.

5. Group the June and July sheets.
   a. Use the custom menu command to apply a light purple fill color to **Cells A7:H8** on the first sheet (June) of the workbook.
   b. Use the custom menu command to apply an outline border to **Cells A7:H8.**
   c. Use the custom toolbar button to insert a column between the CUSTOMER and DAYS UNPAID columns.
   d. Enter **DUE DATE** as the new column heading in **Cell D8.**
   e. Ungroup the sheets.

6. Invoice 139 on the first sheet (June) has been paid. Delete **Row 13** from the report using the Delete Rows button you placed on the toolbar.

7. Calculate the DUE DATE for all invoices on both sheets, by adding 10 days to the INVOICE DATE, which are the terms of payment given to all customers. The DUE DATE results should be in Date format.

8. Save the **10.1OEPAgingReport** file.

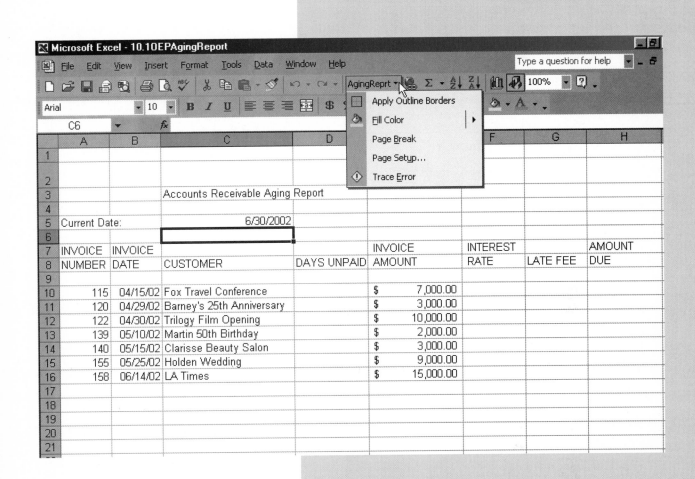

The spreadsheet shows:

	A	B	C	D	E	F	G	H
1								
2								
3			Accounts Receivable Aging Report					
4								
5	Current Date:		6/30/2002					
6								
7	INVOICE	INVOICE			INVOICE	INTEREST		AMOUNT
8	NUMBER	DATE	CUSTOMER	DAYS UNPAID	AMOUNT	RATE	LATE FEE	DUE
9								
10	115	04/15/02	Fox Travel Conference		$ 7,000.00			
11	120	04/29/02	Barney's 25th Anniversary		$ 3,000.00			
12	122	04/30/02	Trilogy Film Opening		$ 10,000.00			
13	139	05/10/02	Martin 50th Birthday		$ 2,000.00			
14	140	05/15/02	Clarisse Beauty Salon		$ 3,000.00			
15	155	05/25/02	Holden Wedding		$ 9,000.00			
16	158	06/14/02	LA Times		$ 15,000.00			
17								
18								
19								
20								
21								

Menu shown: AgingReprt ▾
- Apply Outline Borders
- Fill Color ▸
- Page Break
- Page Setup...
- Trace Error

Cues for Reference

Add a Custom Menu
1. Click **Tools, Customize,** and **Commands** tab.
2. In Categories box, select **New Menu.**
3. In Commands box, click **New Menu** and drag it to toolbar on which you want menu to appear.
4. Right-click **New Menu** on toolbar. Enter a name for menu in Name box. Press **Enter.**
5. Click name of custom menu so that you get an empty box.

6. Locate commands you want by looking first in Categories box, then in Commands box.
7. Click and drag commands from Commands box to Custom Menu box you created.
8. Close Customize dialog box.
9. Save and close file.

Add a Button to a Toolbar
1. Click **Tools, Customize,** and **Commands** tab.

2. Locate button you want by looking first in Categories box, then in Commands box.
3. Click and drag button from Commands box to toolbar on which you want it to appear.
4. Close Customize dialog box.

Remove a Button from a Toolbar
1. Hold down **Alt.**
2. Click and drag button you are removing off toolbar.

TRYOUT

TASK 2

 GOAL

To practice using the following skill sets:

✴ Create, edit, and run macros **M**
- ✴ Create macros
- ✴ Use relative reference macros
- ✴ Run macros
- ✴ Edit macros using the Visual Basic Editor
- ✴ Delete a macro

Create, Edit, and Run Macros

> A *macro* is a series of actions you record to allow you to complete a task quickly and efficiently. In a macro, you can record any set of instructions that you perform over and over, such as selecting commands from a menu, formatting, and writing labels and formulas. Saving instructions in a macro means they are readily available for use at a future time. When you are ready to use the macro, you simply perform a few keystrokes and the macro plays. The macro performs all of the steps you have recorded.

> Excel records macros in the *Visual Basic Editor,* a module in Excel that uses the Visual Basic programming language. You can edit the commands that Excel records by using the syntax of Visual Basic.

Create Macros

> The process of creating macros involves the following general sequence of steps:

- Name the macro.

- Assign the shortcut keys for playing back the macro.

- Perform the sequence of steps you want to record in the macro.

- Stop recording the macro.

> To begin creating a macro, click Tools, select Macro, and click Record New Macro. The Record Macro dialog box opens, as shown in Figure 10.4. Or, you can click the Record New Macro button that you can place on your toolbar or custom menu, as you did earlier in this lesson.

TRY*it*OUT

1. Open the file **10.2TOAging** from the Data CD.

2. Select **Cell C2.**

3. Click **Tools,** select **Macro,** and click **Record New Macro.**

4. Enter the following in the Macro name box:

   `Heading`

5. Enter the following in the Description box:

   `Heading for Time Out Sporting Goods`

6. Enter **t** in the Shortcut key box.

7. In the Store macro in box, select **This Workbook.**

8. Click **OK.**

9. Click **Format, Cells,** and **Font.** Select **Bold Italic** and **16 pt.**

10. Click the **Alignment** tab. Select **Center** in the Horizontal box. Click **OK** to end.

11. Enter the following:
    `TIME OUT SPORTING GOODS`
    Press the **Enter** key.

12. Click the **Stop Recording** button. Save and close the file.

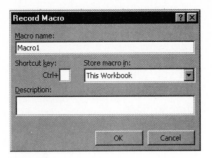

Figure 10.4 Record Macro dialog box

> Enter the name of the macro in the Macro name box. Use a name that will help you remember what the macro does.

Note: A macro name must start with a letter. No special characters or spaces are allowed in macro names, but you can use the underscore character (_) to separate parts of a name.

> Select the existing text in the Description box and enter your description of what the macro does.

> Click in the Shortcut key box and enter a letter that you can use with the Ctrl key to run your macro. You should not use letters that are already assigned to perform commands with the Ctrl key; for example, Ctrl+P for Print or Ctrl+X for Cut. If you do, the macro will override these commands.

Note: You cannot use numbers or special characters as shortcut keys.

> Specify the location in which Excel will store the macro. In the Store macro in box, you can select one of three options:

• Select Personal Macro Workbook if you want to use the macro whenever you use Excel. Excel stores the macro in a hidden workbook that is always open. To see the hidden Personal Macro Workbook, click Window, Unhide.

• Select This Workbook to store the macro in the current workbook only. Choose this option if you use the macro only for tasks in the current workbook.

• Select New Workbook to store the macro in a new or specified workbook. Select this option if you use the macro for some workbooks, but not for all of them. You will have to open the workbook that contains the macro before you can use it.

> Click OK. The Status bar displays the word Recording. The Stop Recording toolbar, as shown in Figure 10.5, appears on the worksheet.

Figure 10.5 Stop Recording toolbar

> Enter the series of steps you want to record in the macro. Press the Enter key. Then click the Stop Recording button on the Stop Recording toolbar.

Note: Take time to plan your steps carefully since Excel will record every action you take.

Use Relative Reference Macros

> If the macro you create contains a range of cells, Excel records them as absolute cell references. This means that the macro plays only on those designated cells. If you want to use the macro in other cell ranges, you must click the Relative Reference button on the Stop Recording toolbar before you record the macro. The Relative Reference button appears indented when it is active. When you record a macro with the Relative Reference button on, the macro can be applied to any cell in the worksheet.

> Once you have created a macro, each time you reopen the file the message shown in Figure 10.6 appears. It warns you that the file contains macros and gives you the option of disabling or enabling macros. If you want to make the macros functional, click Enable Macros.

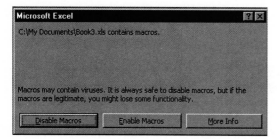

Figure 10.6 Enabling and disabling macros

T R Y *i t* O U T

1. Open the file **10.2TOAging** that you saved in the previous Try it Out.

2. In the dialog box that opens, click **Enable Macros.**

3. Click **Tools,** select **Macro,** and click **Record New Macro.**

4. Enter the following in the Macro name box:
   `Underline`

5. Enter the following in the Description box:
   `Heavy underline`

6. Enter **b** in the Shortcut key box.

7. In the Store Macro in box, select **Personal Macro Workbook.**

8. Click **OK.**

9. Click the **Relative Reference** button on the Stop Recording toolbar.

10. Select **Cells A5:G5.** Click **Format, Cells,** and **Border.** Select the heavy line across the bottom of the cells. Click **OK** to end.

11. Click the **Stop Recording** button on the Stop Recording toolbar.

12. Click **Tools,** select **Macro,** and click **Record New Macro.**

13. Name the macro: `Border`
    Shortcut key: `r`
    Description: `Border around column titles`
    Store macro in: `This workbook`

14. Click **OK.**

15. Make sure the Relative Reference button is not depressed.

16. Select **Cells A7:G8.** Click **Format, Cells,** and **Border.**

17. Click the **Stop Recording** button on the Stop Recording toolbar.

18. Keep the file open.

Run Macros

> To run a macro, select the cell where you want the macro to start playing. Then press the keys that you designated for the particular macro (e.g., Ctrl+letter).

> Another way to run a macro is to click Tools, select Macro, and click Macros. The Macro dialog box opens, as shown in Figure 10.7. Select the name of your macro from the list and click Run.

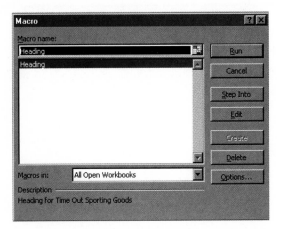

Figure 10.7 Macro dialog box

> You can also open the Macro dialog box by pressing the Alt+F8 keys. Then select the macro from the list and click Run.

> If you placed the Macros button on a toolbar or custom menu, you can click it to open the Macro dialog box. Select the macro and click Run.

T R Y *it* O U T

Note: Continue to work in
10.2TOAging.

1. On Sheet 2, click **Cell C2.**

2. Press the **Ctrl + t** keys.

3. On Sheet 2, click **Cell C5.**

4. Press the **Ctrl + b** keys.

5. On Sheet 2, click **Cell A14.**

6. Press the **Ctrl + r** keys.

7. Keep the file open.

Edit Macros Using the Visual Basic Editor

> If you want to make changes in your macro, you must use the *Visual Basic Editor* that is located in a module attached to your worksheet.

> To begin editing, click Tools, select Macro, and click Macros (or click the Alt+F8 keys). Select the macro you want to edit and click Edit. The Visual Basic Editor appears, as shown in Figure 10.8. Excel lists the commands in the macro in the window. Select and reenter, delete, or add commands. The way to make changes may be obvious for some of the commands, but if you want to learn more about the syntax for programming commands, click Help and Microsoft Visual Basic Help. When you have finished making your changes, close the Visual Basic Editor.

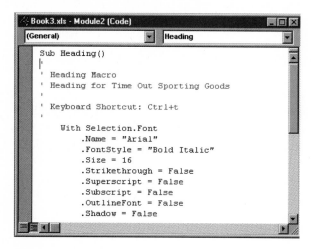

Figure 10.8 Example of a Visual Basic module

Delete a Macro

> To delete a macro, click Tools, select Macro, and click Macros. Select the macro you want to remove and click Delete.

Note: If the macro is stored in the Personal notebook, you must unhide it to view and delete the macro.

TRY *it* OUT

Note: Continue to work in 10.2TOAging.

1. Click **Tools**, select **Macro**, and click **Macros.**

2. Select the **Heading** macro. Click **Edit.**

3. Scroll down the list of commands until you see: .Font Style = "Bold Italic."

4. Delete **Italic.**

5. Close the Visual Basic Editor.

6. Go to Sheet 3 and click **Cell C2.**

7. Press the **Ctrl** + **t** keys. Keep the file open.

TRY *it* OUT

Note: Continue to work in 10.2TOAging.

1. Click **Tools,** select **Macro,** and click **Macros.**

2. Select **Heading** and click **Delete.**

3. Click **Window, Unhide.**

4. Click **OK** in the Unhide dialog box.

5. Click **Tools,** select **Macro,** and click **Macros.**

6. Select **Underline** and click **Delete.**

7. Click **Window, Hide.**

8. Close the workbook. Do not save.

REHEARSAL

TASK 2

 GOAL
To create an accounts receivable aging report

SETTING THE STAGE/WRAPUP
File name: 10.2OEPAgingReport

WHAT YOU NEED TO KNOW

> Accounts receivable are reviewed monthly to determine which invoices are unpaid and have exceeded the terms allowed. Finance charges may be imposed to encourage payment within the terms of the sale.

> In this Rehearsal activity, you create, edit, and run macros to complete the aging report for Occasions Event Planning for two months. You will name, describe, and establish shortcut keys for the macros that relate to their purpose.

> You will use the macros with the custom menus and toolbars created earlier to create an accounts receivable aging report more efficiently.

DIRECTIONS

1. Open **10.2OEPAgingReport** or use the file you worked on in the last Rehearsal, **10.1OEPAgingReport.**

2. Click **Cell C2.** Create a macro that does the following:
   a. Enter the following heading for the report, as shown in the illustration on the next page:
      Occasions Event Planning
   b. Format in Comic Sans MS, Bold Italic, 18 pt.

3. Go to the sheet labeled July and run this macro in **Cell C2.**

4. Edit the macro so that bold is removed.

5. Run the edited macro in the sheets for June and July in **Cell C2.**

6. In **Cell E10** for June, create a macro that does the following:
   a. Enters the formula for calculating the number of days an account is unpaid. (*Hint: Subtract the DUE DATE from the Current Date, which must be an absolute cell reference.*)
   b. Formats the result for General numbers (no decimal places).

7. Use the fill handle to copy the formula to the remaining invoices.

8. Go to the sheet for July and run this macro in **Cell E10.** Use the fill handle to fill in the remaining values for the column.

9. Group the June and July sheets and do the following:
   a. Enter the lookup table below beginning in **Cell B22.**

Unpaid Days	Interest Rate
1	0.000
15	0.005
30	0.010
60	0.015
90	0.020

   b. Name the lookup table: **Table**
   c. In the Interest Rate column, enter a formula using the LOOKUP function in Excel, and the name of the table, to determine the interest rate for each customer.
   d. Format **Column G** for Percent with one decimal place.

Continued on next page

e. Use the fill handle to fill in the remaining values for the column.

f. Ungroup the sheets.

10. In **Cell H10,** on the June sheet, create a macro that does the following:

    a. Enters the formula to calculate the late fee due.

    b. Formats the result for currency.

    c. Fills in the remaining values for the column.

11. In **Cell I10,** create a macro that does the following:

    a. Enters the formula for calculating the total amount due.

    b. Formats the result for Currency.

    c. Fills in the remaining values for the column.

12. On the July sheet, run the macros for the late fee and total amount due in **Columns H** and **I,** respectively.

13. Print a copy of this workbook.

14. Save and close the **10.2OEPAgingReport** file.

	A	B	C	D	E	F	G	H	I
1									
2	Record macro to create								
3	heading here		Accounts Receivable Aging Report						
4							Enter macros to create		
5	Current Date:			6/30/02			formulas for these values		
6									
7	INVOICE	INVOICE				INVOICE	INTEREST		AMOUNT
8	NUMBER	DATE	CUSTOMER	DUE DATE	DAYS UNPAID	AMOUNT	RATE	LATE FEE	DUE
9									
10	115	04/15/02	Fox Travel Conference	04/25/02		$ 7,000.00			
11	120	04/29/02	Barney's 25th Anniversary	05/09/02		$ 3,000.00			
12	122	04/30/02	Trilogy Film Opening	05/10/02		$ 10,000.00			
13	140	05/15/02	Clarisse Beauty Salon	05/25/02		$ 3,000.00			
14	155	05/25/02	Holden Wedding	06/04/02		$ 9,000.00			
15	158	06/14/02	LA Times	06/24/02		$ 15,000.00			
16									
17									
18	Group sheets and enter lookup table here						Group sheets and enter lookup formulas here		
19									
20									
21									
22									

Cues for Reference

Create a Macro

1. Click **Tools,** select **Macro,** and click **Record New Macro,** or click **Record Macro** button you have placed on toolbar.
2. In Record Macro dialog box:
   a. Enter name of macro in Macro name box.
   b. Enter a description of macro in Description box.
   c. Enter letter you will use (with Ctrl key) to enable macro in Shortcut key box.
   d. Select location in which to store macro in Store macro in box.

3. Click **OK.**
4. If macro will be used in any location on worksheet, click **Relative Reference** button.
5. Enter commands for macro and press **Enter.**
6. Click **Stop Recording** button.

Run a Macro

1. Click **Tools,** select **Macro,** and click **Macros.**
   or
 • Click **Macros** button you have placed on toolbar.

2. In Macro dialog box, click name of macro and click **Run.**

Edit a Macro

1. Click **Tools,** select **Macro,** and click **Macros.**
   or
 • Click **Macro** button you have placed on toolbar.
2. Select name of macro you want to edit. Click **Edit.**
3. Make changes in commands in Visual Basic Editor module.
4. Close Visual Basic Editor.

PERFORMANCE

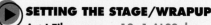
WHAT YOU NEED TO KNOW

Act I

The Boston office of the Air Land Sea Travel Group is setting up a workbook for its sales to customers who have agency accounts. Since most customers use bank credit cards, the company only has a small number of sales to customers who use the agency billing system. The workbook will be used to track invoices prepared for agency account customers. Open the file **10p1.ALSSales** from the Data CD. You will create a custom menu and add several buttons to the Standard toolbar. You will create a macro to format dates on the worksheet. You will use these customized features to work in the sales report.

Follow these guidelines:

★ Create a custom menu named: `Sales`

★ Make sure the Customize dialog box is open when you are naming and adding commands to the custom menu.

★ Add the following commands to the menu:
Insert, Rows
Edit, Delete Rows
Format, Currency Style
Format, Fill Color

★ Put the following buttons on the Standard toolbar if they are not already there:
Tools, Macros
Tools, Record New Macro
Tools, Trace Error
Tools, Search

★ Delete the **Search** button from the Standard toolbar.

★ Enter a formula to calculate Date Due, using the terms and invoice date.

★ Use the customized toolbar buttons to record a macro to format dates in any column to dd-mmm-yy format.

★ Run the macro to format all dates.

★ Use the customized menu to format Amount Due for Currency.

✴ Include the following sales for the last two days of the week:

Invoice Date	Invoice Number	Trip Date	Customer	Terms-Days	Amount
7/5/02	2442	8/15/02	Marvin Franks	30	$1500.00
7/6/02	2443	8/23/02	Lance Scully	30	$ 674.50
7/6/02	2444	7/28/02	Helen Reid	20	$ 235.65

✴ Use the customized menu, toolbar buttons, and macro as needed to complete all sales records.

✴ Print a copy of the report.

✴ Save your work. Close the file.

Act II

Odyssey Travel Gear is preparing a workbook to handle its accounts receivable aging reports. Open **10p2.OTGAging** from the Data CD. Create macros for the corporate heading and all of the necessary formulas on the sheet labeled July. Then run the macros in the appropriate locations on the sheet labeled August.

odyssey travel gear

Follow these guidelines:

✴ The Tools, Macros and Tools, and Record New Macro buttons should be on the toolbar.

✴ Create a macro to enter the corporate heading that can be used in any cell. In **Cell A1,** enter: **Odyssey Travel Gear**

✴ Use Bold Italic, 14 pt. Center the heading horizontally across **Columns A:I** using the Merge and Center button.

✴ Edit the macro for the corporate heading so that it appears in 18 pt. Run the heading macro again in **Cell A2.** Delete the heading in **Cell A1** and remove the merge cells format from **Row 1.**

✴ In **Cell D9,** create a macro to enter the formula to calculate the due date of the invoice; format the results for dates in the mm/dd/yy format. (All customers are given 30 days to pay their bills.) Use the fill handle to fill in the values for all of the invoices.

✴ In **Cell E9,** create a macro to enter the formula computing the number of days an invoice is unpaid, i.e., the number of days past the due date. Use the General number format for the results. Use the fill handle to fill in the values for all of the invoices.

✳ The lookup table below should start in **Cell A20** and should be entered on both sheets.

UNPAID DAYS	INTEREST RATE
1	0.00
30	0.01
60	0.02
90	0.03

✳ In **Cell G9,** use the LOOKUP function in Excel to find the interest rate for all customers using a named range for the table. Format the interest rate for Percent with one decimal place.

✳ In **Cell H9,** create a macro to compute the late fee for each customer. Use the fill handle to fill in the values for all of the customers.

✳ In **Cell I9,** create a macro to compute the total amount due for each invoice. Use the fill handle to fill in the values for all of the invoices.

✳ For the month of August, the following invoices are still unpaid: 265, 324, 387, and 453. In addition, there is one more invoice that has not been paid: Invoice 524, dated 7/1/02, to Bender's, for $300. Copy the data for the August aging report by copying **Columns A:F** data for the invoices that are still unpaid. Enter the new unpaid invoice.

✳ Run all of the appropriate macros on the sheet for August.

✳ Print the report and save the file.

TRUE / FALSE

Circle **T** if the statement is true or **F** if the statement is false.

T F 1. To name a custom menu, the Customize dialog box must be open.

T F 2. A macro is edited in the Visual Basic Editor.

T F 3. An accounts receivable aging report allows a business to identify delinquent customers.

T F 4. If you want a macro to run only in the specific workbook in which you recorded it, you should save it in the Personal Macro Workbook.

T F 5. A macro cannot contain a formula.

MULTIPLE CHOICE

Identify the letter of the choice that best completes the statement or answers the question.

6. The purpose of a custom menu is to:
    A. Create commands Excel does not have.
    B. Group the Excel commands you use most frequently for a given task.
    C. Record a series of keystrokes.
    D. Create a template.

7. Most of the actions necessary to create a custom menu use the:
    A. Macro Record dialog box.
    B. Stop Recording toolbar.
    C. Customize dialog box.
    D. View drop-down menu.

8. A drop-down menu that contains the commands and buttons you use most often is called a:
    A. Macro.
    B. Custom menu.
    C. Customized toolbar.
    D. Visual Basic Editor.

9. To add a button to a toolbar:
    A. Click Tools, Customize, and the Commands tab.
    B. Click the Start Recording button.
    C. Click Tools, Macros.
    D. Click Insert, Buttons.

10. Which of the following is permissible as a macro name?
    A. Total_Sales
    B. Total Sales
    C. Total@Northeast
    D. 2002Heading

11. The toolbar that appears when you are recording a macro is called the:
    A. Macro toolbar.
    B. Customize toolbar.
    C. Stop Recording toolbar.
    D. Personal Workbook toolbar.

12. The Visual Basic Editor:
    A. Is another spreadsheet.
    B. Contains programming statements for macros.
    C. Does not allow you to make changes in macros.
    D. Cannot be accessed directly from your workbook.

13. One way to play back a macro is to:
    A. Use the shortcut keys you designated when you created the macro.
    B. Press the Shift, Alt, and Delete keys.
    C. Click View, Toolbars.
    D. Press the X button in the upper right corner of the worksheet.

14. You want to record the keystrokes that format and label a company name. The Excel function you should use is a:
    A. Template.
    B. Lookup function.
    C. AutoSum function.
    D. Macro.

15. A record of amounts of money owed to a business by its customers is called:
    A. Accounts payable.
    B. Accounts receivable.
    C. A payment form.
    D. A debit form.

COMPLETION

Complete each sentence or statement.

16. The sequence of actions you take to create a custom menu is to click Tools, _____.

17. A report that provides an analysis of how many days payments from customers are overdue is called _____.

18. Accounts that shows the amount of money owed to a company by its customers are called _____.

19. A series of actions you record in order to complete a task quickly and efficiently is called a _____.

20. The module that contains the program codes for macros is called the _____.

LESSON 11

Data Lists

In this lesson, you will learn to use several features of Excel that allow you to manage data lists such as personnel, real estate, and inventory lists. These features include sorting a list and using subtotals, filters, group and outline criteria, and data validation.

Upon completion of this lesson, you should have mastered the following skill sets:

- Create and sort a list
  - Create a list
  - Sort a list
- Use subtotals with lists and ranges Ⓜ
- Define and apply filters Ⓜ
  - AutoFilter
  - Advanced Filter
- Add group and outline criteria to ranges Ⓜ
  - Group data
  - Outline data
- Use data validation Ⓜ
  - Error messages

Terms
MOUS-related
Record
Field name
Subtotal
Filter
Criteria range
Data validation
Document-related
Personnel list
Real estate list
Inventory list

TRYOUT

TASK 1

 GOAL
To practice using the following skill sets:
* Create and sort a list
  * Create a list
  * Sort a list
* Use subtotals with lists and ranges **M**

WHAT YOU NEED TO KNOW

Create and Sort a List

> In addition to its spreadsheet functions, Excel has many features that allow you to create, manage, and obtain information from lists. In other words, Excel performs many database functions. Businesses can use these functions to store and analyze information about employees, customers, product inventories, and sales, to name just a few examples.

Create a List

> To create a data list, you must follow a number of conventions:

* The data for one person or unit, called a *record,* goes across a row.

* Place a label, or *field name,* for the data in each column above the first row of data. The field name format (i.e., font, cell border, alignment, capitalization style, etc.) should be different from that of the data entries. Excel uses these labels to find and perform operations on the data.

* The data for each record must correspond to the labels or field names in the first row, or the column labels for the list.

* Put only one list on a given worksheet.

* Do not put blank rows or columns within the list.

* If there is other data on the worksheet, leave at least one blank row or column between that data and the list.

TRY*it*OUT

1. Open the file **11.1PersList** from the Data CD.

2. Click **Data, Form,** and **New.**

3. In the dialog box, enter the following information for each field:
   LAST: **Sullivan**
   FIRST: **Karen**
   LOCATION: **CT**
   IDNO: **42898**
   HIRED: **02/20/02**
   DEPT: **Sales**
   WKSAL: **$325.00**

4. Click **New** and **Close.**

5. Add a column to the left of **Column H.**

6. In the new column, click **Format, Cells, Alignment,** and check the **Wrap text** option. Click **OK.**

7. Label the column: **DATE OF LAST PERFORMANCE REVIEW**

8. Click **Data, Form** and use the navigation buttons to view the previous records.

9. Leave the file open.

- Avoid storing data to the left or right of the list, since filtering can hide that data. Figure 11.1 shows an example of a list with its components.

Field name

	A	B	C	D	E	F	G
1	LAST	FIRST	LOCATION	IDNO	HIRED	DEPT	WKSAL
2	Notting	Deirdre	CT	42980	02/25/99	Sales	$ 325.60
3	Edwards	Henry	CT	42859	03/07/98	Sales	$ 400.89
4	Martin	Hester	NJ	43449	04/05/01	Stock	$ 250.76
5	Wendt	Jack	NY	44689	05/24/00	Stock	$ 275.66
6	Rogers	James	CT	42785	05/04/01	Stock	$ 248.77
7	Brown	James	NY	44783	06/12/00	Admin	$ 495.82
8	Bartlett	Jane	NY	44132	01/05/99	Sales	$ 362.33
9	Selman	Jean	CT	42234	05/30/96	Admin	$ 600.45
10	McCarthy	Joan	NY	44675	03/14/00	Sales	$ 322.79
11	Sullivan	Karen	CT	42898	02/20/02	Sales	$ 325.00
12	Dodge	Kiley	NJ	43212	04/16/98	Sales	$ 460.96
13	Yaeger	Kimberly	NY	44332	04/19/99	Sales	$ 390.68
14	Smith	Lisa	NJ	43989	05/17/99	Sales	$ 378.56

Record for one person

Figure 11.1 Example of a data list

> To add a new record to a list, click Insert, Row at the appropriate place in the list and add the data. You can also click Data, Form, so that the Data Form dialog box opens, as shown in Figure 11.2. The data form displays the names for every data field you have created in the list. It also lets you view all of the information for each record, one record at a time. By using the data form, you can add new records, delete records, edit records, move to the next or previous record, and find records based on criteria that you apply.

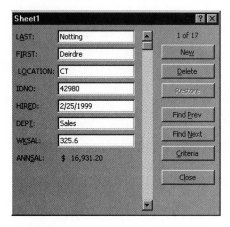

Figure 11.2 Data Form dialog box

> To add a new column or field, click Insert, Column, and add the appropriate field name and data.

Note: A data list in Excel requires that all column labels (or field names) fit in one cell above the data. Thus, you must format long field names with the Wrap Text feature. Click Format, Cells, click the Alignment tab, and select the Wrap text option.

Sort a List

> Excel allows you to sort the data in a list according to the criteria you specify. For example, you can sort the data alphabetically, numerically, or according to groups (e.g., all those who work in the states of New York or Connecticut).

> To sort data, select a cell in the field by which you want to sort. Click Data, Sort. The Sort dialog box opens, as shown in Figure 11.3. In the box labeled Sort by, select the field name by which you want Excel to sort the data.

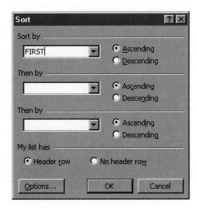

Figure 11.3 Sort dialog box

> Check the box to indicate whether you want to sort in ascending or descending order. If you want to arrange the data alphabetically, from smallest to largest or from oldest to most recent, select Ascending. If you select Descending, the reverse order results.

> You can sort records by several fields in successive order.

> Once you sort a list, the original order of the data is lost. To retain a copy of the original order of the data list, create a field name called Record Number (or any name that indicates the numbers below it are in sequence). Then number each record sequentially. Later, when you want to sort the data back to the original order, you can sort by Record Number.

> To undo a sort, click Edit, Undo Sort.

Use Subtotals with Lists and Ranges

> Excel provides a quick way to obtain a *subtotal,* a summary of a subset of data that is arranged in a list. You should sort the data for which you want to create a subtotal according to the relevant criterion, so that data in each subgroup appears together.

> To create a subtotal, click Data, Subtotal to open the Subtotal dialog box, as shown in Figure 11.4.

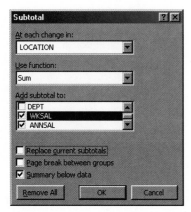

Figure 11.4 Subtotal dialog box

> In the box labeled At each change in, select the field name of the data that determines the groups for which you will obtain subtotals.

> In the box labeled Use function, select the mathematical operation you want to perform. You can select from Sum, Count, Average, Max, Min, Product, or several statistical functions.

> In the box labeled Add subtotal to, select the data on which you want to perform the mathematical function.

> Check the box Replace current subtotals if prior subtotals have been computed and you want to replace them.

> Check the box Page break between groups if you want each of the subtotals to appear on a separate page.

> Check the box Summary below data if you want to compute a grand total.

> Click OK.

*Note: Continue to work in **11.1PersList.***

1. Click **Data, Sort.** Sort the list by **LOCATION** and then by **LAST.** Click **OK.**

2. Click **Data, Subtotals.**

3. In the Subtotal dialog box, in At each change in, select **LOCATION.**

4. In the Use function box, select **SUM.**

5. In the Add subtotal to box, check **WKSAL** and **ANNSAL.**

6. Check **Summary below data.** Click **OK.**

7. As shown in Figure 11.5, click each **Hide Detail** button in the far left column, starting with those on the right in Column Level 2 and then in Column Level 1. Then click the **Show Detail** buttons in succession, starting with Column Level 1 and then Column Level 2.

8. Close the file. Do not save.

> You can use the outline controls on the far left column of a subtotaled list to hide or show the elements in the subtotaled list, as shown in Figure 11.5. Click the Show Detail button to display the data that makes up a subtotal. Click the Hide Detail button to collapse the data so that just the subtotal shows.

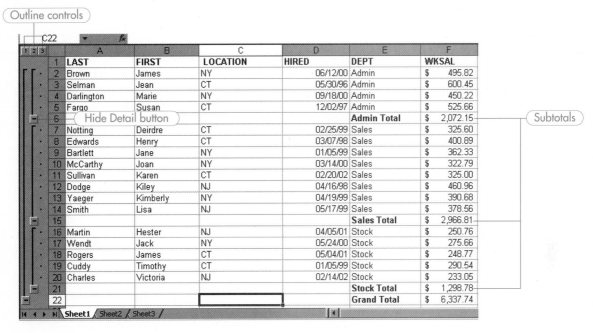

Figure 11.5 Outline controls on a list

> If you want to remove subtotals, click Data, Subtotals, and click the Remove All button in the Subtotals dialog box.

REHEARSAL

TASK 1

 GOAL
To use the list, sort, and subtotal
functions in Excel on a personnel list

SETTING THE STAGE/WRAPUP
File name: 11.1Personnel

WHAT YOU NEED TO KNOW

> Businesses need to keep database information on their employees to store essential facts, such as when individual employees were hired, their rates of compensation, and the departments in which they work. The record of all employees and their associated information is called a *personnel list.* The database functions in Excel allow you to manipulate the list to arrange the data in different ways and to summarize different components of the list.

> In this Rehearsal activity, you will work with the Occasions Event Planning personnel list. You will add new records to the list, sort the list, and add subtotals to create a report of salaries according to region.

DIRECTIONS

1. Open the file **11.1Personnel** from the Data CD and use the illustration on the next page as a guide for this activity.

2. Add a column to the left of **Column A** and select the **Wrap text** option. Label it `Record Number` and use the fill handle to number each record from 1 to 14.

3. Change the label for **Column D** to: `OFFICE LOCATION` Set the alignment to Wrap text, so that both lines appear in one cell.

4. Format the column for WKSAL in Accounting style.

5. Add a column to the right of **Column H** labeled: `ANNSAL` Format the column in the Accounting style.

6. Enter a formula to calculate the annual salary.

7. Add the following employee records to the end of the list and fill the record numbers down for each new employee:

LAST	FIRST	OFFICE LOCATION	IDNO	DATE HIRED	DEPT	WKSAL
Smith	Rebecca	CA	20749	6/24/01	Sales	455
Trent	Robert	OR	21980	6/30/01	Sales	435

8. Click **Data, Form** to add the following new employees' records to the list using a data form:

LAST	FIRST	OFFICE LOCATION	IDNO	DATE HIRED	DEPT	WKSAL
Leary	Gina	CA	20998	7/15/01	Sales	455
Orroz	James	WA	23999	8/30/01	Sales	430

9. Sort the list according to two fields: first by Office Location and then by Last (name).

10. Obtain a subtotal for the weekly and annual salaries according to office locations. In addition, obtain grand totals.

11. Print the worksheet.

12. Collapse the data so that only the subtotals for each region show in the report. Print the report.

13. Expand the data so that all of the elements in the original database are visible.

14. Remove the subtotals.

15. Re-sort the list so that it is back to the order it was in at the start of this exercise.

16. Sort the list according to annual salaries with the highest salary on top.

17. Save and close the file.

	A	B	C	D	E	F	G	H
1	LAST	FIRST	LOCATION	IDNO	HIRED	DEPT	WKSAL	
2	Birney	Mary	CA	20456	2/15/1997	Sales	650	
3	Darby	Marge	OR	21567	6/1/1999	Admin	625	
4	Ajello	Anthony	WA	23143	3/2/2000	Sales	460	
5	Kearney	Sharon	CA	21980	8/24/2001	Sales	455	
6	Weeks	David	OR	21486	9/25/1999	Admin	480	
7	Cacher	William	CA	20998	4/13/2000	Sales	490	
8	Gilchrest	Cindy	OR	21222	5/15/2000	Sales	445	
9	Lakoff	Brian	WA	23886	5/15/1999	Admin	500	
10	Williams	Todd	CA	20648	2/15/1997	Admin	650	
11	Carey	Barbara	WA	23846	9/24/2001	Sales	445	
12	Sanderson	David	OR	21778	8/28/2000	Sales	465	
13	Penney	Jason	CA	20846	2/20/1997	Sales	565	
14	Murphy	Janelle	WA	23112	6/15/1999	Sales	480	
15	Gibbons	Dorothy	OR	21668	6/15/1999	Sales	495	
16								
17								

Cues for Reference

Add a Record to a List
1. Click **Insert, Row.**
2. Enter appropriate data to correspond to field names in first row.
   or
1. Click **Data, Form,** and **New.**
2. Enter data for each field name in dialog box.
3. Click **Close.**

Sort a List
1. Click **Data, Sort.**
2. Select field name by which you want Excel to sort data.
3. Click **Ascending** or **Descending.**
4. Click **OK.**

Obtain Subtotals
1. Click cell in database.
2. Click **Data, Subtotals.**
3. Select field name to sort by in At each change in box.

4. Select function in Use function box.
5. Select field for subtotals in Add subtotal to box.
6. Check boxes that apply: **Replace current subtotals, Page break between groups,** and **Summary below data.**
7. Click **OK.**

Remove Subtotals
1. Click **Data, Subtotals.**
2. Click **Remove All.**

T R Y O U T

▶ **GOAL**
To practice using the following skill sets:
✶ Define and apply filters M
  ✶ AutoFilter
  ✶ Advanced Filter

TASK 2

Define and Apply Filters

> A *filter* allows you to display only the data you want from a data list. For example, certain data may be confidential or you might want to present only a portion of the data on a printout or report. You have already learned how to use AutoFilter to perform some of these actions. In this lesson, you learn how to create and apply custom filters.

AutoFilter

> One way to customize the information you select for display is to use AutoFilter to create a specified range of values as the criteria for filtering.

> Click Data, select Filter, and click AutoFilter. List arrows appear next to each field name.

> Click the list arrow next to the field name you want to filter.

> Click Custom. The Custom AutoFilter dialog box opens, as shown in Figure 11.6. Enter or select the filtering criteria you want to use in each of the boxes. For example, you may want to display records for which the data equals, is greater than, or is less than a specified value. In addition, you may want to specify one criterion and another, or one criterion or another.

T R Y *it* O U T

1. Open **11.2RealEstate** from the Data CD.

2. Select any cell in this list. Click **Data,** select **Filter,** and click **AutoFilter.**

3. Click the **list arrow** next to **TYPE.**

4. Select **Custom.**

5. In the Custom AutoFilter dialog box, select **TYPE equals.** Click the **list arrow** in the box on its right and select **A-frame.**

6. Click the **Or** button. In the next box, click **equals.** Click the **list arrow** in the box on its right and select **Ranch.**

7. Click **OK.** The records with Ranch and A-Frame types appear.

8. Click the **list arrow** next to **TYPE.** Select **All.**

9. Leave the file open.

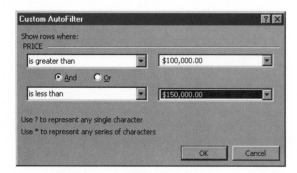

Figure 11.6 Custom AutoFilter dialog box

> Click OK. Only the records that meet the filtering criteria you select appear. The other records remain in the data list, but Excel hides them.

> To show all of the records again, click the list arrow next to the field name you are using to filter the data and click All.

> Another way to show all of the records again is to click Data, select Filter, and click AutoFilter to deselect it.

Advanced Filter

> Another way to specify filtering criteria is to use the Advanced Filter feature in Excel. The Advanced Filter allows you to name more complex criteria for filtering and to copy the filtered records to another location on the worksheet. You can then view the filtered records, as well as the original data list, at the same time. You can also manipulate the data in the filtered list (e.g., sort or delete records) without affecting the original data list. In contrast to AutoFilter, list arrows do not appear next to each field name when you use the Advanced Filter.

> To use the Advanced Filter, click a cell in the data list. Then click Data, select Filter, and click Advanced Filter. The Advanced Filter dialog box opens, as shown in Figure 11.7.

Figure 11.7 Advanced Filter dialog box

> You must first specify whether you want Excel simply to filter the records in the current location of the worksheet or to filter and copy them to a new location. Click the appropriate Action button in the dialog box.

> Next, select the range that contains the data you want to filter. The field names should be included in this range. You can enter the cell references, or click the Collapse Dialog Box button and select the appropriate cells. Then click the Expand Dialog Box button to redisplay the Advanced Filter dialog box.

 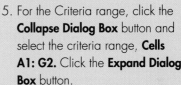

> Specify the range of cells on the worksheet that contains the filtering criteria. This means that beforehand, you must create a duplicate of the field names of the original data list. The values of the specific filtering criteria for an advanced filter are entered under the relevant field names in the location called the *criteria range,* as shown in Figure 11.8. An easy way to do this is to copy the field names from the data list and paste them to the criteria range. You can enter one or more criteria, and Excel displays only the records meeting all of those criteria. If you enter a specific value under a field name, Excel filters only records matching that criterion. Other operators used to set criteria are given in the table below:

SYMBOL	EXAMPLE	RESULT
= (equal to)	=A-frame	Lists all A-frame houses
<> (not equal to)	<>Ranch	Lists all houses except ranches
> (greater than)	>$150,000	List all houses with selling prices greater than $150,000
< (less than)	<$100,000	List all houses with selling prices less than $100,000
>= (greater than or equal to)	>=$150,000	Lists all houses with selling prices of $150,000 or higher
<= (less than or equal to)	<=$100,000	Lists all houses with selling prices of $100,000 or less

> Try to plan the best place to put the criteria range so that it does not interfere with the entry of new data in the list. Figure 11.8 shows an example of a criteria range created for the data in the file 11.2RealEstate. It is located at the top of the data list so new entries to the data list do not overlap it.

Figure 11.8 Example of criteria range

> If you are copying the filtered list to another location, specify the range of cells that will contain the filtered data. Click OK.

Note: You can specify the first cell to which you want to copy the filtered data and Excel will fill in the rest of the values. You cannot select another worksheet as a destination for the filtered data, but you can copy it to another worksheet later.

> To de-activate filtering, click Data, select Filter, and click Show All.

REHEARSAL

TASK 2

GOAL
To generate various real estate lists
using the filtering functions in Excel

SETTING THE STAGE/WRAPUP
File name: 11.2FourCorners

WHAT YOU NEED TO KNOW

> A *real estate list* is a data list that
contains a real estate company s
current inventory of homes and
apartments for sale or rent. By

 DIRECTIONS

1. Open **11.2FourCorners** from the Data CD and use the
illustration on the next page as a guide for this activity.

2. Add the following listings to the data list by clicking **Data, Form:**

LOCATION	TOWN	LISTED	TYPE	BR	BATHS	PRICE
12 Loring Drive	Bakersfield	July 30	Cape	3	2	$162,000
33 Wayside Road	Tilton	July 31	Ranch	3	2	$172,000

using the filtering functions in
Excel, you can select properties
according to the criteria specified
by buyers or real estate brokers.

> In this Rehearsal activity, you apply
custom filters to create various
reports from the data in a real estate
list for Four Corners Realty.

3. Use the Custom feature of AutoFilter to create a list of three-
bedroom properties priced at $170,000 or less. Copy and
paste this list to another worksheet and print the report. Label the
worksheet tab: **3br<170**

4. Remove all of the filters.

5. Copy the field names to **Row 1.**

6. Use the Advanced Filter to generate a list of all properties in
Farmington that are priced at $150,000 or less. Place the
criteria range above the data list and under the field names you
copied. Copy the filtered list to another worksheet and label the
worksheet tab appropriately. Print the report.

7. Use the Advanced Filter to generate a list of all Contemporary
homes with four bedrooms priced above $190,000. Copy the
filtered list to a new worksheet and label the worksheet tab
appropriately.

8. Sort the resulting filtered list by date from most recent to less
recent and print the report.

9. Use the Advanced Filter to generate a list of three-bedroom
homes priced under $160,000. Filter the list on the original
worksheet. Print the report.

10. Delete the list from the last filter and all criteria entries.

11. Use the Advanced Filter to generate a list of all Cape-style homes with three or more bedrooms and two baths priced less than $172,000. Copy the filtered list to a new worksheet and label the worksheet tab appropriately. Sort the resulting filtered list by date from most recent to less recent and print the report.

12. Return to the real estate list sheet and sort the list by town and then by date listed. Use subtotals (sums) to find the total value of listings for each town and the total value of all real estate listings. Print a copy of this report.

13. Save and close the file.

	A	B	C	D	E	F	G	H
3								
4	LOCATION	TOWN	LISTED	TYPE	BR	BATHS	PRICE	
5	11 Neeland Way	Farmington	6-May	Tudor	2	2	$ 150,000.00	
6	212 Conran Street	Santa Ana	15-May	Ranch	3	2	$ 165,000.00	
7	89 Second Street	Bakersfield	1-Jun	Ranch	4	3	$ 200,000.00	
8	55 Brighton Road	Farmington	30-May	Cape	3	2	$ 145,000.00	
9	67 Lithgow Drive	Farmington	10-Jun	Contemporary	4	3	$ 230,000.00	
10	8 Rolling Hills Road	Santa Ana	20-May	Tudor	3	2	$ 180,000.00	
11	88 Mountain Drive	Santa Ana	14-Jun	Contemporary	3	2	$ 189,000.00	
12	43 Brook Road	Bakersfield	2-Jun	Cape	2	1	$ 135,000.00	
13	65 Summer Street	Farmington	1-Jul	Ranch	3	2	$ 165,000.00	
14	10 Forsyth Street	Tilton	3-Jun	Cape	4	2	$ 170,000.00	
15	14 King Street	Tilton	20-Jun	Contemporary	3	2	$ 180,000.00	
16	5 Holly Road	Farmington	19-May	Ranch	2	1	$ 139,000.00	
17	200 Winston Drive	Bakersfield	28-Jun	Tudor	3	2	$ 160,000.00	
18	314 Third Avenue	Bakersfield	19-May	Ranch	4	3	$ 205,000.00	
19	6 Ridley Drive	Santa Ana	30-Jun	Contemporary	4	2	$ 197,000.00	
20	95 Simon Street	Tilton	27-May	Ranch	4	2	$ 188,000.00	
21	14 Pine Street	Bakersfield	28-Jun	Cape	2	1	$ 139,000.00	
22	73 George Street	Tilton	3-Jul	Ranch	3	2	$ 159,000.00	
23	68 Corcoran Drive	Bakersfield	20-Jul	Contemporary	3	2	$ 159,000.00	
24								

Cues for Reference

Use Custom Filters with AutoFilter
1. Select cell in data list.
2. Click **Data,** select **Filter,** and click **AutoFilter.** Select **Custom** from drop-down list next to appropriate field name.
3. Select filtering criteria you want to use.
4. Click **OK.**

Remove Filters
1. Click **Data,** select **Filter,** and click **AutoFilter.**
2. Click **AutoFilter** to de-select it.

Use Advanced Filter
1. Click cell in data list.
2. Click **Data,** select **Filter,** and click **Advanced Filter.**

3. Specify whether to filter in place or at new location.
4. Specify range of data to filter.
5. Create criteria filter range. Insert values for filtering criteria.
6. Specify range for destination of filtered list if you are copying it to new location.
7. Click **OK.**

TRYOUT

TASK 3

GOAL

To practice using the following skill sets:

✴ Add group and outline criteria to
   ranges M
   ✴ Group data
   ✴ Outline data
✴ Use data validation M
   ✴ Error messages

Add Group and Outline Criteria to Ranges

> Under certain circumstances, you might want to display only a subset or a summary of information in a data list. For example, when the data list is very large, you might want to display only certain similar items from that subset. Or, you might want to show only the subtotals or results of other calculations that Excel has performed on a set of records. To do so, you can use the Group and Outline feature in Excel.

Group Data

> One way that you can display a subset of a list is to create groups of records.

> To create a group, first select the records in the data list that will comprise the group. Click Data, select Group and Outline, and click Group.

> The Group dialog box opens, as shown in Figure 11.9. Click Rows or Columns, depending on which defines the nature of your group, and click OK.

Figure 11.9 Group dialog box

Note: You can create groups within groups by applying the above procedures to the smallest group first, and then successively larger groups.

TRY *it* OUT

1. Open the file **11.3Inventory** from the Data CD.

2. Select **Cells A5:F7.**

3. Click **Data,** select **Group and Outline,** and click **Group.**

4. In the Group dialog box, select **Rows** and click **OK.**

5. Select **Cells A5:F10.**

6. Click **Data,** select **Group and Outline,** and click **Group.**

7. In the Group dialog box, select **Rows** and click **OK.**

8. Select **Cells A5:F13.**

9. Click **Data,** select **Group and Outline,** and click **Group.**

10. In the Group dialog box, select **Rows** and click **OK.**

11. Leave the file open.

> Figure 11.10 shows a group created from a larger data list. Notice the Hide Detail button in the leftmost column. When you click the Hide Detail button, Excel removes the group from view. When you click the Show Detail button, the group reappears.

	4	Item No.	Description	Color	Quantity in Stock	Co
	5	21-202	Sports bags	Black	20	$
	6	21-203	Sports bags	Navy	15	$
	7	21-204	Sports bags	Green	18	$
	8	Hide sports bags detail		White	25	$
	9	23-302	Soccer balls	Black trim	30	$
	10	23-303	Soccer balls	Red trim	23	$
	11	Hide A5:F10 detail		White	25	$
	12	24-161	Soccer T's	Gray	18	$

Figure 11.10 Example of grouped data

> To remove a group, select the data in the group. Then click Data, select Group and Outline, and click Ungroup.

Outline Data

> The outlining functions in Excel work just like the grouping functions, but apply only to data lists that contain formulas.

> To outline data, click Data, select Group and Outline, and click Auto Outline. Excel automatically groups any data that is summarized in the worksheet. You can click the Hide and Show Detail buttons, as you did above, to collapse and expand the data.

Note: As mentioned earlier in this lesson, Excel automatically adds outline features when it computes subtotals.

> To remove an outline, click Data, select Group and Outline, and click Clear Outline. The outline symbols no longer appear on the worksheet.

TRY *it* **OUT**

Note: Continue to work in 11.3Inventory.

1. Click the **Hide Detail** button in **Column 3, Column 2,** and **Column 1.**

2. Click the **Show Detail** button in **Column 1, Column 2,** and **Column 3.**

3. Select **Cells A5:F13.**

4. Click **Data,** select **Group and Outline,** and click **Ungroup.** Select **Rows** and click **OK.**

5. Select **Cells A5:F10.**

6. Click **Data,** select **Group and Outline,** and click **Ungroup.** Select **Rows** and click **OK.**

7. Select **Cells A5:F7.**

8. Click **Data,** select **Group and Outline,** and click **Ungroup.** Select **Rows** and click **OK.**

9. Leave the file open.

TRY *it* **OUT**

Note: Continue to work in 11.3Inventory.

1. In **Cell A15,** enter: **TOTAL**

2. In **Cell F15,** apply the AutoSum feature to obtain the sum of the Valuation column.

3. Click **Data,** select **Group and Outline,** and click **Auto Outline.**

4. Click the **Hide Detail** button that appears over **Column F.**

5. Print the report.

6. Click **Data,** select **Group and Outline,** and click **Clear Outline.**

7. Keep the file open.

Use Data Validation

> *Data validation* is a feature that helps you ensure that the correct data is entered on a worksheet or in a data list. You specify what data is valid for particular cells or cell ranges. You can also create messages to alert the person entering the data that there is an error.

> Some of the ways that you can specify valid entries include the following:

   • Restrict entries to whole numbers, percentages, or text.

   • Define a list of valid entries.

   • Limit the number of characters that you can enter.

   • Compare the entry to a formula in another cell to determine if it is valid.

> To use data validation, select the range of data that is subject to validation. Click Data, Validation. The Data Validation dialog box opens, as shown in Figure 11.11.

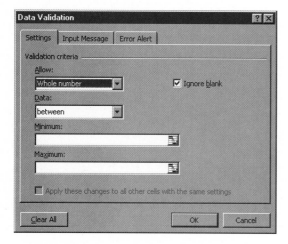

Figure 11.11 Data Validation dialog box

> Click the Settings tab. In the Allow box, select the type of entries that are permitted.

> For whole numbers, decimals, dates, and times, you can specify the values that are valid, such as the Minimum and Maximum values.

> For text, you can specify the length that is permissible.

> If you select List, you can designate a worksheet location that contains the specific values that you can enter. If the list is not long, you can enter the values in the dialog box, separated by commas.

> If you select Custom, you can write a formula to test the validity of a data entry.

TRY*it* **OUT**

Note: Continue to work in 11.3Inventory.

1. Select the range **B4:B20.**

2. Click **Data, Validation,** and the **Settings** tab.

3. In the Allow box, select **Text length.**

4. In the Data box, select **between.**

5. In the Minimum box, enter: **1**

6. In the Maximum box, enter: **12**

7. Click **OK.**

8. In **Cell B14,** enter:
   Soccer Sweatshirts
   Press the **Enter** key and notice the error message that appears. Click **Cancel** on the message.

9. Keep the file open.

Error Messages

> If you want to create a message that provides information about the data entry error, click the Error Alert tab, as shown in Figure 11.12.

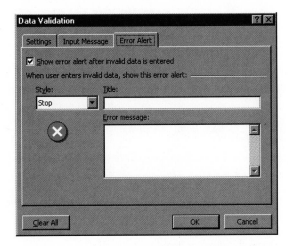

Figure 11.12 Error Alert tab

> In Style, select the action you want Excel to take when a mistake in entry is made.

> In Title, enter the title of the error message you want to display.

> In Error message, enter the text describing the nature of the error.

> Click OK.

TRY*it*OUT

Note: Continue to work in **11.3Inventory.**

1. Click **Data, Validation** and click the **Error Alert** tab.

2. In the box labeled Style, select **Stop.**

3. In the box labeled Title, enter:
   Entry too long

4. In the box labeled Error message, enter: **Text is limited to 12 characters.**
   Click **OK.**

5. In **Cell B15,** enter:
   Referee Uniforms
   Press the **Enter** key. Notice the error message that appears.

6. Close the file. Do not save.

REHEARSAL

Again

TASK 3

 GOAL
To use the Group and Outline and Validation features in Excel on an inventory list

SETTING THE STAGE/WRAPUP
File name: 11.3TOInventory

WHAT YOU NEED TO KNOW

> Companies that sell products and goods must maintain an *inventory list* to keep track of their stock on hand, cost of goods, and other information, such as suggested retail price.

> In this Rehearsal activity, you create data validation tests for the inventory list for the Baseball Department in the suburban Time Out Sporting Goods store. You also apply Group and Outline criteria and use filters to generate four summary reports of stock on hand.

DIRECTIONS

1. Open the file **11.3TOInventory** from the Data CD and use the illustration on the next page as a guide for this activity.

2. Write the formula for the **Valuation** column. Use the fill handle to fill in the rest of the values.

3. Set data validation for **Item No.** so that only numerical entries between 5000 and 9999 are permitted. Create an appropriate error message.

4. Test the data validation by entering a value of **4000** in **Cell A19.** Click **Cancel** on the error message.

5. Set data validation for **Description** so that only text 12 or fewer characters in length is permitted. Create an appropriate error message.

6. Test the data validation by entering **Baseball t-shirts** in **Column B19.** Click **Cancel** on the error message.

7. Set data validation for **Cost** so that no values greater than $100.00 are permitted. Create an appropriate error message.

8. Test the data validation by entering **$200** in **Cell E19.** Click **Cancel** on the error message.

9. Create a group that includes all equipment (baseballs, bats, gloves, and helmets).

10. Create a group that contains all of the items in the inventory.

11. Hide the portion of the inventory that includes equipment. Print a report that lists the inventory for accessories (pants and sports bags).

12. Show all of the details in the inventory list. Remove all of the groups.

13. Apply outline criteria to the inventory list.

14. Hide the details in the list so that **Quantity in Stock** and **Cost** are not visible. Print the report.

15. Use Advanced Filter to create a report of all the items in inventory that need to be re-ordered. Re-ordering occurs when the quantity on hand drops below one dozen, or 12 units. Move the report to another sheet, create a heading, and print the report.

16. Find subtotals (sums) for the valuation of each description in the inventory and for the total inventory. Print a copy of the report.

17. Save and close the file.

	A	B	C	D	E	F	G
1	*TIME OUT SPORTING GOODS*						
2	*Inventory--Baseball*						
3							
4	Item No.	Description	Size	Quantity in Stock	Cost	Valuation	
5	5001	Baseballs	4	30	$ 1.50		
6	5002	Baseballs	5	15	$ 1.50		
7	5003	Baseballs	6	25	$ 1.50		
8	6001	Bats	32	15	$ 25.00		
9	6002	Bats	33	12	$ 25.00	Enter a formula to calculate the valuation for each item	
10	6003	Bats	34	24	$ 30.00		
11	6500	Gloves	Small - left	10	$ 21.00		
12	6501	Gloves	Small - right	6	$ 21.00		
13	6601	Gloves	Medium-left	13	$ 23.00		
14	6602	Gloves	Medium-right	8	$ 23.00		
15	6701	Gloves	Large - left	15	$ 23.00		
16	6702	Gloves	Large - right	6	$ 23.00		
17	7001	Helmets	Small	10	$ 10.00		
18	7002	Helmets	Medium	12	$ 10.00		
19	7003	Helmets	Large	10	$ 10.00		
20	8001	Pants	Small	20	$ 8.00		
21	8002	Pants	Medium	15	$ 8.00		
22	8003	Pants	Large	15	$ 8.00		
23	9001	Sports bags	Medium	10	$ 9.00		
24	9002	Sports bags	Large	10	$ 9.00		

Cues for Reference

Data Validation
1. Select range of cells for data validation settings.
2. Click **Data, Validation,** and **Settings** tab.
3. Select type of entries that are permitted and any restrictions on their values.
4. In Error Alert tab, title alert and enter error message.
5. Click **OK.**

Group Data
1. Select range of cells that comprise the group.

2. Click **Data,** select **Group and Outline,** and click **Group.**
3. Click **Rows** or **Columns,** depending on how your group is defined.
4. Click **OK.**
5. Click **Hide Detail** button to view collapsed format.
   or
• Click **Show Detail** button to view in detailed format.

Remove Groups
1. Select data in a group.

2. Click **Data,** select **Group and Outline,** and click **Ungroup.** Select **Rows** or **Columns** and click **OK.**

Outline Data
1. Click **Data,** select **Group and Outline,** and click **Auto Outline.**
2. Click **Hide Detail** and **Show Detail** buttons to view data in collapsed or detailed formats.

Remove Outlines
1. Click **Data,** select **Group and Outline.**
2. Click **Clear Outline.**

PERFORMANCE

WHAT YOU NEED TO KNOW

Act I

Trilogy Productions is assessing its personnel costs for three offices, Los Angeles, New York, and London. Open the file **11p1.TrilogyPers** from the Data CD and organize the data to enable an analysis of the employee expenses associated with each office.

Follow these guidelines:

✴ Label Column H ANNSAL and format the column for the Accounting style. Write the formula for annual salary in **Cell H2** and fill in the values for the rest of the employees.

✴ Create data validation for the following columns:

- IDNO should be a whole number between 1000 and 9999. Create an error alert message for this column.

- HIRED should be a date greater than May 30, 1996. Create an error alert message for this column.

- WKSAL should be a decimal number between $400 and $1500. Create an error alert message for this column.

✴ Insert the following new records by clicking **Data, Form:**

LAST	FIRST	LOCATION	IDNO	HIRED	DEPT	WKSAL
Bergen	Cory	New York	1022	3/20/01	Production	$400
Molina	Tracy	Los Angeles	2044	10/30/01	Marketing	$400

✴ Generate a report summarizing weekly and annual salaries by location.

- Sort the list first according to location and then by date hired. Each should be in ascending order.

- Obtain subtotals (sums) for WKSAL and ANNSAL for each location, as well as a grand total. Collapse the data so that only the subtotals and grand total show. Remove all irrelevant field names. Label the report with an appropriate title. Print the report.

- Remove the subtotals.

- Generate a report by departments within a location, summarizing weekly and annual salaries.

- Sort the list according to the departments in which people work and then by location.

- Obtain subtotals (sums) for WKSAL and ANNSAL for each department. Collapse the data so that only the subtotals and grand total show. Label the report with an appropriate title. Print the report.

Act II

An inventory list for the Luggage Department in Odyssey Travel Gear's Boston store is found in the file 11p2.OTGInventory on the Data CD. You will conduct several analyses of the inventory to determine the cost of goods for several categories of items. You will also assess categories of items for which merchandise needs to be replenished.

Follow these guidelines:

✴ Format **Column F** in Accounting style. Write the formula for the valuation of goods in **Cell F5.** Fill in the values for the rest of the column.

✴ Generate a report of all items for which stock quantities are five or fewer. Use the Advanced Filter to conduct this analysis. Copy the report to a new worksheet. Delete all irrelevant columns. Label the sheet appropriately and print the report.

✴ Generate a report of all items that meet airline specifications for carry-on bags, 27" or less. Use any filtering technique you prefer to conduct this analysis. Copy the report to a new worksheet.

✴ Delete any irrelevant columns. Label the sheet appropriately and print the report.

✴ Sort the list in this report according to description and then cost. Copy the report to a new sheet.

✴ Use subtotals (sum) to summarize the Valuation column by description. The data should be outlined. Collapse the data so that only the total Valuation figures are given for each type of item. Print the report.

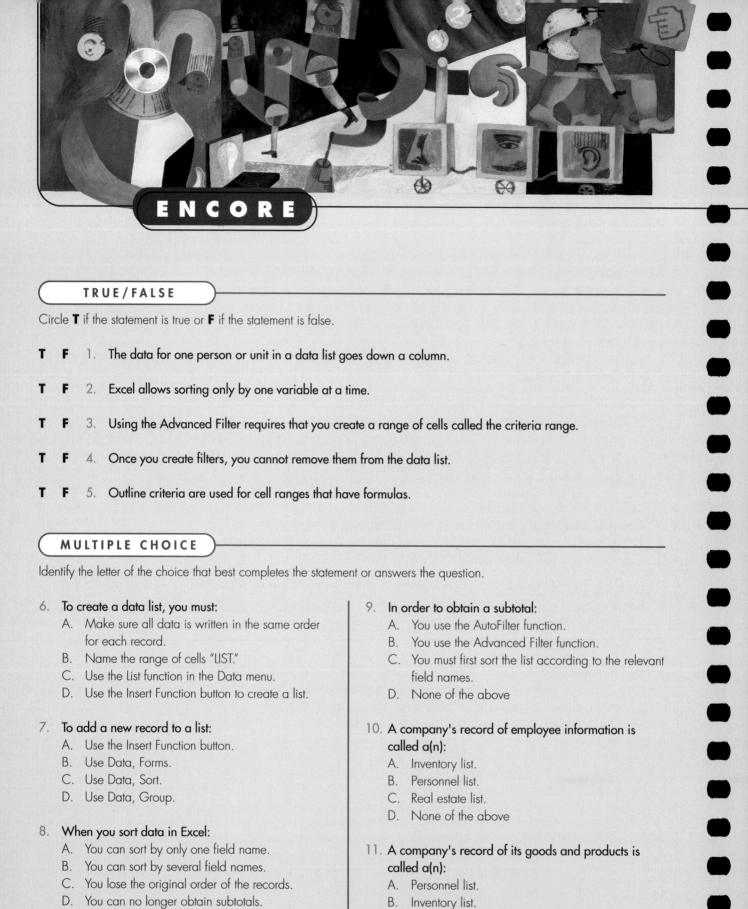

ENCORE

TRUE/FALSE

Circle **T** if the statement is true or **F** if the statement is false.

T F 1. The data for one person or unit in a data list goes down a column.

T F 2. Excel allows sorting only by one variable at a time.

T F 3. Using the Advanced Filter requires that you create a range of cells called the criteria range.

T F 4. Once you create filters, you cannot remove them from the data list.

T F 5. Outline criteria are used for cell ranges that have formulas.

MULTIPLE CHOICE

Identify the letter of the choice that best completes the statement or answers the question.

6. **To create a data list, you must:**
   A. Make sure all data is written in the same order for each record.
   B. Name the range of cells "LIST."
   C. Use the List function in the Data menu.
   D. Use the Insert Function button to create a list.

7. **To add a new record to a list:**
   A. Use the Insert Function button.
   B. Use Data, Forms.
   C. Use Data, Sort.
   D. Use Data, Group.

8. **When you sort data in Excel:**
   A. You can sort by only one field name.
   B. You can sort by several field names.
   C. You lose the original order of the records.
   D. You can no longer obtain subtotals.

9. **In order to obtain a subtotal:**
   A. You use the AutoFilter function.
   B. You use the Advanced Filter function.
   C. You must first sort the list according to the relevant field names.
   D. None of the above

10. **A company's record of employee information is called a(n):**
    A. Inventory list.
    B. Personnel list.
    C. Real estate list.
    D. None of the above

11. **A company's record of its goods and products is called a(n):**
    A. Personnel list.
    B. Inventory list.
    C. Real estate list.
    D. None of the above

12. You can customize the way Excel filters data by using:
   A. AutoFilter.
   B. Advanced Filter.
   C. Both A and B
   D. None of the above

13. When you use the Advanced Filter:
   A. You must specify a criteria range.
   B. You must have the filtered data placed on a new worksheet.
   C. You can only filter up to two field names.
   D. All of the above

14. You want Excel to cluster four records in a data list so that you can show or hide them according to your needs. There are no formulas in the records. You should use:
   A. Outline criteria.
   B. Grouping criteria.
   C. Sorting.
   D. Subtotals.

15. You want an error message to appear any time an erroneous data entry is made. You should use:
   A. Sorting.
   B. Advanced Filter.
   C. Data validation.
   D. Outline criteria.

COMPLETION

Complete each sentence or statement.

16. A list of a company's employees and information about them, such as their salaries, is called a(n) _____.

17. Brokers who list all the homes and apartments they have for sale or rent are using a(n) _____.

18. A list of a company's products or goods is called a(n) _____.

19. The Excel function that allows you to display only the data that are specified by certain criteria is a(n) _____.

20. The data for one person or unit in a data list is a(n) _____.

LESSON 12

Marketing and Sales Reports

In this lesson, you will learn to import data from other sources, including external databases and the Web, into Excel. You will also learn to export data from Excel to other applications and to publish your worksheets to the Web. This ability to move data across different applications is helpful in producing and sharing various types of marketing and sales reports.

Terms
MOUS-related
Importing data
Exporting data
Interactivity
Round-tripping
Query
Microsoft Query
Extensible Markup Language (XML)

 Upon completion of this lesson, you should have mastered the following skill sets:

✶ Import data into Excel from external sources Ⓜ
   ✶ Bring information into Excel from an external file
   ✶ Bring information into Excel from other external sources
   ✶ Obtain data from a Web page Ⓜ
✶ Export data from Excel Ⓜ
✶ Publish worksheets and workbooks to the Web Ⓜ
   ✶ Add interactivity to a Web page
✶ Retrieve external data and create queries Ⓜ
   ✶ Delete and edit database queries
✶ Create Extensible Markup Language (XML) Web queries Ⓜ

TRYOUT

TASK 1

 GOAL

To practice using the following skill sets:

* Import data into Excel from external sources M
  * Bring information into Excel from an external file
  * Bring information into Excel from other external sources
  * Obtain data from a Web page M
* Export data from Excel M
* Publish worksheets and workbooks to the Web M
  * Add interactivity to a Web page

WHAT YOU NEED TO KNOW

Import Data into Excel

> The data you need to conduct analyses and create marketing and sales reports may be found in a variety of locations, such as a corporate database, a file created in an application other than Excel, or on the Web. Instead of re-entering the data, you can import the data into your Excel worksheet and then conduct analyses or create reports. *Importing data* is the process of bringing information into Excel from a source other than an Excel file.

Bring Information into Excel from an External File

> Excel can read data written in several other file formats. Among them are the following:

* Access
* Microsoft SQL Server
* dBASE
* Lotus 1-2-3
* Quattro Pro
* Oracle
* Web pages (HTML)
* Text

TRY*it* OUT

1. Open a blank Excel worksheet and click a cell. Click **Data,** select **Import External Data,** and click **Import Data.**

2. In the Select Data Source dialog box, click the **My Data Sources** list arrow and locate the drive that contains the Data CD.

3. In the Files of type drop-down menu, click **Access Databases.** Click the file **12.1HomeData.** This is an Access database file with the extension .mdb.

4. In the Import Data dialog box, click **Existing worksheet.** Enter or click **Cell A1** as the destination for the imported data. Click **OK.** The Access file appears in the worksheet.

5. Close the file. Do not save.

> In most cases, you can bring external data into Excel by opening a blank worksheet and clicking Data, selecting Import External Data, and clicking Import Data. The Select Data Source dialog box opens, as shown in Figure 12.1.

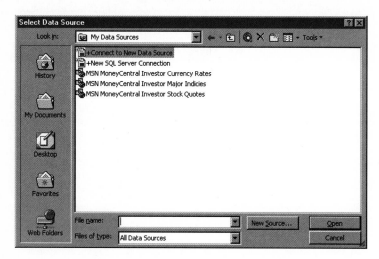

Figure 12.1 Select Data Source dialog box

> If the data you want to import is in a file on your computer or network drive, click the My Data Sources list arrow and select the location that holds your file. Select one of the file types in the Files of type drop-down menu. Select the file you want to import and click Open. The Import Data dialog box opens, as shown in Figure 12.2.

Figure 12.2 Import Data dialog box

> If you want to place the data on your current worksheet, click Existing worksheet. Enter or click the cell on your worksheet where you want the data range to start and click OK.

> If you want the data to appear on a new worksheet, click New worksheet and click OK. Excel adds a new worksheet to your workbook and places the data, beginning in the upper-left cell.

Bring Information into Excel from Other External Sources

> You can also bring data into Excel by other means. Many applications, such as Access, offer the option of saving a file in an Excel format. For example, if you have a file open in Access, you can click Export and choose Excel as your file format. Select a location in which to save your file. After you close the file, you can reopen it and work on it in Excel.

> Use the Copy and Paste features to import text files in table format into Excel. For example, if the data is in a Word file, open the file, select the data, and click the Copy button. Make sure Excel is open in another window. Click the Paste button to place the data in its appropriate location on the Excel worksheet.

> Alternatively, you can drag-and-drop the data from Word into Excel. Open the Word and Excel windows so that they are both visible on the screen. (Right-click the taskbar to tile the windows.) Select the data you want to import from the Word document. Hold down the Ctrl key and drag the data to the Excel worksheet.

Obtain Data from a Web Page

> You can also import data from a Web page written in HTML (Hypertext Markup Language) into Excel with the drag-and-drop method. Follow these steps:

  • Open both the HTML page and Excel.

  • Arrange the windows so that they are both visible on the screen.

  • Select the data you want to import from the HTML page.

  • Hold down the Ctrl key and drag the data to the Excel worksheet.

Export Data from Excel

> You can send data from Excel to many other applications, such as databases or text files, with a process that is called *exporting data.*

> To export data from Excel, click File, Save As. Click the list arrow in the Save as type box. A number of file type options appear, including several text and database formats. Select the file format of the application you want and save the file. You should then be able to use the data originally created in Excel in the other application. If you are saving the worksheet as a Text (Tab delimited) file for use in Word, you can only save one sheet at a time. This file type does not support multiple page workbooks.

> If you want to export data to an existing Access database, you must first make sure to arrange the data in a list. Arrange the data in rows, with a label in each column above the first row of data. Arrange the information in each row in the same way, with no blank rows or columns. Save and close the Excel file and then switch to Access to import the file.

> If the Convert to MS Access, MS Access Report, or MS Access Form commands are not available on the Data menu, you need to load the AccessLinks add-in. The AccessLinks add-in program is available from the Excel Download Web site.

> If you want to convert data created in Excel to a new Access database file, click Data, Convert to MS Access. Then click New database and click OK. The directions in AccessLinks will guide you through the conversion process.

TRY it OUT

1. Open the Excel file **12.1RegionalSales** from the Data CD.

2. Click **File, Save As.**

3. In the Save as type drop-down menu, click **Text (Tab delimited).** Click **OK** to save the current sheet. Name the file: `RegionalSalesText` Click **Yes** if you are prompted to preserve worksheet format.

4. Click **Save.** Close the file.

5. Switch to Word and open the file **RegionalSalesText.**

6. Realign the columns of data using the **Tab** key, if necessary.

7. Print and close the file.

Publish Worksheets and Workbooks to the Web

> Businesses often publish financial reports to the Web to disseminate information to customers, shareholders, employees, and the general public. You do not need to know HTML to create a Web page from your Excel workbook.

> To save an Excel file as a Web page, open the Excel workbook you want to publish. Click File, Save as Web Page. The Save as Web Page dialog box opens, as shown in Figure 12.3.

Figure 12.3 Save as Web Page dialog box

> If you want to publish the entire workbook and do not want to add interactivity to the Web page, select Entire Workbook. *Interactivity* means that viewers of the Web page can manipulate the data in a browser. Leave the Add interactivity box blank, name the file, and click Save.

Note: The instructions above describe the only way in which you can eliminate interactivity from an entire workbook.

TRY*it***OUT**

1. Open the Excel file **12.1RegionalSalesWeb** from the Data CD.

2. Click **File, Save as Web Page.**

3. Click **Publish.**

4. In the Choose box, click **RegionalSales Sheet All contents.**

5. In the Viewing options section, do not check Add interactivity with.

6. In the File name box, enter:
   `C:\MyDocuments\`
   `RegionalSalesPage.htm`

7. Check **Open published web page in browser.**

8. Click **Publish.** You can view your Web page in the browser.

9. Close the page and the file.

> If you want to publish portions of a workbook, or if you want to remove interactivity from portions of a workbook, click Publish. The Publish as Web Page dialog box opens, as shown in Figure 12.4.

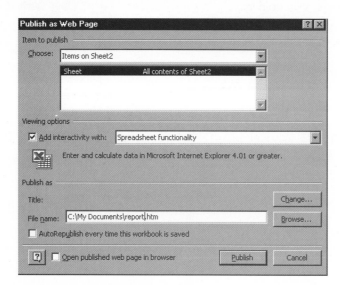

Figure 12.4 Publish as Web Page dialog box

> In the Choose box, select whether you want to publish the entire workbook, a specific worksheet, specific items on a worksheet (such as chart or filtered list), or a range of cells on a worksheet.

Note: You can publish only one item at a time. If you want to publish multiple items from a workbook, you must repeat the publishing steps described here.

> Click Change to add a title to the Web page you are publishing. The Set Title dialog box opens, as shown in Figure 12.5. Enter the title you want and click OK.

Figure 12.5 Set Title dialog box

> In the File name box, enter the path to the location for your Web page. Or, you can click Browse to find the location and select it.

> If you want to republish the page automatically after making changes in the Excel file, check the box AutoRepublish every time this workbook is saved.

> To view the page after you publish it, check the box Open published web page in browser.

> Click Publish.

Add Interactivity to a Web Page

> If you want to add interactivity to your Web page so that users can work in the worksheet, you must choose different options in the Publish as Web Page dialog box.

  • In the Viewing options section, select Add interactivity with.

  • Select the type of interactivity you want: Spreadsheet, PivotTable, or Charts.

Note: Viewers of your page must have Internet Explorer 4.1 or later in order to work with data published from Excel. They must also have a license to use Office.

> To edit your Web page, you can use a process called *round-tripping,* which routes you back to Office from your browser and back again, after edits are complete.

  • If you have saved your Excel worksheet as a Web page, open the published page in a browser and click Edit on the browser toolbar.

  • You can choose from several applications to edit, including Word, Excel, and Notepad. Select one.

  • Make the changes to your Web page.

  • Click File, Save on the browser toolbar.

  • Close the browser.

T R Y *it* O U T

1. Reopen the Excel file **12.1RegionalSalesWeb** from the Data CD.

2. Click **File, Save as Web Page.**

3. Click **Publish.**

4. In the Choose box, click **RegionalSales Sheet All contents.**

5. In the Viewing options section, check **Add interactivity with.** Select **Spreadsheet functionality.**

6. Click **Change** and enter **Four Corners Realty** for the title.

7. In the File name box, enter: **C:\My Documents\ RegionalSalesPage2.htm**

8. Check **Open published web page in browser.**

9. Click **Publish.** You can view your Web page in the browser.

10. Within the browser, sort the regions alphabetically.

11. Click **Edit** on the browser toolbar. Click **Word.**

12. Change the data in **Cell B16** to: **10**

13. Click **File, Save** on the browser toolbar.

14. Close the page.

REHEARSAL

TASK 1

 GOAL
To create a marketing report by importing and exporting data

SETTING THE STAGE/WRAPUP
File names: 12.1SeniorMembers
12.1SeniorMembers.xls
12.1Competition

WHAT YOU NEED TO KNOW

> In-Shape Fitness Centers maintain an Access database of all of their members. The membership coordinator would like to give a special, one-time promotional discount of 15% for the monthly membership fees of all members who are age 55 and over. She also found information about a competitor's discounts on a Web page. She would like to include all of this information on a Web page published by In-Shape Fitness Centers.

> In this Rehearsal activity, you import the In-Shape Fitness Centers Access database into Excel. You perform the appropriate analyses in Excel to calculate the one-time promotional discount. You also import their competitor's information from an HTML page. After creating the Excel report with some of the information from the competitor's page, you publish it to a Web page for In-Shape Fitness Centers.

▼ DIRECTIONS

1. The file **12.1SeniorMembers** on the Data CD is an Access database file. Import this file into a blank worksheet in Excel, starting in **Cell B5.** Use the illustration on the next page as a guide for this activity.

2. In **Cell B2,** enter and format the title:
In-Shape Fitness Centers

3. Insert the current date in **Cell C1.**

4. In **Cell I5,** create a new column labeled: **Age**
Enter a formula to calculate each member's age in **Cell I6.** *(Hint: Use the YEAR function to compute the difference in years between two dates, e.g., =YEAR (C1) -YEAR (G7). Make sure the date in Cell C1 is an absolute cell reference and that the result is in the Number format.)*

5. Use the fill handle to fill in the rest of the values for each member.

6. Sort the data by age, so that the oldest members are at the top of the list.

7. Filter the data, so that only the members age 55 or older are displayed.

8. Label **Cells J4** and **J5: 15% Discount**

9. Write a formula in **Cell J6** that computes 15% of the individual's membership fee and fill in the values for each member.

10. Label **Cells K4** and **K5: Promo Fee**
Compute the promotional membership fee by applying the discount to the membership fee.

11. Format the column in Accounting style and fill in the values for each member.

12. Delete all columns except for Name, Address, City/Town, Date of Birth, Member Fee, 15% Discount, and Promo Fee. Delete any other unnecessary information.

13. Format all of the column labels so they are in bold. Adjust column widths as necessary.

14. Save the file as **12.1SeniorMembers.xls.**

15. Use Word or your browser to open the HTML file **12.1Competition** on the Data CD. Copy the table to your Excel worksheet, starting in **Cell C27.**

16. In the Excel worksheet, label each table appropriately, e.g., **Our Discounts** in **Cell B3**; **Competition's Discounts** in **Cell B26**.

17. Enter the following above the table with the imported data (Cell B23): **We give better discounts than our competition!**

18. Format labels created in Steps 16 and 17 for bold and set an appropriate font size.

19. Publish the worksheet as a Web page. View the Web page in a browser. Use the browser editor to make any changes in formatting you think are necessary.

20. Save and close the file.

	A	B	C	D	E	F	G	H	I	J	K
1											
2			IN-SHAPE FITNESS CENTERS		◄ Enter and format title				Add new column headings		
3			Enter today's date here								
4										15%	Promo
5		ID	Name	Address	City/Town	Gender	Date of Birth	Member Fee	Age	Discount	Fee
6		1	Smith, Harry	32 Pine Ridge	Centerville	M	04/12/1940	$55			
7		8	Neely, Caren	114 First Avenue	Townsend	F	06/16/1960	$75			
8		9	Hanson, Neal	15 Rawley Street	Centerville	M	12/02/1982	$75	Enter formulas		
9		10	Gretel, Conor	33 King Street	Springfield	M	11/04/1973	$75			
10		11	Henry, Grace	782 Main Avenue	Springfield	F	03/15/1945	$65			
11		12	Stanton, Joan	89 Forest Avenue	Townsend	F	05/07/1976	$75			
12		13	Rogers, Thomas	201 Fox Run	Centerville	M	09/23/1977	$75			
13		14	Topher, Eric	52 Queen Street	Springfield	M	10/01/1943	$60			
14		15	Loring, Stephen	11 Brigham Street	Centerville	M	01/25/1980	$75			
15		2	Prouty, Shannon	2 Lyme Street	Townsend	F	08/04/1949	$75			
16		3	Houston, Debra	57 North Street	Springfield	F	12/16/1939	$55			
17		4	Gingrich, John	45 Elm Street	Centerville	M	04/27/1944	$60			
18		5	Deutsch, Lyle	6 Hancock Road	Townsend	M	06/14/1963	$75			
19		6	Manion, Kris	86 Noon Street	Centerville	F	11/17/1968	$75			
20		7	O'Connor, Timothy	19 Newtown Road	Townsend	M	05/19/1979	$75			
21											
22											
23			Copy competitor's rates here								
24											
25											
26											
27											

Cues for Reference

Import Data to Excel

1. Open blank Excel worksheet and click **Data,** select **Import External Data,** and click **Import Data.**
2. Click **My Data Sources** list arrow and select location that holds your file.
3. Click **Open.**
4. Indicate whether you want file to go to an existing or a new worksheet.
5. Click **OK.**

Getting Data from a Web Page

1. Open HTML page and open Excel.
2. Arrange windows so that both are visible on screen.
3. Select data you want to import from HTML page.
4. Hold down **Ctrl** and drag data to Excel worksheet.

Export Data from Excel

1. Click **File, Save As.**
2. Specify new file type for Excel file.
3. Click **OK.**
4. Open file in alternate application.

Publish Worksheets and Workbooks to the Web

1. Click **File, Save as Web Page.**
2. Click **Publish.**
3. In Choose box, select whether to publish workbook, worksheet, or specific range of cells.
4. In Viewing options section, decide if you want to add interactivity and what type.
5. Click **Change** to add a title to Web page.
6. In the File name box, enter or select location in which you want to save your file.
7. Check any other options you want to enable, such as AutoRepublish or Open web page in browser.
8. Click **Publish.**

TRYOUT

TASK 2

WHAT YOU NEED TO KNOW

Retrieve External Data and Create Queries

> A useful way to obtain external data in Excel is to create a query. A *query* is a text file that includes information about a data source and information you would like to extract from it. Instead of importing the whole database as you did earlier in this lesson, you can specify which portions of a database you want. In other words, you can ask questions of, or query, the database. You can also filter and sort the data, according to the criteria you specify, before the data is imported into Excel.

> You can save queries if you want to extract the same information from a database in the future. If you apply a saved query at a later time, any changes to the database are reflected in the query results. You can also share saved queries with other users.

Note: Queries have .odc or .dgy file extensions.

> The easiest way to create a query is to use the Microsoft Query feature, which contains the Query Wizard. *Microsoft Query* is an application that allows you to retrieve specified information from external sources and is automatically activated when you initiate a query. If it does not activate, you will have to install it using the Custom Installation option for Excel.

> To create a query, first open an Excel worksheet. Click Data, select Import External Data, and click New Database Query.

TRY*it* OUT

1. Open a new Excel worksheet. Click **Data,** select **Import External Data,** and click **New Database Query.**

2. In the Choose Data Source dialog box, click **MS Access Database.** Click **OK.**

3. In the Select Database dialog box, locate the Access file **12.2Transactions** on the Data CD and click **OK.**

4. Click the plus sign to the left of **Transactions.** Move the following field names to the **Columns in your query** section: **Customer, Transaction Description, Number of Units, Stock, Buy or Sell Price.** Click **Next.**

5. Filter the data so that only the records for customer Smith are selected.
   a. In Columns to filter, select **Customer.**
   b. In Only include rows where, select **equals.**
   c. Enter **Smith** in the next box on the right. Select **And.**

6. Filter the data so that only the records where the Transaction Description is Buy are selected.
   a. In Columns to filter, select **Transaction Description.**
   b. In Only rows where, select **equals.**
   c. Enter **Buy** in the next box on the right.
   d. Click **Next.**

7. Click **Next** to skip the sorting.

Continued on next page

> The Choose Data Source dialog box opens, as shown in Figure 12.6. Make sure the box Use the Query Wizard to create/edit queries is checked. Select the type of file you want to access and click OK.

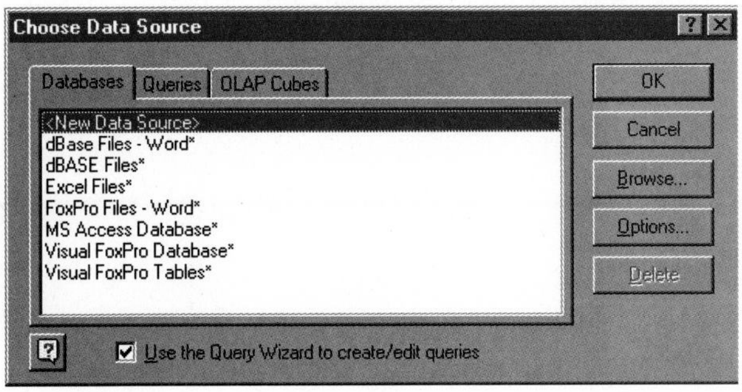

8. Select **Return Data to Microsoft Excel.** Click **Finish.** The results of the query appear in Excel.

9. Save the file as **12.2Transactions.** Keep the file open.

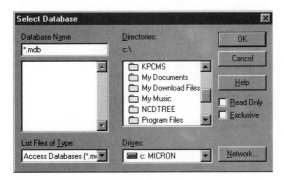

Figure 12.6 Choose Data Source dialog box

> The Select Database dialog box opens, as shown in Figure 12.7. Find the location that contains the file you want to access, select the file name, and click OK.

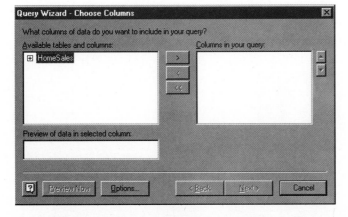

Figure 12.7 Select Database dialog box

> The Query Wizard-Choose Columns dialog box opens, as shown in Figure 12.8. Click the plus sign to the left of the database name. All of the field names in the database then appear. To bring a field into Excel, select it and click the > button to bring it into the Columns in your query box. Use the up and down buttons on the far right to change the order of the fields. Click Next.

Figure 12.8 Query Wizard-Choose Columns dialog box

> The next dialog box gives you the opportunity to filter the data. Select your filtering criteria and click Next. Simply click Next if you do not want to filter the data.

> The next dialog box gives you the opportunity to sort the data. Select your sorting criteria and click Next. Simply click Next if you do not want to sort the data.

> The Query Wizard-Finish dialog box opens, as shown in Figure 12.9. Click Save Query if you want to save the query for future use. Select the location in which you want to save it in the Save As dialog box that opens. (Usually queries are saved in the Queries folder.) Indicate if you want to place the results of the query in an Excel worksheet or if you want to edit or view the data in the query. Click Finish.

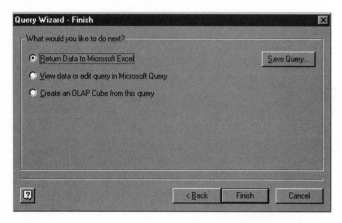

Figure 12.9 Query Wizard-Finish dialog box

Note: When you initiate Microsoft Query, it runs in the background while you work on your Excel worksheet. You can view it or minimize it like any other window that appears in the taskbar at the bottom of your screen.

> When you create a query and click a cell that contains data from an external source, the External Data toolbar appears, as shown in Figure 12.10. If you click the Refresh Data button, data linked to an external source is updated if there have been any changes in the original database.

Figure 12.10 External Data toolbar

Delete and Edit Database Queries

> If you need to delete a database query, click the name box and select the named range for the query, as shown in Figure 12.11. When you press the Delete key, you are prompted to confirm the deletion of the query.

	A	B	C	D	E	F
1	Customer	Transaction Description	Number of Units	Stock	Buy or Sell Price	
2	Smith	Buy	100	Microsoft	70	
3	Smith	Buy	100	IBM	90	
4	Smith	Buy	100	Hewlett Packrd	25	
5	Smith	Buy	100	Intel	25	
6	Smith	Buy	100	Lucent	20	
7	Smith	Buy	75	Cisco	65	

Figure 12.11 Selected query range

> Microsoft Query and the Query Editor let you edit the query to display other information. To edit an existing query, click Data, select Import External Data, and click Edit Query, or use the Edit Query button on the External Data toolbar. You are returned to the Query Wizard in the Choose Columns screen (see Figure 12.8), where you can begin to change your query selections.

TRY it OUT

Note: Continue to work in 12.2Transactions.

1. Copy the data on Sheet1 to **Sheet2** and **Sheet3.**

2. On Sheet2, click **Insert, Name, Define,** and select the **MS Access Query.**

3. Click **Delete** and confirm the deletion.

4. Switch to **Sheet3.**

5. Click **Data,** select **Import External Data,** and click **Edit Query.**

6. Click **Next** in the Choose Columns dialog box.

7. Filter the data so that only the **Sell** records for customer Hudson are selected.
   a. In Columns to filter, select **Customer.**
   b. In Only include rows where, select **equals.**
   c. Enter **Hudson** in the next box on the right. Select **And.**
   d. In Columns to filter, select **Transaction Description.**
   e. In Only rows where, select **equals.**
   f. Enter **Sell** in the next box on the right.
   g. Click **Next** two times to complete the query.

8. Select **Return Data to Microsoft Excel.** Click **Finish.** The results of the query appear in Excel.

9. Switch to **Sheet1.**

10. Do not close the file.

Create Extensible Markup Language (XML) Web Queries

> Excel has several features that let you obtain data from Web pages and import it to a worksheet. Once the data is in Excel, you can analyze it and use it in reports just as you would with any other data in Excel. You can also refresh or update data that you import to your worksheet. For example, as stock quotes or sales figures on the Web change, you can update them in your worksheet and include them in any formulas you create.

> To obtain data from the Web, create a Web query. Click Data, select Import External Data, and click New Web Query. The New Web Query dialog box opens, as shown in Figure 12.12. In the Address box, enter the Web address that contains the data you want to import and click Go.

Figure 12.12 New Web Query dialog box

> Select the tables you want to import by clicking the yellow arrows that appear next to the tables on the Web page. As you click each arrow, it turns into a green checkmark. Once you select your data, click Import.

Note: If you want to import the whole page, click the yellow arrow in the upper left corner.

TRY*it* **OUT**

Note: Continue to work in **12.2Transactions.**

1. Click **Data,** select **Import External Data,** and click **New Web Query.**

2. In the New Web Query dialog box, enter the following address: **http://moneycentral.msn.com** Click **Go.**

3. In the left column of the browser window, under the MSN logo, locate the box in which you can obtain stock quotes. Enter **MSFT** (the Microsoft stock symbol) within the browser.

4. Click the **yellow arrow** next to the current value.

5. Click **Import.**

6. In the Import Data dialog box, indicate that you want to place the data starting in **Cell H3** of the existing worksheet. Click **OK.**

7. In **Cell I2,** enter: **Current Value**

8. In **Cell I3,** enter the formula that gives the customer s total valuation of Microsoft stock: **(=D3*H3, number of shares*current price)**

9. Save and close the file.

10. Reopen the file at another time and click the **Refresh Data** button.

> The Import Data dialog box opens, as shown in Figure 12.13. Indicate whether you want the data to go into an Existing worksheet or a New worksheet. Click OK.

Figure 12.13 Import Data dialog box

> Click the Refresh Data button on the External Data toolbar if you want to update the data in the table.

> You can also bring data on a Web page into Excel with a shortcut. Right-click the data on the Web page and choose the Export to Excel option. This activates a Web query.

> Many Web pages now use *Extensible Mark-Up Language (XML)* as a format for presenting data. XML, like HTML, is a commonly used language that employs tags to separate data from other information on the page. Because of its widespread use, data sharing through the Web is easier. Excel takes advantage of XML format to locate data on a Web page. In addition, you can save any Excel file in XML format (in the Save As option) for eventual publication to the Web.

REHEARSAL

TASK 2

 GOAL
To create a sales report that retrieves data from an external source and from the Web

SETTING THE STAGE/WRAPUP
File name: 12.2ForeignOrders

WHAT YOU NEED TO KNOW

> Time Out Sporting Goods maintains a database of its transactions in several foreign countries. A manager wants to create a summary report of all sales that took place in Denmark, Sweden, and Switzerland during one month. As she prepares the report, she also wants to keep track of currency conversion rates on the Excel worksheet.

> On the currency conversion Web site used in this Rehearsal, the current currency rates are quoted "In U.S. dollars" and "Per U.S. dollar." Use the appropriate "Per U.S. dollar" rate multiplied by the U.S. dollar amount to calculate the foreign currency equivalent. Or, to obtain the U.S. equivalent of foreign funds, use the "In U.S. dollars" rate and multiply by the foreign currency amount.

> In this Rehearsal activity, you create a query for Time Out Sporting Goods to obtain data from the database and import it into Excel. You also create a Web query to obtain currency conversion rates that you can update periodically.

DIRECTIONS

1. Open a blank Excel workbook.

2. The file **12.2ForeignOrders** on the Data CD is an Access database file. Create a query to import data from this file to your Excel workbook.

3. In your query, include all of the columns in the database except for ID.

4. Filter the data in your query so that only the orders from Denmark are imported.

5. Place the data starting in **Cell B5** of the Excel worksheet. Use the illustration on the next page as a guide for the rest of this activity.

6. Label the top of the sheet: `Sales in Denmark: March` Format the title in 14 pt. bold.

7. In **Cells G4** and **G5,** enter: `Total Due U.S.$` Format in bold. Enter the formula that computes the total amount due for each order. Format the column for U.S. currency and fill in the values for the rest of the orders.

8. In **Cells H4** and **H5,** enter: `Conversion Factor` Format in bold and adjust the column width if necessary.

9. In **Columns I4** and **I5,** enter: `Total Due Krone` Format in bold.

10. In **Cell A16,** create a Web query to find the conversion factor to change the U.S. dollar amount in Column G to Danish krone. One place to find the current currency conversion rates is: http://moneycentral.msn.com/investor/market/rates.asp

    *Note: If you use the suggested Web site, the entire table of conversion rates is labeled with the yellow arrow, rather than individual rates. Have the query place the currency conversion table in **Cell B16.** If you do not have Internet access, copy the data from **12.2conversion** on the Data CD to **Cell B16.***

11. Copy the currency conversion factor for Danish krone to **Cell H6** and make it an absolute reference. (Use the Per U.S. dollar conversion factor.) Fill in the value for the rest of the column.

12. In **Cell I6,** enter a formula to multiply the Total Due U.S.$ data by the Conversion Factor to convert to Danish krone. Fill in the values for the rest of the column.

13. Rename the sheet: `Sales-Denmark`

14. Make two copies of the sheet and rename them:

`Sales-Sweden`
`Sales-Switzerland`

15. Edit the queries to locate orders from Sweden for Sheet2 and from Switzerland for Sheet3, enter appropriate new headings, and use the appropriate conversion rates (with an absolute reference) to complete the analysis for Swedish and Swiss sales. The formulas on the copied sheets will work with the new data.

16. Format the Krona and Franc columns for two decimal places.

17. Print a copy of the workbook.

18. Save and close the file; name it: `12.2ForeignOrders`

19. Reopen the file at another time. Click **Cell B16** and click the **Refresh Data** button on the External Data toolbar. Check the changes in the conversion rates.

20. Save and close the file.

	A	B	C	D	E	F	G	H	I
1									
2		**Sales in Denmark: March**			← Enter and format title		Enter new column titles		
3									
4							Total Due	Conversion	Total Due
5		Company	Country	Item	Quantity	Price/Unit (U.S.$)	U.S.$	Factor	Krone
6		Krump	Denmark	4590-Sweats	10	12			
7		Hanover	Denmark	2343-Bags	20	14			
8		Martine	Denmark	4590-Sweats	15	12			
9		Zugspits	Denmark	2343-Bags	30	14			
10		Krump	Denmark	832-Sneakers	15	19		Enter	
11		Krump	Denmark	162-T-shirts	24	6		formulas	
12		Hanover	Denmark	162-T-shirts	12	6			
13									
14								Copy	
15								appropriate	
16		←		Create Web				conversion	
17				Query to find				factor from	
18				the conversion				Web query	
19				table and place				conversion	
20				here				table here	
21									

Retrieve External Data with Queries

1. Open an Excel worksheet.
2. Click **Data,** select **Import External Data,** and click **New Database Query.**
3. In Choose Data Source dialog box, select file type and click **OK.**
4. In Select Database dialog box, select name and click **OK.**
5. In Query Wizard-Choose Columns dialog box, click plus sign to left of database name. Move each of fields you want into Columns in your query section. Click **Next.**
6. Filter data, if needed. Click **Next.**
7. Sort data, if needed. Click **Next.**

8. In Query Wizard-Finish dialog box, indicate if you want to save query and if you want to place it in an Excel worksheet. Click **Finish.**

Edit Database Query

1. Position mouse cursor within external data range.
2. Click **Data,** select **Import External Data,** and click **Edit Query.**
3. Edit Query Wizard settings as necessary.
4. Complete Query Wizard-Finish dialog box, as indicated in Step 8 above. Click **Finish.**

Create Web Queries

1. Click **Data,** select **Import External Data,** and click **New Web Query.**

2. In New Web Query dialog box, enter Web address that contains data you want to import in Address box. Click **Go.**
3. Select tables you want to import by clicking yellow arrows next to tables on Web page. Click **Import.**
4. Indicate whether you want data to go to existing or new worksheet. Click **OK.**
5. Click **Refresh Data** button on External Data toolbar if you want to update data in table.

Delete External Data Ranges

1. Click **Insert, Name,** and **Define.**
2. Select data range to delete.
3. Press **Delete.**
4. Confirm deletion and click **Yes.**

PERFORMANCE

WHAT YOU NEED TO KNOW

Act I

A marketing analyst for the Air Land Sea Travel Group would like to publish a Web page that provides information about the regions of the world to which the company's customers travel. The page will also include similar information from a national data bank. The company data is currently in a text file. The national data is on the Web. You will import the relevant information from these sources to an Excel file and then publish the worksheet as a Web page.

Follow these guidelines:

✷ The file that contains the company information is a Word file, **12p1.Travelers.doc,** on the Data CD. Import the data into Excel and make any necessary adjustments to the format of the table.

✷ Insert a line below Oceania and compute the total number of travelers who went overseas. Label that row.

✷ Compute the total number of travelers for all destinations at the bottom of the table and label it.

✷ Obtain information about national travel statistics from: http://tinet.ita.doc.gov

✷ Go to the page that gives the following table: Basic Market Analysis Program U.S. Citizen Air Traffic to Overseas Regions, Canada & Mexico 2000. (Use the most current data. If you do not have Internet access, use the data in the **12p1.national data** file, found on the Data CD.)

✷ Import the table into your Excel worksheet.

✷ Delete all columns from the national data except YTD Total.

✷ Add text to label all information on the page for viewers. Add any clip art or formatting that you think will make the page attractive and readable.

✷ Save the file as a Web page; name it: **12p1.Travelers**
Open and view your page in a browser. Make any modifications you think are necessary to improve the page. (You can use round-tripping to edit in Excel from your browser.)

✷ Print the page.

✷ Close and save the file.

Act II

Odyssey Travel Gear has an Access database that keeps track of all orders. A portion of that database is available in **12p2.Orders** on the Data CD. A manager would like to obtain a summary of the sales orders originating in Brazil, Chile, and Argentina for the month of June. For this exercise, you will import the database information into Excel and filter the data three times to show the orders from each country on a separate worksheet. You will also add information about Brazil's currency to compute the total amount due for each order. You will create a Web query to obtain the current currency conversion factor and use it for future updates of the information.

Follow these guidelines:

✴ Open a worksheet in Excel and create a database query linked to the Access file **12p2.Orders.** Include the Company, Country, Item, Quantity, and Price/Unit data.

✴ You will create a report showing the Sales Order Summary for Brazil. Enter a title for the worksheet that includes the company name and the report title.

✴ Add columns to the table that are labeled:
```
Total Due (U.S.$)
Conversion Factor
Total Due (Reals)
```

Note: Brazil's currency is the real. Format the labels and adjust the column widths to make your table attractive and readable.

✴ Create a Web query to locate the conversion factor for U.S. dollars to Brazilian reals. A good source for this information is:
http://moneycentral.msn.com/investor/market/rates.asp

✴ Fill in the data and formulas for the columns Conversion Factor and Total Due (Reals). Be sure to make the conversion factor an absolute reference so that it will fill in correctly.

✴ Copy this sheet to the next two sheets, and edit the query on each sheet to display the orders from Chile and Argentina. Edit the worksheet title, column headings, sheet names, and conversion formula reference as necessary. Save and close the file; name it:
```
12p2.Orders
```

✴ Reopen the file at another time and refresh the data.

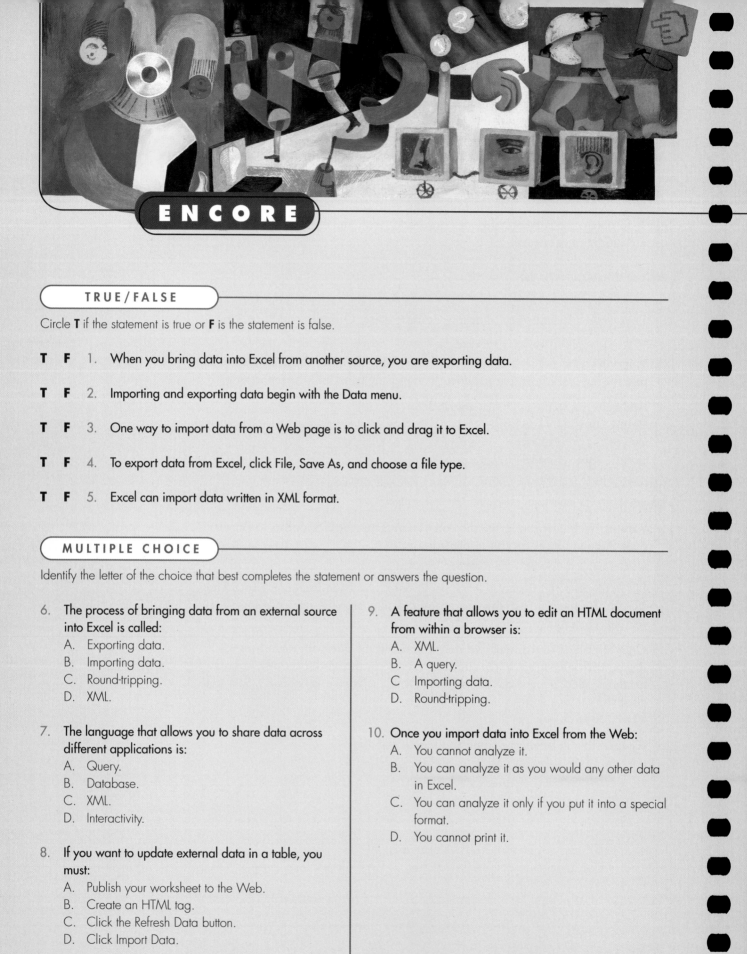

ENCORE

TRUE/FALSE

Circle **T** if the statement is true or **F** is the statement is false.

T   F   1. When you bring data into Excel from another source, you are exporting data.

T   F   2. Importing and exporting data begin with the Data menu.

T   F   3. One way to import data from a Web page is to click and drag it to Excel.

T   F   4. To export data from Excel, click File, Save As, and choose a file type.

T   F   5. Excel can import data written in XML format.

MULTIPLE CHOICE

Identify the letter of the choice that best completes the statement or answers the question.

6. The process of bringing data from an external source into Excel is called:
   A. Exporting data.
   B. Importing data.
   C. Round-tripping.
   D. XML.

7. The language that allows you to share data across different applications is:
   A. Query.
   B. Database.
   C. XML.
   D. Interactivity.

8. If you want to update external data in a table, you must:
   A. Publish your worksheet to the Web.
   B. Create an HTML tag.
   C. Click the Refresh Data button.
   D. Click Import Data.

9. A feature that allows you to edit an HTML document from within a browser is:
   A. XML.
   B. A query.
   C Importing data.
   D. Round-tripping.

10. Once you import data into Excel from the Web:
   A. You cannot analyze it.
   B. You can analyze it as you would any other data in Excel.
   C. You can analyze it only if you put it into a special format.
   D. You cannot print it.

Complete each sentence or statement.

11. When you bring data into Excel from another application, you are _____ data.

12. When you send data from Excel to another application, you are _____ data.

13. _____ is the process of editing an HTML document in a browser.

14. Extensible Markup Language is often abbreviated as _____.

15. An application that allows you to retrieve specified information from external sources is _____.

16. A _____ is a text file that contains information about a data source and the elements you can extract from it.

17. _____ refers to publishing an Excel file to a Web page so that viewers can interact with it.

18. To update information brought into Excel from an external source, you click the _____ button on the External Data toolbar.

19. To publish an Excel workbook to the Web, click File, _____.

20. When you create a Web query to obtain data from the Web, each yellow arrow you click to select data turns in to a(n) _____ .

Data Analysis

In this lesson, you will learn to use several Excel features to analyze data and create financial reports. Among these are PivotTables and PivotCharts, forecasting, and scenarios. You will also learn how to create and print reports using the Report Manager add-in.

Upon completion of this lesson, you should have mastered the following skill sets:

- Create PivotTables and PivotTable reports Ⓜ
- Modify and format PivotTables Ⓜ
- Create PivotCharts and PivotChart reports from a PivotTable Ⓜ
- Create PivotCharts and PivotChart reports from a data list Ⓜ
- Forecast values with what-if analysis Ⓜ
  - Chart forecast data
- Create and display scenarios Ⓜ
- Create and print reports with the Report Manager add-in

Terms

MOUS-related
- PivotTable
- PivotTable report
- PivotChart
- PivotChart report
- What-if analysis
- FORECAST
- Trendline
- Scenario
- Report Manager

Document-related
- Personnel list
- Sales forecast
- Aging report
- Budget

TRYOUT

 GOAL

To practice using the following skill sets:

* ✴ Create PivotTables and PivotTable reports Ⓜ
* ✴ Modify and format PivotTables Ⓜ
* ✴ Create PivotCharts and PivotChart reports from a PivotTable Ⓜ
* ✴ Create PivotCharts and PivotChart reports from a data list Ⓜ

TASK 1

WHAT YOU NEED TO KNOW

Create PivotTables and PivotTable Reports

> Excel contains a powerful tool for data analysis called a PivotTable. A *PivotTable* is an interactive function that allows you to manipulate data in a list in order to summarize, analyze, or arrange it in a specific way. With the PivotTable feature, you can work with data using different functions (e.g., Sum, Average, Maximum), select which portions of the data to view, and rearrange (or *pivot*) the layout of your summary. These features are especially useful when you have a large database or list and want to analyze trends or select a portion of the information for a closer look. When you have completed your PivotTable analysis, you can generate a report that contains its contents. It is important to remember that no matter how you pivot or rearrange the data, the original data in your worksheet remains intact.

> To create a PivotTable, first click a cell in the data list. Click Data, PivotTable and PivotChart Report. The PivotTable and PivotChart Wizard opens and guides you through the following sequence of steps:

TRY*it*OUT

1. Open **13.1PersList** from the Data CD. Click a cell in the data list.

2. Click **Data, PivotTable and PivotChart Report.**

3. In Step 1 of the PivotTable and PivotChart Wizard, click **Microsoft Excel list or database.** Click **PivotTable** as the kind of report you want to create. Click **Next.**

4. In Step 2 of the Wizard, the range of cells should already be designated as **A1:H18.** Enter that range if it does not appear in the Range box. Click **Next.**

5. In Step 3 of the Wizard, click **New worksheet.** Click **Finish.**

6. Drag the following field buttons from the PivotTable field list to the designated locations:
   a. Drag **LOCATION** to the Page Fields area.
   b. Drag **DEPT** to the Column Fields area.
   c. Drag **WKSAL** to the Data Items area. (This action automatically creates the Sum function.)
   d. Leave the Row Fields area blank.

7. Click the list arrow for **LOCATION,** click **CT,** and click **OK.**

8. Click the list arrow for **DEPT,** select only **Sales,** and click **OK.**

9. Keep the file open.

- Step 1 of the PivotTable and PivotChart Wizard, as shown in Figure 13.1, asks you to select the data source you want to analyze. Select a data list or database contained in an Excel workbook or an external data source. Then select whether you want to create a table or chart. For this section of the lesson, select PivotTable and click Next.

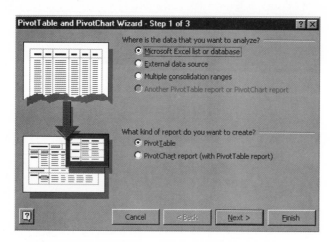

Figure 13.1 PivotTable and PivotChart Wizard—Step 1

- Step 2 of the Wizard, as shown in Figure 13.2, asks you to identify the range of the data you want to use. If the data is in an active list, the range of cells it occupies is indicated by default. You can change the default range or click Browse if you want to locate data that is contained in another file. Then click Next.

Figure 13.2 PivotTable and PivotChart Wizard—Step 2

- Step 3 of the Wizard, as shown in Figure 13.3, asks you to select the destination for the PivotTable report. Indicate whether you want it to go to a new or existing worksheet. If you select a new worksheet, Excel puts the result on a sheet labeled Sheet 4 in your workbook. Click Finish.

Figure 13.3 PivotTable and PivotChart Wizard—Step 3

> The layout view of the PivotTable appears, as shown in Figure 13.4.

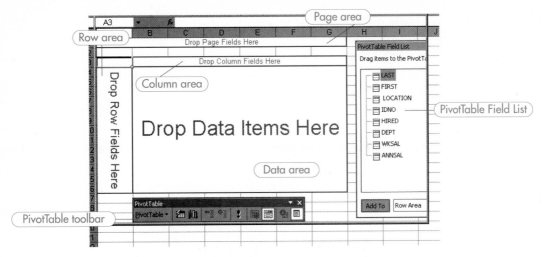

Figure 13.4 Layout view of the PivotTable

> This screen contains the following components:

- The PivotTable toolbar, as shown in the lower portion of Figure 13.4, contains buttons that activate a number of commands, including formatting the PivotTable report, making a chart, selecting the function to apply to the data, and refreshing the data. (See also Figure 13.7.)

- The PivotTable Field List, at the right in Figure 13.4, includes the field names from the original data list. You can drag-and-drop the field names you need to the appropriate locations on the PivotTable layout.

- The upper-left portion of the screen contains the different sections, or drop zones, into which you can drag-and-drop data and field names. You can place field names from the original data list in rows or columns or you can use them to label a page. When you drag-and-drop a field name in any part of this screen, a small replica of the layout appears next to the mouse pointer with the shaded region indicating exactly where Excel will place the field name. The sections are:

  a. Page area—The data field you place in the page area is the data that will be displayed in the PivotTable. It acts as a filter. For example, if you have a list of employees and each employee is in one of three locations, you could use Location as the page field. This would give you a report showing the employees in one of the locations. If you change the location, you could view each of the other employee lists.

  b. Row area—Creates row labels for each unique item within the page field. For example, to count employees in each department in each location, you could use Department as the row field. The PivotTable would then automatically count the number in each department for the location selected. This same analysis could be done using the column area.

  c. Column area—Creates column labels for each unique item within the page field. This is similar to the row field; it is a category to use to summarize the data. For example, if you want to find out the salaries for each department, for each location, you could use Department as the column field. This same analysis could be done using the row area.

d. Data area – The field name for the data to analyze or summarize goes in the section labeled Drop Data Items Here. Weekly Salary would be the data field to get a summary of salaries, by department, in each location. In Figure 13.5, Location is in the Page field, Department is in the Column field, and Weekly Salary is being dragged to the Data field.

Note: You must always put at least one data field in the data area.

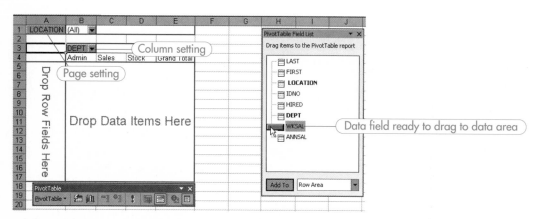

Figure 13.5 PivotTable layout with Page and Column field settings and Data field in process

> An alternate way to set up the layout of a PivotTable is to click Layout in Step 3 of the Wizard. The Layout dialog box opens, as shown in Figure 13.6. Click and drag the field names you want to their appropriate locations in the layout section.

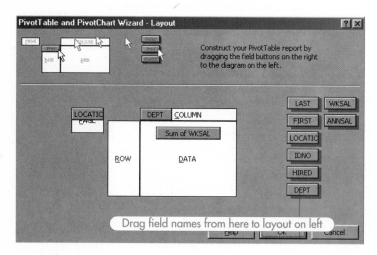

Figure 13.6 PivotTable and PivotChart Wizard Layout dialog box and resulting PivotTable

Modify and Format PivotTables

> A useful feature of PivotTables lets you easily modify them by using the drag-and-drop technique. For example, to add another field name or additional data to the PivotTable, drag it from the PivotTable field list and drop it in the appropriate place on the PivotTable layout. When you first begin, try to keep your PivotTable simple. Adding too many field names or data fields can make the report difficult to interpret.

Note: The PivotTable field list appears only when a cell in the PivotTable is active.

> You can remove field names or data from the PivotTable by dragging them to a blank portion of the worksheet.

> To undo your most recent change to a PivotTable, click Edit, Undo Pivot.

> You can activate many editing features for a PivotTable from the PivotTable toolbar, as shown in Figure 13.7.

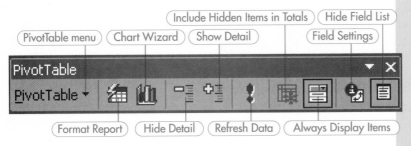

Figure 13.7 PivotTable toolbar

> To change which function is operating on the data, click the Field Settings button on the PivotTable toolbar. The PivotTable Field dialog box opens, as shown in Figure 13.8. Insert the name of the data you want to summarize in the Name box. Select the function (e.g., Average, Minimum, Maximum, etc.) you want to apply in the Summarize by box. Click OK.

Note: You can also change the function used on the data by double-clicking the name of the data.

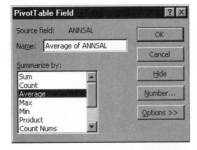

Figure 13.8 PivotTable Field dialog box

TRY_it_**OUT**

Note: Continue to work in **13.1PersList.**

1. Click **Edit, Undo Pivot.** The data for all departments should reappear.

2. From the PivotTable field list, click and drag **ANNSAL** to the cell labeled **Sum of WKSAL.**

3. Click **LOCATION** on the PivotTable and drag it to a blank portion of the worksheet.

4. Click **Sum of WKSAL** and click the **Field Settings** button on the PivotTable toolbar. Sum of WKSAL should appear in the Name box. In the Summarize by box, click **Average** and click **OK.**

5. Click **Sum of ANNSAL** and click the **Field Settings** button on the PivotTable toolbar. Sum of ANNSAL should appear in the Name box. In the Summarize by box, click **Average** and click **OK.**

6. On Sheet 1, change the value in **Cell G2** to: **$375**
   Go back to the PivotTable and click the **Refresh Data** button on the PivotTable toolbar.

7. Click the **Format Report** button on the PivotTable toolbar. Click **Report 3** as the format and click **OK** (see Figure 13.9).

8. Select **Columns B** and **C.** Click **Format, Cells.** In the Format Cells dialog box, click the **Number** tab, click **Accounting** as the format, and click **OK.**

9. Click **File, Print.**

10. Save the file. Keep the file open.

> To apply an automatic format to the PivotTable, click the Format Report button on the PivotTable toolbar. You can select from several formats or choose None from the AutoFormat dialog box, as shown in Figure 13.9. Click OK.

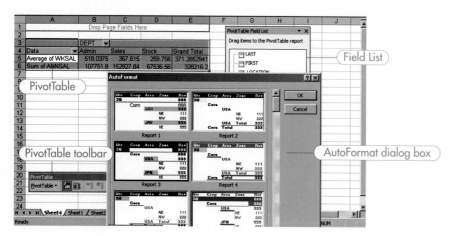

Figure 13.9 AutoFormat dialog box

> If the data in the original list changes, you can update the PivotTable by clicking the Refresh Data button on the PivotTable toolbar.

Note: The different buttons on the PivotTable toolbar function only when a cell in the PivotTable is active.

> You can reactivate the PivotTable and PivotChart Wizard by clicking the PivotTable drop-down menu on the PivotTable toolbar and clicking Wizard.

> You can print the results of a PivotTable analysis in the form of a *PivotTable report.* Click a cell in the worksheet that contains the PivotTable and click File, Print, or click the Print button on the toolbar.

Create PivotCharts and PivotChart Reports from a PivotTable

> It is often helpful to see the results of a PivotTable analysis in the form of a chart. A *PivotChart* is a graphical representation of the contents of a PivotTable. To create a PivotChart, click a cell in the PivotTable. On the PivotTable toolbar, click the Chart Wizard button (see Figure 13.7). A graph of the data in the PivotTable appears on a new worksheet.

  • As Figure 13.10 shows, data located in the rows of the PivotTable are placed on the x-axis of the chart. Usually, the x-axis represents categories into which you can place the numerical data.

  • Information in the Data Items area of the PivotTable is represented on the y-axis. The y-axis usually displays numerical values such as dollars or frequency counts.

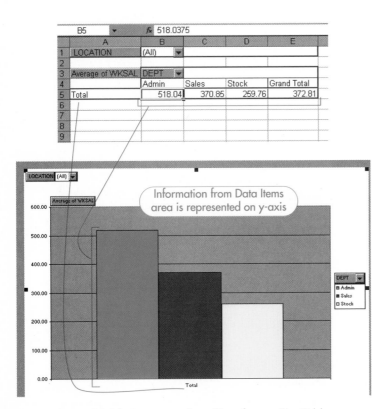

Figure 13.10 Creating a PivotChart from a PivotTable

> You can change the type of chart that appears by clicking the Chart Wizard button on the Standard toolbar or by selecting the chart and clicking Chart, Chart Type. Common graphs are column, bar, line, and pie charts.

TRY*it***OUT**

Note: Continue to work in 13.1PersList.

1. Click **Average of WKSAL** on the PivotTable and drag it to a blank spot on the worksheet.

2. Click the **Chart Wizard** button on the PivotTable toolbar. The chart should appear on a new sheet.

3. Click the **chart legend** to activate it. Delete the **legend,** since there is only one type of data represented in this graph.

4. Click the list arrow for **DEPT.** Click **Admin** and **Sales.** Click **OK.**

5. Click **Chart, Chart Options.** In the **Titles** tab of the Chart Options dialog box, enter the following in the Chart title box:
   `Average Weekly Salaries for Administration and Sales`
   Click **OK.**

6. Click and drag **LOCATIONS** from the PivotTable field list to the Page Fields section of the PivotChart.

7. Print the report.

8. Save and close the **13.1Pivot** file.

> You can make changes in labels for axes, legends, and other aspects of the chart format by clicking the Chart Wizard button and following the steps in the Wizard, or by selecting the chart and clicking Chart, Chart Options.

- A chart should have a title that explains the information that is represented.

- The x- and y-axes should be properly labeled.

- If you are presenting more than one data type, columns, bars, lines, or pie slices appear with different colors to distinguish them. Make sure there is a legend that accurately describes the data that each color represents.

Note: Remember, you can also change the formatting of the chart by double-clicking the relevant portion and selecting a color or other style options from the dialog boxes that open.

> PivotCharts contain many of the interactive features that are found in PivotTables. For example, you can add and remove field names from the layout of the chart. Field names also appear with drop-down menus that allow you to select different values for a given field.

> You can print the results of a PivotChart analysis in the form of a **PivotChart report.** To create the report, select the worksheet that contains the PivotChart. Then click File, Print or click the Print button on the toolbar.

Create PivotCharts and PivotChart Reports from a Data List

> If you want to create a PivotChart before you create a PivotTable, you can use the PivotTable and PivotChart Wizard to create a PivotChart directly from a data list. Click Data, PivotTable and PivotChart Report.

- In Step 1 of the Wizard, select the data source. Click PivotChart report as the type of report you want to create and click Next.

- In Step 2, indicate the range that contains the data. The data list should appear as the default range. If it does not, enter the correct range and click Next.

- In Step 3, indicate where you want to locate the PivotChart, either on a new or an existing worksheet. Click Finish.

> The layout view of the PivotChart appears, as shown in Figure 13.11. The layout contains locations for Page Fields, Category Fields, and Data Items. As with the PivotTable, you can click and drag field names from the PivotTable field list to the appropriate sections of the chart layout. Drag the data to analyze to the Data Items section.

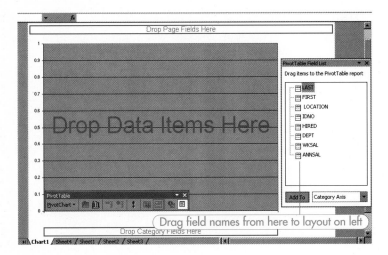

Figure 13.11 PivotChart layout view

> To remove a field name from the chart, click and drag it to an empty section of the sheet.

> When you create a PivotChart, Excel automatically creates a PivotTable on a separate sheet. A PivotChart can be created without first creating a PivotTable, but it is always linked to a PivotTable.

TRY it OUT

1. Open **13.1PersList** from the Data CD.

2. Click **Data, PivotTable and PivotChart Report.**

3. In Step 1 of the Wizard, click **Microsoft Excel list or database.** Click **PivotChart report** as the type of report and click **Next.**

4. In Step 2, the range should already be designated as **A1:H18.** Enter that range if it does not appear in the Range box. Click **Next.**

5. In Step 3, click **New worksheet** and click **Finish.**

6. Drag the following field buttons from the PivotTable field list to the designated locations:
   a. Drag **LOCATION** to the Page Fields area.
   b. Drag **DEPT** to the Category Fields area.
   c. Drag **WKSAL** to the Data Items area.

7. Click the **Sum of WKSAL** button. Click the **Field Settings** button on the PivotTable toolbar. In the Summarize by box, click **Average** and click **OK.**

8. Click and drag **LOCATION** to a blank area on the sheet.

9. Click the chart title and change it to:
   Average of Weekly Salary by Department

10. Click **File, Print.**

11. Save the **13.1PivotChart** file. Close the file.

REHEARSAL

TASK 1

 GOAL
To analyze the data in a personnel list by creating a PivotTable and PivotChart report

SETTING THE STAGE/WRAPUP
File name: 13.1Personnel

WHAT YOU NEED TO KNOW

> You have already learned that businesses usually keep a *personnel list,* a record of all employees and their associated information. Businesses often need to analyze the data in a personnel list, for example, how many employees work in each department or office location or the payroll totals for specific departments or office locations. A PivotTable and/or PivotChart analysis is an excellent way to conduct these data analyses.

> In this Rehearsal activity, you will conduct several analyses of the data contained in the personnel list for Occasions Event Planning. You will produce a PivotTable report of average weekly salaries, by department, for each office location. You will also produce a PivotChart report showing annual salaries for each department for all locations combined. Finally, you will produce a PivotChart report that shows the number of employees who work in each department.

DIRECTIONS

1. Open **13.1Personnel** from the Data CD. Use the illustration on the next page to guide you through the sequence of steps below.

2. Sort the list by **LAST** (name).

3. Format **Column G** using the Accounting style.

4. Write a formula to compute annual salary in **Column H.** Label the column **ANNSAL** and format it in the Accounting style. Fill in the values for all of the employees.

5. Create a PivotTable report to summarize the average weekly salaries of employees for each department and office location. Use the following settings for the PivotTable layout screen:
   a. Drag **LOCATION** to the Page Fields area.
   b. Drag **DEPT** to the Column Fields area.
   c. Drag **WKSAL** to the Data Items field.
   d. Change the function for weekly salaries from Sum to **Average.**

6. Format the report using one of the AutoFormats provided by Excel. Create a PivotTable report for each of the three locations. Print each report.

7. Create a new PivotChart report that shows average annual salaries for each department for all locations combined. Do not base this report on existing data. Use a column graph to display the data.
   a. Drag **LOCATION** to the top or page field.
   b. Drag **ANNSAL** onto the PivotChart.
   c. Change the function for **ANNSAL** from Sum to **Average.**
   d. Drag **DEPT** to the bottom of the chart to the category axis. Title the chart as follows: `Average Annual Salary by Department`

8. Print the PivotChart report.

9. Use the PivotChart to find the number of employees in each department across all locations. *(Hint: To obtain this number, change Average of ANNSAL to **Count of ANNSAL** with the Field Settings button.)*

10. Change the graph to a pie chart using the Chart Wizard button on the PivotTable toolbar. Enter the following for the title of the chart: `Number of Employees by Department`

Continued on next page

11. Print the PivotChart report.

12. Save the **13.1Personnel** file.

	A	B	C	D	E	F	G	H
1	LAST	FIRST	LOCATION	IDNO	HIRED	DEPT	WKSAL	ANNSAL
2	Birney	Mary	CA	20456	2/15/1997	Sales	330	
3	Darby	Marge	OR	21567	6/01/1999	Admin	400	
4	Ajello	Anthony	WA	23143	3/01/2000	Sales	275	
5	Kearney	Sharon	CA	21980	8/24/2001	Sales	255	
6	Weeks	David	OR	21486	9/25/1999	Admin	380	
7	Cacher	William	CA	20998	4/13/2000	Sales	275	
8	Gilchrest	Cindy	OR	21222	5/15/2000	Sales	275	
9	Lakoff	Brian	WA	23886	5/15/1999	Admin	400	
10	Williams	Todd	CA	20648	2/15/1997	Admin	500	
11	Carey	Barbara	WA	23846	9/24/2001	Sales	255	
12	Sanderson	David	OR	21778	8/28/2000	Sales	270	
13	Penney	Jason	CA	20846	2/20/1997	Sales	330	
14	Murphy	Janelle	WA	23112	6/15/1999	Sales	350	
15	Gibbons	Dorothy	OR	21668	6/15/1999	Sales	350	
16	Smith	Rebecca	CA	20749	6/24/2001	Sales	255	
17	Trent	Robert	OR	21980	6/30/2001	Sales	255	
18	Leary	Gina	CA	20998	7/15/2001	Sales	255	
19	Orroz	James	WA	23999	8/30/2001	Sales	250	
20								
21	Sort data list							
22	by last name							
23								
24								

Add column and calculate annual salary

Format using Accounting style

Cues for Reference

Create a PivotTable
1. Click cell on worksheet containing data list.
2. Click **Data, PivotTable and PivotChart Report.**
3. In Step 1 of Wizard, select data source and select PivotTable as type of report. Click **Next.**
4. In Step 2, enter range of cells to include in analysis or accept default range. Click **Next.**
5. In Step 3, select location for PivotTable. Click **Finish.**
6. Drag field names from PivotTable field list to Page Fields, Row Fields, or Column Fields areas on layout screen.
7. Drag field name for data you are analyzing to Data Items area on layout screen.
8. To change function used to operate on data, click data field name and click **Field Settings** button on PivotTable toolbar.

Create a PivotChart
1. If you already have created a PivotTable:

a. Click cell in PivotTable and click **Chart Wizard** button on PivotTable toolbar.

b. Click **Chart Wizard** button on toolbar to make changes to layout and contents of chart.

2. If you have not yet made a PivotTable:

a. Click **Data, PivotTable and PivotChart Report.**

b. In Step 1, select data source and select **PivotChart** as type of report you want to create. Click **Next.**

c. In Step 2, enter range of cells to include in analysis or accept default range. Click **Next.**

d. In Step 3, select location for PivotChart. Click **Finish.**

e. Drag field names from PivotTable field list to Page Field or Category Field areas on layout screen.

f. Drag field name for data you are analyzing to Data Items area on layout screen.

Change the Function in a PivotTable and/or PivotChart Report
1. Click data field name on which you are operating.
2. Click **Field Settings** button on PivotTable toolbar.
3. Make sure field name for data appears in Name box.
4. Select operation you want from Summarize by box.
5. Click **OK.**

Create a PivotTable/PivotChart Report
1. Click cell in worksheet that contains PivotTable or PivotChart.
2. Click **File, Print,** or click **Print** button.

Format a PivotTable
1. Click cell in PivotTable.
2. Click **Format Report** button on PivotTable toolbar.
3. Select format in AutoFormat dialog box.
4. Click **OK.**

TRYOUT

GOAL
To practice using the following skill sets:
✴ Forecast values with what-if
analysis M
✴ Chart forecast data

TASK 2

WHAT YOU NEED TO KNOW

> Before business managers make important financial
decisions, they often want to evaluate the impact of several
possible courses of action. Past data is generally used in
conjunction with a set of formulas or models to make
predictions about future outcomes. For example, a business
might want to assess the impact on company revenues of
changing interest rates for past due accounts. Or, a business
might want to create a *sales forecast,* a projection of future
sales based on past performance. Actual sales are then
compared to the sales forecast.

> Excel contains a powerful set of commands called *what-if
analysis* tools that allow you to assess how changes in data
affect outcomes. *FORECAST* is one of the functions in
this group of commands. Notice the explanation of the
FORECAST function in Figure 13.12.

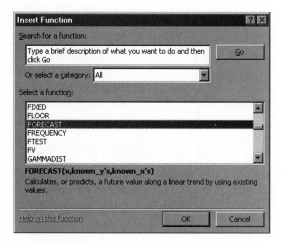

Figure 13.12 Insert Function dialog box

Forecast Values with What–if Analysis

> FORECAST is a what–if analysis function that allows you to project future data values based on data that you have already obtained. For example, suppose you have a list of sales figures for each of six months. Excel can compute the projected values for a subsequent month or months. Excel uses a statistical process called regression analysis to forecast data.

> To forecast data values, click the cell where you want the forecast value to appear. Then click the Insert Function button.

> In the Insert Function dialog box that opens (see Figure 13.12), select All or Statistical in the Or select a category box. In the Select a function box, choose FORECAST. The Function Arguments dialog box opens, as shown in Figure 13.13.

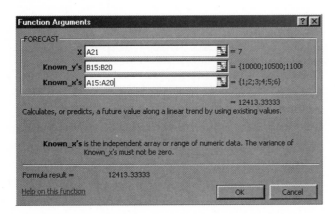

Figure 13.13 Function Arguments dialog box

> Fill in the values as follows:

- In the box labeled X, enter the cell reference for the data point that is associated with the prediction you are making (for example, the month for which you are seeking a forecast sales value). As an alternative, click the Collapse Dialog Box button and click the cell for the data point. Then click the Expand Dialog Box button.

- In the box labeled Known_y s, enter or select the cells that contain the known data of the type you are predicting (for example, past sales figures).

- In the box labeled Known_x s, enter or select the cells that contain known data corresponding with the y-values (for example, months). The x-values must be in numerical form in order for this analysis to work.

TRY *it* **OUT**

1. Open the file **13.2SalesForecast** from the Data CD.

2. Select the range **B6:G6.** Click **Copy.**

3. Click **Cell B15.** Click **Edit, Paste Special, Transpose,** and click **OK.**

4. Click **Cell B21.**

5. Click the **Insert Function** button.

6. Select **Statistical** from the Or select a category list box.

7. Select **Forecast** from the Select a function box and click **OK.**

8. In the Function Arguments dialog box, do the following:
   a. In the box labeled X, click the **Collapse Dialog Box** button and click **Cell A21.** Click the **Expand Dialog Box** button.
   b. In the box labeled Known_y s, click the **Collapse Dialog Box** button and select the range **B15:B20.** Click the **Expand Dialog Box** button.
   c. In the box labeled Known_x s, click the **Collapse Dialog Box** button and select the range **A15:A20.** Click the **Expand Dialog Box** button.
   d. Click **OK.**

9. Use the fill handle to fill in the values for **Cells B22:B23.**

10. Format **Cells B21:B23** for Currency style with no decimals.

11. Copy **Cells B21:B23.** Select **Cell H6.** Click **Edit, Paste Special,** and click the **Values** and **Transpose** options.

12. Keep the file open.

- Arrange the data so that each x-value is in the same row (or column) as its corresponding y-value. In other words, pair the data, as shown in Figure 13.14. Click OK.

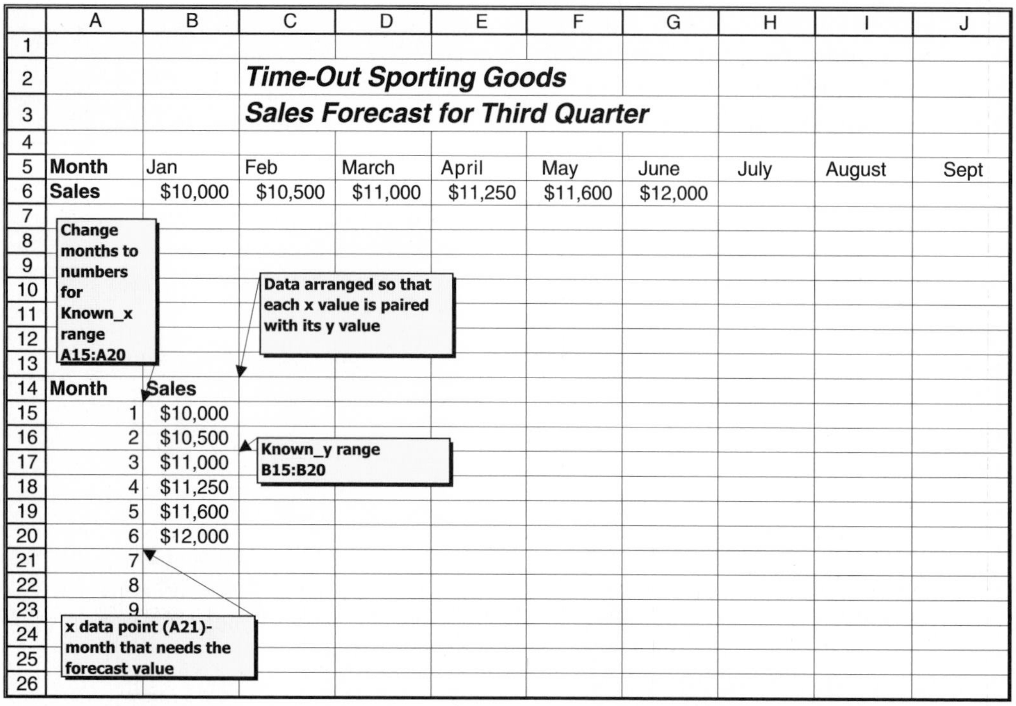

	A	B	C	D	E	F	G	H	I	J
1										
2			**Time-Out Sporting Goods**							
3			**Sales Forecast for Third Quarter**							
4										
5	**Month**	Jan	Feb	March	April	May	June	July	August	Sept
6	**Sales**	$10,000	$10,500	$11,000	$11,250	$11,600	$12,000			
7										
8	Change									
9	months to									
10	numbers for		Data arranged so that							
11	Known_x		each x value is paired							
12	range		with its y value							
13	A15:A20									
14	**Month**	Sales								
15	1	$10,000								
16	2	$10,500	Known_y range							
17	3	$11,000	B15:B20							
18	4	$11,250								
19	5	$11,600								
20	6	$12,000								
21	7									
22	8									
23	9									
24	x data point (A21)–									
25	month that needs the									
26	forecast value									

Figure 13.14 Example of how to arrange data for the FORECAST function

> When creating a paired data list (see Figure 13.14), you can use the Transpose feature in Excel. The Transpose feature changes a horizontal range of data to a vertical range or vice versa. Copy the horizontal data, click the new location, use Paste Special, Transpose to copy, and transpose the horizontal to vertical data.

Chart Forecast Data

> Once you have the forecast values, you might want to display the information in the form of a chart. Simply select the data in the table you have completed, click the Chart Wizard button, and follow the steps in the Wizard.

> You can also add a *trendline,* a graphic representation of any tendencies or patterns shown in the data, as shown in Figure 13.15. Excel offers the option of displaying several types of trends, including a linear, logarithmic, or exponential trend. A common choice is a linear trendline.

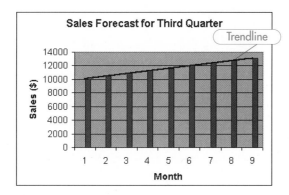

Figure 13.15 Example of a linear trendline

> To insert a trendline into a chart, first click the chart to activate it. Then click Chart, Add Trendline to open the Add Trendline dialog box, as shown in Figure 13.16.

- In the Type tab, select the kind of trendline you want to add to the chart.

- In the box labeled Based on series, select the name of the data for which you want to add the trendline.

- Click OK.

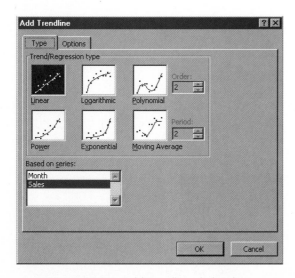

Figure 13.16 Add Trendline dialog box

Note: Continue to work in 13.2SalesForecast.

1. Select the range **A14:B23.** Click the **Chart Wizard** button.

2. Select the **Column** chart type in Step 1 and click **Next.**

3. In Step 2, the data range should already be selected. Select **Series in: Columns** and click **Next.**

4. In Step 3, title the chart:
   `Sales Forecast for Third Quarter`
   Click **Finish.**

5. Click the chart to activate it. Click the **legend** and delete it.

6. Click **Chart, Add Trendline.** In the Type tab, click **Linear.** In the box Based on series, click **Sales, OK.**

7. Click the chart to activate it. Click **Chart, Source Data.** Click the **Series** tab, and in the box Category (X) axis labels, enter the cell range: **B5:J5** Click **OK.**

8. Select each of the last three columns of the chart and format them in **Red.**

9. Add a text box near the last three columns and enter:
   `Forecast Sales`

10. Add an arrow that connects the text box to the last three columns.

11. Close the file without saving it.

REHEARSAL

TASK 2

 GOAL
To create a sales forecast and add a
trendline to a chart

SETTING THE STAGE/WRAPUP
File name: 13.2FCRSales

WHAT YOU NEED TO KNOW

> Four Corners Realty would like
to create a sales forecast for home
sales for the fourth quarter. In this
Rehearsal activity, you will use
home sales data for the first three
quarters to forecast sales for the
fourth quarter. You will create a
chart to display the results and add
a trendline to display an overview
of Four Corners home sales.

▼ DIRECTIONS

1. Open the file **13.2FCRSales** from the Data CD. Use the
illustration on the next page as a guide to the following steps.

2. Starting in **Cell A9,** create a table for sales figures for each
month, using numbers to represent each month.
   a. Label the first column **Month** and the second column **Sales**
   b. Transpose the Sales data to the data list.
   c. Make sure the Month column includes entries for Months 10,
   11, and 12.

3. Forecast the sales figure for Months 10, 11, and 12. Format the
results so they are consistent with the rest of the data table.

4. Use the Paste Special feature with the Values and Transpose
options to copy and paste the forecasted values to **Cells K6:M6.**

5. Create a column chart to represent the past and projected sales.
   a. Label the chart: **Sales Forecast for Fourth
   Quarter**
   b. Label the x-axis: **Month**
   c. Label the y-axis: **Thousands of $**

6. Change the data values in the graph from numbers to the names
of the months.

7. Enhance the chart as follows:
   a. Format the last three columns of the chart in **Red.**
   b. Add a text box that says: **Forecast Sales**
   c. Add an arrow that points from the text box to the last three
   columns of the chart.
   d. Add a linear trendline to the chart.

8. Print the chart.

9. Save and close the file.

	A	B	C	D	E	F	G	H	I	J	K	L	M
1													
2		*FOUR CORNERS REALTY*											
3		*Sales Forecast*											
4													
5	**Month**	Jan	Feb	March	April	May	June	July	August	Sept	Oct	Nov	Dec
6	**Sales (Thousands)**	$250	$300	$500	$550	$600	$500	$700	$750	$700			
7													
8													
9			Transpose										
10			Sales to										
11			this location										
12													
13		Create data											
14		list using											
15		numbers for											
16		months here											
17													

Use the FORECAST Command
1. Click cell where you want result of forecast to appear.
2. Click **Insert Function** button. 𝑓x
3. Select **Statistical** from Or select category list box.
4. Click **FORECAST** in Select a function box. Click **OK.**
5. In box X, enter cell reference for data associated with forecast value (usually a label).

6. In box Known_y's, enter cell references for known data of type you are predicting.
7. In box Known_x's, enter cell references for known data associated with y's. (Data must be numeric.)
8. Click **OK.**

Transpose Data
1. Select data to transpose.

2. Click **Copy.**
3. Click a location for data.
4. Click **Paste Special, Transpose.**
5. Click **OK.**

Add a Trendline
1. Data should be in a chart.
2. Click chart to make it active.
3. Click **Chart, Add Trendline.**
4. Select type of trendline.
5. Click **OK.**

TRYOUT

GOAL

To practice using the following skill sets:

✴ Create and display scenarios

✴ Create and print reports with the Report Manager add-in

TASK 3

Create and Display Scenarios

> A very useful tool in the what-if analysis group is a scenario. A *scenario* is a way to explore the impact of changing data values on numerical outcomes. For example, a company might want to explore the impact of changing specific income or expense values on an overall budget. Or, a business can examine how mailing out statements on different dates affects late fees for delinquent accounts. In some instances, a business might want to develop a best- and worst-case scenario before making a financial decision.

> To create a scenario, click Tools, Scenarios to open the Scenario Manager dialog box, as shown in Figure 13.17. Click Add to start a new scenario.

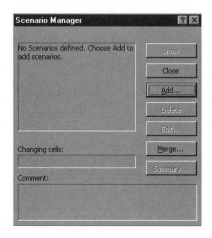

Figure 13.17 Scenario Manager dialog box

T R Y *it* O U T

1. Open the file **13.3AgingReport** from the Data CD.

   *Note: Click **Enable Macros** to be able to use this file properly.*

2. Click the sheet labeled **June.**

3. Click **Tools, Scenarios.**

4. In the Scenario Manager dialog box, click **Add.**

5. In the Add Scenario dialog box, enter the following:
   a. In the Scenario name box, enter:
      Change statement mailing date to: July 15
   b. In the Changing cells box: **C5**
   c. In the Comment box: **Scenario for mailing statements on July 15**
      Click **OK.**

6. In the Scenario Values dialog box, enter: **7/15/2002**
   Click **OK.**

7. In the Scenario Manager dialog box, click **Summary.**

8. In the Scenario Summary dialog box, select **Scenario summary** as the report type. In Result cells, select or enter the range **H10:H15.** Click **OK.**

9. Keep the file open.

> In the Add Scenario dialog box, as shown in Figure 13.18, enter a name for the scenario in the top box. In the Changing cells box, enter the cell reference for the data you want to change. You can add a description of your scenario to the Comment box. Click OK.

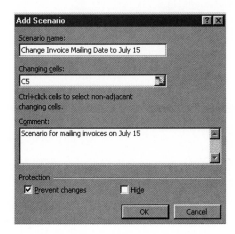

Figure 13.18 Add Scenario dialog box

> The Scenario Values dialog box opens, as shown in Figure 13.19. Enter the value for the data you want to change and click OK.

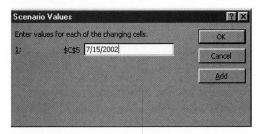

Figure 13.19 Scenario Values dialog box

> The Scenario Manager dialog box opens again. If you want to add another scenario, click Add and repeat the actions in the last two steps.

> To create a report of the outcomes of different scenarios, click Summary in the Scenario Manager dialog box. The Scenario Summary dialog box opens, as shown in Figure 13.20. Select Scenario summary. You will notice that you can also summarize the results of the scenario using a PivotTable. In the Result cells box, enter the cell references for the data for which you want to see results. Click OK.

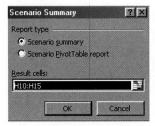

Figure 13.20 Scenario Summary dialog box

> Excel summarizes the results of all of the scenarios in a formatted table on a new worksheet, as shown in Figure 13.21.

Scenario Summary				
		Current Values:		Change statement mail date to July 15
Changing Cells:				
$C$5		6/30/2002		7/15/2002
Result Cells:				
$H$10	$	105.00	$	105.00
$H$11	$	30.00	$	45.00
$H$12	$	100.00	$	150.00
$H$13	$	30.00	$	30.00
$H$14	$	45.00	$	90.00
$H$15	$	-	$	75.00

Notes: Current Values column represents values of changing cells at time Scenario Summary Report was created. Changing cells for each scenario are highlighted in gray.

Figure 13.21 Scenario Summary report

Create and Print Reports with the Report Manager Add-in

> *Report Manager* is an add-in program that allows you to create printed reports containing information from different sections of a workbook, including scenarios. Report Manager does not come packaged with Excel. You must download this program from: www.office.microsoft.com You can tell if Report Manager is already on your computer by clicking the View menu. If Report Manager is not on the drop-down menu, you must download the program from the Web.

Note: You should also click Tools, Add-Ins, to make sure that Report Manager is checked in the Add-Ins dialog box.

> To create a report using Report Manager, click View, Report Manager. In the Report Manager dialog box, as shown in Figure 13.22, click Add to open the Add Report dialog box.

Figure 13.22 Report Manager dialog box

TRY *it* OUT

Note: Continue to work in **13.3AgingReport.**

1. Click **View, Report Manager.**

2. In the Report Manager dialog box, click **Add.**

3. In the Add Report dialog box, enter the following in the Report Name box: **Changing Statement Mailing Date**

4. In the Sheet box, select **June** and click **Add.**

5. In the Sheet box, select **Scenario Summary** and click **Add.**

6. In the Sections in this Report box, select **June** and click **Move Down.**

7. Click **OK.**

8. In the Report Manager dialog box, click **Print.**

9. In the Print dialog box, select **1** copy and click **OK.**

10. Save and close the file.

> In the Add Report dialog box, as shown in Figure 13.23, enter a name for the report in the top box. In the Sheet box, select the sheets you want to use for each portion of the report. Click Add to insert the different sections you have chosen in the report. If you want to add a scenario to the report, check Scenario and select the name of the scenario you want. The Sections in this Report box summarizes the portions you have chosen for the report. Click OK.

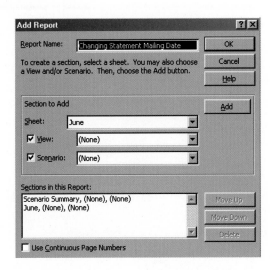

Figure 13.23 Add Report dialog box

> The Report Manager dialog box opens again. Select the action you want to take. You can print, edit, add, or delete reports in this dialog box, as follows:

- To print the report, click Print. In the Print dialog box, select the number of copies you want and click OK. The report is printed in the order shown in the Sections in this Report box.

- To edit the report, click Edit. In the Edit Report dialog box, you can change the title of the report. You can also select different sections of the report and move them up or down in order. Click the name of the section you want to move in the Sections in this Report box. Then click Move Up or Move Down.

- To delete a report, select its name in the Sections in this Report box and click Delete.

REHEARSAL

TASK 3

 GOAL

To create and analyze several worksheets using the Scenario and FORECAST features, and to print a summary report using the Report Manager

SETTING THE STAGE/WRAPUP

File names: 13.3TimeOutAging
13.3TimeOutBudget

WHAT YOU NEED TO KNOW

> You have already learned that an *aging report* is a financial document that shows an analysis of how many days payments from customers are overdue. Scenarios can be very helpful to a business that is trying to determine the effect of changing its credit terms and the interest rates that apply to overdue accounts.

> A *budget* is a proposal for future income and expenses used by a business as a guide for the next business period. The scenario and forecasting tools are valuable for use in preparing a reasonable budget.

> In this Rehearsal activity, Time Out Sporting Goods has asked you to analyze two worksheets they have prepared. You create a scenario for the accounts receivable aging reports for Time Out Sporting Goods. You examine the effect of changing both the credit terms given to all customers from 20 days to 30 days and of raising the interest rate for some delinquent accounts. On the budget worksheet, you create worst-, average-, and best-case scenarios for the budget. In addition, you will use the FORECAST feature to obtain another set of budget proposals. You will also use the Report Manager to print reports of different portions of the workbooks.

DIRECTIONS

1. Open the file **13.3TimeOutAging** from the Data CD. Use the illustrations on the next pages to guide you through the following steps.

2. For the data on the sheet for September, create a scenario for changing three items. The terms for payment in **Cell D6** and the interest rates for 60 and 90 days in **Cells C27** and **C28,** as shown in Illustration A. Use the Ctrl key to select non-adjacent cells. Label the scenario:
   Terms and Interest Rates—Sept

3. Create a scenario summary that shows the impact of the two changes on the late fees in the range **H10:H16.**

4. Repeat Steps 2 and 3 above for the sheet for October. Label it:
   Terms and Interest Rates—Oct

5. Change the sheet label for the first scenario summary to:
   Scenario—Terms and Int—Sept
   Change the sheet label for the second scenario to:
   Scenario—Terms and Int—Oct

6. Use the Report Manager to create a report containing both of the scenario summaries above. Title the report **Impact of Changing Terms and Rates** and print it.

7. Open the file **13.3TimeOutBudget** from the Data CD. Use Illustrations B and C on the next pages to guide you through the following steps.

8. Enter a formula in **Cell D8** that calculates the proposed budget by multiplying the Actual 2002 data by the percent increase in **Cell D6. Cell D6** should be an absolute reference. Fill the formula in for all values.

9. On the Budget Scenarios sheet, create three scenarios that change the percent the budget is of the previous year's data. Label the scenarios as **Worst**, **Average**, and **Best**. The percent in **Cell D6** will be changed in each scenario as follows:
   a. Worst   101%
   b. Average   105%
   c. Best   110%

Continued on next two pages

Illustration A

	A	B	C	D	E	F	G	H	I
1									
2			Time Out Sporting Goods						
3			Accounts Receivable Aging Report		Scenario:				
4					Compare to 30 days				
5	Current Date:			10/31/02					
6			Terms for payment:		20 days				
7	INVOICE	INVOICE					INVOICE	INTEREST	AMOUNT
8	NUMBER	DATE	CUSTOMER	DATE DUE	DAYS UNPAID	AMOUNT	RATE	LATE FEE	DUE
9									
10	100	07/15/02	KM Dept Store	08/04/02	88.00	$ 4,000.00	0.015	$ 60.00	$4,060.00
11	110	07/22/02	Channel	08/11/02	81.00	$ 3,000.00	0.015	$ 45.00	$3,045.00
12	115	07/29/02	Champ's	08/18/02	74.00	$ 11,000.00	0.015	$ 165.00	$11,165.00
13	120	08/17/02	Morton's	09/06/02	55.00	$ 2,000.00	0.010	$ 20.00	$2,020.00
14	133	08/22/02	ABC Sports	09/11/02	50.00	$ 8,000.00	0.010	$ 80.00	$8,080.00
15	145	09/10/02	Quality Dept. Stores	09/30/02	31.00	$ 12,000.00	0.010	$ 120.00	$12,120.00
16									
17									
18									
19									
20									
21									
22		UNPAID	INTEREST						
23		DAYS	RATE		Scenario:				
24		1	0.000		Compare to				
25		15	0.050		changing to				
26		30	0.010		.02 for 60 days and				
27		60	0.015		.03 for 90 days				
28		90	0.020						

Illustration A

Illustration B

	A	B	C	D	E	F
1		Time Out Sporting Goods				
2		Budget Analysis - 2003				
3						
4		Actual	Actual	Budget		
5		2001	2002	Proposals 2003		
6				101%	Create scenarios that	
7	Income:				change the	
8	Net Sales	1,548,911	1,647,778	1,664,256	percent	
9	Less: Cost of Goods Sold	1,002,543	1,045,212	1,055,664	Budget 2003	
10	Gross Profit	546,368	602,566	608,592	is of Actual	
11	Expenses:	413,341	446,049	450,509	2002 data	
12	Net Income before Taxes	133,027	156,517	158,082		
13	Less: Taxes	39,908	46,955	47,425		
14	Net Income after Taxes	93,119	109,562	110,658		

Illustration B

Cues for Reference

Create a Scenario
1. Click **Tools, Scenario.**
2. Click **Add** in Scenario Manager dialog box.
3. In Add Scenario dialog box, enter name for scenario. In Changing cells box, enter cell reference for data you want to change.
4. In Scenario Values dialog box, enter new value for data you want to change. Click **OK.**
5. In Scenario Manager dialog box, click **Summary.**

6. In Result cells box, enter cell references for data for which you want to see results.

Create a Report with the Report Manager
1. Click **View, Report Manager.**
2. In Report Manager dialog box, click **Add.**
3. In Add Report dialog box, enter a name for report in top box. In Sheet box, select sheets to appear in report. Click **Add** after each one. Click **OK.**

Edit a Report with the Report Manager
1. Click **View, Report Manager.**
2. Select report you want to edit. Click **Edit.**
3. To add a section to report, select sheet and click **Add.**
4. To move a section of report, select section in Sections in this Report box. Click **Move Up** or **Move Down.**
5. To delete a section of report, select section in Sections in this Report box and click **Delete.**
6. In Report Manager dialog box, click **Close.**

10. Create a scenario summary that shows the impact of the three changes on the data in the range **D6:D14.**

11. On the Budget Forecast sheet, enter numbers **1, 2,** and **3** as shown in Illustration C, and transpose the data as shown.

12. Use the FORECAST function to calculate the value for year 3 for the y-range **B17:B18.** Copy the formula to all transposed values.

13. Copy the forecast results and use Edit, Paste Special with the Value and Transpose options to place the values in the Budget Forecast column.

14. Delete the work area you created at the bottom of the worksheet.

15. Use the Report Manager to create a report containing the Scenario Summary. Title the report: **Budget Proposals**

16. Use the Report Manager to edit the report so that it now includes the Scenario Summary sheet and the Budget Forecast sheet. Print the report.

17. Save and close both files.

	A	B	C	D	E	F	G	H
1		Time Out Sporting Goods						
2		Budget Forecast - 2003						
3								
4		Actual	Actual	Budget				
5		2001	2002	Forecast				
6								
7	Income:							
8	Net Sales	1,548,911	1,647,778		Copy and Paste Special forecast results, with Values and Transpose options			
9	Less: Cost of Goods Sold	1,002,543	1,045,212					
10	Gross Profit	546,368	602,566					
11	Expenses:	413,341	446,049					
12	Net Income before Taxes	133,027	156,517					
13	Less: Taxes	39,908	46,955					
14	Net Income after Taxes	93,119	109,562					
15								
16								
17	1	1,548,911	1,002,543	546,368	413,341	133,027	39,908	93,119
18	2	1,647,778	1,045,212	602,566	446,049	156,517	46,955	109,562
19	3							
20		Enter numbers and transpose data	Use FORECAST function to forecast year three data					
21								
22								

Illustration C

PERFORMANCE

WHAT YOU NEED TO KNOW

Act I

The Trilogy Film Company is assessing its personnel costs for three offices, New York, Los Angeles, and London. Open the file **13p1.TrilogyPersonnel** from the Data CD. Create the appropriate PivotTable and PivotChart reports so that management can make an analysis of employee expenses by department and location.

Follow these guidelines:

✶ Prepare the worksheet:

- Label Column H: ANNSAL

- Format the column in Accounting style.

- Enter the formula for annual salary in **Cell H2** and fill in the values for the rest of the employees.

- Sort the list first by LOCATION and then by date HIRED. Each should be in ascending order.

✶ Create a PivotTable that shows average ANNSAL by location and department. *(Hint: Put LOCATION in the Columns field and DEPT in the Rows field.)* Format all appropriate cells in Currency format with no decimals.

✶ Use one of the AutoFormats to format the report and print it.

✶ Remove LOCATION from the PivotTable and print a new report that shows average annual salaries by department.

✶ Go to the sheet with the data list and change the WKSAL entry for Judy Harris to: $750.00

✶ Go to the sheet with the PivotTable and refresh the data.

✶ Create a PivotChart from the PivotTable showing average ANNSAL by department. Format the columns so they are green. Title the chart: Average Annual Salary by Department

✶ Label the x-axis: Department

✶ Label the y-axis: Average Salary

✶ Print the PivotChart report.

✶ Save your work.

Act II

Odyssey Travel Gear is preparing a sales forecast for the third quarter. Open the file **13p2.OdysseySales** from the Data CD. Create and print a sales forecast for the third quarter, including a chart with a trendline.

Follow these guidelines:

✻ Arrange the data in a list that represents the months by numbers.

✻ After you have created a tabular version of the forecast, create a column chart that shows the data. Label the chart: `Sales Forecast for the Third Quarter`

✻ Label the x-axis: `Month`

✻ Label the y-axis: `Sales ($)`

✻ Change the values on the x-axis from numbers to the names of the months.

✻ Format the columns that represent the forecast data with a different color. Add a text box that labels the columns for July, August, and September as: `Forecast Sales`

✻ Add a text box that labels the columns for preceding months as: `Actual Sales`

✻ Print the chart.

✻ Save your work.

Act III

The Air Land Sea Travel Group is conducting an analysis to assess the impact of changing interest rates on past due accounts. Open the file **13p3.ALSAging** from the Data CD. Create two scenarios according to the guidelines below and use the Report Manager to print the designated summaries.

Follow these guidelines:

✻ Create the first scenario so that the interest rates for accounts past due appear as follows:

Days Unpaid	Interest Rate
1	0.000
30	0.010
60	0.020
90	0.030

Label the scenario: `Interest Rate Change 1`

✳ For the second scenario, the interest rate for accounts past due should appear as follows:

Days Unpaid	Interest Rate
1	0.000
30	0.020
60	0.030
90	0.040

Label the scenario: Interest Rate Change 2

✳ Create a scenario summary showing the impact of these changes on the late fees.

✳ Create a scenario summary showing the impact of these changes on the total amount due.

✳ Use the Report Manager to print a report of the above two scenario summaries. Title it: Impact of Interest Rate Changes

✳ Edit the report so that it includes the scenario summary for changes in late fees and the data sheet listing the accounts. Print the report.

✳ Save your work.

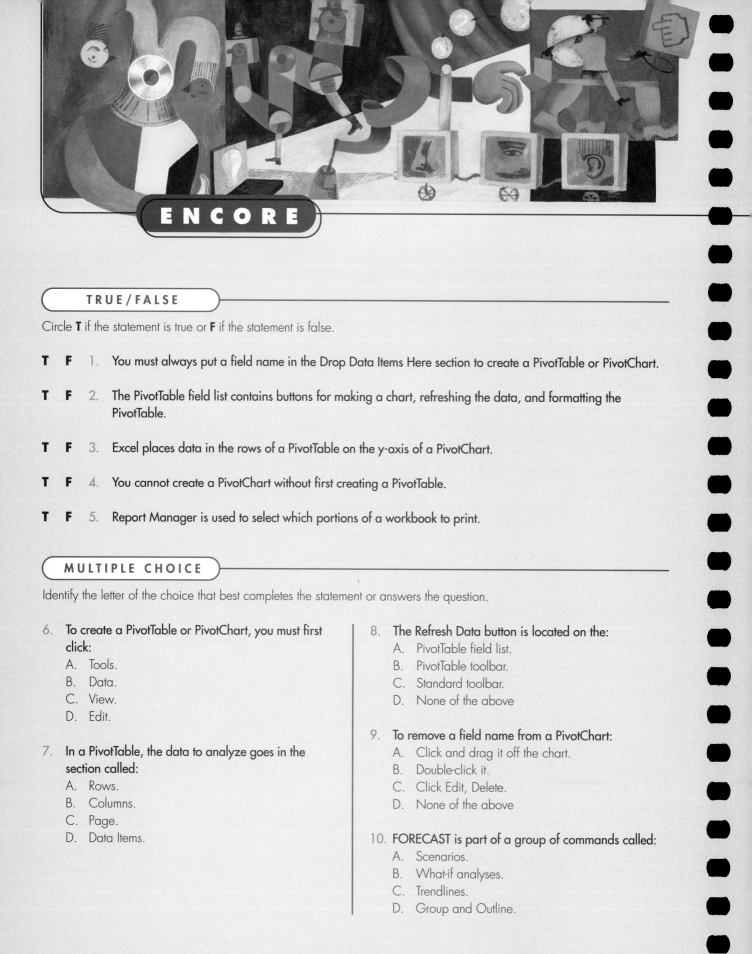

ENCORE

TRUE/FALSE

Circle **T** if the statement is true or **F** if the statement is false.

T F 1. You must always put a field name in the Drop Data Items Here section to create a PivotTable or PivotChart.

T F 2. The PivotTable field list contains buttons for making a chart, refreshing the data, and formatting the PivotTable.

T F 3. Excel places data in the rows of a PivotTable on the y-axis of a PivotChart.

T F 4. You cannot create a PivotChart without first creating a PivotTable.

T F 5. Report Manager is used to select which portions of a workbook to print.

MULTIPLE CHOICE

Identify the letter of the choice that best completes the statement or answers the question.

6. To create a PivotTable or PivotChart, you must first click:
    A. Tools.
    B. Data.
    C. View.
    D. Edit.

7. In a PivotTable, the data to analyze goes in the section called:
    A. Rows.
    B. Columns.
    C. Page.
    D. Data Items.

8. The Refresh Data button is located on the:
    A. PivotTable field list.
    B. PivotTable toolbar.
    C. Standard toolbar.
    D. None of the above

9. To remove a field name from a PivotChart:
    A. Click and drag it off the chart.
    B. Double-click it.
    C. Click Edit, Delete.
    D. None of the above

10. FORECAST is part of a group of commands called:
    A. Scenarios.
    B. What-if analyses.
    C. Trendlines.
    D. Group and Outline.

Complete each sentence or statement.

11. A(n) _____ is an interactive tool that allows you to work on data in a list in order to summarize, analyze, or arrange it in tabular form.

12. A graphical representation of the contents of a PivotTable is called a(n) _____.

13. A(n) _____ is a projection of future sales based on past performance.

14. A(n) _____ is a graphical representation of any tendencies or patterns in data presented in a chart.

15. A(n) _____ is a what-if analysis that allows you to explore the impact on numerical outcomes of changing data values.

16. _____ is an Excel add-in program that allows you to create printed reports containing information from different sections of a workbook.

17. A(n) _____ is a what-if analysis that allows you to project future data values based on data that you have already obtained.

18. _____ is a type of analysis that allows the user to assess how changes in data or formulas affect outcomes. It includes forecasting and scenarios.

19. A printout of a PivotChart analysis is called a(n) _____.

20. A print-out of the contents of a PivotTable is called a(n) _____.

Accounting Department: Shared Files

In this lesson, you will learn to use several features of Excel that are useful when multiple users collaborate and share their work. Specifically, you will learn how to protect cells, worksheets, and workbooks from being changed by others. You will also learn how to share workbooks, keep track of and respond to changes suggested by others, and merge workbooks.

Upon completion of this lesson, you should have mastered the following skill sets:

⭐ Modify passwords, protections, and properties Ⓜ
  ⭐ Protect individual worksheets
  ⭐ Use passwords for protection
  ⭐ Add cell protection
  ⭐ Protect workbooks
⭐ Create a shared workbook Ⓜ
⭐ Track, accept, and reject changes in workbooks Ⓜ
  ⭐ Track changes
  ⭐ Accept and reject changes
⭐ Merge workbooks Ⓜ

Terms
MOUS-related
  Protection
  Password
  Locked cells
  Shared workbook
  Merged workbook
  Track changes
  Accept changes
  Reject changes
Document-related
  Depreciation schedule
  Straight-line depreciation
  Divisional sales report

TRYOUT

TASK 1

 GOAL
To practice using the following skill sets:
- Modify passwords, protections, and properties M
  - Protect individual worksheets
  - Use passwords for protection
  - Add cell protection
  - Protect workbooks

WHAT YOU NEED TO KNOW

Modify Passwords, Protections, and Properties

> Excel provides several features that allow multiple users to work on the same files. There may be situations, however, when you do not want other users to make changes to the data, formulas, or formatting in a file. For example, when you are working on a budget spreadsheet, you may want to prevent others from making changes to a projected budget while allowing them to be able to add data to an actual budget.

> Excel allows you to add protection to specific cells, worksheets, or an entire workbook. *Protection* means that another user can read the data, but cannot make any changes to it until protection is removed or unless a password is used. A *password* is a sequence of letters and/or numbers that a user must enter before access to a worksheet or workbook is allowed.

Protect Individual Worksheets

> One way to restrict access to an Excel file is to add protection to a worksheet. By doing so, you allow other users to open the workbook, but prevent them from making specified changes to that worksheet.

> To protect a worksheet, click Tools, select Protection, and click Protect Sheet. The Protect Sheet dialog box opens, as shown in Figure 14.1.

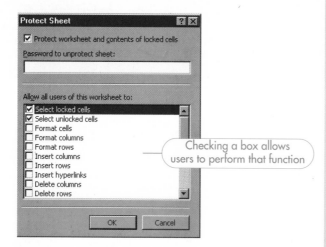

Figure 14.1 Protect Sheet dialog box

> The top box, labeled Protect worksheet and contents of locked cells, should be checked.

> The bottom section of the Protect Sheet dialog box is labeled Allow all users of this worksheet to, and contains a list of commands to which you can regulate access. If you clear all of the boxes, users will not be able to do anything on the worksheet, including selecting a cell. Checking a box allows the user to perform that function. For example, checking Select locked cells allows another user to select a specific cell, but not make changes to it. Checking Format cells allows another user to format cells on the worksheet. Clear the boxes for commands you do not want other users to be able to use. Click OK.

> Once you have added protection to a worksheet, any user attempting to make a change to a locked cell will see the message, as shown in Figure 14.2.

Figure 14.2 Protection warning box

> To cancel protection of the worksheet, click Tools, select Protection, and click Unprotect Sheet.

1. Open the file **14.1Budget** from the Data CD.

2. Click **Tools,** select **Protection,** and click **Protect Sheet.**

3. In the Protect Sheet dialog box, make sure the box **Protect worksheet and contents of locked cells** is checked. Leave the Password field blank. In the box labeled Allow all users of this worksheet to, leave **Select locked cells** and **Select unlocked cells** checked. Click **OK.**

4. Click **Cell D10** and try to change the value to: **3000**

5. Click **OK** when you get the Microsoft Excel warning message.

6. Click **Tools,** select **Protection,** and click **Unprotect Sheet.**

7. Change **Cell D10** to: **3000**

8. Keep the file open.

Use Passwords for Protection

> You can add a password in the Protect Sheet dialog box to allow only designated users to make changes to the worksheet. Enter the password you have selected in the box labeled Password to unprotect sheet. Click OK.

> Reenter the password in the Confirm Password dialog box that follows and click OK.

> The password is optional, but if you do not add a password, any user can remove protection from a worksheet. Once you have added a password, you and any other user must use it to access the worksheet. IMPORTANT: If you lose or forget the password, you cannot make changes on the worksheet.

Note: Passwords can be up to 255 characters long and include letters, numbers, symbols, and spaces. Passwords are case sensitive, so pay attention to whether you are using uppercase or lowercase characters.

> Users who enter the password can remove protection from the sheet and then make changes on it. Click Tools, select Protection, and click Unprotect Sheet. The Unprotect Sheet dialog box opens, as shown in Figure 14.3. Enter the password and click OK. You can now make changes to the worksheet.

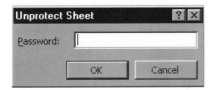

Figure 14.3 Unprotect Sheet dialog box

> To change a password for a protected sheet, you need the original password to unprotect the sheet and then to reprotect it with the new password. Click Tools, select Protection, and click Unprotect Sheet. Enter the current password in the Unprotect Sheet dialog box and click OK. Then click Tools, select Protection, click Protect Sheet, and enter the new password in the box labeled Password to unprotect sheet. Reenter the password in the Confirm Password dialog box and click OK. You will now need to use the new password to access the worksheet.

*Note: Continue to work in **14.1Budget.***

1. Click **Tools,** select **Protection,** and click **Protect Sheet.**

2. In the Protect Sheet dialog box, leave all of the default values: this time, however, enter **BUDGET** in the box labeled Password to unprotect sheet. Click **OK.**

3. In the Confirm Password dialog box, reenter: **BUDGET**

4. Click **OK.**

5. Try to change **Cell D12** to: **600**

6. Click **OK** when you get the warning message.

7. Click **Tools,** select **Protection,** and click **Unprotect Sheet.**

8. In the Unprotect Sheet dialog box, enter the password: **BUDGET**

9. Click **OK.**

10. Change **Cell D12** to: **600**

11. Click **Tools,** select **Protection,** and click **Protect Sheet.**

12. Enter **BUDGET2** in the box labeled Password to unprotect sheet. Click **OK.**

13. In the Confirm Password dialog box, reenter: **BUDGET2**
    Click **OK.** You have changed the password.

14. Close the file. Do not save.

Add Cell Protection

> In some situations, you may want other users to be able to use a worksheet, but you also want to restrict their access to certain cells on the worksheet. In other words, you want to create protected cells, or *locked cells.* This feature is useful when you create a worksheet and want to protect labels and formulas. You can unlock only the cells where another employee can add current data.

> By default, all cells in a workbook are locked, but the locked status becomes enabled only when you protect a worksheet. Therefore, to add cell protection to some portions of a worksheet only, you actually have to unlock the cells you are allowing others to access and then protect the worksheet. The protection will enable locked cells for all cells except the unlocked ranges.

> To unlock specific cells on a worksheet, select the range of cells you want to unlock. Click Format, Cells to open the Format Cells dialog box, as shown in Figure 14.4. Click the Protection tab and clear the Locked box.

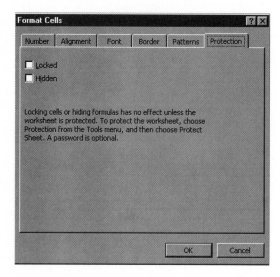

Figure 14.4 Format Cells dialog box

> Next, protect the worksheet. Click Tools, select Protection, and click Protect Sheet. Now, other users can make changes only to the cells you unlocked. You can add a password so that designated users can make changes in the locked cells.

TRY*it*OUT

Tryout Task 1

1. Reopen the file **14.1Budget** from the Data CD.

2. Select **Cells D7:D22,** the range to unlock.

3. Click **Format, Cells,** and the **Protection** tab. Clear the **Locked** box. Click **OK.**

4. Click **Tools,** select **Protection,** and click **Protect Sheet.** Leave the default values and click **OK.**

5. Try to change the value in **Cell C10** to: 2000
   The warning message appears, since the cell is locked.

6. Change the value in **Cell D10** to: 2000
   This cell has been unlocked and you can change it.

7. Close the file. Do not save.

Protect Workbooks

> In some cases, you may want to protect an entire workbook. This means that other users cannot add or delete sheets, rename sheets, or otherwise change the overall structure of a workbook. If you have not added worksheet protection, however, others can make changes to the data on a sheet. To protect a workbook, click Tools, select Protection, and click Protect Workbook. As with protecting a worksheet, you have the option of adding a password to allow designated users to remove workbook protection.

> In the Protect Workbook dialog box, as shown in Figure 14.5, check Structure if you want to prevent others from moving, adding, deleting, renaming, or copying sheets. Check Windows if you want to prevent others from changing the size or position of the windows when the workbook is opened. Add a password if you want to let designated individuals remove workbook protection. Click OK.

Figure 14.5 Protect Workbook dialog box

> To remove protection from a workbook, click Tools, select Protection, and click Unprotect Workbook. Enter the password, if you are prompted to do so. Click OK.

TRY*it*OUT

1. Reopen the file **14.1Budget** from the Data CD.

2. Click **Tools,** select **Protection,** and click **Protect Workbook.**

3. In the Protect Workbook dialog box, make sure the box for **Structure** is checked. Click **OK.**

4. Double-click the tab for **Sheet 1** to try to change its name. Click **OK** in response to the error message.

5. Try to move Sheet 1 to follow Sheet 2 by clicking and dragging the tab for **Sheet 1** to the right.

6. Change the value in **Cell C10** to: **2000** (Worksheets must be protected individually.)

7. Close the file. Do not save.

R E H E A R S A L

TASK 1

 GOAL
To add cell, worksheet, and workbook protection to a depreciation schedule

SETTING THE STAGE/WRAPUP
File name: 14.1Depreciation

WHAT YOU NEED TO KNOW

> Businesses can obtain tax deductions for machinery, buildings, and equipment that are used to produce income. However, the deduction for the cost of such items must extend over the "estimated useful life" of each asset. A *depreciation schedule* is an accounting record that shows the cost of an asset spread over its estimated useful life.

> There are several methods of determining the depreciation of a business's assets. The most common way is called *straight-line depreciation.* This method assumes that the worth of an asset is spread equally over its estimated useful life. Thus, the annual amount of depreciation is calculated by subtracting its value at the end of its useful life (that is, its residual value) from its initial cost, and then dividing by the length of its useful life. For example, to calculate depreciation on a desk costing $1500 with a residual or scrap value of $500, divide the difference of $1000 by the useful life of the desk. For a five year life, the annual depreciation is $200. Expressed as a formula, depreciation is calculated as follows:

Depreciation = (Initial Cost – Residual Value)/Estimated Useful Life)

DIRECTIONS

Note: Follow the guidelines in the illustrations on the next page as you conduct the steps below.

1. Open **14.1Depreciation** from the Data CD. Work on the sheet labeled **2000,** as shown in Illustration A.
Note: Notice that the month (M) and date (D) of the asset purchase are entered in Columns C and D, using the MONTH and DAY function. (See formula bar in Illustration A)

2. In **Cell H7,** enter the formula for Annual Depreciation using the straight-line depreciation method described at left.

3. Enter a formula to calculate 2000 Months, the months the company has owned the asset, using the half-month method. As explained on the next page, to calculate the months owned, you must determine if the asset was purchased after the 15th of the month. (*Hint: Use an IF statement with the D (date) and M (month) column data. =IF(D>15,12-M,12-(M-1))*

4. Enter a formula to calculate 2000 Depreciation. (*Hint: Use an IF statement to determine if the 2000 Months column contains data. If so, the annual depreciation must be prorated by dividing the annual depreciation by 12 and multiplying by the 2000 Months. Annual Depreciation is entered if the 2000 Months column is blank. Use cell addresses in a formula that contains the following: =IF(2000 Months>0,Annual Depreciation/12*2000 Months, Annual Depreciation)*

5. Copy all formulas in **Cells H7:J7,** to fill in the range **H8:J11.**

6. Total the **2000 Depreciation.**

7. Protect the worksheet. Do not use a password. Try to change the cost of the telephone system to: **$6000**

8. Copy the data on **Sheet 2000** to the sheet labeled **2001.** Adjust the width of all cells so that the data appears in each cell.

Continued on next three pages

> To compute the amount of money you should record for depreciation, calculate depreciation for the time that the asset is owned, using the half-month method. The annual depreciation amount is prorated using the following rules:

- If equipment is purchased between the first and the 15th of a month, depreciation is calculated for the entire month.

- If equipment is purchased between the 16th and the end of the month, depreciation is not calculated until the next month.

> In this Rehearsal activity, you will work on a depreciation schedule for assets owned by Occasions Event Planning. You will protect cells, a worksheet, and the workbook and create a password to allow only certain users to make changes to various portions of the workbook. Protection of the data in this workbook is important since the data must be used for tax returns over a period of years. Inadvertent changes by unauthorized users can have serious consequences for the accuracy of a company's tax records.

C7			fx =MONTH(B7)							
	A	B	C	D	E	F	G	H	I	J
1		**Occasions Event Planning**								
2		**Depreciation Schedule - 2000**								
3		Straight-Line Method								
4										
5		Date				Asset	Residual	Annual	2000	2000
6	Asset	Purchased	M	D	Cost	Life	Value	Depreciation	Months	Depreciation
7	1999 White Van	2/18/2000	2	18	$21,000.00	5	$ 8,000.00			
8	Computer	3/21/2000	3	21	$ 2,800.00	3	$ 500.00			
9	Desk	3/24/2000	3	24	$ 1,500.00	5	$ 500.00			
10	Printer	3/24/2000	3	24	$ 800.00	5	$ 200.00			
11	Telephone System	6/18/2000	6	18	$ 5,000.00	5	$ 1,000.00			
12										
13	Total									
14								Enter formulas and protect cells		
15										
16										
17										

Illustration A

9. Copy the **2001 Purchases** sheet data to the appropriate columns on the **2001** sheet, as shown in Illustrations B and C.

10. Fill in the formulas for **Columns C, D, H, I,** and **J** for the new items.

11. Delete the **2000 month data** from the 2001 Months column so that the assets purchased last year show no value in that column. Shade the area that does not apply, as shown in Illustration C.

12. Total the **2001 Depreciation.**

13. Protect the worksheet; do not use a password.

14. Repeat the procedure in Steps 8 -13, using 2002 Purchases and the 2002 sheet. Delete the **2001 month data** from the 2002 Months column and shade the rows that do not apply.

15. Protect the workbook. Use `Occasions` as the password. Try to delete **Sheet 2002.**

16. Use the password to unprotect the workbook. Delete the **2001 Purchases** and **2002 Purchases** sheets.

17. To prepare for the year 2003, insert a new sheet and label it:
    2003
    Copy the **2002** sheet data to the **2003** sheet. Delete the data from **Columns I** and **J.**

18. Unlock **Cells B2, I5,** and **J5.** Protect the worksheet.

19. Try to change the cost of an asset. In **Cells B2, I5** and **J5,** edit the year to read: 2003

20. Protect the workbook. Save and close the file.

Cues for Reference

Protect a Worksheet
1. Click **Tools,** select **Protection,** and click **Protect Sheet.**
2. In Protect Sheet dialog box, check **Protect worksheet and contents of locked cells.**

3. In **Allow all users of this worksheet to,** clear boxes for any functions you do not want other individuals to use.
4. Click **OK.**

Add a Password
1. Click **Tools,** select **Protection,** and click **Protect Sheet.**
2. In Protect Sheet dialog box, enter password in **Password to unprotect sheet.** Click **OK.**
3. Reenter password in **Confirm Password** dialog box. Click **OK.**

Illustration B

	A	B	C	D	E
1		Date		Asset	Residual
2	Asset	Purchase	Cost	Life	Value
3	Computer	2/18/2001	$ 2,200.00	3	$ 500.00
4	Desk	2/18/2001	$ 1,600.00	5	$ 600.00
5	2000 White Van	4/10/2001	$22,000.00	5	$8,500.00
6	Computer	4/25/2001	$ 1,800.00	3	$ 500.00
7	Desk	4/25/2001	$ 1,400.00	5	$ 400.00
8					
9					
10					
11					
12					
13					
14					
15					
16					
17					
18					
19					
20					
21					
22					

Copy the data from this sheet to the appropriate columns on the 2001 Depreciation Schedule

⏮ ◀ ▶ ⏭ \ 2000 / 2001 / 2002 \ 2001 Purchases / 2002 Purchases /

Illustration C

Delete formulas and shade area for assets purchased in 2001

	A	B	C	D	E	F	G	H	I	J
1		*Occasions Event Planning*								
2		*Depreciation Schedule - 2001*								
3		**Straight-Line Method**								
4										
5		Date					Asset	Residual	Annual	2001	2001
6	Asset	Purchased	M	D	Cost		Life	Value	Depreciation	Months	Depreciation
7	1999 White Van	2/18/2000	2	18	$ 21,000.00		5	$ 8,000.00	2600.00		$ 2,600.00
8	Computer	3/21/2000	3	21	$ 2,800.00		3	$ 500.00	766.67		$ 766.67
9	Desk	3/24/2000	3	24	$ 1,500.00		5	$ 500.00	200.00		$ 200.00
10	Printer	3/24/2000	3	24	$ 800.00		5	$ 200.00	120.00		$ 120.00
11	Telephone System	6/18/2000	6	18	$ 5,000.00		5	$ 1,000.00	800.00		$ 800.00
12	Computer	2/18/2001	2	18	$ 2,200.00		3	$ 500.00	566.67	10	$ 472.22
13	Desk	2/18/2001	2	18	$ 1,600.00		5	$ 600.00	200.00	10	$ 166.67
14	2000 White Van	4/10/2001	4	10	$ 22,000.00		5	$ 8,500.00	2700.00	9	$ 2,025.00
15	Computer	4/25/2001	4	25	$ 1,800.00		3	$ 500.00	433.33	8	$ 288.89
16	Desk	4/25/2001	4	25	$ 1,400.00		5	$ 400.00	200.00	8	$ 133.33
17										
18	Total									$ 7,572.78
19										
20										
21										

⏮ ◀ ▶ ⏭ \ 2000 \ **2001** / 2002 / 2001 Purchases / 2002 Purchases /

Cues for Reference *continued*

Protect a Cell or Cells
1. Select cells you want to unlock. All other cells remain locked.
2. Click **Format, Cells,** and **Protection** tab.
3. Clear **Locked** box. Click **OK.**
4. Add protection to sheet following steps above.

Protect a Workbook
1. Click **Tools,** select **Protection,** and click **Protect Workbook.**
2. In Protect Workbook dialog box, check whether you want to protect structure of workbook and/or size and arrangement of windows.

3. Add a password if you want.
4. Click **OK.**

Remove Protection
1. Click **Tools,** select **Protection,** and click **Unprotect Sheet.**
2. Enter password if you are prompted to do so.
3. Click **OK.**

TRYOUT

TASK 2

GOAL
To practice using the following skill sets:
* Create a shared workbook 🗹
* Track, accept, and reject changes in workbooks 🗹
  * Track changes
  * Accept and reject changes
* Merge workbooks 🗹

WHAT YOU NEED TO KNOW

Create a Shared Workbook

> There may be instances in which you want more than one user to work on the same file in order to add or modify data. For example, several people may have responsibility for adding data to files containing budgets, sales reports, or inventories.

> Excel has a feature that allows you to create a *shared workbook,* a workbook that a number of users can edit. When you create a shared workbook, changes made by each user are marked with a comment. You can review these changes and decide whether to accept or reject them. Later, all of the modifications you accept can be put together in the form of a *merged workbook,* a workbook that incorporates the selected changes made by various users of the file.

> To create a shared workbook, click Tools, Share Workbook. The Share Workbook dialog box opens, as shown in Figure 14.6. In the Editing tab, check the box Allow changes by more than one user at the same time. If you are finished at this point, click OK.

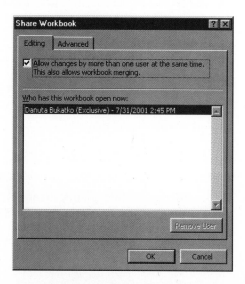

Figure 14.6 Editing tab in the Share Workbook dialog box

TRY*it*OUT

1. Open the file **14.2Sales** from the Data CD.

2. Save the file as **14.2SalesFigures.**

3. Click **Tools, Share Workbook.**

4. In the **Editing** tab, check the box labeled **Allow changes by more than one user at the same time.**

5. In the **Advanced** tab, select **Keep change history for,** and change to **15** days.

6. Click **OK.** Click **OK** at prompt to save file.

7. Close the file.

8. Have another user open this file and change **Cell D9** to:
   $500,000
   If this is not possible, do it yourself.

9. Save the file as **14.2SalesFigures1** and close the file.

> In the Advanced tab, as shown in Figure 14.7, you can select how long you will track changes, how frequently the file will be updated, and what to do when suggested changes conflict with each other. When you have made your selections, click OK.

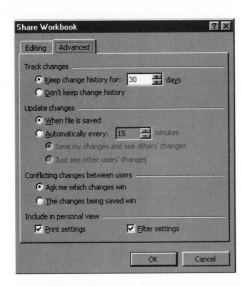

Figure 14.7 Advanced tab in the Share Workbook dialog box

> A good way to avoid confusion when you create a shared workbook is to keep one copy of the shared workbook in a separate file. Do not allow any changes to be made to this copy. Any user that makes changes must start with the shared workbook and save their modified files from it with a new name. When you are ready to merge workbooks, you work with the original shared workbook and the modified workbooks saved from this workbook. If a user saves the modifications without renaming the file, you still have the copy of the original workbook.

Track, Accept, and Reject Changes in Workbooks

Track Changes

> When multiple users are working on a file, you will probably want to monitor the changes made—who made the change and the date and time each person did so. Excel has a feature that permits you to *track changes,* which is to view the modifications made to a file by each user.

> To track changes in a file, click Tools, select Track Changes, and click Highlight Changes. The Highlight Changes dialog box opens, as shown in Figure 14.8.

- Check the box labeled Track changes while editing.

- Check the box labeled When, to select which changes you want to review.

- Check the box labeled Who, to select if you want to track all changes or everyone's changes except your own.

- Check the box labeled Where, if you want to select a specific range of cells for which you want to track changes. Otherwise, the whole worksheet will be tracked.

- Check the box labeled Highlight changes on screen, if you want to view the changes as you enter them.

- The List Changes on a new sheet box is dimmed and only available after the workbook is saved as a shared workbook. It provides a history of changes on a separate history worksheet.

- Click OK.

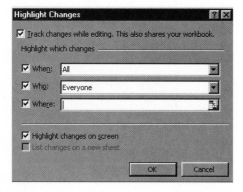

Figure 14.8 Highlight Changes dialog box

1. Open the shared file **14.2SalesFigures** that you saved earlier in this lesson.

2. Click **Tools,** select **Track Changes,** and click **Highlight Changes.**

3. In the Highlight Changes dialog box, check the box **Track changes while editing.** Leave the box labeled **When** checked and the default selection as **All.** Check the box **Highlight changes on screen.**

4. Click **OK.** Click **OK** if a message appears.

5. Change **Cell E9** to: **$800,000** Place the mouse over the cell to view the comment.

6. Save the file as **14.2SalesFigures2.** Close the file.

> Excel then displays a message that the action will save the workbook. Click OK. The title bar will show the file name with [Shared] added to it.

> Once you have enabled Track Changes, any cell for which you make a modification contains a dark triangle in the upper-left corner. When you move the mouse over the cell, a comment appears indicating who made the change and when. The comment also gives the original data contained in the cell. Figure 14.9 shows an example of a comment.

r3	Quarter4
,000.00	$ 800,000.00
,000.00	$ 900,000.00
,000.00	$ 850,000.00
,000.00	$ 850,000.00
,000.00	$ 3,400,000.00

Danuta Bukatko, 7/31/2001 7:59 PM:
Changed cell E9 from ' $800,000.00 ' to ' $850,000.00 '.

Figure 14.9 Example of comment when tracking changes

Accept and Reject Changes

> Once modifications have been made to a file by any user, you can *accept changes,* i.e., decide that the modification should stay on the worksheet. You can also *reject changes,* i.e., decide that the modification should not be made to the worksheet. To implement this feature, click Tools, select Track Changes, and click Accept or Reject Changes.

> The Select Changes to Accept or Reject dialog box opens, as shown in Figure 14.10. You can decide to review changes by time, user, or location on the worksheet. Check any of the relevant boxes labeled When, Who, or Where. Each contains a drop-down menu from which you can make a selection. Click OK.

Select Changes to Accept or Reject
Which changes
☑ When: Not yet reviewed
☐ Who: Everyone
☐ Where:
OK   Cancel

Figure 14.10 Select Changes to Accept or Reject dialog box

TRY*it* OUT

1. Open the file **14.2SalesFigures2** that you saved in the previous Try it Out.

2. Click **Tools,** select **Track Changes,** and click **Accept or Reject Changes.**

3. In the Select Changes to Accept or Reject dialog box, leave the **When** box checked and the selection as **Not yet reviewed.** Click **OK.**

4. In the Accept or Reject dialog box, click **Accept.**

5. Save and close the file.

> The Accept or Reject Changes dialog box opens, as shown in Figure 14.11. Each change made to the worksheet appears, one at a time. You can click Accept or Reject for each change. If you want to accept or reject all of the changes, click Accept All or Reject All.

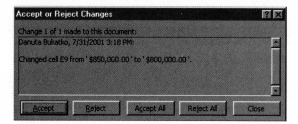

Figure 14.11 Accept or Reject Changes dialog box

Merge Workbooks

> As you learned earlier in this lesson, if several different users have made changes to a file, you will likely want to create a single, or merged, workbook that contains all of the changes.

> Merged workbooks must be created from files saved from the same original shared workbook. Thus, you must first designate the workbook as a shared workbook. All users must start with this workbook and save their modified files from it.

> To create a merged workbook, first open the original shared workbook. Click Tools, Compare and Merge Workbooks. When prompted by Excel about saving the file, click OK.

> The Select Files to Merge Into Current Workbook dialog box opens, as shown in Figure 14.12. Select the file that contains modifications and click OK. If there are additional files you want to merge into the workbook, click Tools, Compare and Merge Workbooks again. Repeat the instructions in this step as many times as necessary.

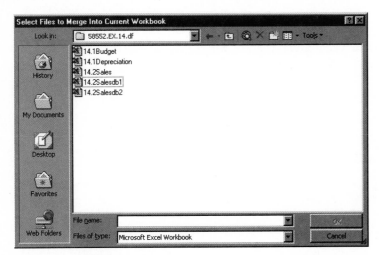

Figure 14.12 Select Files to Merge Into Current Workbook dialog box

TRY *it* **OUT**

1. Open the file **14.2SalesFigures** that you saved earlier in the lesson.

2. Change the data in **Cell E6** to: **$700,000**

3. Save the file as **14.2SalesFigures3.** Close the file.

4. Open the file **14.2SalesFigures** that you saved earlier.

5. Click **Tools, Compare and Merge Workbooks.** In the Select Files to Merge into Current Workbook dialog box, select the file **14.2SalesFigures1.**

6. Click **OK** if you are prompted to accept the change from the **14.2SalesFigures1** file.

7. Repeat Steps 5 and 6 two times, selecting the files **14.2SalesFigures2** and **14.2SalesFigures3** on successive passes through the process.

8. Notice the changes to the workbook.

9. Save the **14.2SalesFigures** file and close it.

REHEARSAL

GOAL
To create a divisional sales report using shared and merged workbooks

SETTING THE STAGE/WRAPUP
File names: 14.2DivisionalSales
14.2cactussales
14.2morelandsales
14.2pueblosales
14.2DivSalesRept
14.2DivCactus
14.2DivMoreland
14.2DivPueblo
14.2DivSalesFinal

TASK 2

WHAT YOU NEED TO KNOW

> Companies with several branches or divisions often need to prepare a *divisional sales report,* a summary of the sales figures for each segment of the company. Because many divisions are feeding data into one report, the ability to share and merge workbooks is very useful for this task.

> In this Rehearsal activity, you will prepare a divisional sales report for In-Shape Fitness Centers. There are five branches reviewing a workbook that contains their revenues for a company quarterly report. Some of the sales data needs to be changed for several branches because they incorrectly recorded gift memberships in the fourth quarter. You create a shared workbook, track changes made by different users, and create a merged workbook from the files saved by several users. You will be making all the changes in this problem, but in practice each corrected worksheet would be saved by users from each branch.

DIRECTIONS

1. Open **14.2DivisionalSales** from the Data CD. Use the illustrations on the next page as a guide to complete the following steps.

2. Enter formulas to complete the Quarterly and Location totals for the year, as shown in Illustration A.

3. Save the file as **14.2DivSalesRept.**

4. Use this file to create a shared workbook.

5. The three branches that had to make changes are Cactus, Moreland, and Pueblo. Assume that the following steps were performed by users at each branch:
   a. Open the **14.2cactussales** worksheet. Notice the corrected sales for the fourth quarter, as shown in Illustration B.
   b. Arrange both worksheets on the screen horizontally. Compare the fourth quarter sales from the updated Cactus report with the Divisional Sales report.
   c. Switch to the **14.1DivSalesRept.**
   d. Track the changes made to this worksheet.
   e. Change the fourth quarter sales data for the Cactus branch, as per the corrected file. Accept this change.
   f. Save the file as **14.2DivCactus.**
   g. Close both files.

6. Reopen the **14.2DivSalesRept** file. Repeat Steps a-g, making the corrections found in the **14.2morelandsales** file, found on the Data CD. Name the corrected report **14.2DivMoreland.** Close both files.

7. Reopen the **14.2DivSalesRept** file. Repeat Steps a-g, making the corrections found in the **14.2pueblosales** file, found on the Data CD. Name the corrected report **14.2DivPueblo.** Close both files.

8. Reopen the **14.2DivSalesRept** file.

Continued on next page

9. Merge the three edited files, **14.2DivCactus**, **14.2DivMoreland**, and **14.2DivPueblo**.

10. Save the merged file as **14.2DivSalesFinal**.

11. Print a copy.

12. Close the file.

	A	B	C	D	E	F	G
1							
2			*In-Shape Fitness Centers*				
3			*Divisional Sales Report (2002)*				
4							
5	**Location**		**Q1**	**Q2**	**Q3**	**Q4**	**Total**
6	Cactus Drive		$ 50,000	$ 75,000	$ 60,000	$ 70,000	
7	Pueblo Street		$ 75,000	$ 100,000	$ 110,000	$ 105,000	
8	Main Avenue		$ 100,000	$ 110,000	$ 125,000	$ 130,000	
9	Pima Street		$ 150,000	$ 160,000	$ 130,000	$ 185,000	
10	Moreland Street		$ 60,000	$ 75,000	$ 130,000	$ 55,000	
11							
12	**Total**						
13							
14							
15			Find Quarterly and				
16			Location totals				
17							

Illustration A

	A	B	C	D	E	F	G	H	I	J
1			*In-Shape Fitness Centers*							
2			*Cactus Drive Sales Report (2002)*							
3							Corrected sales			
4	**Sales**		**Q1**	**Q2**	**Q3**	**Q4**	report from the			
5							Cactus branch			
6	Memberships		$ 36,100	$ 56,570	$ 43,250	$ 42,750				
7	Classes		$ 5,000	$ 7,430	$ 6,000	$ 7,000				
8	Café		$ 8,900	$ 11,000	$ 10,750	$ 11,750				
9										
10	**Total**		$ 50,000	$ 75,000	$ 60,000	$ 61,500	Corrected fourth			
11							quarter sales;			
12							change fourth			
13							quarter sales on			
14							Divisional Sales			
15							Report to this			
16							number			

Illustration B

Cues for Reference

Create a Shared Workbook
1. Click **Tools, Share Workbook.**
2. In **Editing** tab, check **Allow changes by more than one user at the same time.**
3. In **Advanced** tab, make any changes you want in length of time changes are tracked, frequency of file updates, and what to do with conflicting changes.
4. Click **OK.**

Track Changes
1. Click **Tools,** select **Track Changes,** and click **Highlight Changes.**

2. In Highlight Changes dialog box, check **Track changes while editing.** Make any other selections you want for which changes you will review. Check **Highlight changes on screen** to see changes as you enter them.
3. Click **OK.**

Accept or Reject Changes
1. Click **Tools,** select **Track Changes,** and click **Accept or Reject Changes.**
2. In Select Changes to Accept or Reject dialog box, decide whether to review changes by time, user, or location on worksheet. Click **OK.**

3. In Accept or Reject Changes dialog box, as each change appears, click **Accept** or **Reject.** Or, click **Accept All** or **Reject All.**

Merge Workbooks
1. Click **Tools, Compare and Merge Workbooks.** Click **OK** when Excel asks you about saving the file.
2. In Select Files to Merge Into Current Workbook dialog box, select file to merge into open workbook. Click **OK.** Repeat for each file to merge into workbook.

PERFORMANCE

SETTING THE STAGE/WRAPUP

Act I File name: 14p1.Depreciation

Act II

File names: 14p2.DivSales
          14.p2.DivSalesFairfax
          14p2.DivSalesFallsChurch
          14p2.DivSalesAlexandria
          14p2.DivSalesFinal

WHAT YOU NEED TO KNOW

Act I

The Air Land Sea Travel group is preparing a depreciation schedule for all of its office equipment. Much of the data for the schedule has already been entered and must be protected so that it is not changed. Other data must be added, but only by authorized users who have a password. Open the file 14p1.Depreciation from the Data CD. You will add protection to a worksheet, to cells on a worksheet, and to a workbook. You will also create a password to allow only designated individuals to make modifications to the file.

Follow these guidelines:

* Start with the worksheet labeled **2001.** Use the straight-line depreciation method to enter the formula for depreciation in **Cell F8.**

* Enter a formula to calculate the 2001 Depreciation in **Cell H8.** *(Hint: Prorate the annual depreciation by dividing by 12 and multiplying by the number of months owned.)*

* Fill the formulas from **Cells F8:H8** to the range **F9:H18.**

* Copy the information on this sheet to the Sheet **2002.** Adjust the formatting as needed. Protect the sheet labeled **2001.** Add the following password to the protection: `AirLandSea`

* Change the entries on Sheet **2002** as follows:

  * Edit year labels to: `2002`

  * Add the following new assets:

Asset	Date Purchased	Cost	Life	Residual Value
File Cabinets	4/12/2002	$6,350.00	5	$ 700.00
Printer	5/18/2002	$ 750.00	3	$ 150.00

  * Copy the formulas for the new items. Delete the **Months Owned** values for 2001.

  * Edit the 2002 Depreciation formula using an IF statement that enters the Annual Depreciation if the Months Owned column is blank, or else it prorates the Annual Depreciation according to the number of months owned.

  * Protect the worksheet.

✦ Protect the structure of the entire workbook. Use the same password as above.

✦ Unprotect the workbook to add a sheet labeled: Sheet 2003
Protect the workbook again. Save and close the file.

Act II

Green Brothers Gardening is preparing a quarterly sales report that includes data from all three of its locations. Open the file **14p2.DivSales** from the Data CD. You will create a shared workbook so that individuals at each of the three locations can review and make changes to the file. The bookkeepers at each location are reviewing their quarterly totals and have indicated that some revenues were overstated and some were understated for different quarters. They have sent supporting records for the changes they want to make. You will review the changes by tracking and accepting or rejecting the changes made by individuals. Finally, you will merge the files created by several users.

GREEN BROTHERS GARDENING

Follow these guidelines:

✦ Total all data vertically and horizontally.

✦ Create a shared workbook for the file.

✦ The bookkeeper in Fairfax reviews the data and believes the data for **Cell F6** should be changed to: $9500
Change the data in that cell. Save the file as **14p2.DivSalesFairfax.** Close the file.

✦ Reopen the file **14p2.DivSalesFairfax** and enable the Track Changes feature. Reject the change made by the bookkeeper. Save and close the file.

✦ The bookkeeper in Falls Church reviews the data and wants to change **Cell D7** to $24,000 and **Cell E7** to $24,000. Open the file **14p2.DivSales** (the shared file) and change those data values. Save the file as **14p2.DivSalesFallsChurch.** Close the file.

✦ Reopen the file **14p2.DivSalesFallsChurch** and enable the Track Changes feature. Accept the change made by the bookkeeper. Save and close the file.

✦ The bookkeeper in Alexandria reviews the data and wants to change **Cell C8** to $32,000 and **Cell D8** to $33,000. Open the file **14p2.DivSales** (the shared file) and change those data values. Save the file as **14p2.DivSalesAlexandria.** Close the file.

✦ Reopen the file **14p2.DivSalesAlexandria** and enable the Track Changes feature. Accept the change made by the bookkeeper. Save and close the file.

✦ Open the shared file and merge the workbooks created by the three bookkeepers.

✦ Protect the shared workbook so that the shared history cannot be removed.

✦ Save the file as **14p2.DivSalesFinal.**

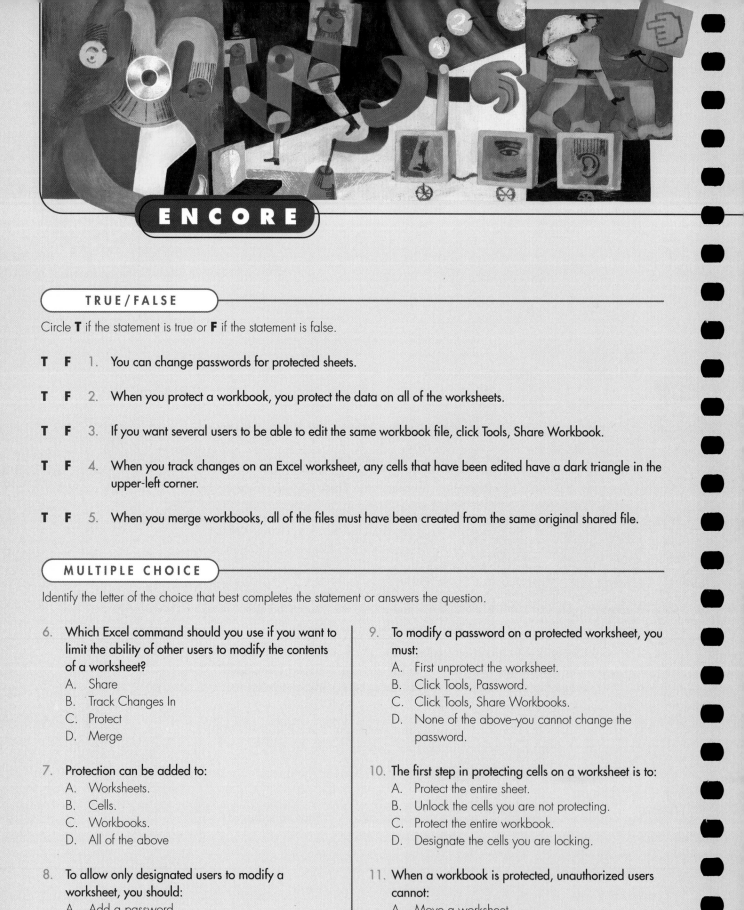

ENCORE

TRUE/FALSE

Circle **T** if the statement is true or **F** if the statement is false.

T F 1. You can change passwords for protected sheets.

T F 2. When you protect a workbook, you protect the data on all of the worksheets.

T F 3. If you want several users to be able to edit the same workbook file, click Tools, Share Workbook.

T F 4. When you track changes on an Excel worksheet, any cells that have been edited have a dark triangle in the upper-left corner.

T F 5. When you merge workbooks, all of the files must have been created from the same original shared file.

MULTIPLE CHOICE

Identify the letter of the choice that best completes the statement or answers the question.

6. Which Excel command should you use if you want to limit the ability of other users to modify the contents of a worksheet?
   A. Share
   B. Track Changes In
   C. Protect
   D. Merge

7. Protection can be added to:
   A. Worksheets.
   B. Cells.
   C. Workbooks.
   D. All of the above

8. To allow only designated users to modify a worksheet, you should:
   A. Add a password.
   B. Share the worksheet.
   C. Track changes on the worksheet.
   D. Merge the workbook.

9. To modify a password on a protected worksheet, you must:
   A. First unprotect the worksheet.
   B. Click Tools, Password.
   C. Click Tools, Share Workbooks.
   D. None of the above–you cannot change the password.

10. The first step in protecting cells on a worksheet is to:
    A. Protect the entire sheet.
    B. Unlock the cells you are not protecting.
    C. Protect the entire workbook.
    D. Designate the cells you are locking.

11. When a workbook is protected, unauthorized users cannot:
    A. Move a worksheet.
    B. Rename a worksheet.
    C. Delete a worksheet.
    D. All of the above

12. A workbook that allows multiple users to make modifications to the data is called:
    A. A merged workbook.
    B. A tracked workbook.
    C. A shared workbook.
    D. A common workbook.

13. If you want to follow the modifications that other users have made to a file, click:
    A. Tools, Share Workbook.
    B. Tools, Track Changes.
    C. Tools, Compare and Merge Workbooks.
    D. Tools, Protection.

14. If you want to accept a change made to a cell by another user, click:
    A. Tools, Share Workbooks.
    B. Tools, Track Changes, Accept or Reject Changes.
    C. Tools, Accept or Reject Changes.
    D. Tools, Protection.

15. The first step in merging workbooks is to:
    A. Open the original shared workbook.
    B. Click Tools, Compare and Merge Workbooks.
    C. Click Tools, Track Changes.
    D. Open all of the modified files.

COMPLETION

Complete each sentence or statement.

16. A feature of Excel that allows another user to read data, but not make changes to it, is called
    _____.

17. A _____ is an accounting record that shows the cost of an asset spread over its estimated useful life.

18. A number of users can edit a _____ workbook.

19. _____ is the process of incorporating changes made by several users into a single workbook.

20. To review the changes made to a file by other users, click _____.

APPENDIX

MOUS Correlation

Microsoft Office User Specialist (MOUS) Certification Correlation Chart

The Microsoft Office User Specialist (MOUS) Certification program provides a benchmark against which you can measure your proficiency with Office XP applications. Certifications provides you with evidence of your level of expertise in using specific Office application. This can be a valuable asset when seeking employment.

There are two levels of certification for each Office tool—Core and Expert. Each level requires that you master a series of skill sets and activities. Certification is achieved by passing an examination, which is administered at an **Authorized Testing Center.** You can locate a testing center by calling 1-800-933-4493 in North America. Each exam costs between $50 and $100, is taken online, and requires that you complete a number of tasks within a specific time period.

Performing with Office XP is officially certified by Microsoft Corporation at the Core user skill level in Word, Excel, PowerPoint, Access, FrontPage, and Outlook. The chart below lists Core MOUS skill sets/activities and correlates them to each lesson and the page numbers in this text where the skill sets are discussed and practiced. The Performance section in each lesson provides additional practice on the lesson's skill sets.

Microsoft Excel 2002 Core Level

Standardized Coding Number	Skill Sets and Skills Being Measured	ICV Performance Based?	Lesson Number	Page Number
EX2002-1-1	**Working with Cells and Cell Data**			
EX2002-1-1	Insert, delete, and move cells	Yes	2 3 5	23, 39 56 101
EX2002-1-2	Enter and edit cell data including text, numbers, and formulas	Yes	2 3	17, 18, 19, 22 38
EX2002-1-3	Check spelling	Yes	2	24
EX2002-1-4	Find and replace cell data and formats	Yes	1 5	10 124, 125
EX2002-1-5	Work with a subset of data by filtering lists	Yes	4	72
EX2002-2	**Managing Workbooks**			
EX2002-2-1	Manage workbook files and folders	Yes	1	11
EX2002-2-2	Create workbooks using templates	Yes	2	28, 29
EX2002-2-3	Save workbooks using different names and file formats	Yes	2	19
EX2002-3	**Formatting and Printing Worksheets**			
EX2002-3-1	Apply and modify cell formats	Yes	2 3 4	18, 37, 38 58 70, 71, 83, 91
EX2002-3-2	Modify row and column settings	Yes	4 5	77 109
EX2002-3-3	Modify row and column formats	Yes	2 4	23 69
EX2002-3-4	Apply styles	Yes	5	122, 123, 124
EX2002-3-5	Use automated tools to format worksheets	Yes	4	82
EX2002-3-6	Modify page setup options for worksheets	Yes	3 4 5	51 70 116, 117
EX2002-3-7	Preview and print worksheets and workbooks	Yes	2 5	24, 25 110
EX2002-4	**Modifying Workbooks**			
EX2002-4-1	Insert and delete worksheets	Yes	4	83

Standardized Coding Number	Skill Sets and Skills Being Measured	ICV Performance Based?	Lesson Number	Page Number
EX2002-4-2	Modify worksheet names	Yes	4	85
EX2002-4-3	Use 3-D references	Yes	4	85
			5	103, 118
EX2002-5	**Creating and Revising Formulas**			
EX2002-5-1	Create and revise formulas	Yes	3	40, 44, 45, 46, 51
			4	76, 77
EX2002-5-2	Use statistical, date and time, financial, and logical functions in formulas	Yes	3	53
			4	88, 89, 90
			5	111
EX2002-6	**Creating and Modifying Graphics**			
EX2002-6-1	Create, modify, position, and print charts	Yes	6	135, 137, 138, 139, 140, 141, 145, 146, 147, 148, 157
EX2002-6-2	Create, modify, and position graphics	Yes	6	152, 153, 154, 155
EX2002-7	**Workgroup Collaboration**			
EX2002-7-1	Convert worksheets into Web pages	Yes	4	78, 79
EX2002-7-2	Create hyperlinks	Yes	5	104, 105
EX2002-7-3	View and edit comments	Yes	3	57
			7	177

Microsoft Excel 2002 Advanced Level

Standardized Coding Number	Skill Sets and Skills Being Measured	ICV Performance Based?	Lesson Number	Page Number
Ex2002e-1	**Importing and Exporting Data**			
Ex2002e-1-1	Import data to Excel	Yes	12	88, 89
Ex2002e-1-2	Export data from Excel	Yes	12	90
Ex2002e-1-3	Publish worksheets and workbooks to the Web	Yes	12	91, 93
Ex2002e-2	**Managing Workbooks**			
Ex2002e-2-1	Create, edit, and apply templates	Yes	8	10, 11
Ex2002e-2-2	Create workspaces	Yes	8	4
Ex2002e-2-3	Use data consolidation	Yes	8	6
Ex2002e-3	**Formatting Numbers**			
Ex2002e-3-1	Create and apply custom number formats	Yes	9	19

Standardized Coding Number	Skill Sets and Skills Being Measured	ICV Performance Based?	Lesson Number	Page Number
Ex2002e-3-2	Use conditional formats	Yes	9	21
Ex2002e-4	**Working with Ranges**			
Ex2002e-4-1	Use named ranges in formulas	Yes	9	25
Ex2002e-4-2	Use Lookup and Reference functions	Yes	9	27
Ex2002e-5	**Customizing Excel**			
Ex2002e-5-1	Customize toolbars and menus	Yes	10	44,45
Ex2002e-5-2	Create, edit, and run macros	Yes	10	49,50,51,52
Ex2002e-6	**Auditing Worksheets**			
Ex2002e-6-1	Audit formulas	Yes	9	31,32
Ex2002e-6-2	Locate and resolve errors	Yes	9	33
Ex2002e-6-3	Identify dependencies in formulas	Yes	9	34
Ex2002e-7	**Summarizing Data**			
Ex2002e-7-1	Use subtotals with lists and ranges	Yes	11	66
Ex2002e-7-2	Define and apply filters	Yes	11	70
Ex2002e-7-3	Add group and outline criteria to ranges	Yes	11	76, 77
Ex2002e-7-4	Use data validation	Yes	11	78, 79 ,80
Ex2002e-7-5	Retrieve external data and create querie	Yes	12	97
Ex2002e-7-6	Create Extensible Markup Language (XML) Web queries	Yes	12	101
Ex2002e-8	**Analyzing Data**			
Ex2002e-8-1	Create PivotTables, PivotCharts, and PivotTable/PivotChart Reports	Yes	13	110, 114, 115, 117
Ex2002e-8-2	Forecast values with what-if analysis	Yes	13	122, 123
Ex2002e-8-3	Create and display scenarios	Yes	13	127
Ex2002e-9	**Workgroup Collaboration**			
Ex2002e-9-1	Modify passwords, protections, and properties	Yes	14	140, 141, 142, 143
Ex2002e-9-2	Create a shared workbook	Yes	14	149
Ex2002e-9-3	Track, accept, and reject changes to workbooks	Yes	14	150, 152
Ex2002e-9-4	Merge workbooks	Yes	14	153

File Management

* Windows Explorer
* Office

Windows Explorer

Windows Explorer is a Windows feature that lets you see the hierarchy of the drives, folders, and files that are stored on your computer. Windows Explorer is used to view, find, copy, delete, move, rename, and reorganize your drives, folders, and files. Windows Explorer also shows any network drives that have been mapped to drives on your computer. The topics below provide a guide to using this feature.

Open Windows Explorer

On some systems, Windows Explorer is located in the Accessories subfolder, while in others it is found in the Programs folder. All illustrations and screens for this appendix use Windows Millennium Edition, which may vary slightly from other versions.

Click Start, select Programs, click Accessories, and click Windows Explorer. Or, if Windows Explorer is in the Programs folder, click Start, select Programs, and click Windows Explorer.

View Folders and Files

When the Windows Explorer screen appears, as shown in Figure B.1, you will see the Explorer menu bar, toolbar, address box, and the screen which is divided into two panes. The Folders pane (the left pane) displays the drives and folders. A folder is a location on a drive in which related files are saved. The right pane displays the contents of the selected folder. Your system may display different items than the illustration below, since every computer contains a different combination of drives, folders, and files.

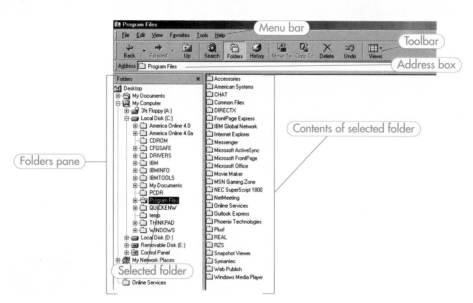

Figure B.1 Windows Explorer screen

To see the contents of the folder in the right pane, click a folder in the left pane. A plus sign next to a folder indicates that there are other folders or files within that folder. A minus sign next to a folder indicates that the folder's contents are displayed. Notice that in Figure B.2, files are displayed with their file type icon, and folders are shown in either a closed or opened position. The folders, folders within folders, and files appear as a hierarchical tree.

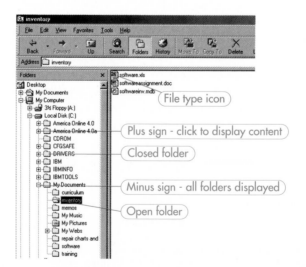

Figure B.2 Opened subfolder

The Windows Explorer Toolbar

The Windows Explorer toolbar provides you with quick access to frequently used features. A description of each button's function is described below.

	Button	Function
←	Back	Returns the insertion point to the last file or folder you accessed.
→	Forward	Reverses a back action.
⬆	Up	Moves the insertion point up to the next folder in the tree.
🔍	Search	Displays a Search pane that allows you to search for text within files or folders.
📁	Folders	Displays the Folders pane.
🕘	History	Displays the History pane, which provides a history of pages visited.
Move To	Move To	Allows you to move the selected item to another location.
📋	Copy To	Allows you to select an item and copy it to another location.
✕	Delete	Removes the selected file or folder.
↺	Undo	Reverses an action.
▦	Views	Provides options for ways to display files and folders.

Size the Windows Explorer Screen

You can size either pane of the window by dragging the bar that separates the two panes.

Change Windows Explorer Views

You can change the way you see the folders or files in the right pane by using the View button. When you click the list arrow to the right of the View button, you are presented with a choice of view options, as shown in Figure B.3. The Details option allows you to view the name, size, and type of the file as well as the date and time it was modified. Clicking the header, as shown in Figure B.4, sorts the files for that field in ascending or descending order.

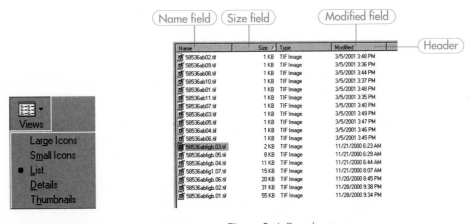

Figure B.3 View options   Figure B.4 Details view

Create A New Folder

To create a new folder, select the drive or folder to receive the new folder, click File, New, Folder on the menu, and enter the name of the new folder.

Rename A Folder or File

You can easily rename a file or folder. To do so, select the folder or file to rename, click File, Rename. You can also right-click the file, click Rename on the shortcut menu, and enter the new name.

Move or Copy A File or Folder

To move or copy files or folders, select the file or folder and click the appropriate toolbar button. A Browse For Folder dialog box opens, as shown in Figure B.5, to allow you to select the destination location. Be aware that both commands place the data in the new location, but the Move command also removes the data from the original folder. You can also use the mouse to drag and drop files and folders to their new location.

Figure B.5 Browse For Folder dialog box

Select Multiple Files Or Folders

You can simultaneously move or copy multiple files or folders that are consecutive or nonconsecutive.

To select consecutive files or folders, click the first item, press and hold the Shift key, and click the last item. (The entire consecutive block is selected.) To select nonconsecutive files or folders, press and hold the Ctrl key, and click each item to select. (Only those items that are clicked are selected.)

If you are using the drag-and-drop method, Explorer displays a shadow of the block of files as you are dragging it to the new location, as shown in Figure B.6.

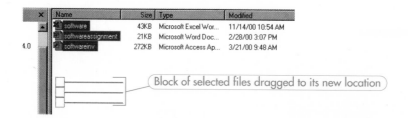

Figure B.6 Files being dragged to new location

Find A File Or Folder

In some cases, you may know the name of a file but do not know where it is. To find a file or folder, you can use the Search feature in Windows Explorer. When you click the Search button, a Search pane appears on the left, as shown in Figure B.7. Enter the name of the folder and set the location for the search. When entering a file name for the search, you may use a wildcard symbol for characters you do not know. For example, if you are looking for a file with a name that ends with the word "memo," but you do not know the full name, you can enter *memo.doc. The asterisk replaces any number of unknown characters before the word memo.

Notice that one of the Find dialog box options is Containing text. Use this feature to search for specific text (such as a name, phrase, or words) in the document.

Figure B.7 Search pane

Office

The default location for saving files in Office is usually the My Documents folder. Office provides other places where you can save or view your work.

When you save (or open) a file, the Save As (or Open) dialog box opens, as shown in Figure B.8. A Places bar appears on the left of the dialog box, which contains buttons that provide access to specialized folders.

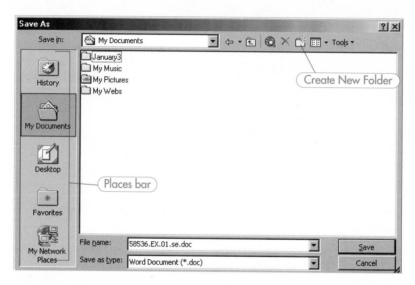

Figure B.8 Save As dialog box

The Places buttons are described below:

- **History** displays a Recent folder, which contains files and folders that you worked on most recently.

- **My Documents** is the default location where files are saved unless you provide another location. You can create subfolders within My Documents to better organize your files.

- **Desktop** is the location to save a file that you want to launch from your desktop.

- **Favorites** folder is a location where you save files that you use most often. You can even save shortcuts to files that are located elsewhere. To save a shortcut, click File, Open and select the file for which you want to create a shortcut. Then click Tools, Add to Favorites. A shortcut to that file will be added to the Favorites folder.

- **My Network Places** allows you to browse folders and files on Web servers.

You can use the Save As and Open dialog boxes to create folders and subfolders. To create a new folder, click the Create New Folder button on the dialog box toolbar, as shown in Figure B.8, and immediately name the folder.

Using the Mouse

You must use the mouse to access many software features. You can also access these features using the keyboard, but for most people, using the mouse is easier and more convenient.

When the mouse is rolled on a tabletop, a corresponding movement of the pointer shows on screen. The mouse pointer changes its appearance, depending on the software tool in use and the object to which it is pointing.

Most mouse actions require using the left mouse button.

The mouse terms and actions in the table below are commonly used when handling a mouse. If you are using the Microsoft IntelliMouse, notice the terms and actions associated with that device in the table on the right.

Term	Mouse Actions
Point	Move the mouse on the tabletop until the pointer is touching a specific item on screen
Click	Press and release the left mouse button
Double-click	Press and release the left mouse button twice in rapid succession
Triple-click	Press and release the left mouse button three times in rapid succession
Right-click	Press and release the right mouse button
Drag	Point and hold down the left mouse button while moving the mouse to a new position; Release the mouse button to drop the dragged object (or text) into the new position

Term	Microsoft IntelliMouse Actions
Scroll	Rotate the wheel forward or back
Pan up or down	Hold down the wheel while dragging the pointer above or below where you first clicked
AutoScroll	• Click the wheel and the software scrolls down; to scroll up, move the pointer above the starting point on the vertical scroll bar; to cancel AutoScroll, click any mouse button • Click the wheel and spreadsheet software scrolls in the direction you subsequently move the pointer
Zoom in or out	Hold down the Ctrl key as you rotate the wheel; rotating the wheel upward increases the magnification; rotating the wheel downward decreases the magnification

Mouse Pointer Shapes

The following chart illustrates common mouse pointer shapes and a description of what each shape indicates. You can customize mouse pointer shapes by selecting Settings and clicking Control Panel, Mouse from the Start menu. In the Mouse Properties dialog box, shown in Figure C.1, click the Pointers tab, click the drop-down menu under Scheme, and select any one of the mouse pointer schemes.

You can also change the speed of mouse actions in the Pointer Options tab. Other options are available in the Mouse Properties dialog box.

Pointer Name	Illustration	Description
Normal Select	⌖	Used to point to objects and toolbar buttons
Help Select	⌖?	Used after clicking "What's This?" on the Help menus; when you point and click on a window item when this pointer is visible, help on that item appears
Working in	⌖⧖	Used to indicate that the system is busy
Busy	⧖	Indicates the computer is processing a command or working in the background; no other work can be completed while this processing is taking place

Pointer Name	Illustration	Description
Precision Select	＋	Used when drawing objects
Text Select	I	Used when selecting or inserting text
Vertical Resize	↕	Used to change the vertical size of objects or windows; horizontal and diagonal resize mouse pointers are also available
Move	✛	Used to move objects
Link Select	☞	Used to indicate and select a hyperlink

Figure C.1 Mouse Properties dialog box

Toolbars, Menus, and Dialog Boxes

Toolbars

Toolbars throughout Windows applications provide you with quick access to features you use frequently. Using the mouse, point to a toolbar button and click once to access a feature. To learn the toolbar button name (and the feature), position the mouse pointer over the button and a ScreenTip displays its name.

If there are more buttons on the bar than can fit across the screen, you can display the hidden buttons by clicking the Toolbar Options list arrow at the end of the toolbar, as shown in Figure D.1.

(Move handle)   (Toolbars Options list arrow)

Figure D.1 Word toolbar

Choosing a Toolbar

Most software comes with numerous toolbars from which to choose. You can add buttons to the predefined toolbars, or you can create entirely new toolbars for those features that you use most frequently. To choose a toolbar, select Toolbars on the View menu, as shown in Figure D.2. You can also right-click a displayed toolbar and select a toolbar on the menu that appears. (Word toolbars are illustrated below.)

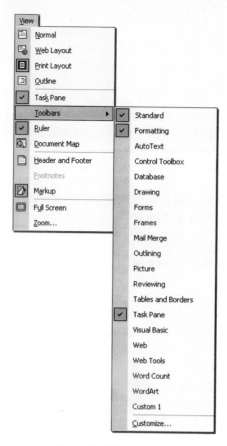

Figure D.2 View menu

Positioning the Toolbar

You can move the toolbar to any location on the screen by dragging the move handle on a stationed toolbar to another location (see Figure D.1). You can also drag the title bar on a floating toolbar and position it as you prefer. If you drag the toolbar to the edge of the application window or to a location alongside another stationed toolbar, it becomes a stationed toolbar as well.

Customizing the Toolbar

After using a software package, you will discover which features you use most frequently. You can then customize the toolbars to give yourself quick access to those features, or you can create new toolbars.

To create a new a toolbar in Office, do the following:

1. Click **Tools.**

2. Click **Customize.**

3. Click the **Toolbars** tab.

4. Click **New.**

5. In the **Toolbar** name box, enter the new toolbar name.

6. In the **Make toolbar available to** box, click the template or document in which to save the toolbar.

7. Click the **Commands** tab.

8. In the **Categories** box, click a category for the command.

9. In the **Commands** box, drag the command you want to the toolbar (which is displayed on the screen).

10. Repeat Step 9 until the toolbar is complete.

11. Click **Close.**

To add a toolbar button, do the following:

1. Display the toolbar to which you want to add a button.

2. Click **Tools.**

3. Click **Customize.**

4. Click the **Commands** tab.

5. In the Categories box, click a category for the command you want.

6. Drag the command from the Commands box to the displayed toolbar.

Or

a. Click the **More Buttons** icon on the displayed toolbar.

b. Click **Add or Remove Buttons.**

c. Select the check box next to the button you want to add.

To remove a toolbar button, do the following:

1. Display the toolbar you want to change.

2. Hold down the **Alt** key and drag the button off the toolbar.

Menus

Menus throughout Windows applications present you with choices for the commands you want the software to perform. The menu bar displays commands across the top of the application screen. The Word menu bar is shown in Figure D.3.

Figure D.3 Word menu bar

Choosing Menu Commands

You can select menu bar items using the mouse or the keyboard. Using the mouse, point to an item on the menu bar and click once. Using the keyboard, press the Alt key and the underlined letter in the menu name.

When you select a menu bar item, a drop-down submenu appears with additional options. Notice the drop-down submenus that appear when you select Edit in Word, as shown in Figure D.4.

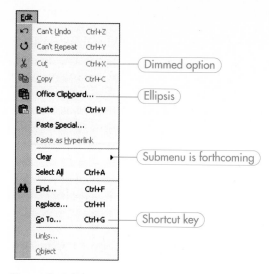

Figure D.4 Edit menu

About Submenus

Notice the following about submenus:

- Some menu options are dimmed, while others appear black. When options are dimmed, they are not available for selection.

- A check mark or bullet next to a drop-down menu item means the option is currently selected.

- Some menu items display shortcut keys that you can use to access a command.

- A menu item followed by ellipsis marks (…) indicates that a dialog box, which requires that you provide additional information to complete a command, is forthcoming.

- An arrow next to a menu item means another submenu is forthcoming.

Shortcut Menus

Shortcut menus appear when you click the right mouse button. The menu items that appear vary, depending on where the mouse is pointing and what task you are performing. Notice the shortcut menu that appears, as shown in Figure D.5, when the mouse is pointing to the Document window in Word.

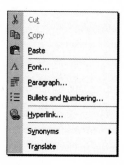

Figure D.5 Shortcut menu

Dialog Boxes

A dialog box presents information about the current settings for a command and allows you to have a "dialog" with it—that is, to change the settings, if necessary. Dialog boxes let you enter information in a variety of ways. Notice the description of each dialog box component in the Word Font and Print dialog boxes shown in Figures D.6 and D.7.

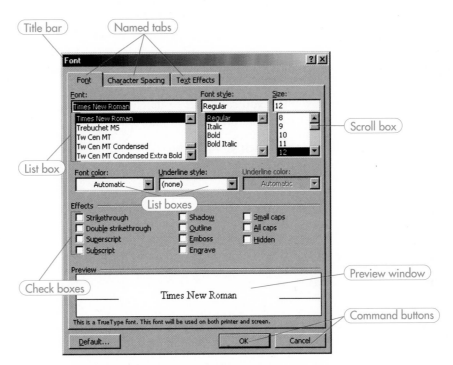

Figure D.6 Font dialog box

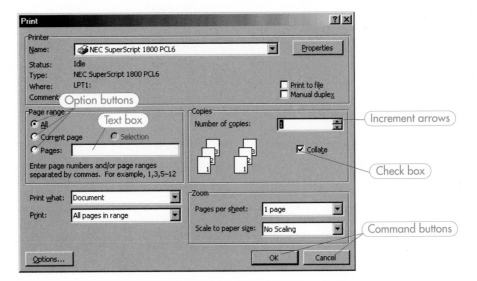

Figure D.7 Print dialog box

- The *title bar* identifies the title of the dialog box.

- A *text box* is a space where you enter information.

- *Command buttons* carry out the actions described on the button.

- An *increment box* provides a space for entering a value. Clicking the up or down arrow (usually to the right of the box) allows you to display the incremental value.

- A *named tab* displays options related to the tab's name in the same dialog box.

- *Option buttons* are small circular buttons marking options in a set. You can choose only one option from the set. A selected option button contains a dark circle.

- A *check box* is a small square box where you can select or deselect an option. A ✓ in the box indicates the option is selected. If several check boxes are offered, you may select more than one.

- A *list box* displays a list of items from which you can make selections. A list box may have a scroll bar that you can use to show hidden items in a list, or the list may be displayed by clicking a down arrow.

- A *scroll bar* is a horizontal or vertical bar containing scroll arrows and a scroll box that you can drag up or down to move through the file quickly.

- A *preview window* allows you to see a sample of the selection you made.

APPENDIX E

Selection Techniques

Before you can perform an action on text in an Excel spreadsheet, you must first select or highlight it. There are numerous mouse as well as keyboard selection techniques and shortcuts, as indicated in Table A below:

Method	To Highlight	Action
Keyboard*	One character left	Shift + ←
	One character right	Shift + →
	To the end of a line	Shift + End
	To the beginning of a line	Shift + Home
	To the end of a word	Shift + Ctrl + →
	To the beginning of a word	Shift + Ctrl + ←

Any action to be performed on numeric or text data in a cell requires that you select the cell. The mouse and keyboard selection techniques are in Table B below:

SELECT WORKSHEET CELLS	
Select a cell	Click the cell
Select the worksheet	Ctrl + A, or click corner box
Select a row	Shift + Space
Select a column	Ctrl + Space

To move quickly through a worksheet, use the keyboard shortcuts listed in Table C below:

NAVIGATE THE WORKSHEET	
Move one cell	Use the left, right, up, or down arrow
Move one screen up or down	Page Up or Page Down
First cell in worksheet	Ctrl + Home
First cell in current row	Home
First cell in current column	Ctrl + ↑
Last cell in current row	Ctrl + →
Last cell in current column	Ctrl + ↓

When you need to move to a different area of a worksheet that requires that the screen display change, use the scroll bars. The mouse actions to use the scroll bars are listed in Table D below:

USE SCROLL BARS	
One column left or right	Click left or right scroll arrows
One row up or down	Click up or down scroll arrows
Scroll quickly	Click and drag scroll bar, press and hold Shift

Portfolio Basics

What is a Portfolio?

A portfolio is a collection of evidence that showcases your skills, abilities, and accomplishments. A portfolio is a way to market yourself to college admissions committees or prospective employers.

Portfolio items may be maintained in a traditional folder or they may be prepared in digital format and burned on a CD. A portfolio may also be created as an electronic portfolio, which is a personal Web site with links to all the required documents. An electronic portfolio will highlight your technical skills and competency with Web site development and design. Digital or electronic formats enable you to include presentations, animations, and graphics which demonstrate your skills in those areas.

What Should A Portfolio Include?

A portfolio should contain your best work samples, a résumé, awards, a letter of introduction, certificates (including evidence of MOUS certification), and letters of recommendation. It may also include works-in-progress that illustrate the ongoing development of a project through various stages of conception and revision.

The Performance phase of this book can provide the work samples for your portfolio; these end-of-lesson activities demonstrate critical thinking and the application of SCANS skills.

How To Organize A Portfolio

A portfolio should be organized in a logical format. It should include a cover page (or home page if it is a Web site), which may include graphics or photographs that reflect your personal expression. A suggested portfolio organization is shown below:

1. Cover (Home Page)

2. Table of Contents

3. Letter of Introduction (see Sample A for content.)

4. Work Sample Cover Sheet (see Sample B)

5. Work Samples

6. Project Cover Sheet (see Sample B)

7. Project

8. Résumé

9. Awards, Certificates

10. Letters of Recommendation

Guidelines for Developing Electronic Portfolios

If you are publishing a portfolio to the Web, be aware of the following:

1. Avoid including your address, phone number, and social security number.

2. Do not include information or ideas you do not want the world to see.

3. Avoid continuous animations.

4. Avoid color, background, and font formats that make pages difficult to read.

5. Avoid using large graphic files that might be difficult to download.

Sample A
Letter of Introduction

A letter of introduction demonstrates your writing ability and provides a framework for what is to follow. It should include the following information:

1. A description of yourself including your college and career goals, your important achievements, and your strengths.

2. A description of your portfolio's contents.

3. A description of what insights you have gained from preparing the portfolio.

Sample B
Work or Project Sample Cover Sheet

A cover sheet that contains the following information should precede each work sample:

Name:
Today's date:
Work sample ☐   **Project sample** ☐
Description of work or project sample included:
If this was a group project, list team members:
1.
2.
3.
Date item was completed:
What was the goal of the project or work sample?
What special skills did you use in completing this work sample?
Explain what you learned by completing this work sample.
Teacher assessment
Teacher's signature
Date reviewed
Comments

APPENDIX G

Proofreader's Marks

Symbol	Meaning	Illustration
bf〰	Boldface	Excellent job!
≡	Capitalize	John l. smith
⌒	Close up space	pres entation
℘	delete	pagees
ds [	Double-space	ds ⌈This is the first time I have ⌊heard about it.
∧	Insert	Where will ∧be? *it*
⋏	Insert punctuation	If you are going I am going too.
˅	Insert apostrophe	It was Johns hat.
#	Insert space	I think it will beuseful.
___	Insert underscore	Time Magazine was ordered last week.

Appendix G   Proofreader's Mark – G1

Symbol	Meaning	Illustration
♂	Move as indicated	This table will be omitted. ⟵ Be sure to remove it from all documents.
[	Move left	[Let's go tomorrow.
]	Move right	]Everything you need is located on the CD.
lc or /	Make lowercase	Her title was Vice President.
¶	New paragraph	It's cold outside.¶The forecast for next week...
___	Replace word	The mouse ~~may~~ be used to access many features. *can*
ss[	Single-space	ss⌈Please be advised that there ⌊will be no delivery service next week.
◯	Spell out	③years ago
stet or	Let the original stand (ignore correction)	The main building was damaged.
∩	Transpose	This is intresting material.

Task Reference

EXCEL TASK REFERENCE, INTRO	
SKILL	**DESCRIPTION**
3-D References, enter	Enter reference; or enter (=) and function and parentheses; select sheet and cell to reference; enter mathematical operator; repeat 2 and 3, and close parentheses; press Enter
AutoSum, use	Select cell; click **Σ ▾**; press Enter; or use mouse to reselect the correct range; press Enter
Borders	Select area; click **▦ ▾**; click border style; or click Format, Cells, Border; select line, color, and style; click OK
Cell comment, add	Select cell; click Insert, Comment; enter comment; click any cell
Cell comment, edit	Select cell; click Insert, Edit, Comment; edit comment; click any cell
Cell, clear contents	Select cell; press Delete; or click Edit, Clear, Contents
Chart, create	Select chart data; click **▦**; select chart type and subtype; click Next; check data range; click Next; click appropriate tab and set chart options; click Next; select placement; click As a new sheet; enter sheet name; or click As object in, accept or enter sheet name; click Finish
Chart, create custom	Select data; click **▦**; select Custom Types; select custom chart type; click Next; complete Chart Wizard steps
Data, edit	Double-click cell or press F2; edit data
Data, move	Select data; click **✂**; select new location; click **▣**; or select data; place cursor; click, hold, and drag
Embed a worksheet/ chart into a Word document	Select the worksheetchart to embed; click **▣**; click the File button; place cursor; click Edit, Paste Special; select Microsoft Excel Worksheet Object or Microsoft Excel Chart Object; click OK
Embedded worksheet/	Double-click worksheet/chart chart, edit
Format, number	Select cell or range; click Percent **%**; Currency **$**; Comma **,**; Increase Decimal **⬚**; Decrease Decimal **⬚**
Formats, clear number	Select cell or range; click Edit, Clear, Formats
Formula, enter range in a	Place mouse; click, hold, and drag
Formulas, enter	Press (=); select formula data; enter mathematical operator; select formula data; repeat 3 and 4 until complete; press Enter
Formulas, revise	Select formula; press F2; edit range
Print Area, clear	Click File, Print Area, Clear Print Area
Print Area, set	Select area; click File, Print Area, Set Print Area
Print Non-adjacent Sections	Hide any columns or rows; click **▣** of Worksheet
Print Titles	Clear merged cells; click File, Page Setup, and the Page tab; select the row or column titles to repeat; click OK
Print, chart sheet	Select sheet; click **▣**
Print, embedded chart on full sheet:	Select chart; click **▣**
Print, embedded chart on worksheet	Select range including chart; click **▣**
Print, with Gridlines	Click File, Page Setup, Sheet tab; click Gridlines box; click Print; click OK
Row or Column, change size	To AutoFit, double-click on column heading right edge; or select column(s) or row(s); place mouse on right edge of last column or bottom edge of row; drag column or row when mouse cursor changes to a double-headed arrow
Row, select	Shift + Space
Rows or Columns, delete	Select row(s) or column(s); click Edit, Delete; click OK
Rows or Columns, insert	Select row(s) or column(s); Click Insert, Column or Insert, Row
Use functions and Formula Bar	Select cell; press equal (=); select function; click **▣**; select range; click **▣**; press OK

EXCEL TASK REFERENCE, INTRO

SKILL	DESCRIPTION
Add a password	Click Tools, select Protection, click Protect Sheet; enter password in Password to unprotect sheet box in Protect Sheet dialog box; click OK; reenter password in Confirm Password dialog box; click OK
Advanced Filter, use	Click cell in the data list; click Data, select Filter, click Advanced Filter; specify whether to filter in place or at new location; specify range of data to filter; create a criteria filter range; insert values for filtering criteria; specify range for destination of filtered list if you are copying it to new location; click OK
AutoFilter, use custom filters	Select cell in the data list; click Data, select Filter, click AutoFilte; select Custom from drop-down list next to appropriate field name; select filtering criteria you want to use; click OK
Button, add to toolbar	Click Tools, Customize, and Commands tabl; locate button you want by looking first in Categories box, then in Commands box; click and drag button from Commands box to toolbar on which you want it to appear; close Customize dialog box
Button, remove from toolbar	Hold down Alt; click and drag button you are removing off toolbar
Cell(s), protect	Select cells you want to unlock; all other cells remain locked; click Format, Cells, and Protection tab; clear Locked box; click OK; add protection to sheet following steps above
Changes, accept or reject	Click Tools, select Track Changes, click Accept or Reject Changes; in Select Changes to Accept or Reject dialog box, decide whether you will review changes by time, user, or location on worksheet; click OK; in Accept or Reject Changes dialog box, as each change appears, click Accept or Reject; or click Accept All or Reject All
Conditional formatting, use	Click Format, Conditional Formatting; select Cell Value Is; select conditions you want to apply to data; enter value with which to compare data points; click Format and select fonts, styles, and colors you want to apply if conditions are met; click OK; click Add and repeat Steps 2 through 5 to add up to two more conditions; click OK
Consolidate data	Open new workbook; Enter any labels; select cell where consolidated table will begin; click Data, Consolidate; select function you want to use; add references for each worksheet from which you are consolidating data; click Add after each one; check the box Create links to source data; click OK
Custom number formats, create and apply	Select cells you want to format; click Format, Cells, and Number tab; select Custom in Category box; enter format codes in Type box; click OK
Data ranges, delete external	Click Insert, Name, and click Define; select data range to delete; click Delete; confirm deletion; click Yes
Data validation	Select range of cells for data validation settings; click Data, Validation, and Settings tab; select type of entries that are permitted and any restrictions on their values; title alert and enter error message in Error Alert tab; click OK
Data, export from Excel	Click File, Save As; specify new file type for Excel file; click OK; open file in alternate software
Data, obtain from a Web page	Open HTML page and open Excel; arrange windows so they are both visible on screen; select data you want to import from HTML page; hold down Ctrl; drag data to Excel worksheet
Data, group	Select range of cells that comprise group; click Data, select Group and Outline, click Group; click Rows or Columns, depending on how your group is defined; click OK; click ▶ to view collapsed format or click ▬ to view in detailed format
Data, import to Excel	Open blank Excel worksheet; click Data, select Import External Data, click Import Data; click My Data Sources drop-down menu; select location that holds your file; click Open; indicate whether you want file to go to existing or new worksheet; click OK
Data, outline	Click Data, select Group and Outline, click Auto Outline; click ▶ and ▬ to view data in collapsed or detailed formats
Data, remove groups	Select data in a group; click Data, select Group and Outline, click Ungroup; select Rows or Columns; click OK
Data, remove outlines	Click Data, select Group and Outline, click Clear Outline
Data, retrieve external with queries	Open Excel worksheet; click Data, select Import External Data, click New Database Query; select type of file to access in Choose Data Source dialog box; click OK; choose Columns dialog box in Query Wizard; click plus sign to left of database name; move each of fields you want into Columns in your query section; click Next; filter data, if needed; click Next; sort data, if needed; click Next; indicate in Query Wizard-Finish dialog box if you want to save query and if you want to place it in Excel worksheet; click Finish
Data, transpose	Select data to transpose; click Copy; click location for data; click Paste Special, Transpose; click OK
Filters, remove	Click Data, select Filter, click AutoFilter; click AutoFilter to de-select it

FORECAST command, use	Click cell where you want result of forecast to appear; click ▦; select Statistical from Or select category list box; click FORECAST in Select a function box; click OK; enter cell reference in box "X," for data associated with the forecast value (usually a label); enter cell references, in Known_y's box, or known data of type you are predicting; enter cell references in Known_x's box, for known data associated with y's (data must be numeric); click OK
Formula, audit (trace dependents)	Click Tools, select Formula Auditing, click ▦, or use Formula Auditing toolbar
Formula, audit (trace precedents)	Click Tools, select Formula Auditing, click ▦, or use the Formula Auditing toolbar
Formulas, identify dependencies	Click Tools, Options, and View tab to see both dependents and precedents; check Show all under Objects; to remove tracer arrows, click Tools, select Formula Auditing, click Remove Tracer Arrows, or use Formula Auditing toolbar
Formulas, locate and resolve errors	Click Tools, select Formula Auditing, click ▣, or use Formula Auditing toolbar; to see step-by-step computation in formula, click Tools, select Formula Auditing, click Evaluate Formula, or use the Formula Auditing toolba; to see all of formulas in cells and other cells they are linked to, click Tools, select Formula Auditing, click Formula Auditing Mode, or use Formula Auditing toolbar
HLOOKUP and VLOOKUP, use	Click cell where outcome of lookup function will go; click ▦; select Lookup & Reference; select HLOOKUP (if data in lookup table is arranged in rows); select VLOOKUP (if data is arranged in columns); enter cell reference you are evaluating in Lookup_value; enter location or named range of lookup table in Table_array; in Col_index_num, enter row or column in lookup table that contains result
List, add a record	Click Insert, Row; enter appropriate data to correspond to field names in first row or click Data, Form, and New; enter data for each field name in dialog box; click Close
List, sort	Click Data, Sort; select field name; click Ascending or Descending; click OK
Macro, create	Click Tools, select Macro, click Record New Macro, or click ▦ that you placed on toolbar; in Record Macro dialog box, enter name of macro in Macro name box; enter description of macro in Description box; enter letter you will use (with Ctrl key) to enable macro in Shortcut key box; select location in which to store macro in Store macro in box; click OK; click Relative Reference button on Stop Recording toolbar if macro will be used in any location on worksheet; enter commands for macro; press Enter; click Stop Recording button on Stop Recording toolbar
Macro, edit	Click Tools, select Macro, click Macros; or click ▦ that you placed on toolbar; select name of macro you want to edit; click Edit; make changes in commands in Visual Basic Editor module; close Visual Basic Editor
Macro, run	Click Tools, select Macro, click Macros; or click ▦ that you placed on toolbar; click name of macro in Macro dialog box; click Run
Menu, add custom	Click Tools, Customize, and Commands tab; select New Menu in Categories box; click New Menu in Commands box and drag to toolbar on which you want menu to appear; right-click New Menu on toolbar; enter name for menu in Name box; press Enter; click name of custom menu so that you get an empty box; locate commands you want by looking first in Categories box, then in Commands box; click and drag commands from Commands box to Custom Menu box you created; close Customize dialog box; save and close file
PivotChart, create	If you already have created a PivotTable, click cell in the PivotTable; click Chart Wizard button on PivotTable toolbar; click Chart Wizard on toolbar to make changes to layout and contents of chart; if you have not yet made a PivotTable, click Data, PivotTable and PivotChart Report; in Step 1, select data source and select PivotChart as type of report you want to create; click Next; in Step 2, enter range of cells to include in analysis or accept default range; click Next; in Step 3, select location for PivotChart; click Finish; drag field names from PivotTable field list to Page Field or Category Field areas on layout screen; drag field name for data you are analyzing to Data Items area on layout screen
PivotTable, create	Click cell on worksheet containing data list; click Data, PivotTable and PivotChart Report; in Step 1 of Wizard, select data source; select PivotTable as type of report; click Next; in Step 2, enter range of cells to include in analysis or accept default range; click Next; in Step 3, select location for PivotTable; click Finish; drag field names from PivotTable field list to Page Fields, Row Fields, or Column Fields areas on layout screen; drag field name for data you are analyzing to Data Items area on layout screen; to change function used to operate on data, click data field name; click ▦ on PivotTable toolbar
PivotTable, format	Click cell in PivotTable; click ▦ on PivotTable toolbar; select format in AutoFormat dialog box; click OK
PivotTable/PivotChart Report, change function	Click data field name on which you are operating; click ▦ on PivotTable toolbar; make sure field name for data appears in Name box; select operation you want from Summarize by box; click OK
PivotTable/PivotChart Report, create	Click cell in worksheet that contains PivotTable or PivotChart; click File, Print, or click ▦ on toolbar
Queries, create Web	Click Data, select Import External Data, click New Web Query; enter Web address that contains data you want to import in Address box in New Web Query dialog box; click Go; select tables you want to import by clicking yellow arrows that appear next to tables on Web page; click Import; indicate whether you want data to go to existing or new worksheet; click OK; click ▦ on External Data toolbar if you want to update data in the table

Query, edit database	Position mouse cursor within external data range; click Data, select Import External Data, and click Edit Query; edit Query Wizard settings as necessary; indicate in Query Wizard-Finish dialog box if you want to save query and if you want to place it in Excel worksheet; click Finish
Range, name	Select cells you want to name; click in Name box and enter name; press Enter
Range, use a named reference in a formula	Enter formula by entering name you gave to range, instead of entering cell ranges; enter name of range in appropriate box if you are using Insert Function button
Report Manager, create a report	Click View, Report Manager; click Add in the Report Manager dialog box; enter name for report in top box in Add Report dialog box; select sheets to appear in report in Sheet box; click Add after each one; click OK
Report Manager, edit a report	Click View, Report Manager; select report you want to edit; click Edit; to add a section to report, select sheet and click Add; to move a section of report, select section in Sections in this Report box; click Move Up or Move Down; to delete a section of the report, select section in Sections in this Report box; click Delete; click Close in Report Manager dialog box
Scenario, create	Click Tools, Scenario; click Add in Scenario Manager dialog box; enter name for scenario in Add Scenario dialog box; enter cell reference for data you want to change in Changing cells box; enter new value for data you want to change in Scenario Values dialog box; click OK; click Summary in Scenario Manager dialog box; enter cell references for data for which you want to see results in Result cells box
Subtotals, obtain	Click a cell; click Data, Subtotals; select field name to sort by in At each change in box; select function in Use function box; select field for subtotals in Add subtotal to box; check boxes that apply: Replace current subtotals, Page break between groups, and Summary below data; click OK
Subtotals, remove	Click Data, Subtotals; click Remove All
Track changes	Click Tools, select Track Changes, click Highlight Changes; in Highlight Changes dialog box, check Track changes while editing; make any other selections you want for which changes you will review; check Highlight changes on screen, if you want to see your changes as you enter them; click OK
Trendline, add	Data should be in form of a chart; click chart to make it active; click Chart, Add Trendline; select type of trendline; click OK
Workbook template, create	Create and format worksheet with appropriate labels, fonts, and formulas; click File, Save As; name file; click list arrow in Save as type box; select Template as file type; click Save
Workbook, create new based upon a user-created template	Click File, New, and General Templates in task pane; double-click appropriate template in General ab; tenter values for appropriate locations in template; click File, Save As; name workbook; save it as a workbook file
Workbook, create shared	Click Tools, Share Workbook; check Allow changes by more than one user at the same time in Editing tab; in Advanced tab, make any changes you want in length of time changes are tracked, frequency of file updates, and what to do with conflicting changes; click OK
Workbook, edit template	Click File, Open; locate file containing template; make changes to items contained in template; click File, Save As; use same template name or rename it; save as Template file type
Workbook, protect	Click Tools, select Protection, click Protect Workbook; in Protect Workbook dialog box, check whether you want to protect structure of workbook and/or size and arrangement of windows; add password if you want; click OK
Workbook, remove protection	Click Tools, select Protection, click Unprotect Sheet; enter password if you are prompted to do so; click OK
Workbooks, merge	Click Tools, Compare and Merge Workbooks; click OK when Excel asks you about saving file; in Select Files to Merge Into Current Workbook dialog box, select file you want to merge into open workbook; click OK; repeat for each file you want to merge into workbook
Worksheet, protect	Click Tools, select Protection, click Protect Sheet; in Protect Sheet dialog box, check Protect worksheet and contents of locked cells; in Allow all users of this worksheet to, clear boxes for any functions you do not want other individuals to use; click OK
Worksheets and workbooks, publish to the Web	Click File, Save as Web Page; click Publish; select whether to publish workbook, worksheet, or specific range of cells in Choose box; decide if you want to add interactivity and what type in Viewing options section; click Change to add title to Web page; enter or select location in which you want to save your file in File name box; check any other options you want to enable, such as AutoRepublish or Open web page in browser; click Publish
Workspace, create	Open each workbook; size and position each file on screen; click File, Save Workspace; enter name of the workspace; click Save

APPENDIX I

LESSON 1

Office Basics

In this lesson, you will learn about the Office XP suite of applications, including how to start an application, navigate application windows, work with multiple applications, and close applications. You will also learn to use the Help options available in Office XP.

 Upon completion of this lesson, you should have mastered the following skill sets:
* About Office XP
* Start an Office application Ⓜ
* Switch between applications
* Close an application Ⓜ
* Default settings
* Explore Office screen elements
    * Title bar
    * Menu bar
    * Toolbars
    * Scroll bars
    * Status bar
    * Task pane
* Get Help
    * Ask a Question box
    * The Office Assistant
    * Help window
    * ScreenTips
    * Help on the Web

Terms
MOUS-related
Office XP
Desktop
Taskbar
ScreenTip
Close button
Defaults
Title bar
Window control buttons
   Minimize button
   Restore button
   Maximize button
Menu bar
Ellipsis points
Dialog box
Shortcut menu
Formatting toolbar
Standard toolbar
Scroll bars
Scroll arrow
Scroll box
Status bar
Spelling check
Task pane
Hyperlink

TRYOUT

TASK 1

 GOAL
To practice using the following skill sets:
- About Office XP
- Start an Office application 🔳
- Switch between applications
- Close an application 🔳
- Default settings
- Explore Office screen elements
  - Title bar
  - Toolbars
  - Status bar
  - Menu bar
  - Scroll bars
  - Task pane
- Get Help
  - Ask a Question box
  - The Office Assistant
  - Help window
  - ScreenTips
  - Help on the Web

WHAT YOU NEED TO KNOW

About Office XP

> *Office XP* is a suite of software programs that provides a full range of powerful computer applications that you can use independently or in an integrated fashion. Office includes Word (word processing), Excel (spreadsheet), Access (database), PowerPoint (presentations), FrontPage (Web page design), and Outlook (desktop information manager). This text includes instruction on all programs.

> The following icons represent each application program found in Office XP.

    🔳 Word

    🔳 Excel

    🔳 Access

    🔳 PowerPoint

    🔳 FrontPage

    🔳 Outlook

> To use the features found in Office, you must be comfortable using the mouse. If you are not familiar with mouse actions and terminology, refer to Appendix C.

Start an Office Application

> When you start your computer, the first window you see is the *desktop*, the area that displays program and file icons. You also see the *taskbar*, located at the bottom of the Windows screen, which displays the Start button, the Quick-Launch toolbar, as well as open documents and programs. When clicked, the Start button displays menus to start a variety of program options.

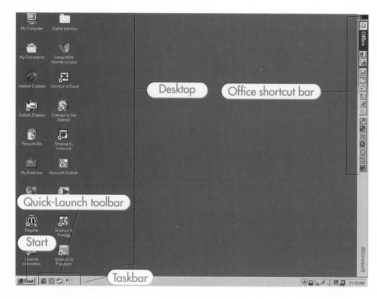

Figure 1.1 Desktop

> You might also see the Office shortcut bar, if it has been installed. You can customize the shortcut bar to show the buttons that access those resources you use most often. To install the Office shortcut bar, click Start, highlight Programs, point to Office Tools, then click the Office shortcut bar.

> You can customize the desktop to include icons of those programs you use most frequently. Therefore, your opening screen may vary from the illustration as shown in Figure 1.1.

> There are several ways to start an Office application.

- Click the Start button on the taskbar, highlight Programs, then click the application you want on the Program menu, as shown in Figure 1.2.

- Click the Start button on the taskbar, click New Office Document, then double-click the application you want to open (Blank Document, Blank Workbook, Blank Presentation, Blank Database) in the New Office Document dialog box, as shown in Figure 1.3.

- Click an application button on the Office shortcut bar. You can also click the New Office Document button, which also appears on the Office shortcut bar, as shown in Figure 1.4.

- Double-click an application button on the desktop, as shown in Figure 1.5.

Figure 1.2 Program menu

Figure 1.3 New Office Document dialog box

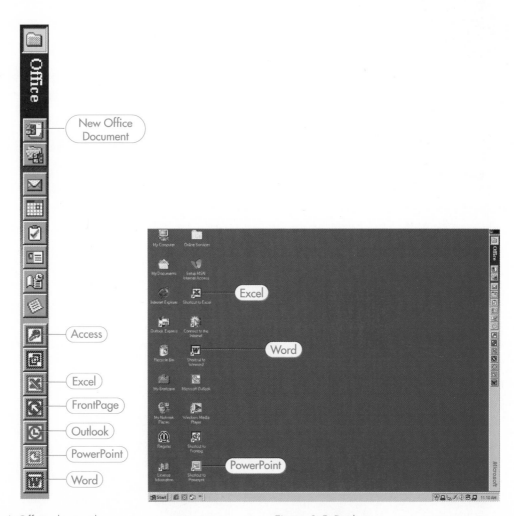

Figure 1.4 Office shortcut bar

Figure 1.5 Desktop

Switch Between Applications

> When you start an application, a button appears on the taskbar, showing an application icon and part of the document name. When you point to an application/document button, a pop-up window known as a *ScreenTip* displays the full document and application name.

> To switch between applications/documents on the taskbar, click the button for the application/document you to want display, as shown in Figure 1.6.

Figure 1.6 Taskbar with open applications

Close an Application

> To exit quickly from an application using the mouse, click the *Close button* on the program window, the ✕ in the uppermost right corner of the window, as shown in Figure 1.7.

Document1 - Microsoft Word   _ ☐ ✕

Figure 1.7 Close button on the program window

TRY*it*OUT

1. To switch to the Word application, click the **Word** button on the taskbar.

2. To switch to the Excel application, click the **Excel** button on the taskbar.

(Close button)

3. Click the **Close** button on the program window.

4. Start the PowerPoint application.

5. Click the **Close** button on the program window.

6. Click the **Close** button on the program window again to exit all programs and return to the desktop.

Default Settings

> Office XP has established certain settings within each application, called *defaults*.

> When you start a program, margins, font size, and text alignment, for example, are already set. You can, however, change those settings to suit your needs.

Explore Office Screen Elements

> After launching an Office application, you see its opening screen. The common parts of all Office application windows are illustrated and discussed using the Word window, as shown in Figure 1.8. The specific screen parts that apply to each Office application are discussed in the related units of this book. Each application window contains the following common elements:

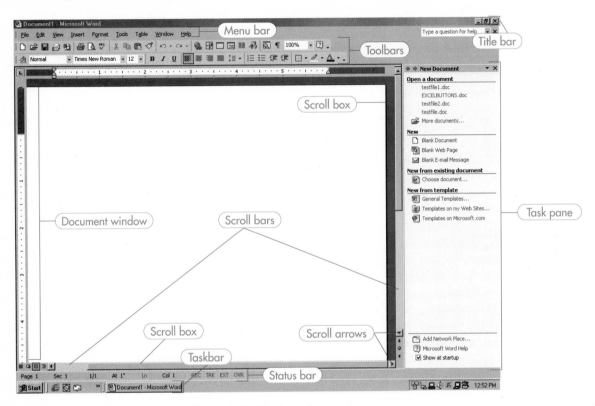

Figure 1.8 Word window

Title Bar

> The *title bar,* located at the top of the application window, as shown in Figure 1.9, displays the document name, followed by the program name. An application-specific generic name will be displayed until you provide a name during the save process.

> The title bar also includes *window control buttons* to minimize, restore, and close the program window. The *Minimize button* reduces the window to a button on the taskbar. The *Restore button* returns a minimized window to its previous size. After you click the Restore button, a *Maximize button* replaces the Restore button. When you click this button, the document or program window returns to its full size. The Close button on the program window exits or closes the application.

Minimize

Restore

Maximize

Figure 1.9 Title bar

Menu Bar

> The *menu bar,* located below the title bar, displays items that you click to execute commands. The Type a Question for Help box and the Close button on the document window appear on the right. The Word menu bar is illustrated in Figure 1.10.

Figure 1.10 Word menu bar

Type a question for help box   Close button

> You can choose menu bar items using the mouse or the keyboard. With the mouse, point to an item on the menu bar and click once. On the keyboard, press the Alt key plus the underlined letter in the menu name.

> When you select a menu bar item, a submenu appears with additional options. The menus that appear when you click Edit and Format in Word are illustrated in Figures 1.11 and 1.12 respectively.

Figure 1.11 Word Edit menu

Figure 1.12 Word Format menu

> Notice the following about menus:

- Some menu options are dimmed, whereas others appear black. Dimmed options are not available for selection at this time.

- A check mark next to a menu item means the option is currently selected.

- Some menu items display shortcut keys to access a command.

- An arrow next to a menu item means a submenu will be forthcoming.

- Some menu items display a toolbar button, if one is associated with them.

> A menu item followed by *ellipsis points* (...) indicates that a dialog box will be forthcoming. A *dialog box,* as shown in Figure 1.13, presents information about the current settings for a command and allows you to have a "dialog" with it—that is, to change the settings, if necessary. Notice the dialog box that appears after clicking File, Print. The parts of a dialog box are described in detail in Appendix D. To close a dialog box, click its Close button.

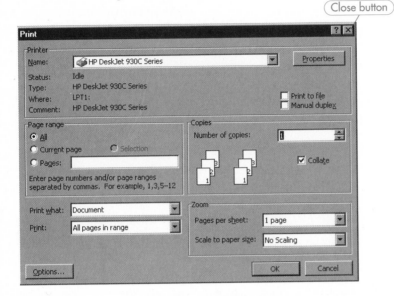

Close button

Figure 1.13 Print dialog box

TRY *it* **OUT**

1. Click **Start,** click **Programs,** and click **Word.**

2. Click the **Minimize** button.

3. Click the **Word** button on the taskbar (to redisplay the Word screen).

4. Click **Edit.** Notice the menu selections that appear.

5. Rest the mouse pointer on the other menu items. Notice the selections that appear.

6. Position the insertion point in the middle of the document window and right-click. Notice the Shortcut menu that appears. Click off the Shortcut menu to close it.

7. Click the **Close** button on the document window. Notice that the document window closes.

8. Click the **Close** button on the program window.

> A *Shortcut menu,* as shown in Figure 1.14, appears when you press the right mouse button. The menu items will vary, depending on where the mouse is pointing and what task you are performing. Notice the Shortcut menu that opens when you right-click the document window in Word.

Figure 1.14 Shortcut menu

Toolbars

> A toolbar, located below the menu bar, provides quick access to features you use frequently. There are more buttons on the bar than will fit across the screen. To display the hidden buttons, click the Toolbar Options list arrow and choose Show Buttons on Two Rows. These two rows constitute the Standard and Formatting toolbars.

> The *Standard and Formatting toolbars* appear in every application. These toolbars contain common buttons as well as application-specific buttons, and are shown in Figures 1.15 and 1.16.

> Other toolbars are available within each application and are displayed by clicking View, Toolbars. When you are working on certain tasks, it is convenient to have task-specific toolbars displayed.

T R Y *i t* **O U T**

1. Click **Start,** click **Programs,** and click **Word.**

2. Point to and rest the pointer on a toolbar button to display its name. Do this for all buttons on the toolbar.

3. Click the **Toolbar Options** list arrow and choose **Show Buttons on Two Rows.** If the buttons are already on two rows, notice the available options.

4. Click **View, Toolbars.** Notice the toolbars available in Word.

5. Click **Formatting** to deselect it. Notice that the Formatting toolbar is no longer displayed.

6. Click **View, Toolbars.**

7. Click **Formatting** to select it. Notice that the Formatting toolbar is redisplayed.

Figure 1.15 Word Standard and Formatting toolbars

Toolbar Options list arrow

Figure 1.16 Excel Standard and Formatting toolbars

Scroll Bars

> Use the *scroll bars* located at the right and bottom of the window to display areas of the screen that are not in view (see Figure 1.8).

> You can click a vertical or horizontal *scroll arrow,* drag the vertical or horizontal *scroll box* on the scroll bar, or use the numerous other screen navigation techniques that are explained in each application unit.

Status Bar

The *status bar,* located at the bottom of the window (shown in Figure 1.8), displays information about the current status of the document. The information shown on the status bar depends on the application that is open.

Task Pane

> A *task pane,* located on the right side of the screen, appears when the application is launched. In the New Document task pane, as shown in Figure 1.17, options for opening a new document are displayed.

> To close the task pane, click the Close button in the top-right corner of the task pane. You can open and display other task panes by clicking the Other Task Panes list arrow to the left of the Close button. The navigation arrows allow you to move forward and back between open task panes. If the task pane is not displayed, you can display it by clicking View, Task Pane.

> When you position the mouse pointer over a task pane option, a hyperlink appears. A *hyperlink* is an underlined word that provides a shortcut to other information. To access a task pane option, click its hyperlink.

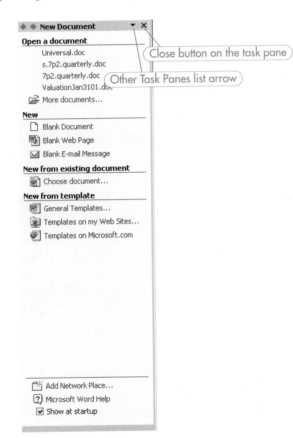

Figure 1.17 New Document task pane in Word window

Get Help

> There are several forms of Help available in each Office application. You can use the Type a Question for Help box, the Office Assistant, the Help window, ScreenTips, and/or Help on the World Wide Web. The Type a Question for Help box and the Office Assistant ultimately bring you to the Help window.

Type a Question for Help Box

> The Type a Question for Help box, as shown in Figure 1.18, appears on the menu bar in every application. Enter a question in the box and press the Enter key. A list of topics is displayed that responds to your question. Click on a topic to view an explanation.

> How do I hide toolbars?|

Figure 1.18 Type a Question for Help box

The Office Assistant

> The Office Assistant is an animated graphic that provides Help topics and tips on tasks you perform as you work. It will appear only when the user requests help or when help seems necessary.

> You can customize the Office Assistant to display tips and messages and to make sounds. A light bulb next to the Assistant displays the tip when you click it. To access the Assistant, press F1, click the Word Help button on the toolbar, or click Help, Word Help on the menu bar. The Assistant appears with the What would you like to do? question box, as shown in Figure 1.19. Enter a keyword, phrase, or question in the box, and click Search. The Office Assistant displays a list of possible matching topics. Clicking a topic displays additional information in the Word Help window (see Figure 1.21).

> **What would you like to do?**
> Type your question here and then click Search.
> Options   Search
> Open a
> te

Figure 1.19 Office Assistant question box

> If you find the Assistant distracting, you can turn it off by right-clicking the Assistant, then clicking Options. In the Office Assistant dialog box, as shown in Figure 1.20, click the Use the Office Assistant check box to deselect it, then click OK.

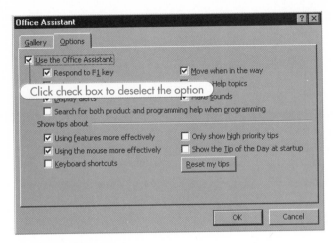

Figure 1.20 Office Assistant dialog box

Help Window

> When you turn off the Office Assistant, Help is available directly through the Help window. To access the Help window, press F1, click the Word Help button on the toolbar, or click Help, Word Help the menu bar, and select Microsoft Word Help.

> The Word Help window, as shown in Figure 1.21, has three tabs in the left pane—Contents, Answer Wizard, and Index. The right pane displays information about the topic selected from any tab in the left pane. To access further information about a topic, position the insertion point over the topic, and click the link.

> The Contents tab displays Help contents by topic in the current program.

> The Index tab provides Help topics in alphabetical order. Entering the first few letters of a topic displays those topics that closely match the search entry.

> The Answer Wizard tab provides another opportunity to enter a keyword or a question in its question box.

> You can print Help screens by clicking the Print button on the Help toolbar. The Help toolbar also contains navigation buttons, which allow you to move back and forth between topics.

> If the tabs are not visible in the Help window, click the Show/Hide button on the Help toolbar.

TRY *it* **OUT**

1. Click the **Help** button on the toolbar.

2. Click the **Contents** tab.

3. Double-click **Getting Started with Microsoft word** and notice the subtopics that display.

4. Click **what's new in Microsoft Word.**

5. Click **Show All** on the top of the right Help pane to expand the information about the topic.

6. Click **Hide all.**

7. Click the **Answer Wizard** tab.

8. Enter `How do I print?` in the What would you like to do? question box and click **Search.**

9. Print the topic.

10. Click the **Index** tab.

11. Enter `Tool` in the Type keywords text box.

12. Double-click **toolbar.** Notice the 53 topics that display.

13. Click the **Close** button on the Help window.

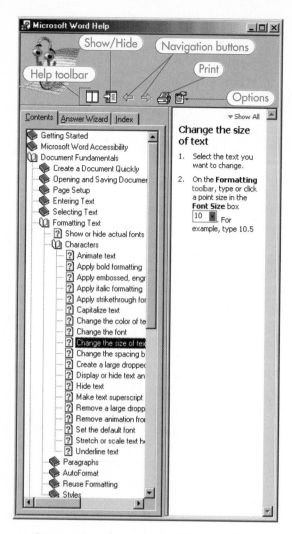

Figure 1.21 Microsoft Word Help window

ScreenTips

> ScreenTips show information about different elements on the screen.

> To get help with a menu command, toolbar button, or screen area, click Help, What's This?, and click on the location on which you want help.

> To get help with a dialog box option, click the Help button in the dialog box title bar, as shown in Figure 1.22, then click the option.

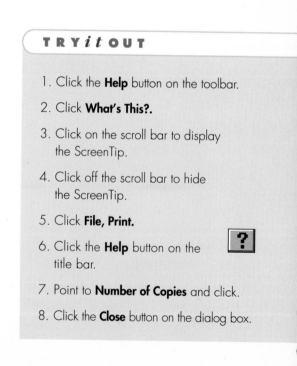

T R Y *it* **O U T**

1. Click the **Help** button on the toolbar.

2. Click **What's This?.**

3. Click on the scroll bar to display the ScreenTip.

4. Click off the scroll bar to hide the ScreenTip.

5. Click **File, Print.**

6. Click the **Help** button on the title bar.

7. Point to **Number of Copies** and click.

8. Click the **Close** button on the dialog box.

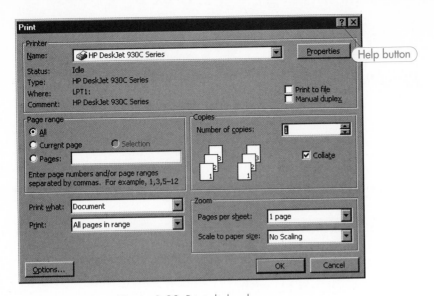

Figure 1.22 Print dialog box

Help on the Web

You can get help on the World Wide Web within any Office application by clicking Help on the menu and clicking Office on the Web. See Lesson 3 in this unit for Internet Basics.

Figure 1.23 Office on the Web

REHEARSAL

 GOAL
To explore Office screen parts (using Word) and use the Help feature

TASK 1

WHAT YOU NEED TO KNOW

> When many files are open at once, the buttons on the taskbar become smaller. When the taskbar contains too many buttons, an up/down arrow will appear. Click an arrow to cycle through the buttons and display the document you want.

> Another way to exit an application is to use the File, Exit option on the menu bar.

> In this Rehearsal activity, you will open several Office applications, change the formatting of windows, and use the Help feature.

DIRECTIONS

1. Start Word.

2. Close the task pane.

3. Start Excel.

4. Start PowerPoint.

5. Switch to Excel.

6. Click to minimize the window.

7. Click to maximize the window.

8. Hide the Formatting toolbar.

9. Display the Office Assistant, if it is not already displayed.

10. Press the **F1** key to access Help.

11. Enter **Office Assistant** in the text box.

12. Click **Search.**

13. Find information about selecting a different Office Assistant.

14. Print the topic.

15. Follow the directions on the printout to change the Assistant.

16. Turn off the Office Assistant.

17. Switch to PowerPoint.

18. Close all applications.

Formatting toolbar hidden

Search box

Office Assistant

Shortcut bar

Open applications on taskbar

Start Office
1. Click **Start** on the taskbar.
2. Click **Programs.**
3. Click the program name.
   or
- Click the program icon on the desktop or on the Office shortcut bar.

Switch Between Applications
Click the desired application/document button on the taskbar.

Close an Application
Click the **Close** button on the program window.

Change Toolbars
1. Click **View, Toolbars.**
2. Select or deselect toolbars as desired.

Close the Task Pane
Click the **Close** button on the task pane title bar.

Use Help
- Press **F1.**
   or
- Click the **Help** button.
   or
1. Click **Help, Microsoft Word Help.**
2. Enter a question in the Type a Question for Help box.

3. Click **Search.**
4. Choose the appropriate topic.
5. Click **Search.**
6. View the Help screen.
7. Click the **Close** button on the Help window.

Show/Hide the Office Assistant
1. Click **Help.**
2. Click **Show** or **Hide** the Office Assistant.

Turn Off the Office Assistant
1. Right-click the Office Assistant.
2. Click **Options.**
3. Click the **Use the Office Assistant** check box to deselect the option.

ENCORE

Identify the letter of the choice that best completes the statement or answers the question.

1. **A dimmed menu item indicates that:**
   A. The option is currently selected.
   B. A dialog box will be forthcoming.
   C. Another submenu will follow.
   D. Menu items are not available for selection at this time.

2. **Ellipsis points (…) mean that:**
   A. The option is currently selected.
   B. A dialog box will be forthcoming.
   C. Another submenu will follow.
   D. Menu items are not available for selection at this time.

3. **A check mark next to a submenu item means that:**
   A. The option is currently selected.
   B. A dialog box will be forthcoming.
   C. Another submenu will follow.
   D. Menu items are not available for selection at this time.

4. **The name of the program as well as the name of the document can be found on the:**
   A. Title bar.
   B. Menu bar.
   C. Office shortcut bar.
   D. Toolbar.

5. **Which one of the following statements regarding the Office Assistant is *not* true?**
   A. You can change the way the Office Assistant appears.
   B. The Office Assistant displays a light bulb when it is providing you with a tip.
   C. The Office Assistant can be turned on and off.
   D. The Office Assistant is available only in Word and PowerPoint.

6. **The New Document task pane contains:**
   A. Hyperlinks that provide a shortcut to another location.
   B. Options for opening a new document.
   C. Information about the current status of a document.
   D. A and B
   E. None of the above

7. **Which one of the following statements is *not* true:**
   A. You can choose menu items using the mouse or the keyboard.
   B. To select a menu item with the keyboard, click Alt + the underlined letter in the menu name.
   C. Some menu items display shortcuts.
   D. All menu items have a toolbar button associated with them.

8. **Which of the following is *not* a way to start Microsoft Office?**
   A. Click Start on the taskbar, highlight Programs, then click the desired application.
   B. Click Start on the taskbar, click New Office Document, then double-click the application you wish to open.
   C. Double-click an application icon on the desktop.
   D. Click a ScreenTip.

9. Which one of the following statements about toolbars is *not* true?
   A. Toolbars provide you with quick access to frequently used features.
   B. There are more buttons on the toolbar than will fit across the screen.
   C. You cannot display hidden buttons by clicking the Toolbar Options list arrow and choosing Show Buttons on Two Rows.
   D. The buttons on toolbars cannot be changed (customized).

10. Which one of the following window controls do you click to reduce the current window to an icon?
   A. Maximize button
   B. Minimize button
   C. Restore button
   D. Close button

TRUE/FALSE

Circle the **T** if the statement is true or the **F** if the statement is false.

T F 11. The desktop displays programs and file icons.

T F 12. Clicking on a menu bar item displays a submenu.

T F 13. The shortcut menu that appears depends on where the mouse is pointing and what task is being performed.

T F 14. Standard and Formatting toolbars appear only in Word and Excel.

T F 15. The task pane appears when an application is started.

T F 16. The Office Assistant provides Help topics and tips on tasks you perform.

T F 17. The most convenient way to access Help while you work is to use the Type a Question for Help box on the menu bar.

T F 18. Window control buttons are available on the title bar of every application.

T F 19. The taskbar contains the Start button and the Quick-Launch toolbar, as well as buttons for open documents and programs.

T F 20. You cannot customize the desktop.

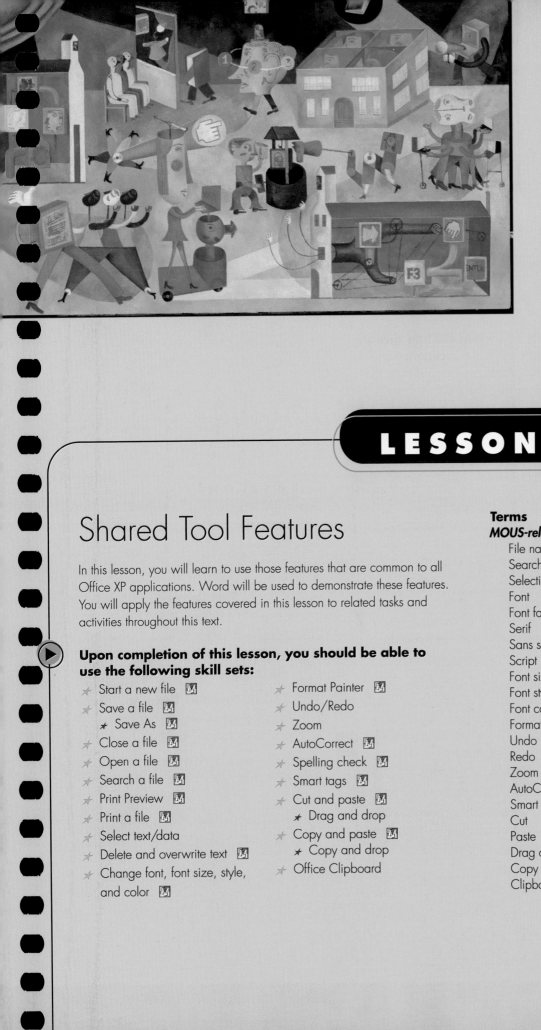

LESSON 2

Shared Tool Features

In this lesson, you will learn to use those features that are common to all Office XP applications. Word will be used to demonstrate these features. You will apply the features covered in this lesson to related tasks and activities throughout this text.

Upon completion of this lesson, you should be able to use the following skill sets:

- Start a new file 🅼
- Save a file 🅼
  - Save As 🅼
- Close a file 🅼
- Open a file 🅼
- Search a file 🅼
- Print Preview 🅼
- Print a file 🅼
- Select text/data
- Delete and overwrite text 🅼
- Change font, font size, style, and color 🅼

- Format Painter 🅼
- Undo/Redo
- Zoom
- AutoCorrect 🅼
- Spelling check 🅼
- Smart tags 🅼
- Cut and paste 🅼
  - Drag and drop
- Copy and paste 🅼
  - Copy and drop
- Office Clipboard

Terms
MOUS-related
File name
Search criterion
Selecting text
Font
Font face
Serif
Sans serif
Script
Font size
Font style
Font color
Format Painter
Undo
Redo
Zoom
AutoCorrect
Smart tags
Cut
Paste
Drag and drop
Copy
Clipboard

TRYOUT

TASK 1

GOAL
To practice using the following skill sets:
- Start a new file
- Save a file
- Save As
- Close a file
- Open a file
- Search a file
- Print Preview
- Print a file

WHAT YOU NEED TO KNOW

About Files and Folders

It is important to understand files and folders and how they are organized on your computer. Therefore, it is recommended that you review Appendix B, File Management, to review file management procedures before starting this unit.

Start a New File

> When you launch an Office tool, an opening screen appears, showing a work window and a task pane. The work window allows you to begin your work in that application.

> The task pane provides you with options for opening a new or existing file. Once you open an Office tool, you have actually created a new file in that application. The file is assigned a generic name until you provide a name during the save process.

> Using Word as an example, the opening screen is a blank document, which has been assigned the name Document1, as shown in Figure 2.1. To create another new file, click Blank Document on the task pane or click the New Blank Document button on the Standard toolbar. A new blank document will appear with Document2 as its name.

> As each new file is opened, a corresponding button will appear on the taskbar. To switch between open documents, click the desired button.

TRY*it* OUT

1. Start Word.

2. Enter your first and last name in Document1.

3. Click the **Blank Document** link on the task pane. Notice that you have created Document2.

4. Enter your home address, city, and state in Document2.

5. Click the **New Blank Document** button on the toolbar. Notice that you have created Document3.

6. Enter your telephone number in Document3. Notice the buttons on the taskbar for the three open documents.

7. Switch to Document1.

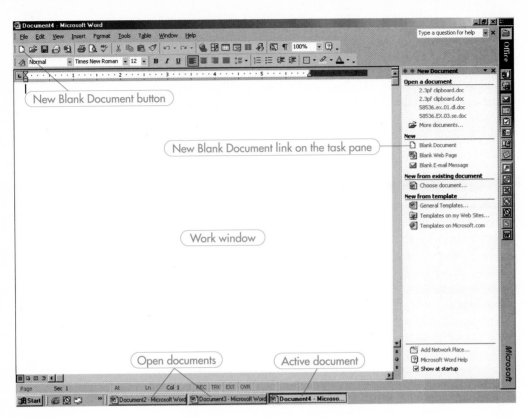

Figure 2.1 Opening Word screen

Save a File

> If you want to save the file you created, you must give it a name for identification. A *file name* may contain a maximum of 255 characters and can include spaces. File names are automatically assigned a tool-specific file name extension, as shown in Figure 2.2. Sample file names with their tool-specific file name extensions (in italic) are shown below:

- Letter.*doc* = Word file
- Table.*xls* = Excel file
- Tal.*ppt* = PowerPoint file
- Guest list.*mdb* = Access file
- My page.*htm* = FrontPage file

> To save a file for the first time, click the Save button on the Standard toolbar or click File, Save.

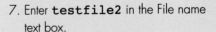

TRY*it*OUT

1. Click **File, Save** on Document1.

2. Click the **Save in** list arrow and choose a location to save the file, if necessary. Check with your teacher.

3. Enter **testfile** in the File name text box.

4. Click **Save.**

5. Switch to Document2.

6. Click the **Save** button on the Standard toolbar.

7. Enter **testfile2** in the File name text box.

8. Click **Save.**

9. Switch to testfile.

10. Click **File, Save As,** and name the file testfile4.

11. Click **Save.**

> In the Save As dialog box, as shown in Figure 2.2, you must indicate the name of the file as well as where you want to save it; My Documents is the default save-in folder. The large area below the Save in box displays the contents of the selected folder.

> Enter a file name in the File name text box and click Save to save the file. Once you have saved the file, the file name appears on the title bar and the document remains on screen.

> To update changes to a saved document, click the Save button on the Standard toolbar.

Figure 2.2 Save As dialog box — tool-specific file extension

> If you wish to save a file to a location other than the default, click the Save in list arrow and choose another location, as shown in Figure 2.3. For example, to save to a removable disk, double-click 3½ Floppy (A:).

> You can also choose a location by clicking one of the options on the Places bar.

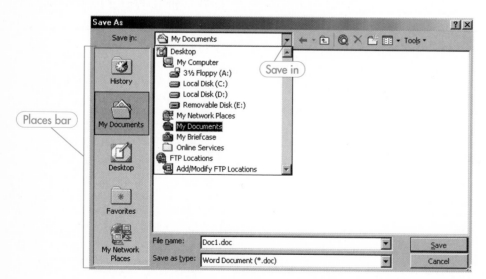

Figure 2.3 Save As dialog box with Save in list

Save As

> To save a document under a different file name or to a different location, click File, Save As. In the Save As dialog box, you can enter the new file name and/or location. The original file will remain intact.

Close a File

> As indicated earlier, when you save a file it remains on screen. To clear the screen, click File, Close, or click the Close button on the document window, as shown in Figure 2.4. If you attempt to close a file you have not yet saved, you will be prompted to save it.

> When several files are open at once, you can save or close all of them simultaneously by holding down the Shift key and clicking File, Save All or File, Close All.

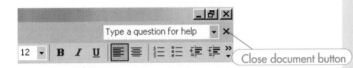

Figure 2.4 Close button on the document window

TRY*it* OUT

1. Display **testfile4** if it is not already displayed.

2. Click **File, Close.**

3. Display Document3 if it is not already displayed.

4. Click **File, Close** to close Document3. You will be prompted to save it.

5. Click **Yes** and name the file **testfile3.** The file is saved and closed.

6. Click the **Close** button on the **testfile2** document window.

7. Click the **New Blank Document** button on the Standard toolbar and enter the name of your school.

8. Click the **New Blank Document** button again and enter today's date.

9. Hold down the **Shift** key and click **File.**

10. Click **Close All.** Do not save.

Open a File

> The last four files you saved are listed in the New Document task pane, as shown in Figure 2.5, as well as at the bottom of the File menu.

> To open a recently saved file, click the file name in the task pane or click File on the menu bar and choose a document from those listed at the bottom of the menu, as shown in Figure 2.6.

> To open a file that has not been recently saved, click File, Open, or click the Open button on the Standard toolbar, or click More documents in the New Document task pane (see Figure 2.5). In the Open dialog box, as shown in Figure 2.7, double-click the file name to be opened from those documents listed. If the desired file is not shown, click the Look in list arrow and close the drive or folder where the document was saved.

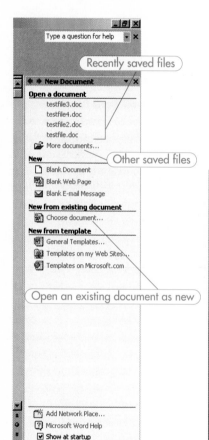

Figure 2.5 Recently saved files in task pane

Figure 2.6 Recently saved files on File menu

1. Click **File.**

2. Click **testfile** at the bottom of the File menu.

3. Click **View, Task Pane** to display the task pane.

4. Click **testfile2** in the task pane.

5. Click **File, Open.**

6. Click **testfile3.** If the file name is not listed in the Open dialog box, click the Look in list arrow and choose the directory/folder where the file has been saved.

7. Click **Open.**

8. Click **Choose document** in the task pane.

9. Click **testfile3** in the New from Existing Document dialog box.

10. Press the **Enter** key once.

11. Enter your first and last name.

12. Click **Save.**

13. Click **File, Save As,** and name the document **testfile5.**

14. Hold down the **Shift** key and click **File.**

15. Click **Close All.**

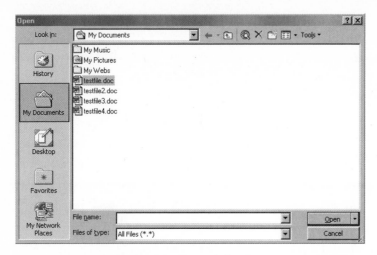

Figure 2.7 Open dialog box

> To use an existing document as a basis for a new document, click the Choose document link below the New from existing document option in the New Document task pane (see Figure 2.5). This opens the New from Existing Document dialog box, where you can choose an existing document on which to base the new file. You can then edit this file and save it under a new name.

Search a File

> You can search for a file you have saved on your computer by its file name or, if you don't remember the file name, you can search for it using unique text that you know is in the file.

> To search for a file, click File, Search on the menu, or click the Search button on the Standard toolbar. This displays the Basic Search task pane, as shown in Figure 2.8, where you can specify a search criterion. A *search criterion* is information provided by the user to help locate the file.

> Begin the search by entering the search criterion in the Search text box. You can specify where to search and the file type. The search returns files that contain the search text whether it is in the body of the file or in the file name. For example, a search for the file name "Letter" would return files named Letter, Letterhead, Letter to Mr. Jones, or any other file in which the word "letter" was used in the document.

> Once you find the file, you can click to open it.

Figure 2.8 Basic Search task pane

Print Preview

> To see how a document will look on the page before printing it, use the Print Preview feature. To preview a document, click File, Print Preview, or click the Print Preview button on the Standard toolbar.

> The Print Preview window, as shown in Figure 2.9, has its own toolbar that includes buttons for the Preview mode. The buttons and their functions are described below:

- Print—prints the document.

- Magnifier—enlarges a portion of the document.

- One Page—shows one page of the document.

- Multiple Pages—displays multiple pages.

- Zoom—sets a magnification percentage.

- View Ruler—shows/hides the Ruler on the Print Preview window.

- Shrink to Fit—fits text data onto one page.

- Full Screen—removes all screen elements except the Preview toolbar.

- Close—closes the Print Preview window.

- Context-sensitive Help—accesses ScreenTips Help.

TRY*it* **OUT**

1. Click the **Print Preview** button on the Standard toolbar (**testfile** should be on screen).

2. Position the mouse pointer, which appears as a magnifying glass, on the text and click to enlarge the text.

3. Click again to reduce the page.

4. Click the **Zoom** list arrow.

5. Change the magnification to **100%.**

6. Click the **View Ruler** button to hide the Ruler.

7. Click the **View Ruler** button to show the Ruler.

8. Click the **Full Screen** button.

9. Click the **Close Full Screen** button.

10. Click the **Close** button on the Preview toolbar.

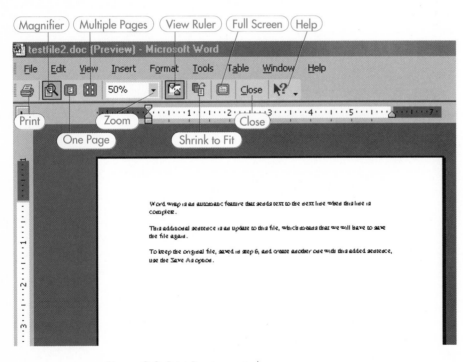

Figure 2.9 Print Preview window

Print a File

> To print a file, click File, Print. The Print dialog box contains options related specifically to that application. The Word Print dialog box is shown in Figure 2.10.

> You can quickly print a document by clicking the Print button on the Standard toolbar. Using this method bypasses the Print dialog box.

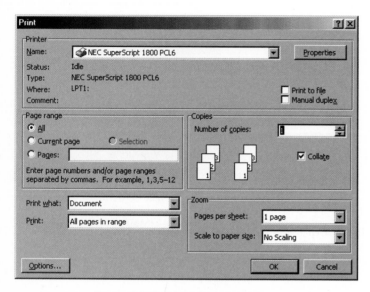

Figure 2.10 Word Print dialog box

TRY*it*OUT

1. Make sure testfile is on screen.

2. Click **File, Print.**

3. Click **OK.**

4. Close testfile.

5. Open testfile3.

6. Click the **Print** button on the Standard toolbar.

7. Close testfile3.

REHEARSAL

GOAL
To create new documents, enter text, change document views, and switch between open documents

TASK 1

SETTING THE STAGE

Margins:	Default	
Start line:	At 1"	
File names:	2.1names	2.1foods
	2.1colors	2.1colorsall

WHAT YOU NEED TO KNOW

> If you want to begin a document again, close the document window by clicking the document Close button, and do not save the file.

> To create a list, press Enter after each item on the list.

> In this Rehearsal activity, you will create and save several documents, then close and print them. You will also open and search for documents that were previously saved.

DIRECTIONS

1. Start Word.

2. Create a list of names by entering your name and the names of three other people. Press the **Enter** key after each name.

3. Save the file; name it **2.1names.**

4. Display the task pane (if it is not already displayed).

5. Open a new blank document from the task pane.

6. Create a list of your five favorite colors.

7. Save the file; name it **2.1colors.**

8. Switch to **2.1names** and close it.

9. Click the **New Blank Document** button to open a new file.

10. Make a list of your four favorite foods.

11. Close the file. When prompted, save the file as **2.1foods.**

12. Open **2.1names** and add one additional name to the list.

13. Save the file.

14. Use the Basic Search task pane to search for a file. Enter a food name you used previously as the search text.

15. Open **2.1foods** from the search results list.

16. In the task pane, create a new document from an existing document by choosing the **2.1colors** file.

17. Add five other colors to the list.

18. Save the file as **2.1colorsall.**

19. Open Print Preview and print the document.

20. Close all files.

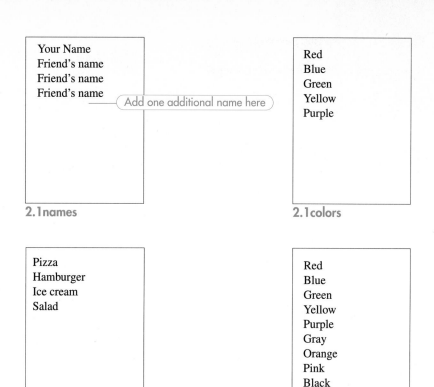

Your Name
Friend's name
Friend's name
Friend's name

Add one additional name here

2.1names

Red
Blue
Green
Yellow
Purple

2.1colors

Pizza
Hamburger
Ice cream
Salad

2.1foods

Red
Blue
Green
Yellow
Purple
Gray
Orange
Pink
Black
Brown

2.1colorsall

Cues for Reference

Start a New File
- Click the **New Blank Document** button on the Standard toolbar.
  or
- Click **Blank Document** in the task pane.
  or
1. Click **File, New.**
2. Click **Blank Document.**

Save a File

To save a file for the first time
1. Click the **Save** button.
2. If necessary, click the **Save in** list arrow to select a drive or folder.
3. Enter the file name in the File name text box.
4. Click the **Save** button.

To overwrite or update a previously saved file
Click the **Save** button.

To save a file with a new name or location
1. Click **File, Save As.**

2. If necessary, click the **Save in** list arrow to select a drive or folder.
3. Enter the file name in the File name text box.
4. Click **Save.**

Save All/Close All Open Documents
1. Press **Shift**.
2. Click **File.**
3. Click **Save All** and/or **Close All.**

Open a File
- Click the **Open** button.
  or
- Click **File, Open.**
  or
- Click the file name or click **More documents** in the task pane.
2. If necessary, click the **Look in** list arrow box to select a drive or folder.
3. Double-click the file name.

Close a File
- Click the **Close** button on the document window.
  or
- Click **File, Close.**

Search for a File
- Click the **Search** button on the Standard toolbar.
1. Click **File, Search.**
  or
2. Click in the Search text box and enter the search word(s).
3. Set other search options as desired.
4. Click **Search.**

Print Preview
Click the **Print Preview** button on the Standard toolbar.

Print
- Click the **Print** button on the Standard toolbar.
  or
1. Click **File, Print.**
2. Click **OK.**

TRYOUT

TASK 2

▶ **GOAL**
To practice using the following skill sets:
- ✷ Select text/data
- ✷ Delete and overwrite text
- ✷ Change font, font size, style, and color M
- ✷ Format Painter M
- ✷ Undo/Redo M
- ✷ Zoom

WHAT YOU NEED TO KNOW

Select Text/Data

> Before you can edit text or data (format, delete, move, or copy it), you must first select it. *Selecting text* highlights a character, word, or block of text or data.

> There are numerous ways to select text; some ways are application specific. The most frequently used technique in all applications is to click and drag the mouse pointer over a block of text or data, or to double-click a word, if you are selecting one word. There are many other shortcuts, which are detailed in Appendix E.

Delete and Overwrite Text

> If you make an error while entering text, press the Backspace key, which deletes the character to the left of the insertion point.

> To delete a word or block of text, you must first select it and then press the Delete key, which permanently removes your selection (unless you undo the action immediately— see Undo below).

> To replace existing text with new text, select the old text and begin to type. The new text will overwrite the highlighted selection.

TRY*it*OUT

1. Start Word.

2. Enter the following without pressing the **Enter** key:
   `Admission to all`
   `Conference events is free.`
   `Please join us`

3. Double-click the word "all" and press the **Delete** key.

4. Double-click the word "events" and enter `sessions`

5. Select the sentence "Please join us."and delete it.

6. Close the file; do not save.

Change Font, Font Size, Style, and Color

> A *font* is a complete set of characters that are designed in a specific face, style, and size. Each design has a name and is intended to convey a specific feeling. The design is called a *font face*.

> There are basically three types of font faces—serif, sans serif, and script. A *serif* face has lines, curves, or edges extending from the ends of the letters (**serif**), whereas a *sans serif* face is straight-edged (**sans serif**), and *script* looks like handwriting (*script*). Each Office application has its own default font, which you can change, if you like.

> You can change font faces, styles, sizes, and colors before or after entering text. You must select existing text before applying a font format.

> To change a font face quickly, click the Font list arrow on the Formatting toolbar and choose a font face, as shown in Figure 2.11.

Figure 2.11 Font list   Figure 2.12 Font Size list

> *Font size* generally refers to the height of the font, usually measured in points. There are 72 points to an inch. The font size used for most text and data ranges between 10 and 12 point.

> To change a font size quickly, click the Font size list arrow on the Formatting toolbar and choose a font size, as shown in Figure 2.12.

> *Font style* refers to the appearance of characters. Bold, italic, and underline are the most common examples of styles. Styles are generally used to emphasize text. You can combine styles to bold, italicize, and underline characters.

> To change a font style quickly, click the Bold, Italic, or Underline button on the Formatting toolbar. These buttons act as toggles to apply or remove the format. You can also use the following keyboard shortcuts to apply styles: Ctrl + B = bold; Ctrl + I = italic; Ctrl + U = underline.

> To apply color to fonts, click the *Font Color* list arrow on the toolbar and choose a color from the palette.

1. Open a new blank document.

2. Enter `blue green red yellow`. Press the **Enter** key after each word.

3. Double-click the word "blue".

4. Click the **Font** list arrow on the Formatting toolbar and click **Arial.**

5. Click the **Font Size** list arrow on the toolbar and click **20.**

6. Double-click the word "green".

7. Click the **Bold, Italic,** and **Underline** buttons on the Formatting toolbar.

8. Double-click the word "red".

9. Click the **Font Color** list arrow, click **Red,** and press the **Ctrl + B** keys to make it bold.

10. Double-click the word "yellow".

11. Click **Format, Font.**

12. Click **Arial** as the font, **Bold** as the style, **24** as the size, and **Yellow** as the color and click **OK.**

13. Right-click the document window and click **Font** on the Shortcut menu.

14. Click **Times New Roman** as the font, **Regular** as the style, **12** as the size, and **Automatic** as the color, and click **OK.**

15. Close the file; do not save.

> To apply fonts, styles, sizes, and colors simultaneously, click Format, Font (or Format, Cells in Excel) from the menu bar, then choose the options you want in the Font dialog box. You can also access the Font dialog box by right-clicking the document window and choosing Font from the Shortcut menu. The Font dialog box, as shown in Figure 2.13, looks slightly different in each application.

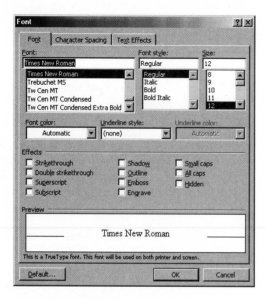

Figure 2.13 Font dialog box

> In most applications it is important to return to your original settings when you are finished applying emphasis styles. Otherwise, the new format will remain in effect as you continue to work on your document.

Format Painter

> The *Format Painter* feature allows you to copy formatting such as font face, style, and size from one block of text to another.

> To copy formatting, select the text or data that contains the formatting you wish to copy, click the Format Painter button on the Formatting toolbar (the insertion point becomes a paintbrush), and select the text to receive the formatting.

> To copy formatting from one location to several, select the text with the formatting you wish to copy and double-click the Format Painter button. You can now "paint" the formatting on several blocks of text or data by clicking a word or highlighting a block. To turn off this feature, click the Format Painter button again.

T R Y *it* O U T

1. Open **2.2pf painter** from the Data CD.

2. Double-click "Blue".

3. Click the **Format Painter** button on the Formatting toolbar. Note that the insertion point changes to a paintbrush.

4. Click "Blueberries".

5. Copy the formatting from the word "Red" to "Apples".

6. Double-click "Green".

7. Double-click the **Format Painter** button.

8. Click "Lettuce", then click "Grapes", then click "Cabbage".

10. Click the **Format Painter** button to turn off the feature.

11. Do not close the file.

Undo/Redo

> The *Undo* feature lets you reverse an action. For example, if you delete a word by mistake, click the Undo button on the Standard toolbar and you will reverse the action. If you click the Undo button repeatedly, you will reverse a series of actions. An application creates a list of actions as you work. To undo a group of actions, click the Undo list arrow and select the group of actions to be reversed. The most recent action appears at the top of the list.

> The *Redo* feature lets you reverse the previous Undo action. If you undo an action by mistake, click the Redo button on the toolbar. As with Undo, you can redo one or a series of Undo actions.

Zoom

> The *Zoom* feature allows you to set the magnification of data on the screen.

> To set a magnification percentage, click the Zoom list arrow on the Standard toolbar, or click View, Zoom and choose a magnification percentage, as shown in Figure 2.14.

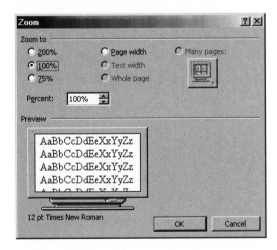

Figure 2.14 Zoom dialog box

TRY *it* **OUT**

Note: **2.2pfpainter** *should still be displayed on your screen.*

1. Click the **Undo** list arrow and note your recent actions.

2. Click the **Undo** button on the toolbar. "Cabbage" should lose its formatting.

3. Click the **Undo** button twice. "Grapes" and "Lettuce" should lose their formatting.

4. Click the **Redo** button enough times to return the formatting to "Cabbage", "Grapes", and "Lettuce".

5. Do not close the file.

TRY *it* **OUT**

1. Scroll to the top of the page.

2. Click the **Zoom** list arrow.

3. Click **200%.**

4. Click **View, Zoom.**

5. Click the **down** increment arrow in the Percent box until it reaches **70%.**

6. Click **OK.**

7. Click the **Zoom** list arrow.

8. Click **100%.**

9. Close the file; do not save.

REHEARSAL

TASK 2

 GOAL
To apply basic formatting (font, style, size, and color to text, to copy formatting and use the Undo/Redo features

SETTING THE STAGE
Margins: Default
Start line: At 1"
File name: 2.2ad

WHAT YOU NEED TO KNOW

> It is important to remember to select existing text before you apply formatting.

> A serif font is typically used for document text because it is more readable. A sans serif font is often used for headlines or technical material. A script font is usually reserved for formal invitations and announcements.

> You should choose typefaces that will make your document attractive and communicate its particular message most effectively. As a rule, use no more than two or three font faces in any one document.

> In this Rehearsal activity, you will apply formatting to unformatted text so that it matches the advertisement in the illustration. You will use the Format Painter, Undo, Redo, and Zoom features in the process.

DIRECTIONS

1. Open **2.2ad** from the Data CD.

2. Change the first two sections to match the font face, size, style, and color of the text in the file to match those indicated in the illustration on the facing page.

   Note: If you do not have the exact font faces indicated in the illustration, substitute others.

3. Use the Format Painter to copy the formatting from section 2 to section 5.

4. Use the Format Painter to copy the formatting from paragraph 4 to paragraph 6.

5. Undo the last change made.

6. Redo.

7. Delete "community" in the second section.

8. Undo the deletion.

9. Set the magnification to **200%.**

10. Print one copy.

11. Set the magnification to **100%.**

12. Save the file **2.2ad.**

13. Close the file.

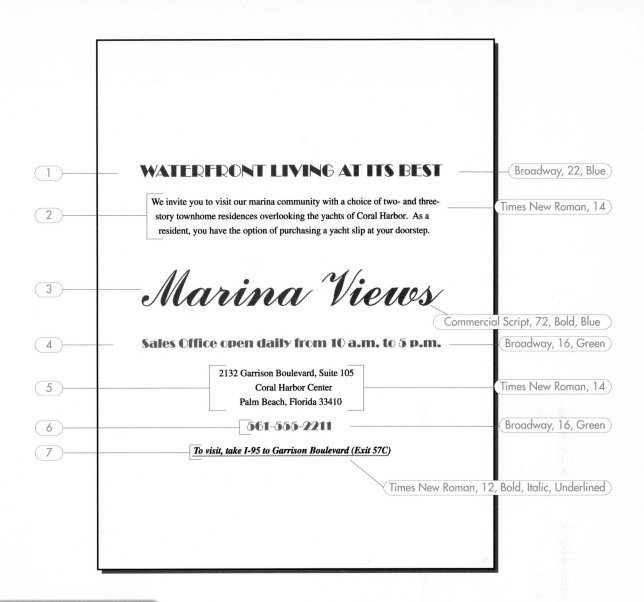

WATERFRONT LIVING AT ITS BEST — ① — (Broadway, 22, Blue)

② We invite you to visit our marina community with a choice of two- and three-story townhome residences overlooking the yachts of Coral Harbor. As a resident, you have the option of purchasing a yacht slip at your doorstep. — (Times New Roman, 14)

③ *Marina Views* — (Commercial Script, 72, Bold, Blue)

④ **Sales Office open daily from 10 a.m. to 5 p.m.** — (Broadway, 16, Green)

⑤ 2132 Garrison Boulevard, Suite 105
Coral Harbor Center
Palm Beach, Florida 33410 — (Times New Roman, 14)

⑥ **561-555-2211** — (Broadway, 16, Green)

⑦ *To visit, take I-95 to Garrison Boulevard (Exit 57C)* — (Times New Roman, 12, Bold, Italic, Underlined)

Cues for Reference

Select Text
See Appendix E for selection techniques.

Delete Text
1. Select the text to be deleted.
2. Press **Delete.**

Change Font, Size, Style, and Color
1. Select the text to be formatted or position the insertion point where the new formatting is to begin.
2. Click **Format, Font,** or right-click the desktop and click **Font.**
3. Make the desired changes.
4. Click **OK.**
   or

- Click the **Font** list arrow on the toolbar and click the desired font.
  or
- Click the **Size** list arrow on the toolbar and click the desired size.
  or
- Click the **Bold** button or press **Ctrl + B.**
  or
- Click the **Italic** button or press **Ctrl + I.**
  or
- Click the **Underline** button or press **Ctrl + U.**
  or
- Click the **Font Color** list arrow and click the desired color from the palette.

Format Painter
1. Select the text with the formatting you wish to copy.
2. Click the **Format Painter** button.
3. Select the text to receive the copied formatting.

Undo/Redo
- Click the **Undo** button.
- Click the **Redo** button.

Zoom
1. Click **View, Zoom.**
2. Set the magnification percentage.
   or
- Click the **Zoom** list arrow and select a magnification percentage.

TRYOUT

TASK 3

GOAL

To practice using the following skill sets:

* AutoCorrect M
* Spelling check M
* Smart tags M
* Cut and paste M
  * Drag and drop
* Copy and paste M
  * Drag and drop
* Office Clipboard

WHAT YOU NEED TO KNOW

AutoCorrect

> The *AutoCorrect* feature automatically corrects common capitalization, spelling, and grammatical errors as you type.

> You can set this feature to insert specific words by entering an abbreviation. For example, you can enter "Mr" and have AutoCorrect replace it with "Mr. Snufulufougus." You can also enter words you commonly misspell into the AutoCorrect dictionary.

> The AutoCorrect feature is on by default. To change settings, turn the feature off. To add to its dictionary, click Tools, AutoCorrect Options. In the AutoCorrect dialog box, as shown in Figure 2.15, make the changes you want. Click the Replace text as you type check box to turn the feature off.

TRY*it*OUT

1. Start Word.

2. Enter each word exactly as shown and note that the correct spelling will appear after pressing the spacebar:
   teh accomodate adn acheive

3. Click **Tools, AutoCorrect Options.**

4. Enter **usa** in the Replace text box.

5. Enter **United States of America** in the With text box.

6. Click **OK.**

7. Enter: **usa**

8. Close the file; do not save.

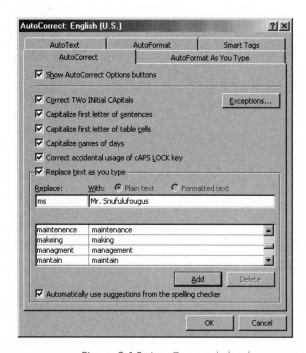

Figure 2.15 AutoCorrect dialog box

Spelling Check

> The *Spelling check* feature compares the words in your file with the words in the application's dictionary.

> In some applications, a wavy red line underlines spelling errors. To correct a misspelled word that is underlined, right-click the word, and a Spelling Shortcut menu, as shown in Figure 2.16, displays a list of suggested corrections. Click the correctly spelled word on the menu to replace the incorrectly spelled word in the document.

> You can add the word you misspelled to the application's dictionary or to AutoCorrect.

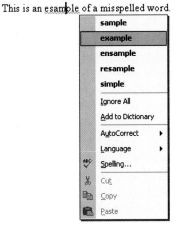

Figure 2.16 Spelling Shortcut menu

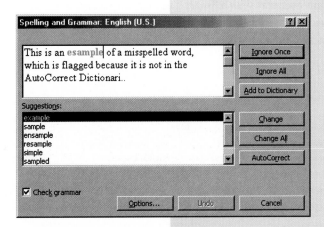

Figure 2.17 Spelling and Grammar dialog box

> To check spelling for an entire document, click the Spelling and Grammar button on the Standard toolbar or click Tools, Spelling and Grammar. (In Word, Spelling includes the Grammar feature. In other applications, the feature includes only Spelling. Spelling and Grammar is described in Word Basics.) In the Spelling and Grammar dialog box, the misspelled word is shown in red, and suggested corrections are listed in the Suggestions box, as shown in Figure 2.17. Choose one of the following command buttons to remedy the error:

- Ignore Once—ignores this occurrence of the error.

- Ignore All—ignores all occurrences of this error.

- Add to Dictionary—adds this word to the application's dictionary.

- Change—replaces the incorrectly spelled word with the selected suggestion.

- Change All—changes all occurrences of this word with the selected suggestion.

- AutoCorrect—adds the word to AutoCorrect.

1. Open **2.3pf spelling** from the Data CD.

2. Right-click "visitt", then click the correctly spelled word on the list.

3. Right-click "comunity", then click the correctly spelled word on the list.

4. Click the **Spelling and Grammar** button on the Standard toolbar.

5. On the next highlighted word ("overloooking"), click the correctly spelled word and click **Change.**

6. On the next highlighted word ("yackhts"), click the correctly spelled word, then click **Change All.**

7. Correct the remaining errors.

8. Close the file; do not save.

Smart Tags

> As you enter certain text or data, Office labels it with a *Smart Tag.* Smart Tags appear as a purple dotted line beneath names, addresses, and other types of data in Word or as an actions button that appears near data as you work. These buttons allow you to choose options without clicking the toolbar or opening a dialog box.

> Smart Tags provide you with numerous actions you can take with the tagged text. For example, you can add a person's name and address from your document to an Outlook Contact folder without copying and pasting it.

> To learn what actions you can take with a smart tag, move the insertion point over text with a Smart Tag indicator until the Smart Tag Actions button appears. Click the button to see the menu of actions, as shown in Figures 2.18 and 2.19.

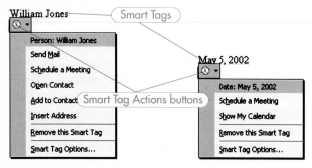

Figure 2.18 Smart Tag name actions

Figure 2.19 Smart Tag date actions

TRY*it* OUT

1. Open a new blank document.

2. Enter your first and last name and press the **Enter** key. Notice the Smart Tag below your name.

3. Position the insertion point over your name and notice the Smart Tag Actions button.

4. Point to the button and click the list arrow. Notice the options.

5. Click **Remove this Smart Tag.**

6. Enter today's date and press **Enter.**

7. Position the insertion point over the date and notice the Smart Tag Actions button.

8. Point to the button and click the list arrow. Notice the options.

9. Close the file; do not save.

Cut and Paste

> *Cut* and *Paste* are features used in all Office applications to move text or data from one location and reinsert it in another.

> To remove text or data, first select it, then click the Cut button on the toolbar, or click Edit, Cut from the menu bar. The text or data is placed temporarily on the Office Clipboard, a temporary storage area.

> To reinsert the text, position the insertion point in the new location and click the Paste button on the Standard toolbar.

> The Smart Tag Paste Options button appears in the lower-right corner of the pasted text selection. When you click the button, a list appears with options for pasting the text into the document. The available options depend on the type of content you are pasting, the program from which you are pasting, and the format of the text in the new location.

TRY*it* OUT

1. Open **2.3pf cut and paste** from the Data CD.

2. Double-click "Two".

3. Click the **Cut** button on the Standard toolbar.

4. Position the insertion point before the "T" in "Three."

5. Click the **Paste** button on the toolbar.

6. Double-click "Four".

7. Hold down the mouse button and drag the selection, then drop it before the "F" in "Five."

8. Close the file; do not save.

Drag and Drop

> *Drag and drop* is another method of moving text. Select the text you want to move and hold down the mouse button as you drag the selection to its new location. When you release the mouse button, the text will drop into place at the insertion point location. Use the Undo button if you make an error.

> The Smart Tag Paste Options button also appears after a drag-and-drop procedure.

Copy and Paste

> *Copy* and Paste are features used in all Office applications to copy text or data from one location and reinsert it in another. Copying leaves text or data in its original location while placing a duplicate in another location.

> To copy text or data, first select it, then click the Copy button on the Standard toolbar or click Edit, Copy on the menu bar. The text or data is placed temporarily on the Office Clipboard.

> To paste the text, position the insertion point in the new location and click the Paste button on the toolbar.

> Because the Cut, Copy, and Paste commands are used frequently, you can use shortcut methods for performing these tasks: Ctrl + X = cut; Ctrl + C = copy; Ctrl + V = paste.

Drag and Drop

> You can also use Drag and drop to copy text. Select the text you want to copy, then hold down the Ctrl key while dragging the selection to its new location. Note that the insertion point displays a plus sign (+), indicating that the selection is being copied.

> When you release the mouse button, the text drops into place at the insertion point location. Release the mouse button before releasing the Ctrl key. Click the Undo button if you make an error.

1. Open **2.3pf copy and paste** from the Data CD.

2. Select "Slow Down."

3. Click the **Copy** button on the Standard toolbar.

4. Position the insertion point in the blank line below "To summarize."

5. Click the **Paste** button on the toolbar.

6. Select "Draw the Line."

7. Hold down the mouse button and press the **Ctrl** key. Drag and drop the selection at the margin below "Slow Down."

8. Use any desired method to copy "Learn to Delegate" and paste it below "Draw the Line."

9. Close the file; do not save.

Office Clipboard

> As indicated previously, when you cut or copy text it is temporarily placed on the Clipboard. The *Clipboard* is a temporary storage area that can hold up to 24 items. To view the Clipboard contents after you cut or copy more than one item, click Edit, Office Clipboard. The Clipboard task pane, as shown in Figure 2.20, lists each copied or cut item.

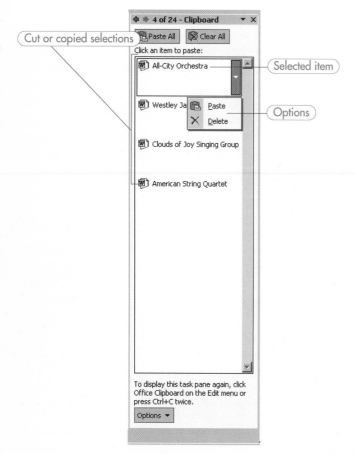

Figure 2.20 Clipboard task pane

> Position the insertion point where you wish to reinsert the cut or copied item and click the item in the Clipboard task pane. A list box next to each item gives you a delete option.

> To paste all or clear all of the selections, click the appropriate button in the Clipboard task pane (see Figure 2.20).

> If you want to display the task pane automatically after you have cut or copied more than one selection, click Options at the bottom of the task pane and choose Show Office Clipboard Automatically.

1. Open **2.3pf clipboard** from the Data CD.

2. Copy each of the following: "American String Quartet," "Clouds of Joy Singing Group," "Westley Jazz Band," and "All-City Orchestra."

3. If the Clipboard task pane does not appear automatically, click **Edit, Office Clipboard.**

4. Position the insertion point below "Mark your calendar with these events:"

5. Click "All-City Orchestra" in the Clipboard task pane and press the **Enter** key.

6. Paste the remaining items from the Clipboard below "All-City Orchestra" in an alphabetical list.

7. Click **Clear All.**

8. Click **Options** at the bottom of the task pane to view the choices.

9. Close the file; do not save.

REHEARSAL

GOAL
To apply basic editing (AutoCorrect, spelling check, cut, copy, and paste) to text, and remove a smart tag.

TASK 3

SETTING THE STAGE
Margins: Default
Start line: At 1"
File name: 2.3color

WHAT YOU NEED TO KNOW

> It is sometimes necessary to insert or delete spaces after completing a move.

> Before you paste the moved text, always place the insertion point immediately to the left of where you want the text reinserted.

> In this Rehearsal activity, you will apply basic editing to a document, including move, copy, and paste techniques. Because multiple selections will be copied, you will use the Clipboard to reinsert the selections. In addition, you will create an AutoCorrect entry to make entering a long name easier.

DIRECTIONS

1. Open **2.3color** from the Data CD.

2. Correct all spelling errors.

3. Use any method to move the words as shown in the illustration on the facing page.

4. Access the AutoCorrect dialog box. Enter the initials **LK** in the Replace text box. Enter **Laboratory Kaleidoscope** in the With text box.

5. Position the insertion point after the last sentence in the paragraph, "Color highlights information." and enter: **Just ask LK**

6. Copy each sentence formatted with color.

7. Display the Clipboard task pane.

8. Paste each selection (in any order) as a list below the word "Remember:"

9. Move "John Williams, President of", and "Laboratory Kaleidoscope" (lines 3 through 5) to become the last lines of the document.

10. Remove the smart tag below John Williams' name.

11. Print one copy.

12. Save the file **2.3color.**

13. Close the file.

Four Reasons Why You Should Design With Color

John Williams
President of
Laboratory Kaleidoscope

move

The (colorfull) world is a place. So why not include color in all of your procesing? Just ask Laboratory Kaleidoscope. **Color increases the visual impact of the message and makes it more memorable.** Don't you want your ads to have (and be impact) noticed? Just ask Laboratory Kaleidoscope. **Color creates a feeling and helps explain the subject.** Greens and blues are cool, relaxxing tones, while reds and organges scream with emphasis. Pastells communicate a gentle tone. **Color Creates a Personality.** You can make your corporate forms and broshures have their own identity and personality with color. Just ask Laboratory Kaleidoscope. **Color highlights information.**

Remember:

Paste
sentences
formatted
in color
here

Cues for Reference

Add to AutoCorrect Dictionary
1. Click **Tools, AutoCorrect Options.**
2. In the Replace text box, enter a code or incorrectly spelled word.
3. In the With text box, enter the correctly spelled word.
4. Click **OK.**

Spelling Check
1. Click the **Spelling and Grammar** button.
2. Click the appropriate command button in the dialog box.
3. Click **OK** when completed.
   or
- Right-click the misspelled word and choose a correctly spelled word from the Shortcut menu.

Smart Tags
1. Position the insertion point over a word that has been tagged.
2. Click the **Smart Tag Actions** button.
3. Choose an option.

Cut and Paste
1. Select the text to move.
2. Click the **Cut** button.
   or
1. Press **Ctrl + X.**
2. Position the insertion point where the text is to be reinserted.
3. Click the **Paste** button.
   or
   Press **Ctrl + V.**

Copy and Paste
1. Select the text to copy.
2. Click the **Copy** button.
   or
1. Press **Ctrl + C.**
2. Position the insertion point where the text is to be reinserted.
3. Click the **Paste** button.
   or
   Press **Ctrl + V.**

Drag and Drop
1. Select the text to move or copy.
2. Point to the selected text.
3. Press the mouse button and drag the text to the new location.
   or
- To copy, press **Ctrl** and drag the text to the new location.

Display Clipboard Task Pane
- Click **Edit, Office Clipboard.**

MULTIPLE CHOICE

Identify the letter of the choice that best completes the statement or answers the question.

1. **Taskbar buttons labeled Document1 and Document2 mean that:**
   A. Those files are open.
   B. Those files are all active.
   C. Those files were closed.
   D. None of the above

2. **A file name extension is:**
   A. Program specific.
   B. Automatically added to a file name.
   C. An identifier of the file type.
   D. All of the above

3. **Use the Save As dialog box to:**
   A. Save a file under a different file name.
   B. Save a file to the desktop.
   C. Give a file a name.
   D. All of the above

4. **When you close a file,**
   A. It is automatically saved.
   B. You may be prompted to save the file.
   C. All of the above
   D. None of the above

5. **To open a file, you can:**
   A. Click a file name at the bottom of the File menu.
   B. Click a file name in the the task pane.
   C. Use the Open dialog box.
   D. All of the above

6. **You can apply fonts, font sizes, styles, and colors by:**
   A. Using the appropriate buttons on the toolbar.
   B. Using the Font option on the Office shortcut bar.
   C. Using the Font dialog box.
   D. All of the above
   E. A and C

7. **The Format Painter is:**
   A. A feature to copy formatting.
   B. A toolbar button.
   C. A and B
   D. Only for setting colors.

8. **AutoCorrect is a feature that:**
   A. Replaces text with other text.
   B. Automatically corrects all spelling errors.
   C. Automatically corrects a list of common spelling errors.
   D. A and C

9. **Copy and paste:**
   A. Moves data from one place to another.
   B. Places a duplicate in another location.
   C. Is the same as cut and paste.
   D. All of the above

10. **The Office Clipboard:**
    A. Is displayed in a task pane.
    B. Shows multiple cuts and pastes.
    C. Can be displayed automatically.
    D. All of the above

Circle the **T** if the statement is true or the **F** if the statement is false.

T F 11. When you select a file under the New from existing document option, you are creating a new file based on one of your old files.

T F 12. If you cannot find a file, you should use the Clipboard task pane.

T F 13. A search criterion is information provided by a user to help locate data or files.

T F 14. To select one word quickly, you can single-click the word.

T F 15. To delete and overwrite the original text, you can select the text and begin to type.

T F 16. You can apply several styles, such as bold, italic, and underline, to one selected block of text.

T F 17. To redo an action that has been reversed, you should click the Undo button.

T F 18. Drag and drop is used only for copy and paste.

T F 19. You can use the Zoom feature to set the magnification of data on the screen.

T F 20. The buttons that appear near certain text entries are Smart Tag Actions buttons.

COMPLETION

21. Multiple cuts and pastes are stored on the _____.

22. To locate a file on your computer when you know only part of the file name, use the _____ feature.

23. If the data on screen is too small, you can use the _____ feature to magnifiy the data.

24. When you move or copy text with the mouse, it is called _____.

25. Serif, sans serif, and script are types of _____.

26. If you wish to reverse an action, use the _____ button.

27. The feature that automatically corrects common capitalization, spelling, and grammatical errors as you enter text is called the _____ feature.

28. A purple dotted line beneath names, addresses, and other types of data it is called a _____.

29. If you wish to copy formatting such as font face, style, and size from one text block to another, use the _____.

30. If you make an error while entering text, press _____, which deletes the character to the left of the insertion point.

Internet Basics

In this lesson, you will learn the basic concepts of the Internet. You will also learn to use a Web browser to access the World Wide Web, copy text and graphics from Web site pages, print Web site pages, and use search techniques to find information on the Internet.

Upon completion of this lesson, you should be able to use the following skill sets:

- ✶ Launch Internet Explorer
- ✶ Navigate the browser window
- ✶ Access a Web site using a Web address (URL)
- ✶ Print Web pages
- ✶ Exit the browser
- ✶ Use Favorites folders
  - ✶ Add a site to Favorites
  - ✶ Open a site from Favorites
- ✶ Organize Favorites folders
  - ✶ Create new folders
  - ✶ Move Favorites sites into new folders
- ✶ Copy from a Web site
- ✶ Save Web pages
- ✶ Search the Internet
  - ✶ Use search engines and directories
  - ✶ Use Boolean operators to refine a search

Terms
MOUS-related
- World Wide Web
- Web browser
- Internet Explorer
- Home page
- Download
- Hyperlink
- Web address
- URL (uniform resource locator)
- Domain name
- Favorites folder
- Search engine
- Directory
- Text string
- Boolean operators:
  - AND, NOT, OR

 T R Y O U T

TASK 1

▶ **GOAL**
To practice using the following skill sets:
* Launch Internet Explorer
* Navigate the browser window
* Access a Web site using a Web address (URL)
* Print Web pages
* Exit the browser

WHAT YOU NEED TO KNOW

Launch Internet Explorer

> The *World Wide Web* is a service of the Internet, in which pages, created by companies, individuals, schools, and government agencies around the world, are linked to one another.

> A *Web browser* is a software program that displays the information you retrieve from the Internet in a readable format. *Internet Explorer* is the Web browser that comes with the Office suite.

> To start Internet Explorer, click the Search the Web button on the Web toolbar in all Office programs, or click the Explorer button on the taskbar, as shown in Figure 3.1.

Figure 3.1 Taskbar

T R Y *it* O U T

1. Start Word.

2. Click **View, Toolbars, Web.**

3. Click the **Search the Web** button to start Internet Explorer.

Navigate the Browser Window

> When you start Internet Explorer, the browser window replaces the program window, and a home page is displayed. The *home page* is the start page of any Web site.

> The Internet Explorer window displays a menu bar, toolbar, Address line, and the page area where the Web page displays. The Status bar displays the status of the information being processed and indicates how much of the page has been downloaded. *Downloading* is the process of copying files from the Internet to your own computer.

T R Y *it* O U T

1. Click a **hyperlink** on the home page. Click another link.

2. Click the **Back** button to return to the previous page.

3. Click the **Forward** button to advance to the next page.

4. Click the **Home** button to return to the start page.

> Web pages contain hyperlinks. A *hyperlink* appears as underlined or colored text or as a graphic, as shown in Figure 3.2. When clicked, a hyperlink takes you to a new page with related information. Clicking on related links to find information is often referred to as "surfing the Web" or "surfing the Net." You can see whether an item on a page is a link by moving the mouse pointer over it; if the pointer changes to a hand, the item is a link.

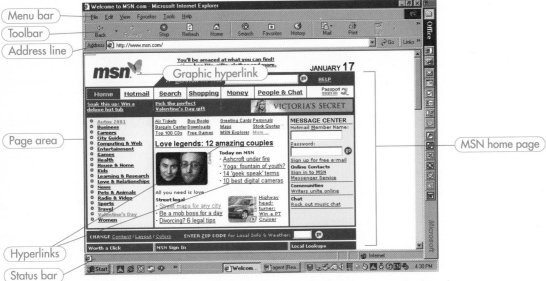

Figure 3.2 Internet Explorer window with the MSN home page displayed

Access a Web Site Using a Web Address (URL)

> Every Web site has a unique *Web address,* which is referred to as a *URL (uniform resource locator).* A URL suffix is called a domain name. A *domain name* identifies the Web site as a commercial (.com), noncommercial (.org), government (.gov), educational (.edu), U.S. military (.mil), or network (.net) organization.

> Each time a Web page downloads, its address appears on the Address line of the Internet Explorer window. To go to another Web page, click a link or enter the correct address on the Address line, as shown in Figure 3.3 and press Enter or click Go to activate the search. An icon to the right of the toolbar rotates while information is being sought or processed.

> To interrupt a search, click the Stop button on the Internet Explorer toolbar.

Figure 3.3 Address line in Internet Explorer

> Internet Explorer records a history list of the sites you have visited and allows you to jump back to a recently visited site. To view a history list, click the list arrow to the right of the Address line. You can also click the History button on the toolbar to view a history of the sites you visited on specific days of the week.

Print Web Pages

Printing Web pages enables you to keep information you research for future reference. To print the current Web page, click the Print button on the Explorer toolbar, or click File, Print on the Explorer menu bar.

TRY*it***OUT**

1. Click another link on the displayed Web page and note the address that displays on the Address line.

2. Enter the following URL on the Address line: www.dell.com

3. Press the **Enter** key.

4. Enter the following URL on the Address line: www.nasa.gov

5. Click **Go.**

6. Click the **Address** list arrow and view the list of the sites visited.

7. Click the **Print** button on the toolbar.

Exit the Browser

To exit Internet Explorer, click File, Close on the menu bar. Exiting the browser does not necessarily mean that you are exiting from your Internet Service Provider (the service that gives you access to the Internet). Check to see that you have disconnected from your service provider so that you are not charged for additional time online.

REHEARSAL

 GOAL
To access Web sites using a Web address, print Web site pages, and exit the browser

TASK 1

WHAT YOU NEED TO KNOW

> Because Web sites change daily, a Web site may display a different home/start page each time you access it.

> If the Standard and Address toolbars are not visible when you start Internet Explorer, click View Toolbars and click to display the toolbars.

> The length of time it takes to open a Web site start page depends on the speed of your modem and the graphics on the page.

> In this Rehearsal activity, you will access a Web site, print Web pages, and exit the browser.

DIRECTIONS

1. Start the Internet Explorer if it is not already running.

2. Display the toolbar if it is not already displayed.

3. Enter the following Web address (URL) on the address line, then press the **Enter** key or click
   Go: www.microsoft.com/windows/iw/tour
   • Click **The Basics.**
   • Click **Basics of the Internet.**

4. Print one copy of the page(s). Read the information and keep the printed copy as a reference.

5. Click the **Back** button.

6. Click the **Forward** button.

7. Click the **Home** button.

8. Access the following Web site: www.nba.com.
   • Click **Teams.**
   • Click a team you are interested in learning more about.

9. Print one copy of the team page.

10. Click the **History** button and click today.

11. Return to the start page. Close the **History** pane.

12. Return to the NBA home page.

13. Click **File, Close** to close the browser.

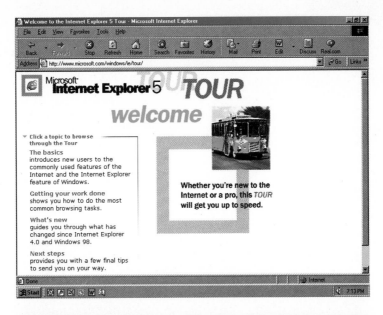

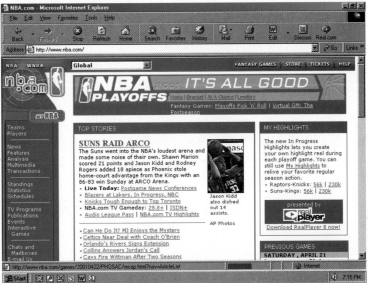

Start Internet Explorer
- Click the **Explorer** button on the taskbar.

  or
1. Start an Office application such as Word or Excel.
2. Click **View, Toolbars, Web.**
3. Click the **Search the Web** button.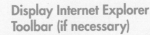

Display Internet Explorer Toolbar (if necessary)
1. Click **View.**
2. Click **Toolbars.**
3. Click **Standard Buttons** and click **Address Bar.**

Access a Web Site
1. Enter the URL on the Address line.

2. Press **Enter** or click **Go.**

  or
- Click a link on the displayed Web page.

Print Web Pages
Click the **Print** button on the Explorer toolbar.

Exit the Browser
1. Click **File.**
2. Click **Close.**

TRYOUT

TASK 2

 GOAL
To practice using the following skill sets:
- Use Favorites folders
  - Add a site to Favorites
  - Open a site from Favorites
- Organize Favorites folders
  - Create new folders
  - Move Favorites sites into new folders
- Copy from a Web site
- Save Web pages

WHAT YOU NEED TO KNOW

Use Favorites Folders

> Internet Explorer enables you to record Web sites that you would like to revisit and save them in a *Favorites folder*. When you save a site, you are actually recording its Web address.

Add a Site to Favorites

> To add a site to the Favorites folder, first display the site on the screen, then click the Favorites button on the Explorer toolbar. This opens the Favorites pane, as shown in Figure 3.4, where favorite sites are listed. To add the on–screen site to the list, click Add.

Figure 3.4 Favorites pane

TRY*it*OUT

1. Start Internet Explorer.

2. Enter www.biztravel.com on the Address line.

3. Click the **Enter** key.

4. Click the **Favorites** button on the Explorer toolbar.

5. Click **Add** in the Favorites pane.

   Note: The Add Favorite dialog box appears, with the Web site address in the Name box.

6. Click **OK** to add the address to the Favorites folder.

7. Enter www.expedia.com on the Address line.

8. Click the **Enter** key.

9. Click the **Favorites** button.

10. Click **Add** in the Favorites pane and click **OK.**

11. Do not close the browser.

> In the Add Favorite dialog box, the name of the site that is on the screen appears in the Name box, as shown in Figure 3.5. Click OK to add the Web address to the Favorites list.

Figure 3.5 Add Favorite dialog box

> The process of saving a site to the Favorites folder is often referred to as "bookmarking" a site.

Open a Site from Favorites

> When you want to revisit a site that you saved in a Favorites folder, click the Favorites button on the Explorer toolbar and click in the Favorites pane the site that you want to open (see Figure 3.4).

Organize Favorites Folders

> It is helpful to organize sites into categories so that you can easily find them. To do this, create and name new Favorites folders and save sites in the appropriate folders.

> You can create new folders before or after saving sites in the default Favorites folder. Organizing files in categories is useful when working in all Office applications.

Create New Folders

> To organize folders, click Organize in the Favorites pane. In the Organize Favorites dialog box shown in Figure 3.6, click Create Folder and enter a folder name when prompted.

Move Favorites Sites into New Folders

> To move existing sites into the newly created folders, in the Organize Favorites dialog box click the Web site you wish to move. Hold down the left mouse button while you drag the selected site and drop it into the correct folder.

TRY *it* **OUT**

1. If the Favorites pane is not displayed, click the **Favorites** button on the Explorer toolbar.

2. Scroll down the Favorites pane and click biztravel.com to return to that site.

TRY *it* **OUT**

1. Click the **Organize** button in the Favorites pane.

2. Click **Create Folder.**

3. Enter **Travel Sites** (the name of the new folder) and press the **Enter** key.

4. Click on biztravel.com (the site you saved previously), which is listed in the Favorites pane.

5. Hold down the left mouse button and drag biztravel.com into the Travel Sites folder.

6. Click on expedia.com.

7. Move the site to the Travel Sites folder.

8. Click **Close** to exit the Organize Favorites dialog box.

9. Do not close the browser.

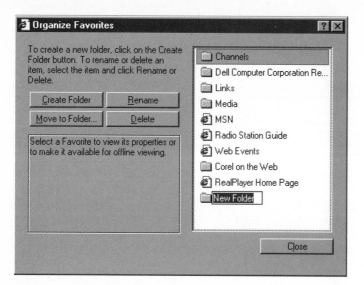

Figure 3.6 Organize Favorites dialog box

Copy from a Web Site

> One reason to use the Internet is to obtain information for a report or other document. You can copy text from a Web site and paste it into an Office application, such as Word, for editing. Select the Web site text to be copied, right-click and choose Copy from the Shortcut menu, as shown in Figure 3.7. Position the insertion point in the Word document to receive the copied text and click Edit, Paste on the Word menu bar. It is important to note the source of the information so that you can give the author credit in your report.

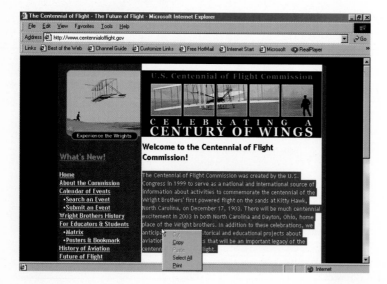

Figure 3.7 Copying text from a Web site

TRY it OUT

1. Enter www.centennialofflight.gov on the Address line.

2. Copy the first paragraph of text on that page.

   Note: Web sites change constantly, so the page you see when you access the Web site may not resemble Figure 3.7.

3. Right-click and choose **Copy.**

4. Click the **Microsoft Word** icon on the shortcut bar.

5. Click **Edit, Paste** on the Word menu bar.

6. Click the **Explorer** button on the taskbar to return to the browser window.

7. Right-click the picture of the White House and choose **Save Picture As.**

8. Enter `firstflight` as the file name.

9. Click the **Save as type** list arrow and choose **Bitmap.**

10. Click **Save.**

11. Click **File, Close** to close Explorer.

> You can also copy a picture from a Web site. The method for copying a picture, however, is different from the method for copying text. Although copied text can be pasted into a document, pictures generally cannot be pasted—they must be inserted. To copy a picture, right-click the picture and choose Save Picture As from the Shortcut menu, as shown in Figure 3.8.

Figure 3.8 Copying a picture from a Web site

> In the Save Picture dialog box, as shown in Figure 3.9, click the Save as type list arrow and choose Bitmap. (A bitmapped file is one that contains a graphic composed of a series of dots.) Enter a name for the picture and click Save. You will learn more about inserting pictures into a document in the Word unit of this text.

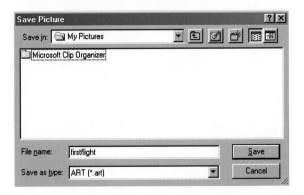

Figure 3.9 Save Picture dialog box

Save Web Pages

Because Web sites change constantly, it is a good idea to save a page that you find valuable. To do so, click File, Save As on the Explorer menu bar. The process of saving a Web page is the same as that for saving a file. A saved Web page displays the Explorer icon next to its file name (See Figure 3.6).

REHEARSAL

 GOAL
To create and organize a favorites folder, to open a site from favorites folder, and to copy text from a Web site and paste it in to a document.

TASK 2

WHAT YOU NEED TO KNOW

> Be sure to cite the source of any Internet material that you use in a document. Failing to do so is called plagiarism. See Word, Lesson 3, to learn how to cite from the Internet.

> If you try to copy a picture and find you are having difficulty, it may be that the picture is not available to you because it has been copyrighted. A copyrighted picture has legal protection and cannot be used unless you obtain written permission from the publisher. Be sure to read Web pages carefully for this information.

> You can move several related sites at one time into a Favorites folder. To do this, hold down the Ctrl key as you click the desired sites and drag the selected group to the new folder.

> Business news sites allow you to learn about up-to-the-minute news and trends. Some sites include real-time (as it is happening) reports of stock trading news. If you plan to purchase computer equipment, you will want to search technology-related sites to learn about new hardware and software products, prices, and computer and technology trends.

> In this Rehearsal activity, you will create Favorites folders for business news sites as well as sites that contain computer-related product information.

DIRECTIONS

1. Start Internet Explorer.
2. Create a Favorites folder; name it **Business News.**
3. Create another Favorites folder; name it **Computer Info.**
4. For each of the following sites, enter the Web address on the Address line, and press **Enter.** Read the content of the site and add it to either the Business News or the Computer Info folder as appropriate.

   www.pcmag.com   www.software.net
   www.bloomberg.com   www.dell.com
   www.businessweek.com   www.ibm.com
   www.forbes.com   www.compusa.com
   www.upside.com

5. Bookmark the following sites (click the **Favorites** button, but do not save in any particular folder):

   www.weather.com   www.cnn.com/WEATHER/
   www.intellicast.com

6. Create a new Favorites folder; name it **Weather.**
7. Move the weather-related sites into the newly created Weather folder.
8. Open the Business News folder.
9. Note the sites that have been added.
10. Return to the Bloomberg site via the Favorites list.
11. Copy the first paragraph of text from the Bloomberg site and paste it into a new, blank Word document.
12. Print one copy of the word document.
13. Return to Internet Explorer and open the **Computer Info** folder.
14. Note the sites that have been added.
15. Return to the Dell site.
16. Print one copy of the first page.
17. Save the Dell site; name it **DELL.**
18. Click the **History** button and note the sites you visited today.
19. Close the browser.

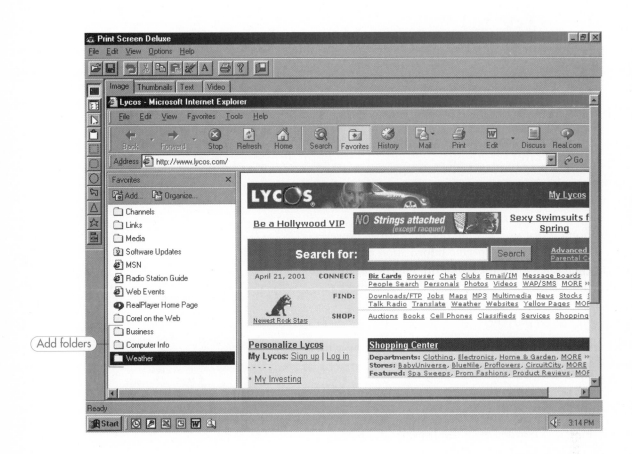

Add folders

Add a Site to Favorites
1. Click the **Favorites** button on the Explorer toolbar.
2. Click **Add.** The Add Favorite dialog box appears, with the Web site address in the Name box.
3. Click **OK.**

Open a Site from Favorites
1. Click the **Favorites** button.
2. Click the desired site to open.

Create a New Folder
1. Click **Organize.**
2. Click **Create Folder.**
3. Enter a name for the new folder and press **Enter.**

Move Favorites Sites into Folders
1. Click the **Favorites** button.
2. Click the site to move.
   Note: To select multiple sites, hold down Ctrl while you select sites.
3. Drag the sites to the newly created folder.
4. Click **Close.**

Copy Text from a Web Site
1. Highlight the text on the Web page to copy.
2. Right-click and choose **Copy.**
3. Position the insertion point in the document to paste the copied text.
4. Click **Edit, Paste** on the menu bar.

Save a Web Site
1. Click **File.**
2. Click **Save.**

TRYOUT

 GOAL

To practice using the following skill sets:
- ✶ Search the Internet
  - ✶ Use search engines and directories
  - ✶ Use Boolean operators to refine a search

TASK 3

WHAT YOU NEED TO KNOW

Search the Internet

> The Internet contains enormous amounts of information. You learned in the previous task that you could enter the Web address of a site in the Address line and find information on that site. It would be impossible, however, to know every site where specific information can be found. Therefore, you must search the Internet to find the information you want. To find the information most efficiently, you need to use the tools that have been developed for this purpose.

> It is important to note the following when working with the Internet:

- Anyone can publish information on the Internet—not all information is accurate.

- Anything downloaded from the Internet can have a virus. Be sure that the computers you are using have virus-protection software installed.

Use Search Engines and Directories

> One of the tools you can use to search for information is a *search engine*—a software program that searches the Web and automatically indexes home pages. The index displays keywords with hyperlinks to new pages. Popular search engines include HotBot, AltaVisa, and Lycos. The term "search engine" is often used to describe both true search engines as well as directories. They are not the same.

> A *directory* displays information by major topic headings, which are broken down into smaller topics that are then broken down further. A search looks for matches only in the descriptions submitted. Yahoo, Magellan, and Infoseek are examples of popular directories.

> Both search engines and directories are often called "Web crawlers" or "spiders," because they crawl the Web looking for information.

TRY*it* OUT

1. Start **Internet Explorer.**

2. Enter the following directory Web address in the Address line:

   www.yahoo.com

3. Enter **British** in theSearch for box and click **Search.** Notice the results.

4. Enter the following search engine Web address in the Address line:

   www.altavista.com

5. Enter **British** in the Search for box and click **Search.** Notice the results.

6. Do not close the program.

> To start a search, access a search engine or directory, such as Yahoo, AltaVista, or Google. Search engine sites always provide a Search box in which to enter the word, words, or phrase you wish to use in your search. This is often referred to as a *text string*. Text strings that contain a single word or phrase are simple; text strings that contain operators (see below) can be more complex. After entering a text string in the Search box, press Enter or click the Search button, as shown in Figure 3.10; the button is sometimes named Go, Go Get It, Seek Now, or Find.

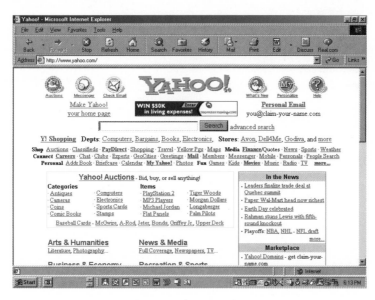

Figure 3.10 Search engine home page

Use Boolean Operators to Refine a Search

> A search can return vast amounts of information that match your request. You can refine your search to return fewer sites by entering more words in the text string or by using advanced search techniques. One such technique is to use Boolean operators as part of the search string.

> A *Boolean operator* is a word or symbol that narrows a search to give you more specific information. Although operators do help filter sites, they are not perfect. The most common Boolean operators are AND, OR, and NOT.

- Use AND or a plus sign (+) when you want the results to include all the words in the text string. ("Kansas AND City Hotels" will find sites that contain both words in the search results.)

- Use OR when you want the results to include one of the words in the text string. ("Kansas OR City Hotels" will find sites that contain either "Kansas" *or* "City Hotels.")

T R Y *it* O U T

1. Click the **Back** button.

2. Enter **British AND Novels** in the Search box.

3. Click **Search** or press the **Enter** key.

4. Enter **British OR Novels**. Notice how the results are different from those of the previous search.

5. Click **File, Close.**

- Use NOT or a minus sign (−) when you want the results to include only the words preceding the NOT operator. (New York NOT City will find sites that contain New York but not sites that contain New York City.) In Figures 3.11 and 3.12, note how the search for British novels was narrowed by using the AND operator in the second search.

> Not all search sites support the use of operators.

Figure 3.11 Search string in Lycos

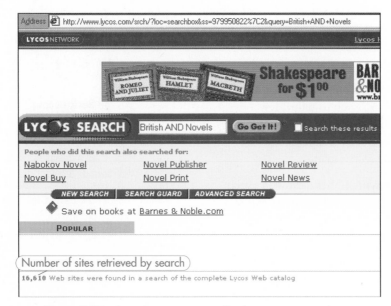

Figure 3.12 Search string using a Boolean operator in Lycos

REHEARSAL

GOAL
To search the Internet using search engines/directories and Boolean operators

TASK 3

WHAT YOU NEED TO KNOW

> Seek out multiple sites when you research a topic. Directories and search engines vary in their content and accuracy and will often yield different results. Therefore, use a directory when you have a broad topic to research.

> Use a search engine when you have a narrow topic to research.

> In this Rehearsal activity, you will search the Internet, add sites to your Favorites folders, and print Web pages.

DIRECTIONS

1. Start Internet Explorer.

2. Enter www.yahoo.com in the Address line. Add this site to Favorites. Enter www.altavista.com in the Address line. Add this site to Favorites. Enter www.lycos.com in the Address line. Add this site to Favorites.

3. Create a new Favorites folder; name it **Search Engines.** Move the saved sites into the newly created Favorites folder.

4. Access the AltaVista site from the Search Engines Favorites folder.

5. Enter the text string **Kansas AND City Hotels** in the Search box and press the **Enter** key.

6. Notice the results and the number of sites this search has yielded. Print one copy of the page.

7. Enter the text string **Kansas OR City Hotels** in the Search box and press the **Enter** key.

8. Notice the results and the number of sites this search has yielded. Print one copy of the page.

9. Enter the text string **Kansas NOT City** in the Search box and press the **Enter** key.

10. Notice the results and the number of sites this search has yielded. Print one copy.

11. Open the Yahoo site from the Search Engines Favorites folder.

12. Repeat steps 8 through 10.

13. Click the **Home** button.

14. Compare the printouts and note the difference between the results of a search engine and a directory when the search is narrowed using Boolean operators.

15. Close the browser.

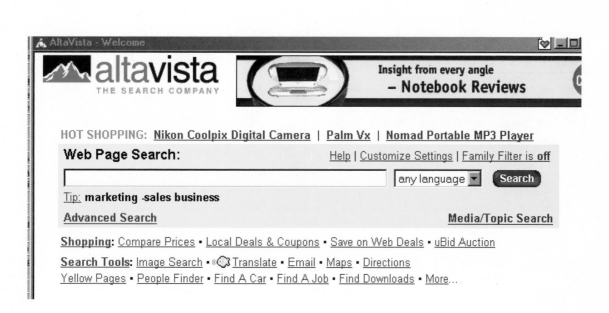

Access a Search Engine or Directory
1. Start Internet Explorer.
2. Enter a search engine or directory site in the Address line.

3. Press **Enter.**

Use a Search Engine or Directory to Refine the Search
1. Enter a text string in the Search box.

Note: You can use a simple text string or one that contains the operators AND, NOT, or OR.

2. Press **Enter** or click the **Search** button.

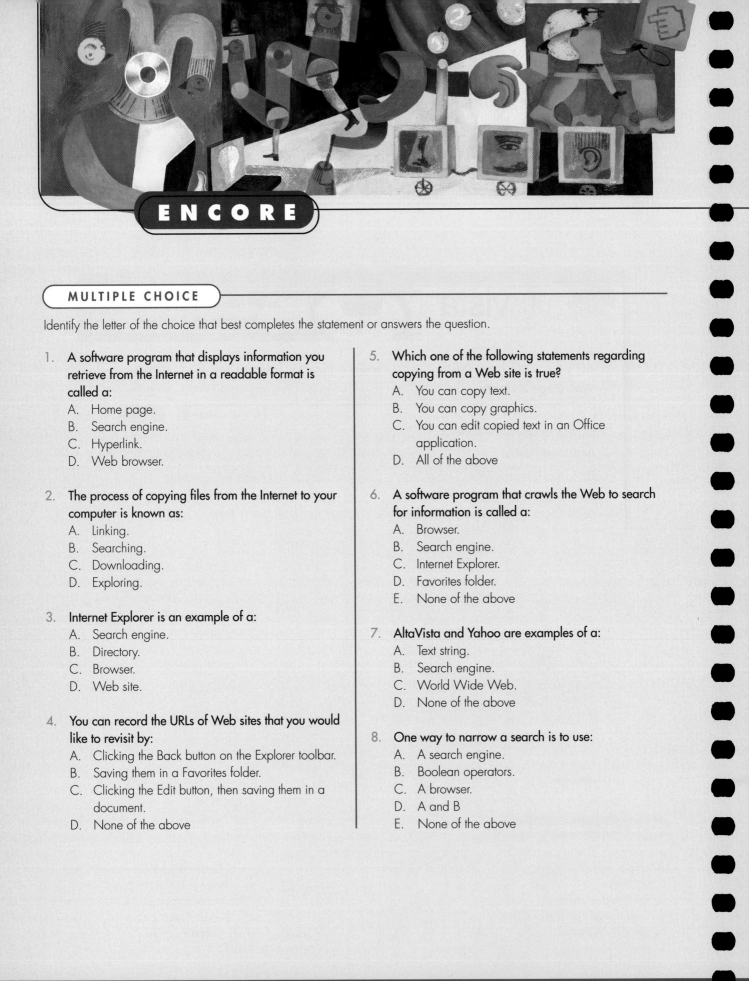

ENCORE

Identify the letter of the choice that best completes the statement or answers the question.

1. A software program that displays information you retrieve from the Internet in a readable format is called a:
   A. Home page.
   B. Search engine.
   C. Hyperlink.
   D. Web browser.

2. The process of copying files from the Internet to your computer is known as:
   A. Linking.
   B. Searching.
   C. Downloading.
   D. Exploring.

3. Internet Explorer is an example of a:
   A. Search engine.
   B. Directory.
   C. Browser.
   D. Web site.

4. You can record the URLs of Web sites that you would like to revisit by:
   A. Clicking the Back button on the Explorer toolbar.
   B. Saving them in a Favorites folder.
   C. Clicking the Edit button, then saving them in a document.
   D. None of the above

5. Which one of the following statements regarding copying from a Web site is true?
   A. You can copy text.
   B. You can copy graphics.
   C. You can edit copied text in an Office application.
   D. All of the above

6. A software program that crawls the Web to search for information is called a:
   A. Browser.
   B. Search engine.
   C. Internet Explorer.
   D. Favorites folder.
   E. None of the above

7. AltaVista and Yahoo are examples of a:
   A. Text string.
   B. Search engine.
   C. World Wide Web.
   D. None of the above

8. One way to narrow a search is to use:
   A. A search engine.
   B. Boolean operators.
   C. A browser.
   D. A and B
   E. None of the above

9. Which one of the following statements about search engines and directories is not true?
   A. Directories and search engines vary in their content and accuracy and will often yield different results.
   B. You should use a directory when you have a broad topic to research; use a search engine when you have a narrow topic to research.
   C. The term "search engine" is often used to describe both true search engines as well as directories.
   D. None of the above

10. The start page of any Web site is called:
   A. Surfing the Net.
   B. A Web address.
   C. A URL.
   D. The home page.

TRUE/FALSE

Circle the **T** if the statement is true or the **F** if the statement is false.

T F 11. The domain name identifies a Web site as belonging to a commercial, noncommercial, government, educational, U.S. military, or network organization.

T F 12. Each time a Web page displays, its address appears in the Address line of the Internet Explorer window.

T F 13. Once you start a search, you cannot stop it.

T F 14. Clicking on related links to find information is often referred to as "surfing the Web."

T F 15. Every Web site has a unique URL.

T F 16. The only way to record a history of the searches you have made is to print Web site pages.

T F 17. Because Web sites change daily, a Web site may display a different home/start page each time you access it.

T F 18. If you have bookmarked related sites, you should organize them in a Favorites folder.

T F 19. Each search engine has its own Web address.

T F 20. You should use the AND operator when you want your search results to include only the words preceding the operator.

GLOSSARY

3-D references A cell reference in a formula that refers to calculating values in a cell or cells in the same location on a group of worksheets in a workbook.

Absolute (cell) reference In Excel, a reference to a particular cell or group of cells that must remain constant even if you copy the contents or formula in one cell to another cell.

Accept changes To decide that a modification of information should remain on a worksheet.

Account An accounting form used to summarize increases and decreases in an item.

Account Statement A monthly summary of the increases and decreases in an account.

Accounts payable Creditors that a business owes money to.

Accounts receivable Customers that owe money to a business.

Accounts receivable aging report A financial document that shows an analysis of how many days payments from customers are overdue.

Active cell The cell in use or the cell that is ready to receive text or a formula.

Active (cell) reference The row and column location of the active cell, which appears in the name box.

Aging report A report prepared to analyze the number of days a company's Accounts Receivable accounts are overdue.

Align center Text alignment in which text is centered between the margins.

Align left Text alignment in which text is even at the left margin and uneven at the right margin.

Align right Text alignment in which text is uneven at the left margin and even at the right margin.

Annual interest Interest rate for the use of money expressed on an annual basis.

AutoComplete The automatic completion of an entry in an Excel column using previously entered column data.

AutoFill The Excel feature that allows you to drag, copy and fill data.

AutoFilter A feature that requires a data table and that allows you to filter lists using arrows that appear at every column heading.

AutoFit Feature to widen columns to fit the longest data in that column.

AutoFormat A feature that provides a predefined format applied to a report, a form, a worksheet, or a table.

AutoShapes Built-in graphic objects, found on the Drawing toolbar that you can place and size.

AutoSum A feature that automatically adds the selected numbers in a column.

Balance sheet A financial report that shows the value of the business, its Assets, Liabilities and Capital, on a specific date.

Benefits statement Report by an employer stating benefits offered or provided to employees.

Bonus table A data table that defines the extra money paid to employees based on some measure of performance.

Border A variety of line styles that border the edge of a cell or range of cells.

Budget An analysis of the projected income and expenses for a future period.

Business form A document format that is developed for an activity that occurs often.

Category labels Identifies values in a chart data series as shown on the horizontal or x-axis.

Cell A location on a worksheet that contains text, values, or formulas.

Cell address The location of a cell as identified by the column letter and row number.

Cell comment A notation or documentation added to a cell in a worksheet.

Cell coordinate The column letter and row number given to a cell. For example, A1 is the coordinate for the cell in the first row, first column.

Cell cursor In spreadsheets, the heavy line that outlines a cell and indicates the active cell.

Chart A visual representation of data. The terms graph and chart are interchangeable.

Chart sheet A separate sheet created to display a chart on a full page.

Chart Wizard A software assistant that steps you through the creation of a chart.

Column Vertical area for data that is identified by letter across a spreadsheet grid.

Column chart Compares individual or sets of values using the proportional height of the columns.

Combination chart A custom chart that plots the data series using two different chart types.

Conditional format The application of specific formats if the content of a cell or range of cells meets certain criteria.

Consolidated budget A business document that shows the planned or actual income and expenses from several departments or companies.

Consolidated income statement An Income Statement that is made up of data from various subsidiaries or divisions.

Criteria range A separate area of the worksheet created using the column headings of a data table that contains criteria for an advanced filter.

Currency conversion table A data table that contains foreign exchange rates for the money of different countries, as well as any computations based on those rates.

Custom menu A set of buttons and commands grouped into a user-created drop-down menu.

Custom number format A user-created format that specifies how Excel displays numbers within a cell.

Data consolidation A way to combine the information from different workbooks or worksheets and store it in another workbook or worksheet.

Data series Is a group of values in a chart identified by a label.

Data validation A feature that helps to ensure that the correct data is entered on a worksheet or in a data list.

Dependents Cells containing formulas that reference the cell you are auditing.

Depreciation schedule An accounting record that shows the cost of an asset over its estimated useful life.

Destination file Receives data from another file.

Divisional sales report A summary of sales figures for each department of a company.

Drag-and-drop A method of moving text using the mouse. Text is "dragged" from its original location and dropped into its new location.

Edit mode Double-click a cell or press F2 to go into worksheet edit mode.

Embedded chart Is a chart object that is placed on a worksheet.

Embedded file An object placed into a destination file that becomes part of that file, but can be edited in its source application.

Expense report A report of money spent by an employee on business travel or expenses.

Exporting data Sending data from Excel to other applications.

Extensible Mark-Up Language (XML) A format for putting structured data in a text file; allows for the exchange of data between different applications.

Field name Label for a particular column of data in a list.

Fill handle The rectangular indicator at the bottom right corner of a cell that is used with AutoFill.

Filter An Excel function that allows you to display only the data specified by certain criteria.

Financial functions Are used to analyze loans, calculate payments, and compute depreciation on assets.

Find and Replace A feature that scans a document and searches for occurrences of specified text, symbols, or formatting and replaces it with other specified text, symbols, or formatting.

Folder A subdivision of a drive that you create to hold files that are related to each other.

Footer The same text or graphic appearing at the bottom of every page or every other page in a document.

FORECAST A what-if analysis that allows you to project future data values based on data that you have already obtained.

Format Painter An Office feature that allows you to copy formats from one set of data to another.

Formula An instruction to the computer to calculate data in a certain way.

Formula bar The formula bar is under the toolbar and shows the entry of data and provides formula assistance.

Freeze Panes Used to keep headings or row data in view when scrolling through a large worksheet.

Function In spreadsheets, a built-in formula that performs special calculations automatically.

Function arguments The cell addresses that make up the data for the function formula.

FV (future value) function Used to calculate the future value of a series of equal payments, at a fixed interest rate, for a specific number of payments.

General ledger Contains the major accounts of a business.

Graphic A line, circle, or box that has been created, or an image or illustration that is imported into the publication.

Group sheets Selecting multiple worksheets as a group so that you can make entries on all sheets simultaneously.

Header The same text appearing at the top of every page or every other page in a document.

HLOOKUP An Excel lookup function used when the data are arranged horizontally in a table.

Hyperlink A shortcut that allows you to jump to another location in another workbook, a file on your hard drive or network, or an Internet address.

IF statement A logical function that tests a condition and performs one action if it is true and another if it is false.

Importing data Bringing information into Excel from a source other than an Excel file.

Income statement A financial report that shows Income, Expenses and Profits for the period..

Insert Function button Used to select and enter a function name and arguments in a formula.

Integration The sharing or combining of data between Office XP applications.

Interactivity A feature added to an Excel file published to a Web page that allows viewers to manipulate data in their browsers.

Inventory list A data list kept by a company to keep track of products and goods, including stock on hand, cost of goods, and other information, such as suggested retail price.

Journal A record of business transactions in chronological order.

Label In spreadsheets, a text entry.

Label prefix Numeric labels are entered with an apostrophe ('), which serves as the label prefix.

Left-alignment To position text along the left margin. See *Align Left*.

Legend The identification of a chart data series showing the colors of the series markers.

Line chart Compares individual sets of values with lines connecting the points of data.

Linked file A shortcut to source file data placed in a destination file. All data changes will update in both locations.

Listing agent In a real estate office, the agent who contracts with the homeowner to sell the property.

Locked cells Specific cells in a worksheet to which protection has been added.

Macro A series of actions you record to allow you to complete a task quickly and efficiently.

Menu bar Appears at the top of the Excel screen and contains lists of commands for each category of features or items on the menu.

Merge and Center button Centers text over a range of selected cells.

Merge cells Removing the dividing lines between cells to create a single, larger cell. This is also referred to as joining cells.

Merging workbooks incorporating changes made by users into a single workbook.

Microsoft Query An application that allows you to retrieve specified information from external sources.

Name box On the Formula bar, the name box shows the cell address of the active cell.

Named range A label applied to a specified range of cells.

Negative numbers Result of a calculation that is a value less than zero.

Nonadjacent selection A selection of worksheet data that is not contiguous accomplished using the Ctrl key.

Nper Number of payments.

Numeric label In spreadsheets, text that begins with a number. Numeric labels cannot be calculated.

Office Clipboard A memory area of the computer where data is stored temporarily.

Order of mathematical operations Formulas are executed in the following order: parentheses, exponents, multiplication and division, and addition and subtraction.

Orientation On charts, the plotting of data in a chart by row or column layout.

Page break Is the location on a page where one page ends and another begins.

Password A sequence of letters and/or numbers that must be entered before access to a worksheet or workbook is allowed.

Paste Link option Connecting the data from one location to another so that if the original data is changed it updates on the linked location.

Paste values A paste option that allows you to paste only the values, not the formulas of copied data.

Payroll register A worksheet that calculates employee's salary, taxes, and net pay.

Personnel list A record of all employees in a business and their associated information.

Pie chart Circular graphs used to show the relationship of each value in a data range to the total of the range.

PivotChart A graphical representation of the contents of a PivotTable.

PivotChart report A print-out of a PivotChart analysis.

PivotTable An interactive tool that allows you to manipulate data in a list in order to summarize, analyze, or arrange it in tabular form.

PivotTable report A print-out of a PivotTable analysis.

PMT (payment) function Used to calculate a loan payment based on the principal (present value of loan), interest rate, and number of payments.

Portfolio A group of investments owned by a person or business.

Precedents Cells that are referenced in a formula.

Principal Present value of a loan.

Print Titles Use to print row or column titles for a large worksheet that prints on more than one page.

Professional invoice An invoice or bill sent for services such as legal, accounting or consulting services.

Protection A feature of Excel that allows another user to read data but not make any changes to it until protection is removed.

Purchase order A form sent by a firm to a vendor to request shipment of items listed on the order.

PV (present value) function Use to calculate the present value of a series of equal payments, at a fixed interest rate, for a specific number of payments.

Quarterly Every three months, or four times a year.

Quarterly budget A statement of income and expenses prepared every three months.

Query A text file that contains information about a data source and the information to extract from it.

Range In spreadsheet applications, one or more contiguous cells.

Rate Interest rate per period.

Real estate list A data list that contains a company's current inventory of properties for sale and/or rent.

Reciprocal Used to calculate the result of subtracting a percentage discount. Subtract the discount percent from 100% to get the reciprocal.

Record The data for one person or unit in a list; it goes across a row in Excel.

Regional sales analysis A financial analysis of sales figures for different sales territories.

Reimbursement A request to be paid for money spent on business expenses.

Reject changes To decide that a modification of information should not be made to a worksheet.

Relative (cell) reference In spreadsheets, cell references that change relative to their new locations when a formula is copied.

Report Manager An Excel add-in program that allows you to create printed reports containing information from different sections of a workbook; it includes scenarios.

Revenue Income or monies received by a business.

Right-alignment To position text along the right margin. See *Align right*.

Round-tripping A feature that allows you to edit an HTML document in a browser using Notepad, Word, or FrontPage.

Row Horizontal area for data that is identified by a number along the side of a spreadsheet grid.

S&P 500 Standard and Poor's 500 stock index is a weighted index made up of the stock prices of 500 blue chip stocks, which reflects market trends.

Sales commission analysis A study of sales performance over a specified period of time in order to identify notable patterns or to select individuals who are above or below certain goals important to a business.

Sales forecast A projection of future sales based on past performance.

Sales invoice A bill prepared by a seller and sent to the customer when goods are supplied, which details items sold and terms of the sale.

Sales journal A record of sales transactions.

Scenario A what-if analysis that allows you to explore the impact of changing data values on numerical outcomes.

Schedule of accounts payable A list prepared monthly of the balances of creditor accounts.

Schedule of accounts receivable A list prepared monthly of the balances of customer accounts.

Scroll bars Located at the right and bottom of the screen and used to move to different areas of the worksheet that are not displayed.

Selling agent In a real estate office, the agent who sells a listed property. The listing and selling agent can be the same person.

Serial value The numeric value of a date which allows you to use dates in formulas and represents the number of days from January, 1900 to the date entered.

Series A list of numbers or text that is in a sequential arrangement that can be produced using AutoFill.

Series labels Identifies charted values and appears in the legend.

Shared workbook A workbook that a number of users can edit.

Source file Provides the data for integrating into another file.

Split cells Reversing the merge cells process and returning cells to their normal size.

Status bar The status bar at the bottom of the Excel screen displays the condition of worksheet calculations and settings.

Straight-line depreciation A method of calculating the loss in value in an asset by dividing the cost of an asset less the scrap value by the estimated useful life.

Style A set of formatting characteristics that can be applied to a paragraph or selected text.

Subtotal A summary of a subset of data that is arranged in a list.

SUM In spreadsheet and database applications, a function used to add numbers in a range or values in a field.

Tab scrolling buttons Allow you to scroll hidden worksheets into view.

Task pane A new feature that displays on start up, on the right side of the screen, and shows options pertinent to the task at hand.

Tax status The number of dependents and marital status of employees, which is used for payroll tax calculations.

Template A workbook that serves as an outline or guide, into which you can place data.

Terms Credit terms given to a buyer that may involve discounts for early payment.

Title bar The shaded bar at the top of a dialog box or application window that displays the title of the box, or the name of the file, and the application.

Toolbar A bar with buttons, located under the menu bar, provides quick access to common features.

Tracer arrows The lines Excel creates in a worksheet to identify dependents and precedents of audited cells.

Track changes The ability to view modifications made to a file by other users.

Transaction A business event or activity that changes the financial status of a business.

Trendline A graphic representation of any tendencies or patterns in data, presented in a chart.

Trial balance A list of all the accounts in a business consisting of debit and credit balances, which must equal to show that the books are in balance.

Value A numeric entry on a worksheet that is able to be calculated.

Vendor A supplier or merchant that provides your company with goods or services.

Visual Basic Editor A module in Excel within which macros are recorded using the programming language Visual Basic.

VLOOKUP An Excel lookup function used when the data are arranged vertically in a table.

Web page Is a location on an Internet server, part of the World Wide Web, which can be reached and identified by a Web address.

What-if analysis A group of commands that allows the user to assess how changes in data or formulas affect outcomes; includes forecasting and scenarios.

Workbook An Excel file made up of several worksheets.

Working folder The default location for saving and opening files.

Worksheet An accounting term for a columnar analysis that uses the Trial Balance and end-of-year adjustments to develop the data for the Income Statement and Balance Sheet reports.

Worksheet One page in an Excel workbook.

Workspace A shared location in which you can store several workbooks.

X-axis In spreadsheet charting, the horizontal scale that typically displays the data series.

Y-axis In spreadsheet charting, the vertical scale that typically displays the scale values.

INDEX